Allenby's Gunners

Allenby's Gunners

Artillery in the Sinai & Palestine Campaigns 1916–1918

Alan H. Smith

Pen & Sword
MILITARY

First published in Australia in 2016 by
Big Sky Publishing Pty Ltd
PO Box 303, Newport, NSW 2106, Australia

Reprinted in hardback format in 2017 in Great Britain by
Pen & Sword MILITARY
An imprint of
Pen & Sword Books Ltd
47 Church Street, Barnsley
South Yorkshire
S70 2AS

ISBN 978 1 52671 465 7

A CIP catalogue record for this book is
available from the British Library

Printed and bound in England
by TJ International Ltd, Padstow, PL28 8RW

Pen & Sword Books Ltd incorporates the Imprints of Pen & Sword Aviation,
Pen & Sword Family History, Pen & Sword Maritime, Pen & Sword Military,
Pen & Sword Discovery, Pen & Sword Politics, Pen & Sword Atlas,
Pen & Sword Archaeology, Wharncliffe Local History, Leo Cooper,
Wharncliffe True Crime, Wharncliffe Transport, Pen & Sword Select,
Pen & Sword Military Classics, The Praetorian Press, Claymore Press,
Remember When, Seaforth Publishing and Frontline Publishing

For a complete list of Pen & Sword titles please contact
PEN & SWORD BOOKS LIMITED
47 Church Street, Barnsley, South Yorkshire, S70 2AS, England
E-mail: enquiries@pen-and-sword.co.uk
Website: www.pen-and-sword.co.uk

DEDICATION

This account of the Sinai and Palestine campaigns from an artillery perspective is dedicated to my two 'historical' mentors, Major James Essington Lewis, ED, and Major General John Stewart Whitelaw, AO, CBE.

Table of Contents

List of photographs 1

List of maps 3

List of tables 5

Foreword 6

Preface 8

Notes on sources 11

Abbreviations 12

Map Legend 14

Narrative One: Background to April 1916 16

1. Middle East Command: an outline of operations 18
2. Cavalry doctrine and the employment of artillery 26
3. Corps artillery: horse, field, siege and heavy artillery brigades 34
4. The Battle of Romani and the early battles of 1916–17 45
5. The Battle of Magdhaba: 23 December 1916 62
6. The Battle of Rafa: 8/9 January 1916 68
7. The First Battle of Gaza: 26–27 March 1917 77
8. The Second Battle of Gaza: 17–19 April 1917 93
9. Aftermath, artillery reorganisation and interregnum 110
10. The guns of XX and XXI Corps prior to Third Gaza 117
11. The cavalry's guns prior to Beersheba: May October 1917 122
12. The Battle of Beersheba: October 1917 125
13. The Third Battle of Gaza: 25 October–7 November 1917 137

Narrative Two: November 1917 to May 1918 154

14. The Great Northern Drive 155
15. The drive north to Junction Station 164
16. Allenby takes Jerusalem 175
17. The Northern Front and the defence of Jerusalem 191

18. The capture of Jericho: 19–21 February 1918 194
19. The Amman raid and the first Es Salt affair 197
20. The April 1918 battles of XX Corps and XXI Corps 204
21. The second Es Salt raid: 30 April–4 May 1918 211
22. The Northern Front 1. Wadi Auja: 18 March 1918 222
23. Summer in the Jordan Valley: May–July 1918 226

Narrative Three: May 1918 to November 1918 238

24. A summer of contemplation and creativity 239
25. The Battle of Megiddo: the first three days 249
26. Chaytor's thrust to Amman and Deraa 268
27. The pursuit to Damascus 272
28. Damascus to Aleppo 280
29. The artillery campaign: a recapitulation 282
30. Artillery summary and conclusions 290
Postscript 294

Appendices: 295

Appendix 1 296
Appendix 2 298
Appendix 3 299
Appendix 4 301
Appendix 5 304
Appendix 6 306
Appendix 7 320
Appendix 8 328
Endnotes 329
Bibliography 351
Index 358

General Edmund Allenby, appointed commander of the Egyptian Expeditionary Force on 27 June 1917.

List of photographs

1. Colonel Charles Rosenthal, Australian commander of the artillery supporting the combined Allied force that defended the Suez Canal against a Turkish attack in early 1915.
2. Major General S.C.U. Smith, Allenby's MGRA.
3. Each squadron of the Australian Light Horse had either horse and/or vehicle-mounted Lewis, Vickers or Hotchkiss machine-guns.
4. Lieutenant General Sir Harry Chauvel, GOC Desert Mounted Corps. The Hong Kong Singapore Mountain Battery training with its light field guns.
5. An 18-pounder field gun and crew. These guns equipped infantry divisional artilleries.
6. An RGA 60-pounder gun and part of its detachment.
7. Brigadier Charles Cox, GOC 1st Australian Light Horse Brigade, and Major General E.W.C. Chaytor, GOC NZMR Brigade. Both were enthusiastic supporters of the '*arme blanche*' cavalry approach to combat.
8. Captured Turkish artillery at Rafa is inspected by the leaders of the cavalry involved.
9. The terrain showing the infantry's approach to Gaza prior to First Gaza. The cactus hedges evident here proved a serious obstacle for the infantry. They were eventually obliterated by shellfire.
10. Australian light horsemen look over a British Mk I female tank prior to the Second Battle of Gaza.
11. The aircraft of No. 1 Squadron, AFC.
12. An Australian soldier operates a wireless set at a field station during the first Amman stunt in March 1918.
13. Cavalry crossing the Jordan River at Ghoraniye by pontoon bridge, one of which was erected by a Canadian engineer bridging unit.
14. The topography of the Jordan Valley and the Musallabeh feature.
15. The Abu Tellul feature was regarded by both the Allies and Turks as tactically important and was contested by both sides. It was the site of a combined German-Turkish defeat.
16. A wagon brings supplies to a detachment — note the tracks (foreground) and dust. Troops were rotated for duty during summer in the Jordan Valley which was noted for its vile climate, sickness, mosquitoes, dust and heat.

17. A scene in the dust at Megiddo (Lejjun) during the advance on Damascus, showing the Australian Light Horse advancing and prisoners by the wayside.
18. Two RA officers stand with a captured German coastal artillery piece (150mm) used against the attackers during the cavalry fight for Haifa.

Note: despite my best efforts I could not locate photographs of the artillery commanders from the cavalry or infantry divisions.

List of maps

Narrative 1

A. The Sinai Desert area of operations in 1916.

1. The Turkish attack on the Romani position showing the furthest extent of the Turkish advance on 5 August 1916 and the positions of the supporting and enemy artilleries.
2. The unsuccessful assault on Bir el Abd by the 1st Australian Light Horse and NZMR brigades and their supporting RHA batteries, Leicester, Ayrshire and Inverness, on 9 August 1916.
3. The Battle of Magdhaba, 23 December 1916, showing the artillery gun positions and the cavalry approaches.
4. The encirclement of Rafa by the NZMR Brigade, 5th Mounted Brigade, five Australian Light Horse regiments and the ICC, with artillery positions indicated.
5. The First Battle of Gaza showing the dispositions of horse, field and heavy artilleries at dusk on 26 March 1917.
6. Second Battle of GAZA showing the cavalry friendly eastern flank on which the Turkish attack was concentrated and repulsed. The Atawine Redoubt was the most important tactical feature.

Narrative 2

B. Map showing the coastal plain and rugged nature of the hinterland, major towns and villages, roads and railways of Palestine where most of Allenby's battles were fought.

7. The Battle of Beersheba (31 October 1917) showing the assault on the town by XX Corps infantry from the west and the eastern and northern DMC cavalry approaches.
8. The Third Battle of Gaza (27 October–7 November 1917) showing the 15-mile corps front from the coast to the eastern perimeter.
9. The beginning of the Great Northern Drive to secure the coastal plain, including the Sheria position.
10. The famous charge of the Bucks Hussars, Worcester and Warwick Yeomanrys at Huj on 8 November 1917 supported by both RGA and RFA batteries.

11. The action at El Mughar by the 5th Mounted Brigade's Dorset Yeomanry and Bucks Yeomanry on 13 November 1917.
12. The northern flank on the Wadi Auja proved vital to tying down the Turkish *VIII Corps* and, ultimately, to the capture of Jerusalem.
13. The battle for Jerusalem lasted a month. This map shows the dispositions of the infantry divisions before the final, successful attempt in December.
14. The Nebi Samwil feature north-west of Jerusalem showing artillery positions at Biddu, the only area suitable for protecting the Zeitoun and El Jib to Beit Iska front line.
15. The raid on Amman from 27 March to 2 May 1918 was a cavalry operation featuring a three-pronged advance which failed due to a lack of artillery support.
16. Map illustrating the loss of nine RHA guns during the debacle east of the Jordan River when the Australian light horsemen were beaten by a superior Turkish force.
17. The actions east of the Jordan — the Es Salt raid, showing the dispositions of the attackers and defenders.
18. The Abu Tellul defence and counter-attack of 14 July 1918 and the positions of supporting artillery.
19. The Battle of Megiddo evolved as General Allenby planned, with the DMC bearing north-east to encircle the Turkish Twentieth Army while the XX Corps infantry and Chaytor's cavalry pinned down the Turks' western front prior to the capture of Amman.
20. The Megiddo left flank showing the preponderance of artillery and infantry tasked with blasting a passage for Chauvel's cavalry to exploit.
21. Map showing Major General Chaytor's cavalry and infantry assault across the River Jordan prior to the force's advance north to eventually join Chauvel's cavalry.

List of tables

1. Field brigade war establishment
2. Siege and heavy battery outline establishments
3. Casualties for the battles of Romani, Katia and Bir el Abd
4. Casualties for the Battle of Rafa
5. Comparable casualty ratios from the battles of Romani, Magdhaba and Rafa
6. Siege brigade order of battle for Beersheba and Third Gaza
7. Heavy artillery battery order of battle for Beersheba and Third Gaza
8. Gas at Gaza
9. Casualties for the Amman raid and first Es Salt
10. Casualties at Berukin
11. Casualties for the second Es Salt raid
12. Abu Tellul casualty count
13. Allenby's progress 25 September–11 October 1918
14. Campaign casualty count
15. Comparison of guns and casualties
16. Summary of total British Commonwealth casualties

Foreword

This book is the latest in a series by prolific military historian Alan Smith, dealing with artillery support for campaigns in which Australian forces have participated. He has focussed this time on how artillery support was provided during the Middle East campaigns of 1916–1918 to the British, Australian and New Zealand forces that took part, ultimately successfully.

Following the total failure of the Gallipoli campaign, the formations and units of the Australian Imperial Force that were committed were evacuated to Egypt. There, after receiving reinforcements, the Australian Imperial Force, light horse units aside, was reorganised into five infantry divisions and trained for deployment to the Western Front. Fortunately, there was a need for the Australian Light Horse to remain in the Middle East to help counter the Ottoman Empire's forays into the Sinai desert and then drive its forces out of Palestine.

As this campaign developed in the Sinai desert east of the Suez Canal, the Australian Light Horse regiments and New Zealand Mounted Rifles had to rely on British Army Royal Artillery units for field, medium and heavy artillery support. Because of this arrangement, Australian historiography has tended to focus on the dash and élan of the light horse in its successful actions at Romani, Gaza, Beersheba and elsewhere. As the author recounts, the British gunners quickly gained the expertise required for success in battles against a skilled and determined enemy and won the confidence of the supported arms.

The author is to be commended for his extensive research in producing a most readable and technically interesting (and, I predict, not only for latter day gunners) account of how effective artillery support was provided. Although fire plans for attacks and associated counter-battery tasks never approached the scale of those on the Western Front, the artillery was required to meet some stiff challenges, especially during General Allenby's great thrusts at Jerusalem and his hook from the left flank that led to the fall of Damascus.

Artillery was to make a major contribution to the success of the campaigns in the Middle East, a contribution of which the Royal Regiment has every reason to be proud. The supported arms were very fortunate to have what proved to be a highly professional force to provide its artillery support.

Foreword

I congratulate Alan Smith for producing a very valuable record of what has been to date a neglected aspect of Australian military history of operations against the Ottoman forces in the Middle East.

Major General Steve Gower, AO, AO (Mil) (Ret'd)
Patron, Royal Australian Artillery Historical Company

Preface

For many years I was curious — no doubt like others with an interest in the Sinai and Palestine campaigns — as to why the contribution of artillery to the most successful campaign of World War I has never been adequately recognised. To me it is clear that these campaigns suffer from the strong historical focus on the France and Flanders operations. While there have been numerous battery histories and articles on World War I in the *Journal of the Royal Artillery*, those relating to the Middle East are few and far between. So, where does one start? While the Australian War Memorial collections hold three important headquarters war diaries and six Royal Horse Artillery Battery war diaries of very poor quality, there are no records from the British and Indian infantry units. A review of the Australian Light Horse regimental and brigade histories provides few — even passing — mentions of artillery cooperation and its effect on tactical outcomes despite the fact that, prior to 1901, two militia units in Victoria, the Rupertswood and Chirmside batteries, were organised in similar fashion to the Royal Horse Artillery. Tellingly, neither unit survived later reorganisation.

Chauvel's biographer, A.J. Hill, allows his Desert Mounted Corps organic artillery a total of six mentions in his index for the campaign as a whole. Yet, as historian Sir Martin Farndale writes, 'the Gunners might not have won many battles, but many would have been lost without them', a point that is apparently lost — in turn — on some historians. For his part, Farndale's contribution in his monumental history of the World War I campaigns is covered in just 50 pages, although there are a few brief references to their overworked field artillery brigades. Even on Anzac Day (25 April in Australia), when military discussion dominates the media, holistic reference to the Sinai and Palestine campaigns other than to the Battle of Beersheba appears to occur more by accident than by design.

Following the Gallipoli campaign and the reconstitution of the Australian Imperial Force there was insufficient manpower to provide an Australian equivalent of the Royal Horse Artillery. This applied similarly to the New Zealand Army. Accordingly, the British Territorial artillery units were allotted that role for the Australian Light Horse and New Zealand Mounted Rifle Brigades, and colonial mountain batteries also became organic. The relationship between these two disparate cultures could not have been more harmonious. Indeed the Ayrshire Battery Scots were keen to adopt the wallaby skin 'pugri' on the slouch hat for their own headwear after the Battle of Romani, while other batteries sought the famed emu plume. Alas, officialdom demurred.

Lieutenant General Sir Harry Chauvel's Desert Mounted Corps, the upscaled Desert Column of the early days of Sinai operations, was given a role by General Allenby in the last six months to October 1918 in which, as it eventuated, there was little use for its artillery support. However that support remained keen and battleworthy, ready to respond if needed, particularly for the most famous battle of all — Megiddo. My emphasis therefore is on both cavalry and infantry operations and on battles from Romani and the coastal plain, the Palestine desert, Jordan Valley and Eastern Escarpment to Amman, until the theatre armistice of October 1918.

As in operations in France in 1917–1918, the light horsemen and gunners owed a great deal to the Australian Flying Corps and Royal Flying Corps for their tactical and offensive bombing and counter-battery work from mid-1917. While the *Royal Artillery Journal* post-World War I published several detailed descriptions of the heavy artillery triumphs and tragedies, this work does not include the anti-aircraft artillery branch of the regiment. Likewise, despite extensive enquiries, detailed accounts of the contribution of the Field Survey Company, Royal Canadian Engineers, to counter-battery work remain to be 'unearthed', although these are acknowledged in many citations. Finally, as the geography of this campaign was familiar as the site of numerous battles in biblical times, these events resonated with some historians who made allusions to historical battles or shrines at various points in their narratives. Nothing much has changed in 2000 years except that many of the smaller place names, now in Yiddish, are not currently used. The campaign also suffers from the lack of a suitable suite of maps illustrating the deployment of artillery. In their absence I have used or created those that best suit my narrative. In terms of photographs, my preference was to highlight the terrain over which battles were fought, rather than retaining a purely artillery focus.

I am indebted to Major General Steve Gower, AO, AO (Mil), for vetting my manuscript and for his suggestions for textual amendments. I regard his interest in my work as a great honour. I am also deeply grateful to the Head of the Army History Unit, Dr Roger Lee, and to Dr Andrew Richardson who provided significant assistance with images and advice on maps. Denny Neave from Big Sky Publishing is responsible for producing this high quality volume and also provided valuable assistance with the technical aspects of publication.

Finally, I wish to thank and acknowledge the assistance of my editor, Cathy McCullagh, who, as usual, has been a model of patience in amending my literary endeavours. My son, Andrew, also provided crucial help with my computer 'difficulties' — indeed, without his timely intervention, there would have been no 'end point'.

Alan Smith
St Ives, New South Wales

Notes on sources

The primary sources I have used for artillery actions associated with the light horsemen and other cavalry include 30 National Archives war diaries and other records and an account of the Honourable Artillery Company's historical record of its A and B batteries by Major G. Goold-Walker. This latter account provides an excellent description of battery operations that can also be assumed to apply to the other Royal Horse Artillery Territorial Force batteries. Colonel R.M.P. Preston's account of the Desert Mounted Corps earned the imprimatur of his commander, Chauvel, and has been a fruitful source of detail. It adds much flesh to Sir Martin Farndale's account in his *Forgotten Fronts and The Home Base, 1914-18* (Part I, Chapter 1, Egypt; Part III, Chapter 5, The Western Desert and Part IV, chapters 6 to 10, Palestine). His is a compressed account in which the exploits of the Royal Horse Artillery batteries are subsumed by the sheer numerical presence of divisional field and corps heavy artilleries during operations — not that this is a bad thing. Few regimental histories — and notably Gullett's Australian *Official History* — describe the effects of their fire or lack of it at crucial times, notwithstanding their long association at brigade and regimental level, although this was to be expected.

I hope readers will forgive an understandable emphasis on the Australian Light Horse and New Zealand Mounted Rifles at the expense, at times, of the British cavalry arm. While the former far outperformed the latter on operations, the British, having gained battle experience and confidence, jointly led the charge at apocalyptic Megiddo.

Three volumes and several maps of the British *Official History* of the campaigns in the Middle East are useful for artillery details 'in the broad', although other sources are selective. In order to place events described from an artillery perspective, I have relied on the Australian *Official History*, H.G. Gullett's *Sinai and Palestine*, Vol. VII (he was on the ground as a war correspondent for the duration) for text and some maps, and on A.J. Hill's biography of Lieutenant General Sir Harry Chauvel with maps drawn by Wendy Gorton, despite the fact that neither work devotes much space to gunnery detail. Another fruitful source has been F.M. Cutlack's *Official History*, Vol. VIII, *The Australian Flying Corps*, chapters III to XII.

Measurements

Distances will be expressed in Imperial as was the practice of the time:

1 mile = 1.6 kilometres

1 yard = 0.91 metres

1 pound = 453.5 grams

Abbreviations

AFC	Australian Flying Corps
AIF	Australian Imperial Force
AMD	Australian Mounted Division
ANZAC	Australian and New Zealand Army Corps
A&NZ	Australian and New Zealand
BAC	brigade ammunition column
BC	battery commander
BEF	British Expeditionary Force
BGRA	Brigadier General Royal Artillery
BHQ	battery headquarters
BSM	battery sergeant major
CO	commanding officer
CRA	Commander Royal Artillery
cwt	hundredweight
DAC	divisional ammunition column
DMC	Desert Mounted Column
DSO	Distinguished Service Order
EEF	Egyptian Expeditionary Force
EFF	Eastern Frontier Force
FAB	field artillery brigade
FOO	forward observer
GHQ	General Headquarters
GOC	General Officer Commanding
GPO	Gun Position Officer
GSO1	General Staff Officer Grade 1
HAC	Honourable Artillery Company
HAG	heavy artillery group
HE	high explosive
ICC	Imperial Camel Corps
IMD	Imperial Mounted Division
MGRA	Major General Royal Artillery
NCO	non-commissioned officer
NZMR	New Zealand Mounted Rifles
OC	officer commanding
OP	observation post

Abbreviations

OPO	observation post officer
RA	Royal Artillery
RE	Royal Engineers
RFA	Royal Field Artillery
RFC	Royal Flying Corps
RGA	Royal Garrison Artillery
RHA	Royal Horse Artillery
RHQ	regimental headquarters
RN	Royal Navy
UK	United Kingdom

Map Legend

GEOGRAPHICAL SYMBOLS

- Settlement
- Train station
- Village
- Coastline
- Country border
- Wadi
- River
- Ridge
- Road or track
- Railway line
- Telegraph line
- Bridge or viaduct
- Elevated ground
- Swamp
- Oasis
- City environs

TURKISH & GERMAN SYMBOLS

- Headquarters
- Infantry
- Cavalry
- Artillery
- Medium machine guns
- XXXX Army
- XXX Corps
- XX Division
- X Brigade
- Regiment or Group
- Battalion
- Battery
- Section
- Defended area
- Limit of attack
- Divisional boundary
- Trench lines
- Positions
- Gun positions
- Direction of movement
- Reserves
- Infantry
- Occupied area
- Observation posts
- Cavalry deployments
- Unit deployments
- Tactical ground
- Planned tactical ground
- Planned direction of movement

ANZAC SYMBOLS

- Headquarters
- Infantry
- Light Horse
- Artillery
- Medium machine guns
- Armour (tracked)
- Australian and Royal Flying Corps
- XXXX Army
- XXX Corps
- XX Division
- X Brigade
- Regiment or Group
- Battalion
- Battery
- Section
- Heavy machine gun
- Cavalry
- Logistics or Admin Installation
- X Objective
- ANZAC front line
- Cavalry deployments
- Unit deployments
- Divisional boundaries
- Direction of movement
- Temporary positions
- Gun battery
- Tactical ground
- Planned tactical ground
- Armoured car positions

Narrative One

Background to April 1916

Narrative One
Background to April 1916

Britain's long-held recognition of the strategic importance of the Suez Canal and its northern and southern approaches from 1880 saw a number of irregular Arab uprisings quelled in Sudan, Aden and Egypt. The latter involved the British Army's cavalry and horse artillery, with the support of service elements, suppressing revolts by the Senussi of the Western Desert in 1915 and other dissident tribes of Arabia in 1916.

From the outbreak of war in 1914 to the evacuation of Gallipoli in December 1915, military operations had not proceeded well for the British, French and Commonwealth armies and navies. On every front the Allied forces were in dire straits. In the Mediterranean the armies of the Central Powers — Turkish and German — campaigning in Gallipoli, Mesopotamia, Palestine-Sinai and Salonika taxed the British Empire's resources. The Russian incursion into Anatolia saw the Turkish high command involved on all four fronts. Salonika siphoned off 115,000 British troops, allied with French divisions, in a nondescript but bloody campaign. Gullett noted that 'Salonika itself was a nightmare for the leader responsible for its control' and, eventually, still bickering with their French allies, the British vastly reduced their commitment there. The Mesopotamian campaign of 1915 by General Townshend's army enjoyed initial successes until routed by the Turks in April 1916 with the loss of 20,000 British troops. By the following February General Maud had retaken Kut and provided a welcome reinvigoration for British Empire prestige.

In January 1916 General Archibald Murray was appointed General Officer Commanding (GOC) the Egyptian Expeditionary Force (EEF) with command of Sinai-Palestine operations. In the aftermath of Gallipoli he was forced to reconstitute the British Army with Australian (Australian Imperial Force) and New Zealand (New Zealand Expeditionary Force) reinforcements, most of which were sent to France. Successful diplomacy saw Murray eventually persuade the Arab tribes of the Hejaz to the Allied cause, although he was less successful in his fight with the War Office to secure the troops he needed to prosecute his campaign against the Turks and their German masters. The Germans and Turks sought to disrupt the Allied war effort and supply chain, to draw Allied Middle Eastern assets to France and thus weaken the Suez Canal defences. With the Allied rearguard retreating along defined wells and oases, the forces of the Central Powers could then deny the British that crucial element of desert warfare — water — and thus exhaust their offensive capacity.

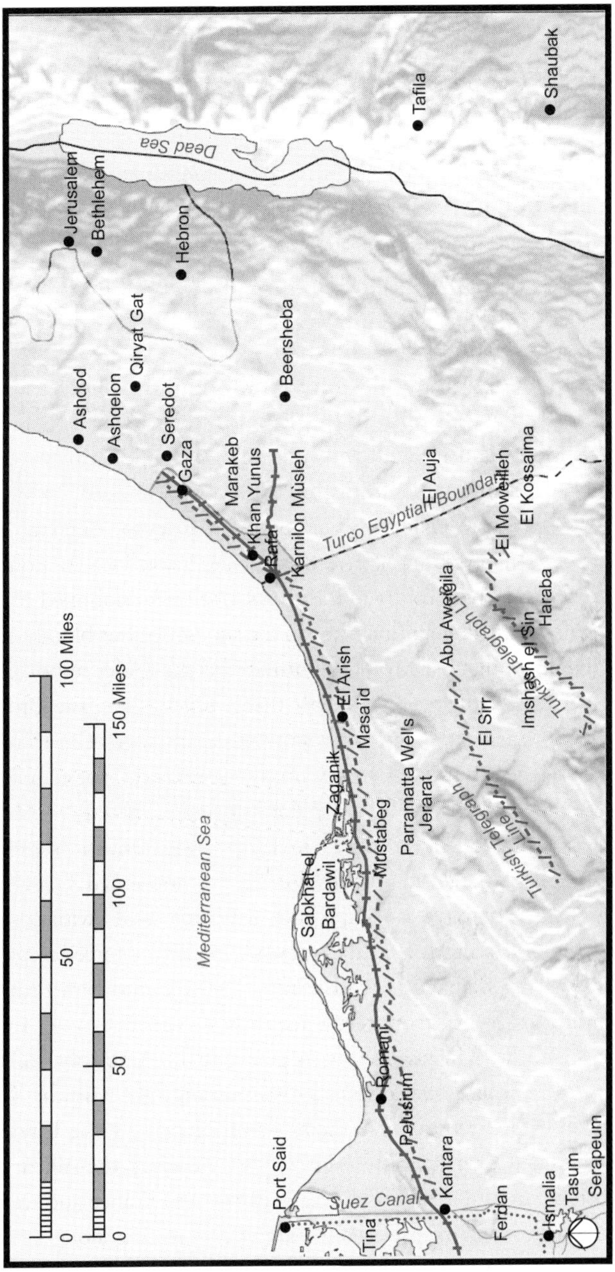

Map A: The Sinai Desert area of operations in 1916.

Chapter 1
Middle East Command: an outline of operations

The desert probably offers as many tactical advantages as disadvantages for gunnery, and while it offers great opportunity for mobility, its frictions make those opportunities harder to exploit. In logistic terms there are few benefits.

J.B.A. Bailey[1]

Historical background

The British Army's presence in Egypt, which dated from 1884, was used some 30 years later as a strategic deterrent based on ownership and the commercial and strategic importance of the Suez Canal. Until October 1914, when Egypt became a British protectorate, the army was employed simply as a 'peacekeeper'. By 1914, however, dissident Senussi tribesmen had begun fomenting insurrection within the nomadic tribes of the Western Desert, drawing on Turkish support to fuel their activities. Having taken advantage of the distraction of Britain's Dardanelles campaign to expand their rebellion, the ringleaders were eventually suppressed by a mobile force despatched from the delta. The seriousness of the unrest varied, usually dependent on the energy and fervour of the local Arab leader and his followers. The actions that eventually suppressed this revolt involved the mounted forces of the Western Frontier Force, including a Royal Horse Artillery (RHA) battery (or more often a section) and Australian troops from November 1915 to May 1916. This coincided with the withdrawal of the British Commonwealth's forces from Gallipoli to Egypt and their subsequent rehabilitation, training and restructuring. The importance of the Suez Canal for access to Europe hardly needs stating, but it was also vital to the economies of the Commonwealth and sundry nations (such as Argentina) which supplied the logistics for the forces in the Middle East and France/Belgium. Britain could not sustain a war against Germany and Austria without the canal.

The British Army's EEF garrisoned Egypt and the canal zone. Its opponents were the Turkish Army infantry and cavalry divisions, corps and armies. The Turkish artillery had learnt much from operations at Gallipoli, where it had played its part in defeating the British, Australian, New Zealand and French troops. Many Turkish infantry regiments had also seen service in the Balkan Wars of 1910–12, where they gained a reputation as first class riflemen, particularly in defence.[2] Artillery had also played a major role in this important but historically neglected campaign. Observers from the major powers drew conclusions on the importance of howitzer fire on trench lines which gave rise to new British Army artillery tactics at the divisional level. Since 1914 the Turk's German allies had stiffened and strengthened their artillery arm with commanders and advisers from Germany, Austria and a smattering from Hungary. Their artillery was to cause the British and Commonwealth forces much grief when it faced them across the dusty Sinai Desert and rugged Palestinian hinterland. The Turkish cavalry, however, was somewhat of an unknown martial quantity.

The terrain

The Middle East area of operations was vast, extending from the Western Desert (Libya) in a crescent to Aleppo in what was the Ottoman Empire. The Suez Canal marked the centre. Amman was the easternmost city and Aleppo the northernmost. The Sinai Peninsula was bounded by the canal, the Gulf of Suez and the border between the Sinai and Palestine representing the north-south border from Rafa on the Mediterranean to the Gulf of Aqaba. The major coastal centres and battles were at Romani, El Arish, Rafa, Magdhaba and Berukin. Operations in southern Palestine focused on Gaza, Beersheba, Hebron, Es Salt and Amman. In northern Palestine they covered locations from Jerusalem, Jaffa, Megiddo, El Afule, Nazareth, Haifa, Deraa and Damascus (in Syria) to Aleppo.[3]

The terrain over which the campaign was waged was vastly different to that on which the British and Antipodean horsemen had trained in their homelands. There was just one aspect common to all operations — the attention and care of horses/camels/mules (first) and men (second). Horses could manage around 24 hours without water in high summer, double that in winter. This period was frequently longer during operations by a factor of two, sometimes three. The terrain over which horse and foot soldiers operated was also a significant consideration in planning, particularly when operations reached the Judean Hills. In terms of horseflesh, the cold climate breeds from Britain were not as resilient as the Waler, renowned for its smaller stature and speed and imported from Australia in its thousands. The less well-known New Zealand remounts were also very hardy, the New Zealanders naturally asserting that their mounts were 'the better'.[4]

Image 1: Colonel Charles Rosenthal, Australian commander of the artillery supporting a combined Allied force which repulsed a Turkish attack on the Suez Canal in early 1915 (AWM H19207).

Chapter 1

The campaign was to be one of the last in modern times when the most precious resource was water from wells and other sources. Its purity and supply was always the primary factor in any advance or operation that sought to bring the Turks to battle. Its provision involved the latest intelligence on well 'status' since retreating Turks regularly poisoned them or blew them up. Pipelines and water-carrying camels in their thousands were required to sustain horses, mules, camels and men on whose wellbeing the success of a campaign depended. The staff calculated that five gallons per man per day was required for the troops, Egyptian levies and others.

Creating the Delta/Palestine Army

The then British Army's commander in the theatre, Major General Julian Byng, had produced an initial military and strategic appreciation which calculated that, from December 1914, he had sufficient troops on the ground (5000), appropriately structured, to achieve his aim. But his force of cavalry and infantry, British and Indian, was notably deficient in artillery. Indeed by late 1915 the force boasted only two batteries — T Battery, RHA, and the 7th Mountain Battery, Royal Garrison Artillery (RGA). He had no medium and heavy/siege guns, as the War Office view was that these were far more useful in France and Flanders than the Middle East.[5]

Byng was recalled to France to command the Canadian Army and General Sir John Maxwell appointed in his stead. Maxwell was born on 11 July 1859 and commissioned in the infantry. He served in command positions in Egypt and was awarded the Distinguished Service Order (DSO) at Suakin. He was appointed Governor of the Nile and established railway lines and other infrastructure during his tenure. In the Second Boer War he commanded a brigade and was promoted major general in 1900. By 1914 Maxwell was GOC Egypt until his recall to Britain in 1916.[6] Lieutenant General Sir Archibald Murray was then elevated to overall command. It was ironic that in 1914 the British Army structured its infantry and cavalry divisions for manoeuvre warfare only to campaign on two static fronts — those of Flanders/Picardy and Salonika and Gallipoli.

The end of the Gallipoli campaign released substantial Turkish forces to strengthen the Ottoman Empire's Palestine and Persian armies. One of the first operations to be mounted at divisional strength was an attempt to seize the Suez Canal. The EEF canal defences were now commanded by Murray, whose headquarters, sited at Ismailia, included the base depots of mounted forces and infantry divisions from Australia and New Zealand.

Assembled in the delta were two Australian divisions (the 1st and 2nd) and several brigades of light horse, together with their service corps. The divisions were destined for France. The light horse brigades and infantry were making good their losses from Gallipoli, while more reinforcements were arriving by convoy from Australia to expand its overseas defence commitment. The creation of two more infantry divisions — the 4th and 5th (the 3rd was raised in Australia) — from the 1st and 2nd divisions doubled the Australian Imperial Force (AIF) artillery strength. When volunteers were requested to transfer from their current corps/regiment to the divisional artillery, some 1198 light horsemen transferred, presumably the attraction of being horsed having retained its appeal.[7] In the event, four infantry divisions reached acceptable strength and were shipped to France, while the Australian Light Horse eventually reached establishment strength.

British cavalry regiments, both regular and territorial, boosted the defences. Many of the cavalry officers brought their own horses and other remounts from Britain but quickly realised that these were less resilient in the harsh desert conditions than the Walers and other blood horses used by the Australians and New Zealanders. It would be some months before the British horses could be acclimatised and suitably mounted as military assets and thus reach their peak, an observation made by both Maxwell and Murray before and after debacles at Oghratina and Katia.[8]

Both the climate and logistics infrastructure were quite different to those of the Western Front. Heat, *khamsins* (dust and sandstorms), flies and insects, lack of infrastructure and a chronic shortage of that military essential — water — bedevilled operations. The delta was at the end of a comparatively long logistic chain from the factories and bread baskets of the United Kingdom (UK), North and South America, Australia, New Zealand and the British colonies. Mobility was vested in the horse, mule, camel and four new artefacts of war: the aeroplane, armoured car, tractor and tank. Between oases there were mud hut settlements, tracks time-worn over centuries, and a few major towns such as Gaza, Beersheba and Jerusalem. A railway line snaked its way south from Turkey, linking Jerusalem to just north of Gaza and Beersheba. From there a single line travelled to Auja and on to El Kossaima. There was also a lateral line towards the coast near Deir el Belah. The Turks relied heavily on this facility and its 'Decauville' type temporary light gauge rail (600mm) which called at isolated posts from time to time. The British light railways connected Cairo, Ismailia and the canal to Port Suez. In 1916 the British built a line from Kantara on the canal to Romani, later adding a spur to the coast at El Arish. It followed that both belligerents also had to rely on horses, camels, mules, oxen, tractors, motor lorries and, at times, Model T Ford cars and Egyptian labourers in their thousands for manoeuvre and supply from the railhead.

The administrative and logistical turmoil associated with the evacuation from Gallipoli, wounded returning to units, drafts from Australia and New Zealand and British colonies, was immense. It fell first to Maxwell to make sense of it all, his principal concern the training of raw troops in a climate of endless shortages, most notably the stores and ammunition to achieve a level of training that he deemed satisfactory. Much has been written on the extensive training regimes pursued in the delta to produce men of Draft Priority 1 standard. Maxwell was hamstrung by shortages of every description. However, despite his recurrent difficulties, four Australian infantry divisions were duly despatched to France, leaving behind all but one light horse regiment to do battle with the Turk.[9]

General Headquarters (GHQ) had estimated that two corps of six divisions were required to defend the canal and develop operations to push the Turks back over their borders. Maxwell ordered the construction of a railway line from the east bank of the canal into the Sinai Desert at Katia. He allocated the 5th Australian Light Horse Brigade to defend the project. However, both this task and the more complex military operations involved required accurate survey and maps for desert navigation and particularly for use by the artillery. The gunners had to rely extensively on reports from Royal Flying Corps (RFC) observers aloft, particularly for the location of enemy batteries. The British had an advantage in that pre-war English archaeologists had developed a fascination for the region which had resulted in the detailed mapping of some key areas which pinpointed the location of wells and provided accurate description of the terrain. This advantage was initially denied to the Turks and their German, Austrian and few Hungarian artillerymen. However the only survey resource available to British forces was a large-scale 'Map of Sinai and Handbook' compiled by a General Staff Section of which one Lieutenant T.E. Lawrence was a valuable member. This was unsuitable for artillery use and the gunners faced the prospect of campaigning with limited battle maps. Indeed, there are no references in accounts of this time to the application of the locating/observation techniques (such as sound ranging, flash spotting and observation balloon sections) to gather artillery evidence on the enemy for which accurate survey was essential. With Allenby's arrival in theatre in June 1917 and given his experience of cavalry corps command in France, it is reasonable to assume that he knew he had to make better use of and strengthen his scarce artillery assets.[10]

Image 2: Major General S.C.U. Smith, Allenby's MGRA (State Library of NSW image).

Sydenham Campbell Urquhart Smith was born in Madras on New Years Day of 1859, a son of the surgeon general of the Madras Army.

He joined the Royal Artillery, Woolwich in 1879. In 1896 while Instructor at the School of Artillery he was selected by Major General George French to command the New South Wales Artillery with the local rank of major. In 1899 as a colonel he commanded the NSW artillery in the Boer War.

His role was both operational and administrative in nature, and he obviously impressed his superiors. His command of officers and gunners he noted was superior others he had to work with.

He returned to UK and was appointed Chief Instructor, School of Gunnery of the RHA and RFA for two years.

His next appointment was Commander, Royal Artillery (CRA) 1911-1914. Appointments to corps staff followed, first as CRA 29 Division at the Gallipoli campaign and ending as MGRA to Murray, then Allenby for the duration of the war. He retired on New Years day, 1919 having been created Knight Commander of the Order of St Michael and St George, and Commander of the Bath.

The artillery available comprised a collection of horse-drawn, mountain and two heavy guns that had arrived in the theatre via Gallipoli or with their divisions/brigades from Britain and India. Major General S.C.U. (Sydenham) Smith was appointed Major General Royal Artillery (MGRA) to supervise this motley grouping. Smith's first command had been as a lieutenant colonel in charge of the Artillery Forces of New South Wales in 1897. He served in the Boer War as commander of A Battery, and was subsequently Commandant of the Northwestern District of Cape Colony. Given the sobriquet of 'Long 'un' — he was six foot four inches tall and a colonel by 1914 — Smith was a practical, persuasive and impressive figure who performed admirably for his two superiors throughout the war.

While by July 1916 Smith had two batteries of 60-pounders, these had just two guns and the organisation of his heterogeneous arsenal was predicated on the structure of Maxwell's army. Indeed the despatch of V Field Survey Company, Royal Engineers (RE), in June 1917 to the theatre under the command of Captain W. Cockburn, Royal Canadian Engineers — which coincided with General Edmund Allenby's appointment — marked the first attempt to provide accurate survey. Several months passed before Maxwell's command crystallised with the formation of Lieutenant General Birdwood's I Australian Corps (1st and 2nd divisions) and Lieutenant General Godley's II ANZAC Corps of the 4th (at Serapeum) and 5th Australian divisions (at Ferry Post) and the New Zealand details. Maxwell's Brigadier General Royal Artillery (BGRA) was Brigadier W.D. Nichol who had oversight of the artillery assets of the Imperial Mounted Division (IMD), Desert Mounted Column (DMC) and six infantry divisions.[11] It was not until July 1917 that additional siege and heavy batteries ensured that the force had sufficient artillery strength for the task that lay ahead. The RFC presence was also weak, with just two squadrons of 48 aircraft available for servicing this vast area of operations.[12]

Chapter 2
Cavalry doctrine and the employment of artillery

The advantage of time and place in all practical actions is half a victory which, being lost, is irrecoverable.

Sir Francis Drake,
in a letter to Queen Elizabeth I

Despite the numerical superiority of the British infantry divisions over the mounted troops gathered in the delta, cavalry operations were to play a significant role in British strategy during the early battles with the Turks and their German advisers. By way of background, it is useful to review the many characteristics of this important arm, particularly its combination with artillery. Up to the time of the Boer War the level of staff attention paid to the cavalry effectively polarised its military hierarchy. In Britain a cavalry association conferred an elevated position in society, particularly for officers. With the development of the rifle, reactionary senior cavalry officers took issue with Captain Ian Hamilton (later to command the Mediterranean Expeditionary Force in the Dardanelles) who stated in 1885 that the 'cavalry and direct fire artillery will become obsolete, and that battles would consist of widely dispersed rifle-armed infantry skirmishers picking each other off at ranges of one mile.' In the 1880s, a young officer named Douglas Haig offered his thoughts on the subject, commenting that 'the ideal cavalry is one that can attack on foot, fight on horseback'. He supported the notion of machine-guns and artillery supporting cavalry. His contemporary, Colonel John French, had similar views. In Australia, British Major General Sir Edward Hutton, Commandant of Colonial Forces, supported the concept of mounted infantry and structured the light horse regiments accordingly. The New Zealanders soon followed suit.[1]

In general terms, the British Army used the Second Boer War (1899–1902) to examine tactical doctrine and it is instructive to review the refinement that ensued following a formal enquiry and several years of study. There were many hard lessons to be learned from South Africa. The comprehensive inquiry that followed the Boer War revealed that British doctrine had been formulated for a

European-style war completely unsuited to the 'guerilla' campaign waged by the Boers. With the raising and training of what became known as mounted infantry, British Army doctrine was enshrined in the 1912 *Yeomanry and Mounted Rifle Training Manual*. This doctrine saw troopers armed with a Lee Enfield .303 rifle replacing their previous issue carbine. Thus a squadron or regiment could apply either dismounted firepower and/or synchronise a charge, using rifle and bayonet, carbine, revolver, lance or sword. The lance and sword were a hangover from the fascination that lingered from the cavalry charge at Omdurman in the Sudan, or perhaps even Balaclava. General Lord Roberts was a firm believer in mounted infantry and, during the Boer War, he was supported by a colonel who would also make his name on the Western Front: Henry Rawlinson.[2]

History has left little hard evidence of 'staff rides' involving cavalry manoeuvres with horse artillery or the advent of Maxim machine-guns with their extended killing range. Used extensively by the Boers, this weapon caused the British horsed troops and infantry much grief on the open veldt. However when the disparate combination of regular cavalry, territorial yeomanry, light horse and mounted rifle regiments of three nations gathered in Egypt in 1916–17 they spoke a similar doctrinal language. Despite this there were significant differences in the standards of training and tactical acumen of their officers, a flaw that was to be revealed in early operations.

The use of barbed-wire barriers to channel cavalry charges onto machine-gun 'killing grounds' (akin to using obstacles to channel tanks onto minefields or within range of anti-tank artillery) was clearly demonstrated on the Somme. What had not been fully realised from the Boer War was that Boer artillery was rendered less effective on several occasions because of the speed or advance and/or the shock of a charge. These observations had relevance for the unfolding scenario in the Sinai and Palestine. During training in Egypt in late 1914, the 4th Australian Light Horse Regiment charged an infantry position. The umpires declared that it had suffered almost 100% casualties from machine-gun fire.[3]

While at this time visual signalling was the key to manoeuvre, on the other hand, command, control and coordination of the fall of shot onto the enemy, whether entrenched, on foot or horsed, were moot points requiring the cavalry and artillery commanders to think 'as one'. The mutual confidence essential to this process could only be gained through training and/or from battle experience. The gunners' aim was to apply fire from a flank position with the artillery battery commander (BC) or observation post officer (OPO) enjoying clear observation of the cavalry objective. Synchronising the fall of shot with the rate of advance was crucial. This would depend on the topography and elevation, and in the

Palestine campaign this varied considerably. The artillery brigade commander generally positioned his affiliated battery about halfway down his column of march with the BC at his side and within signalling distance. The battery's position was usually specified in orders.

There were other contingent factors relating to effective cooperation between gunner and trooper. In terms of colour, the terrain of the Sinai and Palestine hinterland was various shades of khaki. When observing for the battle commander, gunners discovered that a shimmering heat haze made judging distance, and hence using map data for engagement, very difficult. Furthermore, the khaki uniform material blended extremely well with the earth and, to overcome the dangers of not sighting friendly troops, infanteers (and cavalry) used white or black discs to indicate the forward defence line or line held. The terrain also made life difficult for the cavalry scouts. It was here that the inherent skills of the light horseman, who originated primarily from the rural Australian hinterland, proved superior to those of the yeomanry. The contrast between 'field and coppice' and outback Australia could hardly have been more marked.

Official historian H.S. Gullett concluded early in the campaign that 'modern firepower had greatly curtailed the possibility of shock tactics.'[4] Nevertheless, by 1917, there were instances of cavalry charges with supporting artillery which involved few casualties, such as at Beersheba, thus strengthening some commanders' resolve not to relinquish this cavalry capability altogether. In the Sinai the charge was used at Oghratina and also featured in several actions during the advance from Beersheba to Aleppo, as well as for the last classic cavalry charges at Huj and Mughar. This strengthened the case argued by Brigadier Grant, commander of the 4th Australian Light Horse Brigade at Beersheba, who noted that 'the sword permits a more direct line of attack' and, ergo, was to be preferred on that occasion.[5] However, the 'bible' for combined operations, *Field Service Regulations 1912*, noted that:

> Yeomanry and Mounted Rifles ... act chiefly by fire but may, when they have received sufficient training, employ shock actions in special emergencies ... When cooperating with other arms [e.g. artillery, air] their mobility enables a commander to transfer them rapidly from one portion of the field to another, and thus turn to account opportunities which he would otherwise be unable to achieve.[6]

The logic of that 'macro' view did not include the detail of the command, coordination and control factors described above. A successful example of the 'mounted troops with RHA support' genre occurred at Beersheba where the commander of the Desert Column, Major General Harry Chauvel, at the *moment critique* issued his now famous order, 'Put Grant straight at it.'[7] Nor did it stop the marauding light horsemen stalking Turkish gun positions and despatching their detachments, although this was technically 'counter bombardment'.

The light horse, mounted rifle and cavalry regiment

Based on British practice, Major General Hutton's Australian light horse regiments initially comprised four squadrons. However, in the desert their composition changed to A, B and C squadrons and their details. With the addition of regimental headquarters (RHQ), these regiments numbered 530 all ranks. Deployment battle practice comprised a headquarters group of an adjutant, orderlies and signallers (four officers and 37 other ranks), three squadrons (each of six officers and 77 other ranks) and a machine-gun section (one officer and 26 other ranks) which was then equipped with three Maxim or Lewis machine-guns (until 1916). A squadron was organised into four troops each commanded by a subaltern and comprising four 14-man sections. Two trumpeters accompanied the officers. Two or three men from each section were designated horse-holders for the troopers in action. A fully manned section would deploy 12 riflemen. The squadron had signallers, drivers, batmen and six artificers to repair and maintain horses, saddles, harnesses and hooves. All told, a regiment with attached services (medical, veterinary) had 497 riding horses, 59 draught and seven pack animals, usually mules. At B Echelon, there were 15 vehicles, wagons, limbers and bicycles, some 29 in total. On operations, regimental strength was seldom more than 400, the numbers sapped by brigade duties, attendance at schools and courses, medical reasons, but notably very few absent without leave. The British Army cavalry regiment was similarly organised into an RHQ and three squadrons (A, B and C) each of 227 men. RHQ establishment was five officers and 24 other ranks, of whom eight were non-commissioned officers (NCOs), and included four signallers. The regiment had a machine-gun section of one officer and 24 other ranks, their mounts totalling 528 riding horses, 74 draft animals and six packhorses.[8]

As a 'rule of thumb' a full mounted division in order of march covered around 3.5 miles per hour. Sections of four abreast moved in hourly stops, with 40 minutes of marching, 10 minutes of riders leading their horses and 10 minutes resting or cooling. Horses were watered every six hours and carried a total of 250 pounds (lbs). A division took two and half hours to pass a point; indeed the leading squadron could water horses, mess and have a comfort stop while the last squadron was still on the move.[9]

The General Staff quickly recognised that each brigade needed more firepower, so one regiment became a machine-gun regiment (as also occurred in France), with squadrons equipped in 1917 with 12 Lewis and/or Vickers guns, four each dedicated to a regiment. One squadron of machine-gunners accompanied each regiment, or a regiment was attached to a brigade. The squadron's strength was eight officers and 221 other ranks. In April 1917 the Vickers was replaced by the Hotchkiss M1909 and Benet-Mercie weapons. These weapons could be brought into action in less than one minute.[10]

Image 3: Each squadron of the Australian Light Horse had either horse and/or vehicle-(T Model Ford) mounted Lewis, Vickers or Hotchkiss machine-guns (AWM B00460).

Prior to discussion of the artillery, some explanation of the term 'rifles' and 'sabres' is necessary to clarify the numbers provided in the *Official History* when describing the strength of opposing forces. As the term 'rifles' is used freely in this account, it can be taken literally to mean the number of men armed with rifles, or intelligence estimates of effective men available for battle. However the term conceals the main offensive strength of a Turkish formation which lay in its machine-gun battalion of approximately 800 men. The total numbers of guns were seldom given, but these *ahmets* would have been counted as 'rifles'. There were 60 guns per infantry division in a fixed (i.e. establishment) ratio with its organic artillery. The British infantry divisions had around one-fifth fewer, although in the mounted formations the proportion of machine-guns to rifles was higher. The high level of infantry casualties incurred in the first 18 months of operations could possibly be attributed to this discrepancy. 'Sabres' were counted as the number of effective mounted troops available, and many regiments still carried them while armed with the trusty Lee Enfield .303 rifle. Yeomanry/cavalry regiments carried .303 rifles and were trained to infantry musketry standard, but were counted as 'sabres'.

Bringing all the Australian light horse regiments together and organising them into brigades representative of the Commonwealth fell to Chauvel, who had been temporary commander of the 1st Australian Division at Gallipoli. His General Staff Officer Grade 1 (GSO1) was Lieutenant Colonel J.G. Brown, a British regular but an Australian by birth, who had served in South Africa and had been on the staff of Allenby's cavalry corps during the retreat from Mons. Other staff officers selected by Chauvel showed 'marked ability in Gallipoli', and this extended to brigade, regiment and squadron commanders, many of whom were veterans of the Boer War. This experienced cohort of regimental commanders (including one New Zealand officer) was unique. All had a clear appreciation of the extent to which horse artillery could assist mounted operations. Nine had served in South Africa and all were subsequently promoted to general rank.[11]

Chauvel's style as a commander, so ably described by Gullett and a plethora of biographers and historians, will be described in detail later in this narrative. It is not generally known that he led the 1st Australian Division after Major General Bridges was mortally wounded at Gallipoli: 'He left the Peninsula with a reputation of a shrewd, safe leader who made the most of restricted possibilities. Birdwood was quick to appreciate his wise and intimate knowledge of tactics — a sound, sure touch.' Chauvel declined an infantry division command in France, opting to be with his horsemen and following his penchant for mobile operations. He fought to win, but not at any price. He knew his troops, their limitations, and the same dimensions of their mounts. To him they were indistinguishable when they took the field. Chauvel, like his command, was a modest man, somewhat aloof, a front for his shyness. He was, Gullett surmised, 'a far seeing brain rather than the spirit of his force', never to be a hero to them. He earned his laurels as a master of 'far seeing perfect preparation and exact execution rather than flashes of brilliance in moments of crisis.'[12] Chauvel's subordinates were not of the same mould. Grant, Ryrie, Wilson, Meredith, Macarthur-Onslow and Cox had their own distinctive leadership styles to which the men responded. Chauvel's command was soon to include the New Zealand Mounted Rifles (NZMR) Brigade, which was similarly organised and followed the same doctrine as the other national horsemen.[13]

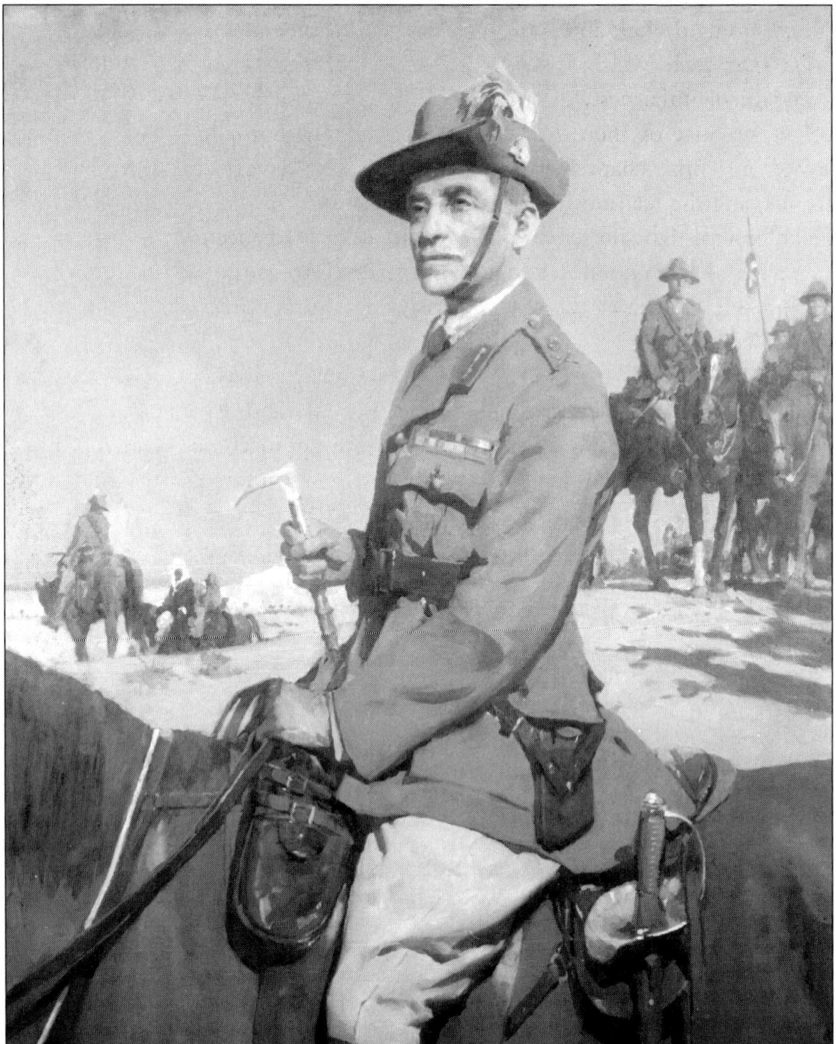

Image 4: Lieutenant General Sir Harry Chauvel, GOC Desert Mounted Corps (AWM ART 13521).

Chapter 2

It is worth summarising the characteristics of this fine group of Australian and New Zealand soldiers who were the power behind Chauvel and his formations. Primarily comprised of reinforcements in 1916 (to make up for Gallipoli casualties and those who transferred to the new 4th and 5th divisions) and a hard core of veterans, this was a unique AIF and New Zealand corps. Gullett's hyperbolic description of the Australian component was, like most generalisations, a sum of its parts. Modest, resourceful, hardy, laconic, no stranger to hard work and sportingly inclined, they were quite different to the English, Scottish, Welsh, Irish and Indian soldiers they supported. Industrious, intolerant of unfairness, discrimination based on birthright and ability, they were a product of their egalitarian society. Light horse historian Jean Bou devotes an entire chapter to an examination of the corps ethos, myths and legends, and the relationships between officers, NCOs and men. Suffice to say the archetypal light horseman was capable of a broad spectrum of behaviours and values — from nobility to baseness — and mirrored the society from which he came. He also shared these characteristics to a greater or lesser extent with his NZMR colleagues.[14]

The soldiers of the British yeomanry/cavalry divisions, where social distinctions and differences were more apparent, and which were initially reflected in their 'sporting' rather than martial approach to soldiering, took some time to reach acceptable operational levels — not so the Indian cavalry regiments which arrived to replace the British later in the war. That said, a typical light horse regimental officer was better educated than most of his troops and had often risen through the ranks. But, as any analysis of combat effectiveness shows, education per se does not correlate highly with leadership at troop, squadron or regimental level.

Chapter 3
Corps artillery: horse, field, siege and heavy artillery brigades

Go where glory waits thee,
But, while fame elates thee,
Oh! Still remember me.

Francis I, 1547

Horse artillery brigades

The Territorial RHA and RGA batteries that accompanied Chauvel's regiments comprised Londoners, Westcountrymen from the Home Counties, Midlanders and Scotsmen. An exception was the Hong Kong and Singapore Mountain Battery RGA, manned by British and Indian personnel.[1] This battery supported almost every cavalry regiment during the course of the war. A battery was generally commanded by a major. An RHA battery establishment of six 13-pounder Erhardt design (and later 18-pounder) guns under 'normal' conditions had to adapt to accommodate the rigours of the desert terrain over which it fought, with pedrails (shoe-like attachments to the wheels) to enable the guns to move over sand. Three batteries comprised a brigade, commanded by a Commander Royal Artillery (CRA), usually a lieutenant colonel. He had a small staff and acted as adviser to the cavalry and infantry commanders. The brigade had its own ammunition column, and it was usual for a senior troop gun position officer, who fought his section of three guns, to be promoted captain and given command of the column. Promotion was then to troop commander, leading to a battery command, depending on vacancies and other extrinsic regional factors. Gun detachments were commanded by sergeants. Low casualty rates throughout the desert campaign, particularly compared to infantry and cavalry units, saw cohesion and teamwork and other morale factors inspire batteries to perform extraordinary feats. When the artillery war began against the Senussi in Egypt, an RHA battery comprised 220 horses and many batteries were equipped with 13-pounders.[2] There were two types of ammunition used: 6 cwt (hundredweight) or 9 cwt high explosive (HE) and shrapnel.[3]

Chapter 3

Image 5: The Hong Kong Singapore Mountain Battery training with its light field guns. Artillery spotters in the top right-hand corner are performing survey work (AWM B01465).

Royal Field Artillery field brigades

The organic artillery support for an infantry division in 1914 comprised three field artillery brigades (FAB) and the divisional ammunition column (DAC). Commanded by a lieutenant colonel, each brigade comprised a headquarters, three batteries each of six guns and an ammunition column. At establishment strength the brigade was 25 officers and 882 other ranks strong requiring 218 riding and 511 draught horses for mobility. On parade it covered an enormous area and in column of march extended almost two miles in length. The total establishment is described in Table 1 below with the duties of some of the other ranks at RHQ and battery headquarters (BHQ) to provide support for the infantry included as 'Notes'.

TABLE 1: FIELD BRIGADE WAR ESTABLISHMENT[4]

	Officers	WO	S/Sgts	Artificers	R&F	Total	Horses	
							Riding	Draught
BdeHQ	3	1	0	1	30	35(a)	23	7
Att BdeHQ	1	0	5	1	6	13	7	0
BTY (x4)	16	0	28(d)(e)	32(b)	476(c)	552	168	332
BAC*	1	4	6	9	134	153	20	172
TOTAL	**21**	**5**	**39**	**48**	**646**	**753**	**218**	**511**

*Brigade Ammunition Column

Notes:

a. Each brigade headquarters had 19 rank and file for the Telephone Detachment. Attached to headquarters were water (6), hygiene and medical (7), veterinary (6) and armament (1) dutymen.

b. Includes lookouts (2) and men trained for signalling duties/telephonists and battery staff (21). Some 51 gunners were supported by 16 drivers of spare horses, vehicles, batmen, etc.

c. Artificers covers the broad trades required to keep the battery operational, including farriers, shoeing smiths, saddlers, fitters/wheelers, etc.

d. This includes four detachment commanders, the battery quartermaster sergeant, the battery sergeant major (BSM) and battery staff sergeant. Gun detachments (sub-sections) of five gun numbers and three horse 'drivers' were commanded by a sergeant, totalling nine in all.

e. Includes 16 spare attached.

The twenty-four 18-pounder guns and four battery headquarters required an enormous logistical tail. For example, to fire an aimed round at a target required almost 32 other personnel per one gunner in every detachment. Eventually, in 1916, the six-gun battery superseded the four-gun battery and the three brigade ammunition columns (BAC) amalgamated to become the DAC, with significant savings in man and horse power where this was practical. In 1918 a corps ammunition column was formed, again to reduce man and animal numbers. In addition to the 18-pounder gun, one battery of a field brigade manned 4.5-inch howitzers. This gave the battery flexibility in engaging targets, the howitzer proving useful where a steep descending trajectory was required to engage enemy guns on reverse slopes and in 'dongas'. This weapon fired both types of explosive shells.

Image 6. An 18-pounder field gun and crew. These guns equipped infantry divisional artilleries (AWM B00580).

Heavy and siege artillery

The rationale behind Britain's use of heavy artillery in 1914 lay in observations recorded during the Franco-Prussian War of 1870–71 which highlighted both the need for mobility and an increase in calibre and weight of shell. The nub of the problem lay in developing the means to deploy a far heavier, mobile weapon. At the same time science was providing a better understanding of the physics and mathematics of ballistics, propellant chemistry and metallurgy for ordnance design. All the major European powers were investing in this emergent technology. The Russo-Japanese War of 1904–05 was the next conflict to demonstrate the importance of a high trajectory weapon for counter-battery roles, a point that was reinforced once again during the Balkan Wars of 1912–13. The British Army soon joined the rush to modernise. British brigades required roughly the same number of men and animals as a field brigade — a major's command of around 500 men and almost as many animals. Siege (four 6-inch howitzers) and heavy (four 60-pounder guns) battery establishments are outlined in Table 2 below:

TABLE 2: SIEGE AND HEAVY BATTERY OUTLINE ESTABLISHMENTS[5]

	Siege: four 6-inch howitzers	Heavy: four 60-pounder guns
Horse-drawn		
Officers	4	5
Other ranks	157	173
Total	**161**	**178**
Horses/mules	204	116
Ammunition column	139	56

The explanatory notes concerning the organisation of and duties within a field brigade applied more or less equally to the employment of heavier ordnance, the key difference the replacement of horses with tractors, providing manpower savings.

In operations during 1916, the divisional batteries could not provide the type of support for targets that required the more destructive power of the 60-pounders and 5.5-inch howitzers. Any counter-battery work was conducted with direct fire or observed from aircraft and, in the early stages of the campaign, Gullett records instances of gun-to-gun duels with the Turks in which the latter's fire proved far more effective. This was due in part to a lack of accurate survey to match the maps of the area and the adherence to outdated doctrine and practices, replicating the problems of infantry support during 1916 and 1917 in France and Flanders. In the early days of the campaign this was attributed to the dearth of experienced officers, inadequate training and shortages of control stores endemic in Kitchener's 'New Armies'. Maxwell simply had to make the best of his scarce resources until he was replaced by General Murray in March 1916. In early Sinai operations the need for heavy and siege artillery was subordinated to the field brigades.

Operationally, the performance of the artillery was influenced by a number of factors such as the lack of prior reconnaissance and unfamiliarity with the ground. When plans went awry, deficiencies multiplied into distressing scenarios such as the abandoning of guns. For example, at Katia and Bir el Abd in August 1916, Gullett notes that 'Chauvel's batteries of horse artillery were matched by as many mountain guns in addition to several "five nine" howitzers …', adding that later the guns 'came under heavy fire from "five nines", mountain guns and anti-aircraft guns' as the attack by the NZMR Brigade regiments (Auckland and Canterbury) of the 3rd Brigade came to a standstill. By 10.30 am the enemy guns were becoming increasingly active along the entire front: 'The duel between the German "5.9s" and the plucky little horse gunners was very one-sided ... Their relative weakness was emphasized by the failure of their observers to discover the enemy heavy batteries while the Germans, knowing the ground in detail, had previously located the British guns.'[6]

Image 7: An RGA 60-pounder gun and part of its detachment (AWM J06536).

These disadvantages were at times partially offset by the presence of two aircraft squadrons (No. 1 AFC — Australian Flying Corps — and No. 14 Squadron, RFC) until the end of 1917, the latter retained in western Egypt. Multi-tasked as fighters and also to perform ground attack, reconnaissance, observation and photography, the latter role was to become No. 1 Squadron's specialty for the remainder of the war. Aircraft were a force multiplier by their very presence, ending the war a fine instrument of air power.

A framework for accurate gunnery

Command and control of a troop or battery involved a diverse range of skills and disciplines for both its observer and gun position officer. One of the most important skills was the ability to map-spot the battery's position and that of the target using accurate topographical maps. These were produced by well-sited survey companies and skilled cartographers who converted their data to graphical form suitable for field artillery use. The most important map spot was that of the pivot gun of a troop or battery from which line and range to a target could be calculated so that the target could be engaged quickly and economically. A regiment had three methods of calculating the range from gun to target: using a map or air photograph, using surveying instruments or through the skilled eye of experienced observers with an intimate knowledge of a given zone who directed battery fire by reference to previous targets based on familiarity with the allocated zone. This had the advantage of allowing for any prior survey discrepancies and meteorological effects. To enhance accuracy, the battery staff could also use either a telemeter or range finder, both of which used simple trigonometrical or optical principles. The artillery telemeter required two men and was far more time-consuming to operate than the range finder which equipped one man to find a range in a matter of minutes. The accuracy of range from gun to target in both cases was more important than the accuracy of map spot of the pivot gun.[7]

Communications

Given the background of the senior cavalry commanders who had seen active service in the Boer War and the subsequent developments in modern communication methods, the cavalry force assembled in the delta was in a fortunate position. Since the Boer War, two new methods — telephone and wireless — had been added to the available modes of communication. While the British Army used these extensively within its infantry divisions, the influence of these new devices on command and control arrangements in cavalry and/or combined operations with infantry in mobile warfare was not readily appreciated However, *Field Service Regulations* developed doctrine to apply to mobile warfare in desert conditions as it had to infantry operations in open country.

In open terrain, the doctrinal preference was for artillery support from the flank. Depending on the phase of war, it was essential for the artillery commander to 'have the means of re-adjusting, from time to time, the tasks assigned to brigades'. Cavalry and artillery commanders thus 'should be in view of each other'. This 'top down' communication had a variety of modes such as heliograph, wireless and orderlies particularly since, at regimental level and above, written orders could only provide a broad picture of the commander's intentions (as distinct from infantry 'schemes').

During the Palestine-Sinai campaign air support was a battle winner, and the primary means of air-to-ground communication involved dropping written messages in a tube with a streamer attached, firing Very lights and sounding a klaxon horn. Ground-to-air signals were usually conveyed with white cloth strips and Very lights.[8] Similar conventions applied to the direction of naval gunfire in coastal operations by the Royal Naval Air Service.

First operations

Two minor campaigns set the scene for operations in 1916 at a point when there was still much to learn — not so much from a gunnery perspective, but in terms of the conditions in which the batteries would see active service. The enormous differences in climate, terrain and insects in the Mediterranean/Levant often presented the most significant problems as the Notts Battery, RHA, which had already seen action in the Egyptian Western Desert, would attest.

Of immediate concern was the security of the Suez Canal, a crucial logistical lifeline from Australia and New Zealand and the East Indies/Malaya. General Maxwell's first offensive operations in 1915 were designed to deal with two threats in Egypt and Aden, both places vital to his supplies and communications. It was to be the first real test of the state of training of his mounted troops and infantry and of the long-established affiliations between artillery and cavalry. For its part, the cavalry was well supported by two mountain batteries with their 2.75-inch ordnance, the 'screw guns' of Kipling's famous poem, while the 13-pounders of the cavalry divisions cooperated with the divisional artillery from time to time. These batteries were former territorial units from London (the Honourable Artillery Company — HAC), Scotland, the midlands and the south/west, and totalled 10 in all. Initially, the Senussi revolt in western Egypt and unrest in Aden saw two HAC batteries (A and B) despatched there following their training in Britain.

Initial horse artillery actions — HAC batteries in the delta

No account of artillery in the Sinai and Palestine campaigns would be complete without a description of the London-based HAC and its A and B batteries. The HAC was one of 10 Territorial Force batteries of four RHA brigades (the 18th, 19th, 20th and 21st) in the theatre. These were the Ayrshire, Berkshire, Essex, Hants, Inverness, Leicestershire, Nottingham (Notts) and Somerset batteries.

As members of the Territorial Force they began their active service just a few days after the declaration of war on 4 August 1914 at their county depots, or in the case of the HAC, in London. They shared similar frustrating months of inactivity before being shipped to the Middle East, where their paths diverged until 'married up' with their brigades and formations.[9]

A Battery, commanded by Major Oliver J. Eugster, was mobilised on 15 August at its barracks in the east end of London, and assembled at Hounslow Heath to begin its training under the battery's seasoned regular and serving officers and NCOs. The unit's strength was at establishment, with 100% of vehicles and 75% of horses. B Battery, under Major the Hon. Robert M.P. Preston, opened its recruiting on 5 August. In October, to the delight of the gunners, the HAC Colonel, Lord Denbigh, addressed them with a translation of the Kaiser's recent speech to his Guards Division on their way to war, which ended with the *double entendre*, 'You are Germans, God Help You!'[10]

In October, to their great mortification, rumours of both batteries' impending departure to the Middle East rather than the charnel houses of France were confirmed. A Battery sailed on the SS *Karoa* on 10 April 1915 and reached Alexandria on 21 April. B Battery sailed from Fordwych nine days later on the SS *Minnesota*, arriving on 19 April.[11]

Once in the Middle East theatre, the batteries' paths diverged. A Battery went west to help quell the Senussi revolt after 'working up' near Kantara. On its return, sections were rotated as integral parts of the canal defences, holding practice shoots with the assistance of the gunboat HMS *Aphis*. On their return from Mersa Matruh, they were delighted to exchange their 13-pounders for four 18-pounders. The battery historian proudly claimed that 'they now had the same equipment as a regular [infantry] unit'. They were impressed by the ease with which South American mules could be handled, but lamented the lack of pedrails to 'shoe' their guns. In June the battery was fired on and bombed several times, but emerged unscathed.[12]

B Battery and the Berkshire RHA Battery were sent to defend Aden from the aggressive Turks, both batteries despatched as part of the 28th Independent Field Force Brigade. They were joined by a combined battery ammunition column. Their transport to Aden on the SS *Japanese Prince* saw them endure conditions which, according to the battery historian, 'rivaled the Black Hole of Calcutta'. Care of their horses was given the highest priority and was perhaps the sole highlight of a forgettable voyage, particularly as all the horses survived their ordeal. The Berkshire Battery came into action at Sheikh Othman, albeit with little effect. B Battery was late arriving and missed the 'show'. Despite some sloppy Turkish tactical dispositions, the Berks were unable to help (with direct fire) the cavalry and infantry rush the trenches with lance and bayonet as mist obscured the Turkish positions. On 14 August, following an exhausting night march, B Battery fired its first shots in anger at 2200 yards' range alongside the Berks battery, coming under fire in the process, but without loss. It was a good omen.[13] B Battery returned to the canal zone to recuperate, and the Berks eventually followed.

The Aden deployment introduced the gunners to the harsh conditions of campaigning in dry, dusty, insect-infested and unsanitary conditions that respected neither man nor beast. According to one A Battery account, 'these surpassed the worst prophecies of the pessimists'. Nonetheless the gunners, now back in the canal zone, managed to amuse themselves with typical flair, finding all sorts of diversions, from duck shooting, swimming, entertaining Royal Navy (RN) and sundry personnel, and making themselves comfortable using their ingenuity to make the best of their circumstances. At El Kubri, for example, a full battery muster of all ranks lifted and moved a large mess tent (60 x 25 feet) complete, without dismantling it, to the battery's own lines. Given the large volume of personnel movement, however, training was always at the forefront. The huge Mena camp proved to have its challenges and pitfalls as, in December 1916, the battery recorded the loss of much desirable equipment from 'the utterly unprincipled units on either side', but by the same token was able to acquire a number of necessities using the same means.[14] In 1917 both batteries entered the Sinai in support of their cavalry colleagues.

The HAC in the Sinai

Following its return from Aden, B Battery recovered its health, reinvigorated with reinforcements, prepared its horses to a high state of fitness at Ballah, and was ready to march across the desert to Romani in October 1916. The men experimented to improve the mobility of their gun teams. Eight-inch iron tyres were fitted to all vehicles. Perhaps the result was not a sight that would have pleased an old horse gunner but, on the first day, all went well for some 24 miles. The second day was diabolical:

> We crossed high dunes of loose, shifting sand in which the horses sank above their fetlocks at every step, and the wheels went so deep in the sand it was sometimes impossible to move the vehicles without the aid of drag ropes. A halt was made each half hour, and at each halt the teams were opened out fanwise to let the air circulate around the exhausted, sweating horses. It was the worst in the war.

The horses never recovered from their ordeal. The battery also received its camel ammunition train and, on its march through the Sinai, was joined by the Notts Battery. Both batteries were attached to the 21st RHA Brigade and their affiliated and re-formed 5th Mounted Brigade of the Imperial (later Australian) Mounted Division, its CRA the Marquis of Exeter. It remained at Romani for seven weeks. There was little work for B Battery, which had 'on the whole an easy time', but suffered from exposure to the elements as the tents had been left behind.[15]

A Battery moved a number of times within the canal zone including during a period of affiliation with the 162nd Infantry Brigade, 52nd (Lowland) Division. The CRA (Royal Field Artillery — RFA), Brigadier E.C. Massy, was rather dismissive of this arrangement. In February 1917 the battery was included in the 20th RHA Brigade and thus affiliated with the 4th Australian Light Horse Brigade, which the battery historian termed a 'stroke of good fortune ... Everyone was glad to be back with the cavalry division [Australian and New Zealand Mounted Division — A&NZ Mounted Division] and the Australians proved to be the best hearted and most cheerful comrades one could wish for.' At Ferry Post the battery trained strenuously for its move across the Sinai. Pedrails were fitted to guns, limbers and ammunition wagons and 14 horse teams trained for the vehicles. Horses were arranged four abreast with an extra pair as leaders, which meant modifications to draught bars and riding positions. Training and proving these refinements occurred through route marches and manoeuvres for 'this novel form of draught'. Pedrails caused their own problems, adding considerable weight to the gun, and were liable to break, although they allowed reduced teams to be used. The battery found it more practical to form two eight-horse teams and change them around every half hour. This method was used in the advance across the Sinai, the horses 'arriving in excellent condition'.

Following the winter rains and cold weather through the new year and into March 1917, A Battery also began its march across the desert en route to Romani with the Berks Battery, a trek of 150 miles, during which the gunners endured harsh conditions and learned the importance of animal husbandry for horse and camel alike. The battery made one of the last desert crossings before the new 'wire-reinforced' road was commissioned. The two ammunition columns required 600 camels.[16] For all the artillery that moved into the Sinai it had been a necessary introduction to desert conditions and all that these entailed — harsh terrain and extremes of weather, the need for innovation, the care of horses and camels — with the exception of serious shot and shell. However this would come soon enough and the batteries would be involved in 'real' active service. The operations of all batteries will be covered in the following chapters with descriptions of specific battles and locations.

Chapter 4
The Battle of Romani and the early battles of 1916–17

And though hard be the task, keep a stiff upper lip.

P. Carey

Romani (including Katia and Bir el Abd): 3–9 August 1916

The mere presence of the Turkish military in Sinai promised an attack on the Suez Canal and it eventuated as the Battle of Romani, fought 23 miles east of the canal on the site of ancient Pelusium. Romani was the strategic railhead which marked the logical start of any advance to the Suez Canal. While this British victory over a joint Ottoman and German force marked the end of the defence of the canal, the defence of Egypt itself continued. This campaign, known to the Germans as the *Offensive zur Eroberung des Suezkanals* and to the Ottomans as the *Ikinci Kanal Harekati*, began on 26 January 1915. The end of operations at Romani also marked the beginning of the Sinai and Palestine campaigns.

This chapter describes the development and application of horse, field, siege, heavy artillery and counter-battery doctrine and practice through analysis of all the important battles of the period from 1916 to 1917. Many of these were 'cavalry only' battles in which no artillery was involved and are included simply to signpost the forces' advance from Romani to Damascus. In each case a broad outline of the commander's plan, relative strengths of opposing forces and, as appropriate, artillery factors and outcomes will be examined.

The order of battle for the defence of the canal comprised:[1]

- the A&NZ Mounted Division
- the British Army Cavalry Brigade
- the RHA, RFA and RGA
- the 42nd and 52nd infantry divisions
- RFC and AFC squadrons

During the Battle of Romani — its first major Sinai battle — the EEF was commanded by Major General the Hon. H.A. Lawrence, whose headquarters were sited at Kantara where he was GOC No. 3 Section of the canal defences. His superior was General Sir Archibald Murray, whose headquarters remained in Ismailia. This was the first of many battles fought to eject the Turk from the Sinai and, eventually, Palestine. It was also the 'baptism of fire' for the British New Army divisions and mounted Anzac troops who had not fought at Gallipoli. Neither Murray nor Lawrence had reconnoitred the ground and at no time during the battle did Lawrence, who had tactical command, move forward. Chauvel, on the other hand, as GOC A&NZ Mounted Division, had made several lengthy reconnaissances east of the canal. The high ground of Romani and that of nearby Oghratina were natural positions for the Turks to occupy as their commander envisaged his renewed advance to the canal. Brigadier Chaytor, commander of the NZMR Brigade, also conducted an aerial reconnaissance to Oghratina during which he was wounded (for the fifth time) by ground fire. This was the genesis of what became known as tactical reconnaissance in the theatre. The Germans also conducted such reconnaissance on a daily basis and, as a consequence, there were no secret dispositions on either side. Oghratina was also tactically important as an outpost for Romani. On 23 April, unaware that the Turks occupied Oghratina, Katia and Dueidar in considerable strength, their dispositions obscured by early morning fog, three and a half squadrons of Brigadier Wiggin's 5th Mounted Brigade cavalry were surprised by the Turks. In short order the Turkish artillery, machine-guns and 2000 rifles inflicted a serious defeat on Wiggin's force at its three locations. The losses amounted to 24 officers, 252 other ranks and 425 horses.

Lawrence's forces had been concentrating around Romani and reacting to the aggressive Turkish raids which were well planned with the help of the Bedouins. On 27 May the 2nd Light Horse Brigade, with two guns from the Ayrshire Battery mounted on pedrails and drawn by two 12-horse teams, demonstrated against Oghratina, six miles to the east. The troopers captured several prisoners and began a series of patrols which, in conjunction with the 1st Light Horse Brigade, continued until the eve of the bigger battle.

On the afternoon of 27 May the Ayrshire guns shelled Hod Um Ugba from the high ground at Oghratina. When enemy air activity increased and RFC reconnaissance reported that the Turks had advanced to Katia, some five miles from Chauvel's front, the light horsemen interpreted this as a signal of the Turks' intention to eventually launch an attack.

In July Chauvel's A&NZ Mounted Division (also known as the Anzac Mounted Division) conducted wide-ranging patrols aimed at depriving the

Turks of water and clearing its front. In one of these forays the 3rd Light Horse Brigade destroyed 23 million litres of stored water, compelling the Turks to use a more difficult logistic route from Palestine. The Germans and Ottomans amended their objective, which was now not to cross the canal, but to capture Romani and establish a strongly entrenched artillery position opposite Kantara from which to bombard shipping in the canal.

The Turkish strength in the Sinai was five infantry divisions and one cavalry division — 30,000 rifles, 2200 sabres, 130 machine-guns and 120 guns (approximately 25 batteries). The Turkish *3rd Division* (ration strength of 16,000 rifles but 14,000 effectives) was located east of Romani with its headquarters in Katia. It was commanded by no less than a titled Bavarian, Major General Friedrich Frieherr Kress von Kressenstein, who had already launched unsuccessful attacks on the Suez Canal in January 1915 and again in April 1916. The Turks' objectives — water and the dumps — were vital to the success of their push to the canal. Romani's water resources were poor in both quantity and quality, with better water located at Etmaler and Pelusium some miles to the rear. To mount his attack von Kressenstein's infantry would have to advance four miles and his artillery would have to move a similar distance to occupy a position safe from cavalry encirclement and counter-battery fire. The Turkish *60th Artillery Battalion* strength for the Battle of Romani was:

- one battery with 2 x 100mm guns
- one battery with 4 x 150mm howitzers
- two batteries with 4 x 210mm howitzers
- three batteries with 12 x 75mm mountain guns (*3rd Regiment*)
- two trench mortar companies

One assessment put the Turkish strength at 30 guns.[2]

Lawrence's artillery comprised:

- four batteries of 6 x 13-pounders (Ayrshire, Inverness-shire, Somersetshire and Leicestershire batteries, RHA)
- four batteries of 16 x 18-pounders (260th and 263rd RFA brigades)
- two batteries of 8 x 4.5-inch howitzers (262nd RFA Howitzer Brigade)[3]
- one battery of 2 x 60-pounders (91st Heavy Battery RGA)

General Lawrence divided command of the defence of Romani between four subordinates, namely Brigadier Smith's Camel Brigade, the 1st and 2nd Light Horse brigades of Chauvel's A&NZ Mounted Division (now reduced to around 1500 effectives), Brigadier Chaytor's NZMR Brigade and Major General W.E.B.

Smith's 52nd Lowland Division. Brigadier Antill's 3rd Light Horse Brigade was near Hod el Aras on the right (southern) flank almost 15 miles away and was under Lawrence's orders rather than Chauvel's. Antill was to guard that flank and respond appropriately.

The Leicestershire and Inverness-shire batteries were supporting two squadrons each from the Warwickshire and Worcestershire regiments and one from the Gloucesters, an arrangement that saw the cavalry placed under three different commands. The 42nd Division was in reserve with one regiment forward. These command arrangements did not enjoy the imprimatur of General Murray, who urged Lawrence to move his headquarters from Kantara to a position where he could exert closer executive control of the battle 'to ensure rapid decision and close coordination of his two forward divisions'.[4]

The Romani front line was a series of low sand hills extending from the sea at Mahmudiyah to Romani railway station and settlement and then to a higher series of crescent-shaped dunes five miles long, terminating at Hod el Enna. Gullett's panorama (north to south) shows the main tactical features of Etmaler to the tactically important Wellington ridge to its south then further south to Mount Meredith.[5] Mount Royston (around 120 feet high) was the highest and westernmost feature, while Hod el Enna represented the southern extremity. The dunes, their ridgelines oriented north-west to south-east, were delineated at their edges by soft sand. The high sand hills were oriented north-north-east to south-west, and enemy occupation of features such as Wellington ridge would endanger troops on the ridges on either side. The vital ground was the Katib Gannit railhead, Canterbury Hill, Mount Meredith and Etmaler. If the Turks moved behind Major General Smith's 52nd Division and then deployed in a static role from the high ground north to the coast, they would gain control of the water and stores held at Romani. The division's 156th Brigade was positioned to the left of Chauvel's light horsemen, and this was considered sufficient to deter the Turks from attacking in force in this sector. Other brigades held a line north to the coast. The plan suggested that this brigade could assist the troopers in the defence, although this was not stated in its orders.[6]

On 1 August, the 3rd Light Horse Brigade's mobile columns were ordered forward and the 212th RFA Brigade's A Field Battery moved to Hill 70 at the southern end of the front. South of the 2nd Light Horse Brigade, the 1st Light Horse Brigade patrolled south towards Katib Ganiel, which the New Zealanders also kept under surveillance. A defensive line of 18 redoubts (defended localities) had been constructed which were some 750 yards apart and garrisoned by 100 rifles and light and heavy machine-guns from the 52nd Division. Wire was used to channel attacking infantry across the duned features.[7]

Chapter 4

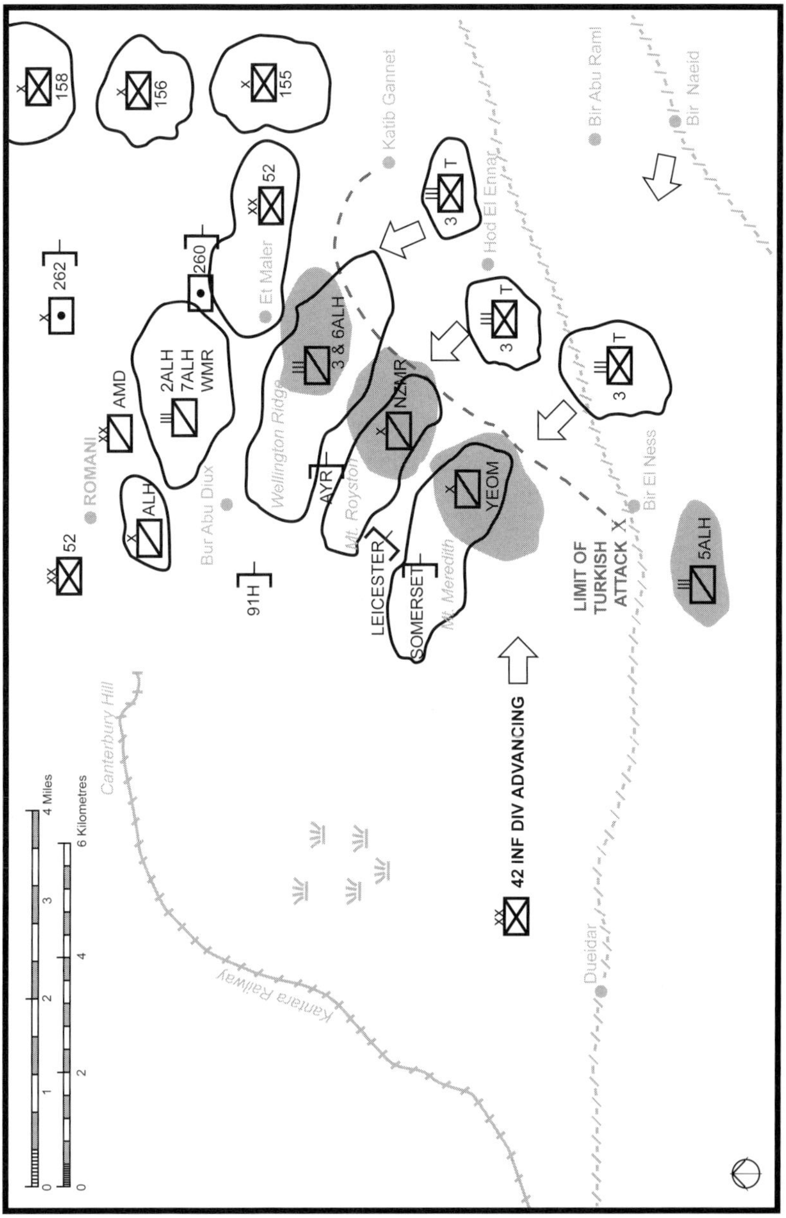

Map 1: The Turkish attack on the Romani position, showing the front line at the furthest extent of the Turkish advance on 5 August 1916 and the positions of the supporting and enemy artillery (source: Gullett, *Official History*, Vol. VII, *Sinai and Palestine*, Map 5).

Murray's overall strategy was to hold the Turkish advance until, either through lack of progress or dehydration, they became disorganised, at which point he planned to assault the enemy flanks with his mounted troops. Lawrence believed the enemy would attack his infantry before turning his right (southern) flank. He planned accordingly, ordering Chauvel to cover his southern flank. Chauvel would then withdraw, luring the Turks into a suitable area for a counter-attack. Concurrently, he would use his troopers and horse artillery to attack the Turkish rear and withdrawal routes. Smith was ordered to deploy three of his four brigades north to the sea. His CRA, Brigadier Parker, split his artillery into No. 1 and No. 2 groups. Lieutenant Colonel G.S. Simpson's No. 1 Group, on the extreme right of the line, placed its guns where the fire could be directed east, south and west. The group's front covered 3000 yards, its last two redoubts in front of the 155th Brigade (21 and 22) covering both front and rear. Should the Turks infiltrate between these two posts, a considerable gap would allow easy penetration routes.

At this point enemy aircraft mounted a bombing offensive aimed at the Romani defences, attacking several of the divisional areas. This exercised the mind of the 52nd's CRA, Brigadier Parker who, having no organic anti-aircraft artillery assets, permitted the Glasgow howitzer detachments of the 262nd RFA Brigade to fix their pieces to a platform that allowed the trail to be dug in, enabling the gun to assume an anti-aircraft role firing shrapnel. The division's historian noted that, as a result, the German machines were forced to bomb from a greater height, with a consequent loss of accuracy.[8]

The GOC 52nd Division was not under Chauvel's command, and Smith was beholden to Lawrence for his orders. This allocation of command responsibilities was a serious matter when sound decisions were required during the first day of battle. Each command had its own artillery 'adviser' with no provision for centralisation in orders. With hindsight, Lawrence's split command arrangements had an adverse effect on the outcome of the battle. To stiffen the defence, Chauvel's attached artillery comprised the 263rd RFA Brigade, situated in the centre, near Romani hod (oasis).

The A&NZ Mounted Division reinforced the garrison on 2 August. There were further skirmishes east until 3 August when the 2nd Light Horse Brigade and the gunners returned to Romani from their screening role at Oghratina, passed through a 1st Light Horse Brigade screen in front of the 2nd Light Horse Brigade and moved into defensive positions. To their south, the 3rd Light Horse Regiment (without horses) and the 2nd Light Horse Regiment were positioned at Hod el Enna. Both the brigades were around half strength. The defence was augmented by two machine-gun companies (160th and 161st) from both the 53rd and 54th divisions. The commanders had expected the Turks to attack earlier, but the protracted process of moving their heavy artillery across the desert had delayed their plans. This in turn had unintended consequences for the infantry attackers whose water rations were insufficient to sustain their troops on the move and in action in very hot conditions once the sun rose.[9]

Just before midnight on 3 August, a strong force of 8000 Turks following the tracks of a returning light horse patrol collided with the 1st Light Horse Brigade screen making its way towards Wellington ridge — just as Murray and Lawrence had anticipated. On a brilliant, starry night the Turks attacked fiercely and confidently. In no time the troopers found themselves outnumbered and in serious trouble, and were forced back to their horses. Chauvel moved Brigadier Royston's 2nd Light Horse Brigade forward and at 4.30 am on 4 August it mounted an unsuccessful attack against the Turks who had occupied what became known as Mount Royston. Enemy artillery now opened fire on the infantry positions and camps to the rear, its shrapnel causing some casualties although, fortunately, HE shells were smothered by the soft sand. There was no artillery support for this withdrawal due to confusion in the dark and the Turkish '5.9s' blasted the dune ridge with shrapnel.[10] At 5.00 am German airmen bombed the British positions, A&NZ Mounted Division headquarters and the railway station.

At 6.00 am the Leicestershire Battery was in action at Etmaler searching for opportunity targets and was eagerly joined by its Ayrshire colleagues. This provoked the Turks to neutralise the Scots gunners. The Australians carried red flags which they placed on the sand to indicate their forward line to gunner observers. On a broader front, the Turks advanced as anticipated with heavy artillery support and, by 7.30 am, held Wellington ridge. The 7th Light Horse Regiment, in the line without mounts, described coming under heavy machine-gun and artillery fire, 'but the damage was not great. It made the men dig deeper, and our own guns did some good shelling.'[11] Since daylight both RHA batteries had been engaging the enemy with observed fire, but it was not sufficiently effective to support another assault and help reclaim the lost ground. To the left of the batteries the Turks were pressing towards the railway, and a battalion commander from the 156th Brigade, on his own initiative, moved two companies of infantry to support the A&NZ Mounted Division troopers on Mount Royston.

From dawn the Scottish infantry were assailed by the Turkish infantry, which was attempting to outflank the 155th Brigade position facing south where the Turkish machine-guns 'punished them severely'. The 155th's commander, Brigadier Pollok-M'Call, concluded that the greater threat lay in an attack from Mount Wellington ridge, where a vigorous firefight with redoubts 21a and 22a was in full swing.[12] The brigade's snipers had a field day, and the attack from that quarter did not threaten the Scots at any stage. They punished the Turks, who sought cover in gullies and hollows where the Lowland C Battery howitzers found them. The Ayrshire Battery's observation posts 'shrapnelled' the Turks with their 18-pounders, augmented by those of the 263rd RFA Brigade howitzers. Further north, the fire was further augmented by that from two companies of the Royal Scots Fusiliers. Thanks to the combined efforts of the gunners, by midday this part of the front had stabilised, notwithstanding the arrival of an enemy party of 250 at noon. They were soon engaged and dispersed.[13]

By mid-morning Chauvel had arranged his dispositions. Lawrence ordered Brigadier A.H. Leggett's 156th Brigade to attack Wellington ridge to support another tilt at Mount Royston. However this attack did not develop, in part because of the confused command arrangements and a miscalculation of the speed at which infantry in battle order could advance to contact in stifling desert conditions. Also at this point the 52nd Division, with the 5th Mounted Brigade under command, was to link with Chauvel and began its march from Pelusium, four miles further back, in preparation to counter-attack, its objective Hod el Enna in support of Chauvel's right flank. The 52nd Division was also to provide close support to Chauvel in his battle for Mount Meredith. Antill's 3rd Light Horse Brigade was to aim for Hod el Enna from the south.[14]

The 91st Heavy Battery had been shelling the attacking Turkish infantry on Wellington ridge, the battery's diarist recording, '1630. Engaged hostile infantry on … where some 1,400 Turks were surrounded.' The Turks were not, in fact, surrounded, but this fire certainly helped break up their attacks. Turkish shelling ceased when their infantry withdrew from part of Wellington ridge, leaving sufficient infantry to maintain their hold on the feature during the gathering dark. By this time the telephone line between Lawrence and Brigadier Chaytor's NZMR Brigade headquarters, the 5th Yeomanry and the 3rd Light Horse Brigade had been cut. Messages had to be routed through Port Said, causing delays. Chauvel had begun to wonder why the force on his right had yet to appear. Their orders, including those covering the Somerset Battery's role, were confused and they belatedly began their deployment to fortify the line on the southern flank.[15] Chauvel sent his reinforcements, the New Zealanders and the 5th Yeomanry Brigade, to Mount Royston. At 6.00 pm the Gloucester Hussars, who had reached the top of Mount Royston, spied a Turkish mountain battery below them around which some sheltering Turkish infantry had assembled, and swooped down on them. Some 500 enemy and their (close support) guns were captured, several Turks admitting during later interrogation that they 'were sick of artillery fire'. Mount Royston was cleared, although the enemy remained on Wellington ridge.

By 4.00 pm the general situation was more favourable, thanks to the tactical wit of Chauvel's mounted commanders who now prompted the Turks to constantly look over their shoulders. The Turks' position was difficult: their water supply lay on the British left while their attacks concentrated on the British right. At 6.45 pm a successful attack by the Scottish Rifles (7th and 8th battalions) was supported by a bombardment of the ridge by all available artillery and extra machine-guns. Once the Scots had consolidated, the front calmed considerably. The defenders were much better placed, having withdrawn towards their resources as darkness descended. Despite their exhaustion, the troops had ample rations and water during the night to maintain their morale for the following day's fighting. That night the Turkish '5.9s' bombarded the railhead. Despite this, Murray in Ismailia was feeling confident of a successful outcome to the battle.

At 6.00 am on 5 August, Lawrence issued new orders from Kantara, beginning with Brigadier Antill's force, hitherto unemployed, which was now to advance to Hamisah. The 5th Mounted Brigade was to come under command of the 42nd Division, and the 52nd and 54th divisions were to advance on either side of Chauvel. Lawrence also issued orders to Chauvel and Smith. As Hill noted, 'The Turks could not have hoped for a less menacing plan.'[16]

Chauvel's original orders were to clear the remaining Turks from their lodgement on Wellington ridge, and hold a line from Katib Gannit to Hod el Enna. In the pale glow of the dawn, the light horsemen met various levels of resistance, from strong to token, before they could declare that, by 5.00 am, no Turks remained there. At 6.30 am Lawrence, having realised that the confused command arrangements had led to unnecessary casualties and confusion, installed Chauvel as overall commander. Chauvel confirmed the 52nd Division's advance to Abu Hamra and Er Rabah, and the 42nd's orders to aim directly for Hod el Enna. The force began its general advance at 10.30 am. Chauvel also knew that he had to capture the Qatya hod and its water by nightfall to maintain pressure on his foes. He was the only divisional commander who had a clear picture of the battle whereas Lawrence, headquartered at Kantara, had reluctantly recognised that his orders and command were less than ideal. Fragmentation of command had resulted in an uncoordinated application of artillery fire, suggesting that, had Lawrence 'been on the spot' and had an artillery adviser, there may have been fewer casualties.[17]

While Romani is generally regarded as a cavalry battle in which RHA supporting batteries won accolades for their excellent support, the few accounts of the infantry operations and their gunners are somewhat revealing. Sand dunes are the least 'friendly' surface on which to detonate HE shells. Shrapnel fire, on the other hand, distributed 'man-killing fragments' in a pattern that was more difficult to avoid. What is missing in the literature are references to command and control of artillery except in the description of resultant casualties to the Turks. Arguably, as a principle of war and artillery employment generally, in night operations where map spotting by various bodies of troops calling for fire would be crucial, there was significant potential for the shelling of friendly troops. Nonetheless, the two-day battle for Romani and the Suez Canal had been won by the British infantry and Australian, New Zealand and British mounted troops. They captured approximately 4000 German and Ottoman soldiers and killed more than 1200. However the main enemy force managed to escape with all its artillery except one captured battery, retreating to its next line of defence.

Katia

Chauvel used the infantry of the 52nd Division to press the Turks' right flank in the direction of Abu Hamra while the cavalry moved to crush the Turkish left flank, and planned to then commit his force to a frontal attack on Katia. However the attack did not materialise. As on the previous day, coordination was lacking and the infantry advanced too late to influence the battle, not moving until 2.00 pm, some eight hours after receiving their orders. Moving in the heat of the day saw them rapidly lose their momentum in the arduous conditions and they lost their value as a fighting resource. Across the front from Hod el Enna to Katib Gannit the enemy surrendered rather than perish from thirst while the remainder straggled towards Qatya and Bir el Abd. At the end of that day a total of 5000 prisoners had been taken. Brigadier Chaytor's NZMR Brigade's objective was Bir el Nuss with exploitation to the limit of the Turkish line, Hamisah and Mageibra by the Camel Column — all designed to conform with the movements of the 3rd Light Horse Brigade.

The 3rd Light Horse Brigade (8th, 9th and 10th regiments) under Brigadier J.M. Antill (an Australian Military Forces permanent force officer) was supported by the Inverness Battery for its first operation as mounted troops. As the brigade advanced towards Hamisah at 9.30 am it made contact with the enemy. The 9th Light Horse Regiment met a troublesome German machine-gun, which was promptly silenced by battery fire. The 10th Light Horse Regiment moved to envelop the enemy from the right and both regiments' enfilade fire caused the Turkish commander to call for artillery support from the '5.9s' behind Qatya. Most of their shells fell short and the Turks, mistaking this for British fire, promptly surrendered. The Australians advanced and, assisted by their machine-gunners, took the Turkish position. The Western Australians of the 10th Light Horse Regiment recorded that 'the Inverness Battery rendered substantial aid. With a couple of extra horses per gun the Highlanders were never far behind our horses. Great credit was due to Major Fraser and his men for their fine effort.'[18] They had fired 500 rounds. The brigade's booty was 425 prisoners and seven machine-guns. As the regiments re-formed they came under shellfire and, as a result of previous delays, were ordered by Antill to retire to Bir Nagid two miles west. Apart from proving that the 3rd Light Horse Brigade was made of the same 'stern stuff' as the 1st and 2nd brigades, this was, as Gullett recorded, 'an event of very little consequence'. However, Gullett's assessment was wrong. Antill's decision, taken without consultation, deprived Chauvel of his freshest troops at the very time he was advancing on Katia. It was the end of Antill's career with Chauvel, as he had made little effort to join the battle until ordered. Later, Chauvel readily supported Antill's acceptance of an offer to join an infantry brigade in France.[19]

Another important action occurred further east, where the cavalry (1st and 2nd Light Horse brigades, the NZMR Brigade and the 5th Yeomanry Brigade) advanced on Qatya. After receiving their orders, and having been joined by the Ayrshire, Leicestershire, Inverness and Somersetshire batteries, and A Battery, 212th RFA Brigade, the force set off in pursuit. In these very trying conditions the two RHA batteries came into action and at once drew fire from the heavier Turkish guns, suffering severely. The Turks made good use of the oasis palms and the strong defensive 'ground' to their front. The swamp and salt pan presented what appeared to be firm ground, inducing the troopers to charge with bayonets fixed. The force became bogged, came under fire from machine-guns sited at El Rabah and, despite resolute minor tactics, the attack petered out some 600 yards from the hod. The troopers then withdrew, badly mauled. At the same time, the RHA batteries which were in the open fought an unequal duel with the Turks. Katia presented a different story to Hamisah. Chauvel's force almost succeeded after strenuous hand-to-hand fighting, but failed to penetrate the Turks' well-sited defensive positions. By nightfall the exhausted troopers were forced to retreat. The horse artillerymen had advanced close behind their regiments but, as Gullett noted, 'they sustained an unequal duel against the heavier and more numerous guns of the enemy. Whereas the former were in the open, the Austrian and German gunners were well concealed, and the British shot without serious effect.'[20] By the end of 5 August, Chauvel was in an invidious position. He had to take the fight to the Turks with a force physically spent from its manifest exertions and numerous casualties in furnace-like heat, no rest and mounted on horses that had been without water for 60 hours. He reluctantly ordered his troops back to Romani which was now garrisoned by the six infantry brigades of both divisions, the 42nd having moved into the line during the day.

On the following day (6 August) a pursuit of the retreating Turks was ordered and three brigades of mounted troops (NZMR Brigade, the 5th Yeomanry and the 3rd Light Horse brigades) investigated Oghratina and Badich, some six miles from Romani. Both of these had been strongly held but were discovered to have been evacuated on 8 August as the enemy had moved further back along his interior lines by evacuating Qatya. He did so with all of his artillery intact, ready to cause Chauvel more grief.

Bir el Abd to 9 August 1916

Chauvel now moved his headquarters to Oghratina and contemplated his next advance to Bir el Abd, an oasis on the telegraph and railway route. Some 4000 yards to its north lay a swamp — El Ruag — and south about the same distance was Bada. The Turkish defences were set in dunes, and scattered palm trees dotted the landscape. Intelligence estimated that the enemy force numbered 6000 rifles. The Turkish line of defence ran north to south and then curved east, a front of 12,000 yards. The mounted attacking force of 3000 rifles was widely dispersed, the distance between the New Zealanders and the 3rd Light Horse Brigade around a mile. The artillery affiliations (north to south) were:

1st Light Horse Brigade	Leicester Battery
2nd Light Horse Brigade	Ayrshire Battery
NZMR Brigade	Somerset Battery
3rd Light Horse Brigade	Inverness Battery[21]

The gunners were positioned some 1500 to 2000 yards behind the troopers. Resistance was expected to be slight, as enemy troops had been observed moving to the rear. H Hour was 4.00 am on 9 August, and the first artillery action occurred when the '5.9s' opened fire, their shells falling just clear of the approaching column of Royston's advancing 2nd Light Horse Brigade. The New Zealanders made early headway, at one stage looking down on Bir el Abd and being counter-attacked for their trouble. This attack was broken up by supporting fire from the Somerset Battery. Royston's brigade was then engulfed by heavy artillery fire from the '5.9s', anti-aircraft guns and 'sustained shafts of machine gun fire'.[22] The 3rd Light Horse Brigade had come to a halt after receiving similar Turkish attention. At 10.30 am enemy artillery fire increased in intensity, its accuracy a product of the Turkish observers' intimate knowledge of the ground. Little could be done to counter this fire as the RHA observation posts could not locate their adversaries. Eventually Chauvel asked for RFC observation. The gunners brought their guns forward and 'pushing up behind their cavalry, waged an unequal contest with admirable courage and reckless tenacity'.[23] The four batteries assisted by engaging the enemy rear, but everywhere the Turk held firm. The Allied line was still two and half miles from the wells.

At midday the enemy rose from their trenches and counter-attacked, by which time Chauvel's reserve, the Warwickshire Yeomanry, had moved to bolster the Kiwis in the centre where the Turks threatened. The Turkish heavy guns found the range of the Ayrshire Battery, one salvo killing four men and 37 horses and wounding several others. The relentless Turkish pressure prompted the BC to use the troopers' horses to rescue his guns from being overrun. All along the front the Turks pressed forward confidently, and all along the front the troops and squadrons retired in copybook fashion, with not one troop 'broken'. At 5.30 pm Chauvel ordered a withdrawal in line with his orders which directed him to retire if he had not secured water by nightfall.[24]

Following Romani, Chauvel moved his headquarters to Oghratina, taking his now depleted regiments and his wounded. He sent the yeomanry, New Zealanders and the 3rd Light Horse Brigade to continue to harass the enemy. On 12 August the New Zealanders discovered Bir el Abd to be unoccupied and then began to harry the Turkish rearguard as they withdrew to Salmana, five miles east, the Kiwis' efforts supported by the 3rd Light Horse Brigade and yeomanry with their artillery. At Salmana the Turks made a token stand, engaged at maximum range by the horse gunners, but no attack was launched. The Turks withdrew on 13 August to make their next stand at El Arish on the coast.

Of the total casualties, the Ayrshires lost seven officers wounded while one soldier was killed and 13 wounded. The Leicesters lost one officer and four gunners wounded. At Romani, the 42nd and 52nd divisions suffered 195 casualties from Turkish gunfire. There were 10 gunner casualties, all from the Glasgow Battery of the 262nd. Yeomanry Brigade losses were light. The 42nd Division saw little comparable action. Gullett wrote that the mounted men of Australian and New Zealand squadrons had suffered unequally. He concluded that:

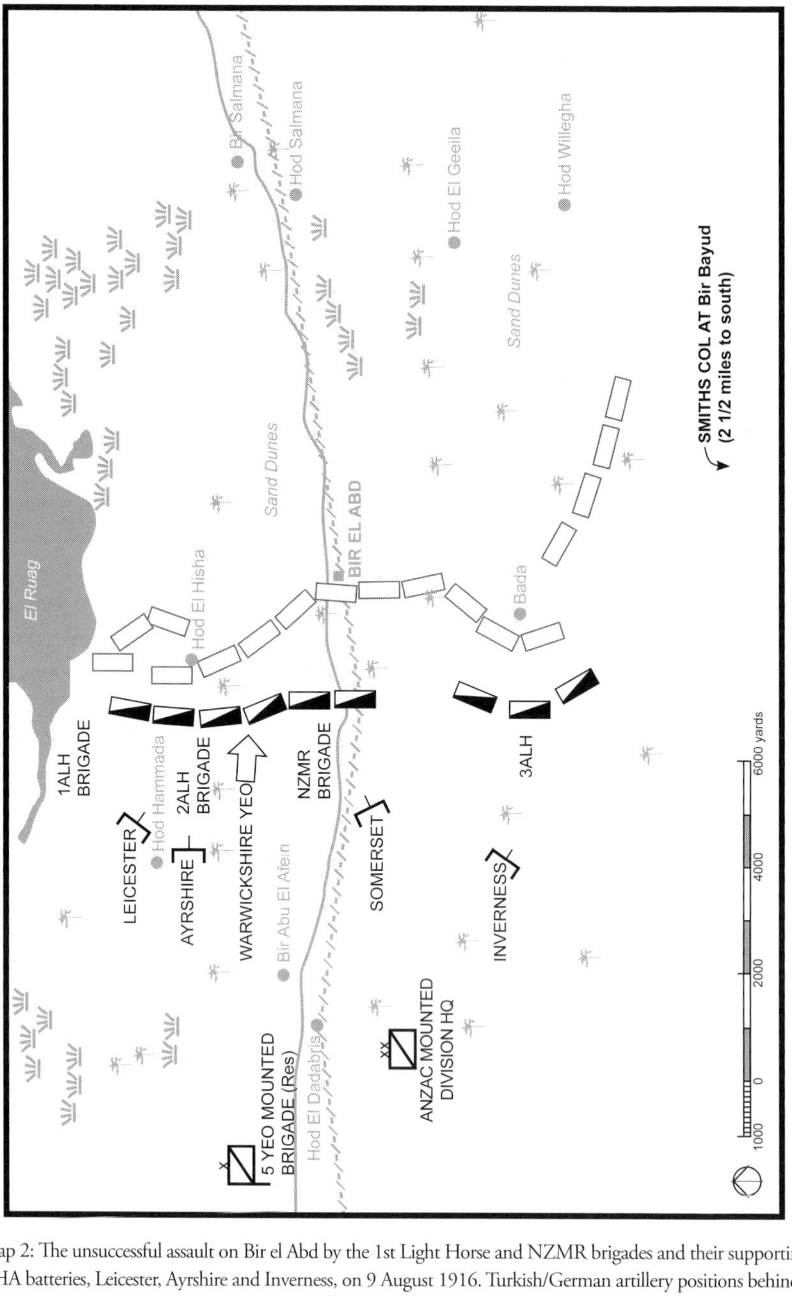

Map 2: The unsuccessful assault on Bir el Abd by the 1st Light Horse and NZMR brigades and their supporting RHA batteries, Leicester, Ayrshire and Inverness, on 9 August 1916. Turkish/German artillery positions behind their lines are not indicated (source: Gullett, *Official History*, Vol. VII, *Sinai and Palestine*, Map 8).

> Throughout the operation there was evidence that, although much plain warning had been given of the Turkish intention … the blow had come before British arrangements were complete. The 42nd Division was late at every stage, not because its leader failed, but because of the miscalculations of the High Command, namely lack of coordination regarding the 3rd LH Brigade at Mount Royston, Colonel Smith's cameleer column on the right flank, and between the two divisions [at Romani].

This may have been a fair comment concerning Romani but, over the whole period, the British also seem to have taken more than their fair share of casualties while primarily occupying defensive positions or advancing in open order. Chauvel outlined the reasons for a less than stunning victory more succinctly. He believed that Murray had erred as early as the end of July by not appointing Lawrence, since he would have been more *au fait* with the terrain and its use in the battle.[25]

The Anzac casualty lists were inflated by the scandalous lack of medical arrangements and uncoordinated staff work devoted to moving wounded at Romani to the hospitals at Kantara. Chauvel was incensed that the number of his recommendations for bravery eventually awarded was minuscule compared to those given to members of British units which he thought, mistakenly, had seen comparatively little action. He was personally offered an award and rejected it as an insult to his troopers' achievements.[26]

Yet there is no doubt that Chauvel's attack on Bir el Abd was unduly optimistic. To commit 3000 tired troopers against an invigorated enemy of 6000 with an artillery advantage ran counter to the conventional wisdom of a ratio of attackers to defenders of three to one in manpower, and an advantage in the lethality of shell and, if possible, numbers available. An assessment of the artillery performance suggests that it was weak in attack but well supported in defence. The absence of heavier artillery and its firepower remained the underlying cause of increased casualties to mounted troops. Nonetheless, the spoils from the battle were considerable. Some 4000 prisoners, 2300 rifles and one million rounds of small arms ammunition were captured, and 100 horses and mules and 500 camels bolstered the Allies' stocks. Two complete field hospitals helped ease the condition of the Turkish wounded in their captivity.[27]

Chauvel was deeply moved by his troops' performance: 'their pluck, dash and endurance is beyond all description. I don't mean only the Australians and New Zealanders but the Horse Artillery Territorials as well.' There were congratulatory messages from the King, Generals Birdwood and Edward Hutton. Archibald

Murray, in his subsequent dispatch, noted of Chauvel's division, 'I cannot speak too highly of the gallantry, steadfastness and untiring energy shown by this fine division throughout operations.'[28]

Aftermath

The Romani campaign also included a minor operation by a mixed Australian and British cavalry group. This comprised an attempt to capture Bir el Mazar, 50 miles east of Romani, by two light horse brigades and a battalion of the Imperial Camel Corps (ICC), with the Ayrshire and Inverness batteries and the Hong Kong and Singapore Mountain Battery in support. A dawn attack on the position in a pincer movement from the west took the outlying defences 800 yards from their second line. All batteries occupied enfilading positions and, against densely manned trenches, inflicted 'considerable loss'. Under orders not to attack entrenched positions, the A&NZ Mounted Division force achieved its objectives, at one stage occupying the enemy trenches despite retaliatory shellfire from the garrison. On 13 October the force scored a minor success in capturing 18 prisoners, but as at Katia and Bir el Abd, did not succeed in beating the Turk. Despite this, after Romani and the raid on Bir el Mazar, the Turks lost the initiative, never to regain it, although they were withdrawing along interior lines and would remain a tough, capable adversary if well supplied. Gullett's view of Romani was that 'the high command did not excel … but the battle was still a far reaching triumph for British arms.'[29]

The Battle of Romani was the first large-scale mounted and infantry victory by British forces in the First World War. It occurred at a time when the Allied nations had experienced nothing but defeat: in France, at Salonika and in the occupation of Kut in Mesopotamia. The battle has been widely acknowledged as a strategic victory and a turning point in the campaign to restore Egypt's territorial integrity and security, and marked the end of the land campaign against the Suez Canal. The tactics employed by the A&NZ Mounted Division were to prove effective throughout the coming campaigns in the Sinai and Palestine (Levant). The key to the mounted rifles and light horse's approach was to quickly move to tactical ground and then effectively operate as infantry once dismounted. In defence, the artillery and machine-guns wrought havoc on enemy attacks and, during the mounted advance, covered and supported the mounted force.[30]

So ended the battles of Romani, Katia and Bir el Abd. Casualties for the five-day battle are illustrated in Table 3 below:

TABLE 3: CASUALTIES FOR THE BATTLES OF ROMANI, KATIA AND BIR EL ABD

	Officers			Other Ranks			
Force	**KIA**	**WIA**	**Missing / POW**	**KIA**	**WIA**	**Missing / POW**	**Total**
Turks:	-	-	-	1250	4000	3900	9150
British:	22	81	1	80	801	45	1030
Chauvel's	8	33	6	65	210	30	328
Total	**30**	**114**	**7**	**145**	**1011**	**75**	**1358**

Between Romani and Magdhaba in December there was a reorganisation of commands and the divisional artilleries. Lieutenant General Sir Charles Dobell assumed command of the canal and Eastern Frontier Force (EFF), headquartered at Ismailia. In the 42nd and 52nd divisional artilleries, the 18-pounder batteries were increased to six guns and a number of batteries were renumbered, split or broken up, primarily to accommodate the howitzer elements.

Chapter 5
The Battle of Magdhaba: 23 December 1916

In military operations timing is everything.

Arthur Wellesley,
Duke of Wellington

Following Romani, General Murray created the Desert Column with Chauvel's A&NZ Mounted Division as its major component, the remainder comprising Imperial regiments, including the ICC. He placed Sir Philip Chetwode in command for the important push up the coast. The nondescript seaport of El Arish constituted the left flank of Murray's thrust towards Palestine, and its capture would ease logistical constraints on the troops, except in the matter of water supplies. Chauvel drove his mounted men hard, notwithstanding that Christmas would soon be upon them. His troops were motivated to capture the town as a 'Christmas present' for their commander. However, at the eleventh hour, an RFC aircraft reconnaissance reported that El Arish had been evacuated, and its troops concentrated at Magdhaba.

Magdhaba was a village astride the route to El Rafa and Rafa, the latter village some 30 miles distant. In brief, the decision by the Ottoman (German) commander Kress von Kressenstein to garrison Magdhaba was the result of disruptions to his coastal supply route which had been interdicted by British and French naval forces. These forces boasted armaments that saw them engage targets up to 16,000 yards inland using seaplane and balloon observation. This was the second significant use of naval heavy guns in the Sinai campaign, a proxy for General Murray's non-existent or immobile heavy artillery groups. They had certainly proved their worth during the canal battles. It was also the third option for him in a strategic sense. The coastal route was initially serviced by light rail (a broad gauge Decauville type) from El Auja to El Arish, although the railway was removed just prior to the British attack.

Initially, Chetwode planned a two-pronged advance to contact against Magdhaba and Rafa, stipulating that all wheeled vehicles be left at Sheikh Zowaiid. This decision was later to embarrass the Scots battery and New

Zealand riflemen. Aerial reconnaissance showed that Magdhaba was held by a stronger force than intelligence estimates had suggested. Chauvel's force was faced with an approach march of 20 miles in harsh desert conditions. Adequate water supply was an ever-present consideration for the attackers in most desert actions. Accordingly, a detachment of Australian engineers conducted a bold reconnaissance to assess whether Wadi el Arish held water. This natural feature was known to flow during winter rains, or to hold water that could be obtained by boring. Intelligence also revealed that the Turks had destroyed the wells at Bir el Lafan on the banks of the wadi. The engineers had only bad news for Chauvel — water would have to be carried. This delayed the now depleted division, from which the 2nd Light Horse Brigade and Ayrshire and Leicester batteries had been withdrawn for rest.[1]

On 22 December 1916, No. 1 Squadron AFC (led by Major R. Williams) overflew the village to assess enemy strength and dispositions and dropped 120 bombs. This action prompted a response from the enemy anti-aircraft defences, thereby betraying their positions. The serpentine nature of the wadi dictated the Turkish placement of redoubts and their covering artillery in an area two miles long and somewhat shorter in width. Three redoubts faced south (Nos. 2, 3 and 4) and had been filled with sand by a *khamsin*. A mountain battery of four guns (*M1873* and the 75mm guns of the *1st Mountain Regiment*) lay roughly in the centre, covered by No. 5 redoubt on the east and No. 1 at the western extremity. The Turkish forces comprised the *2nd* and *3rd battalions*, *80th Regiment*, *27th Division* and ancillary troops. While it was primarily a defensive force, it lacked defence stores.[2]

Chauvel's division moved out at midnight and, in clear, cold conditions, made good progress. Four hours later his forward elements, including battery observing parties, were four miles from their objective. Chauvel's three brigades comprised the 3rd Light Horse (Cox), NZMR (Chaytor) and the ICC Brigade (Smith). The 1st Light Horse Brigade was in reserve, and between it and the main force were the Somerset and Inverness batteries, and the Hong Kong and Singapore Mountain Battery. Aerial observation at first light coincided with ground reconnaissance by Chauvel and his brigadiers. This took around an hour as some of the defiles were filled with smoke. Once it had cleared, Chauvel set up his headquarters some four miles from the town, a location that provided him with good observation. It was co-located with the 1st Light Horse Brigade, the two batteries and Smith's brigade headquarters. The New Zealanders and the 3rd Light Horse Brigade were sited to the east. Chauvel's plan involved a three-point attack. Ultimately, however, he was able to concentrate his offensive power at a decisive point, helped by the 'indiscretion' of one of his brigade commanders.[3]

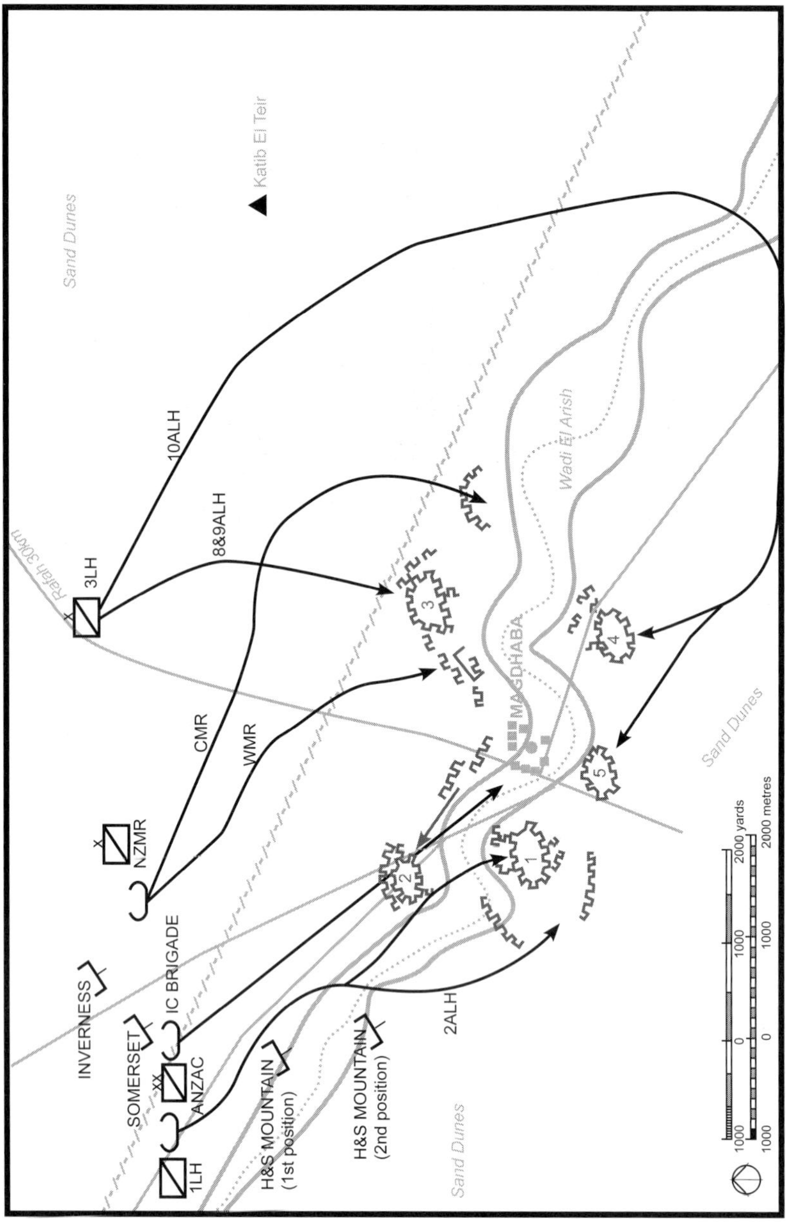

Map 3: The Battle of Magdhaba, 23 December 1916, showing the artillery gun positions relative to five cavalry objectives during their encircling movements. 'HK & S' refers to the Hong Kong and Singapore Mountain Battery (source: Hill, *Chauvel of the Light Horse*, p. 88).

Image 8: Brigadier Charles Cox, GOC 1st Australian Light Horse Brigade, and Major General E.W.C. Chaytor, GOC NZMR Brigade. Both were enthusiastic supporters of the '*arme blanche*' cavalry approach to combat (AWM B00602).

The 10th Light Horse Regiment had the longest ride to its assaulting position opposite Nos. 4 and 3 redoubts, on the south side of the wadi, covering some five miles of sand and scrub. The 8th and 9th regiments attacked the gun area and redoubt north-east of the settlement. Royston's brigade had two machine-gun sections. This was also the area assigned to the Canterbury and Wellington troopers. The cameleers had the shortest approach march (camels were slower than horses) so as to coordinate better with the horse-mounted forces in a synchronised assault. The 1st and 2nd Light Horse regiments had to approach No. 2 redoubt by crossing the wadi. The Indian gunners established their fire position in the wadi and, as the battle developed, moved it an additional 1100 yards to flat ground further east.[4]

As the 10th Light Horse Regiment captured a large body of Turks in the wadi, an RFC observer dropped his flagged message holder literally on Chaytor's doorstep, advising that the 'enemy was making off and might yet escape envelopment'. He was referring to the prisoners in the wadi, and Chaytor decided to request Cox's brigade to advance straight towards the settlement. At 10.30 am the 3rd Light Horse Brigade attacked up the wadi. Elsewhere the fighting was sporadic, the gunners having some difficulty locating the Turk's mountain guns because of the residual 'smoke' effect, but still shooting effectively. By 3.00 pm Chauvel must have considered that 'here was another Bir el Abd', where success appeared to elude him and, without water, he was yet again facing retirement. As it happened Cox's men and the 3rd Battalion of the Camel Brigade were close to No. 2 redoubt in what proved to be the crucial moment of the battle. If the redoubt could not be taken, Chauvel knew he would have to withdraw. Deciding that success was unlikely, he issued the order to withdraw. As the orderly handed it to Cox, 'Fighting Charlie' turned a Nelsonian eye to its content, and told his orderly, 'Take the damned thing away and let me see it for the first time in half an hour.' As Gullett noted of Chauvel's dilemma, 'so narrow was the margin between victory and failure, that even as No. 2 redoubt was falling, Chauvel was . . . giving earnest consideration to ... a general withdrawal.' Cox's men and the 3rd Battalion of the Camel Brigade closed on No. 2 redoubt and took it, much to Chauvel's relief, for Chetwode was pushing him to fight on into the next day, 'even at the cost of some horses'.

As the afternoon wore on and close-quarter fighting seemed inevitable, Chauvel ordered his batteries to cease firing. With No. 2 redoubt captured, the way was opened for the cameleers approaching from the north and the New Zealanders and the 8th and 9th Light Horse regiments to capture No. 3 redoubt followed by No. 1 and the enemy battery. Chauvel's brigades had done him proud in routing the Turkish defences. During the action the Inverness Battery fired all 498 rounds of first line ammunition — its reserve was back with its B Echelon. The Somersets did not have the same problem, but the New Zealand machine-gunners did. The three batteries were ordered to march to El Arish immediately after the battle, arriving just after midnight.[5]

The Turkish losses amounted to just under 100 killed, 300 wounded and almost 1300 taken prisoner, with four mountain guns, 1250 rifles and 1,000,000 rounds of small arms ammunition captured. A considerable amount of 'tibbin' — fodder for horses — was also captured, as were 50 camels and their commander, Kadri Bey. Chauvel's losses totalled five officers killed and seven wounded, while 17 soldiers and troopers were killed and 117 wounded. Due to Magdhaba's relative isolation, evacuation of wounded was a traumatic experience, not helped by more poor staff arrangements at Chetwode's headquarters.[6]

Historians note that the battle of Magdhaba lasted 24 hours from mounting to finale. It was a classical mounted infantry operation beginning with 'its night ride of 50 miles to contact, fought 23 miles from their water supply and 50 miles from their railhead, surprised and beat a strongly placed enemy.' Other factors, such as a rapid approach, dashing leadership, astuteness of the troopers, effective use of machine-guns and bayonet were also noteworthy. For the horse artillery, it says much for the divisional gunner's logistic administration to have 500 rounds for each battery 50 miles from a railhead. Gunner casualties were nil and they demonstrated the same stamina as the troopers.[7]

With the end of the Battle of Magdhaba, there were no more Turks in the Sinai.

Epilogue

A recent scholarly study by Woerlee (with the great benefit of hindsight) included further examination of the records and hypothesised what other actions Chetwode and Chauvel could have taken following the capture of Magdhaba.[8] He raised a number of salient points:

a. Victories at Bir el Abd and Magdhaba were less victories for British forces than part of a planned general withdrawal by Kress von Kressenstein.
b. Communication by telephone between Chetwode's headquarters at Kilo 149 on the coast and Chauvel at Magdhaba were open, as they were to Ismailia. Hence Chetwode's message to fight it out.
c. Chauvel could have detached a brigade and battery to investigate Abu Aweigila and force the surrender of its garrison. A squadron could then have taken an outpost at Um Shihan. His force's morale was high, it was a relatively easy march and it could have been supplied from materiel captured at Magdhaba. The failure to follow up meant that this Turkish force could reinforce El Auja. This garrison primarily comprised service troops and explains von Kressenstein's panic over likely Allied moves.
d. It was almost 40 miles from El Auja to Beersheba, a 12-hour march with water all the way (Magdhaba to Beersheba is 66 miles). A squadron mounted on captured rolling stock with machine-guns moving to Beersheba could have split the town down the middle.

Since the fall of Magdhaba saw the end of Turkish forces in the Sinai, the German air force, which had enjoyed clear operational advantages with superior machines, was now conspicuously absent from the skies. This was even more curious given that the first of the British anti-aircraft guns (3-pounders) had not yet arrived in theatre. During this phase of the campaign the airmen conducted lengthy reconnaissance flights (up to seven hours in duration) and bombing flights to Beersheba. Cutlack's analysis suggests that German air power 'could have derailed Murray's advance over the desert'.[9]

Chapter 6
The Battle of Rafa: 8/9 January 1916

He who hesitates is lost.

Proverb

Just 25 miles from Magdhaba lay the town of Rafa. However the key consideration for any further British advance was the arrival of rail and water supplies. Major General Chetwode had decided to capture Rafa, which included the well-defended locality of El Maghruntein. His DMC comprised the 5th Mounted Yeomanry Brigade, ICC Brigade and the A&NZ Mounted Division (less the 2nd Light Horse Brigade) under Chauvel. Also included were seven patrol cars of the 7th Light Armoured Car Patrol (Model T Fords), mounted with Vickers machine-guns.[1] The Leicester, Inverness and Somerset batteries (twelve 13-pounders) with their affiliated brigades set out at 4.00 am on 8 January 1917 and, after at pause at Sheikh Zowaiid, crossed the border into Palestine at 1.00 am the next morning, reaching the battle site at dawn. B Battery HAC (four 18-pounders) supported the 5th Mounted Brigade. Two brigades marched in an easterly direction to move to the rear of the position, the remainder taking the coastal route.[2]

The Turks opposed the Allied force with around 2000 infantry and two mountain guns based behind El Maghruntein in the centre of their circular position. There was a token force at Rafa settlement which was soon overcome by the New Zealanders, who rode down a machine-gun post and captured six German and two Turkish officers and 163 soldiers. This was the easy part of the battle.[3] Chetwode's plan envisaged his three brigades enveloping the 255 feature (Towaiil el Emir) between El Maghruntein and Rafa. He sited his headquarters four miles to the west. Chauvel's headquarters was located nearby on a feature that provided good observation. He conducted his reconnaissance with his CRA, Colonel Sir Joseph Laycock and, at 9.00 am, issued orders for the attack to begin at 10.00 am, with a preliminary bombardment to start at 9.30 am and last 30 minutes.

The redoubts around this feature were designated A, B and C (west to east). Each brigade would have a specific redoubt as its objective. The Australians would aim for redoubt C while the NZMR Brigade, supported by the Inverness Battery, blocked the escape route to and from Rafa. The Inverness Battery also supported the Australians, both Leicester and Somerset and the cameleers, who were to take redoubt B. The HAC Battery's objective was redoubt A. The battery had been placed under General Chetwode's direct command and was ordered forward to support the Australian brigade.

The artillery began deploying at 7.20 am and three batteries, including the Hong Kong and Singapore Battery, but excluding the Inverness Battery on the northern flank, were located south of the battle area. The gunners soon began to register their targets, their initial positions some 2000 to 2200 yards from these. There was no covered approach to the redoubts or to the town. Despite this, early aircraft observation could not locate the position of the Turkish artillery although, later in the day, the airmen reappeared and rendered substantial assistance to the artillery.

Once the bombardment concluded, the troopers dismounted and advanced. The Turks waited until they were some 1000 yards away before opening fire and, in some cases, were able to bring enfilade fire to bear. For the first time in the campaign, AFC observers directed artillery fire and reported enemy movements for most of the day. As the engagement continued the horse gunners on the southern flank moved their guns closer to increase their effectiveness, advancing by sections to maintain their fire. Eventually they engaged their targets over open sights, assisting the mounted rifles and cameleers. In the middle of the afternoon, B Battery HAC's officer commanding (OC) decided to gallop the battery into action in the open to a point less than 1000 yards short of A redoubt. As they moved into position, the order 'Halt! Action Front!' was given and, with perfect drill, the detachments stopped their iron-mouthed mules just in time to drop trails and come into action. This was long enough for their mules to gallop down the firm slope towards the enemy trenches with limbers still attached. It was, according to the battery historian, 'a glorious sight — never before in the history of warfare had the limbers of a battery charged the enemy army alone, closely supported by the fire of their own guns.'

Following this action, B Battery HAC came under command of the 5th Mounted Brigade once again on the left flank. Here the battery learned the lesson of having alternative means of communication when the observer, Lieutenant Hawkings, used semaphore to direct his guns while exposed to continuous fire. The 5th Brigade was again readied for an assault and the BC sent the left section to support it while its commander (Lieutenant Rushbrooke) made excellent use of ground to gain cover for his guns and teams some 2000 yards from the trenches under heavy fire with only one man and three horses hit. Brigadier FitzGerald, a spectator for this action, commented later, 'He got the range quickly, raked the trenches, in part enfilade, with rapid and most accurate fire … this fine piece of work was followed by the best shooting the Battery ever did during the course of the war.' The brigade captured its objective at dusk.[4]

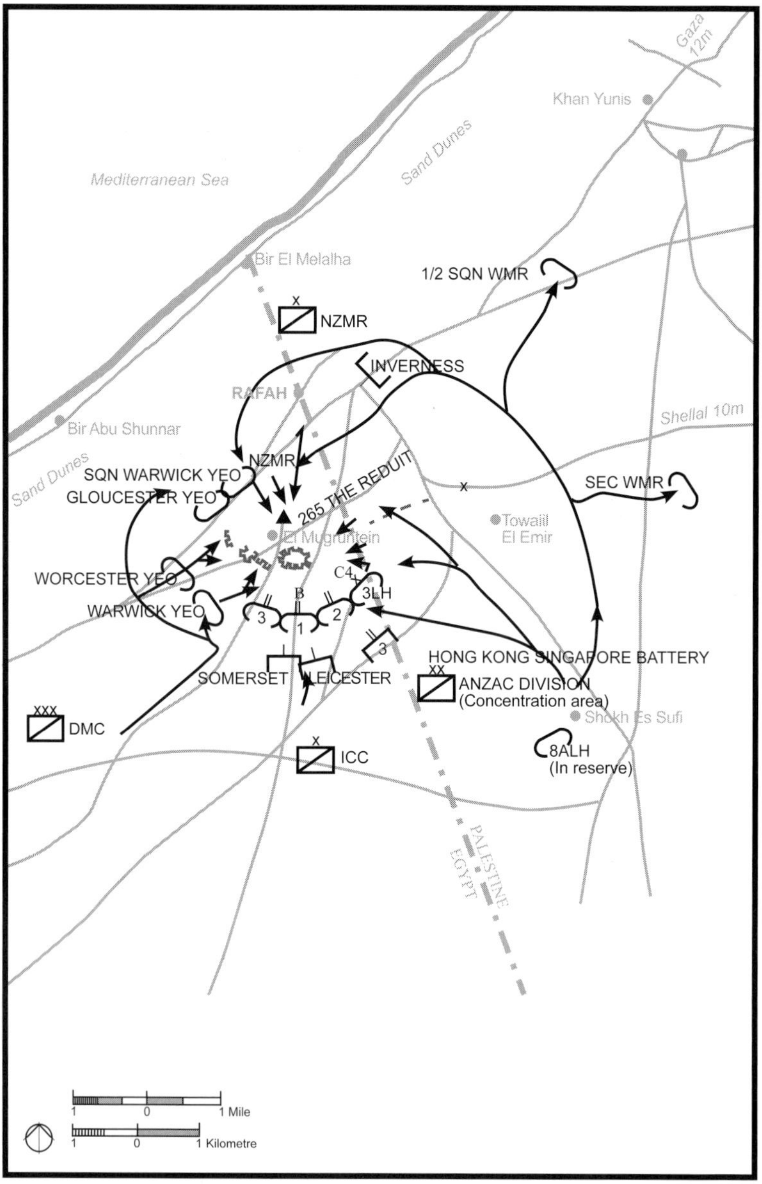

Map 4: The encirclement of Rafa by the NZMR Brigade, 5th Mounted Brigade, five Australian Light Horse regiments (1st, 2nd, 3rd, 9th and 10th) and the ICC. The gun positions of the four RHA batteries involved, Inverness, Somerset, Leicester and the Hong Kong and Singapore Battery, were north and south of the settlement (source: Gullett, *Official History*, Vol. VII, *Sinai and Palestine*, Map 11).

Chapter 6

The Hong Kong and Singapore Mountain Battery's Indian gunners manhandled their weapons to within 1000 yards of their targets and were able to reduce the volume of fire directed at the cameleers. The 10th Light Horse Regiment recorded that 'our batteries [were] sweeping the whole Turkish position with shrapnel and HE, and [were themselves] under heavy artillery and machine gun fire. The batteries were brought up to the firing line — and nearly fired their last shells.' Gullett wrote that 'All day the gunners shot with fine precision at the exposed targets, but although they harassed the enemy riflemen, the material effect of their light weapons on earthworks was insignificant.'[5]

But, however hard the dismounted men tried, the Turks appeared to have the upper hand, and Chetwode's forces were unable to overcome the defences with superior firepower at a critical point. At the same time, a patrol from the 8th Light Horse Regiment and aerial observers reported enemy reinforcements arriving from Khan Younis, a force estimated at two battalions, some 2500 men. At 4.45 pm Chetwode advised Chauvel to call off the fight and withdraw. Coincidentally, in a near repeat of Cox at Magdhaba, two regimental commanders, a New Zealander in the north and a cameleer in the south, decided to cover the 1000 yards to the feature 255, Towaiil el Emir (key to the defences), with a bayonet charge and the other at redoubt B4 respectively, without the assistance of artillery fire.[6] The success of these actions forced the surrender of the garrison within the hour. The Inverness Battery supporting the New Zealanders expended all but 19 rounds of its ammunition (471 rounds) and repaired to its B Echelon before receiving the order to withdraw. Its ammunition had to be replenished from Karm Ibn Musleh, although this did not alter the tactical situation. Similar expenditures were recorded for the other batteries.[7]

B Battery's withdrawal was a severe test of water and march discipline, the battery historian recording that, after replenishing rations at Sheikh Zowaiid for their return to El Arish, the combined effects of battle fatigue, hot weather and other exertions, were among the worst the gunners had endured. Men fell asleep at halts (every 30 minutes) standing or while riding. Shortly after midnight the moon rose and bathed the desert in an eerie light and several men experienced strange hallucinations. With dawn, the pace of the horses picked up and the force rode into El Arish at 8.30 am, 'weary, dirty and unshaven but full of satisfaction at the successful result of the capture.' The horses had been 42 hours without water and had covered 70 miles. Major Preston was awarded the DSO.[8] Casualties for the battle are listed in Table 4 below.

Image 9: Captured Turkish artillery at Rafa is inspected by the leaders of the cavalry involved (AWM J03188).

Chetwode's forces withdrew to Sheikh Zowaiid and bivouacked there while the 3rd and 8th Light Horse regiments guarded the battlefield from the depredations of the Bedouins and the field ambulances completed their work. Rafa was the first significant advance into Palestine or, from von Kressenstein's perspective, another stage in a planned withdrawal. It was the first battle fought on firm ground in which light artillery fire could be more effective than in desert sand and scrub due to ease of manoeuvre.[9]

Artillery critique

At this point it is appropriate to analyse the results achieved by the RHA and Hong Kong and Singapore Mountain Battery where they were allotted to Chetwode's forces. Farndale claims that, 'against considerable ground, weather and logistic problems the artillery had done well at Romani, Magdhaba and Rafa' and 'were hard seasoned campaigners, capable of quite complex artillery tactics, and above all had earned the respect of the … cavalry and infantry.'[10] British forces at two of the battles he cites enjoyed numerical superiority (in rifles and sabres) and in the other they were outnumbered. In two of the encounters the attackers approached laboriously and assaulted over open ground, across salt pan, sand dunes and sandy scrub, while at Rafa firm ground made an encircling manoeuvre easier but the attack more perilous. In all battles, Chetwode and Chauvel had a numerical superiority in light artillery, but at Qatya and Bir el Abd the Turks had a clear advantage with more and heavier calibre weapons. In all the engagements in which the troopers defeated their opponents it was at the point of a bayonet after rushes or fire and movement minor tactics by troopers, sections, troops and squadrons. In describing these engagements the literature mentions the severity of enemy machine-gun fire, almost until the troopers leapt into the trenches and redoubts. So the question arises, how effective was artillery fire and why? Did it enable the troopers' last 100-yard dash to the trench when the Turks' heads were down and, if so, how well controlled was it? One answer can be found at Rafa in an examination of the Turkish trenches by the 5th Mounted Brigade Field Ambulance. B Battery HAC's guns (18-pounders) were able to enfilade B redoubt trenches. While searching for wounded, Royal Army Medical Corps personnel found 200 Turks killed or wounded by shrapnel fire. Had they been using their 13-pounders would the same attrition have occurred? Perhaps.

The use of some statistics may partially answer this question, with some 'givens'. The first is that a number of machine-guns (on both sides) operated with impunity and added to casualty lists. Table 4 lists the toll of casualties:

TABLE 4: CASUALTIES FOR THE BATTLE OF RAFA

Force	KIA	WIA	POWs	Total
Brit/Aus:	71	415	486	942
Turks:	200	168	1434	1802

Four Turkish mountain guns and machine-guns were also captured.[11]

The second 'given' is that advances to contact and assaults were over open ground with good visibility (except for shellfire dust) giving the defenders a tactical advantage in respect of observed fire accuracy. Yet another factor is the lethality of an HE shell on firm ground compared to sand, with one account noting that a man was safe six yards from a '5.9' burst and also from lesser calibre HE (ground) burst.[12] However, there was agreement among the cavalrymen and infanteers, both officers and men, that they appreciated the artillery support and recognised the difficulties encountered by the gunners. Comparable casualties for the battles of Romani, Magdhaba and Rafa are outlined in Table 5 below:

TABLE 5: COMPARABLE CASUALTY RATIOS FROM THE BATTLES OF ROMANI, MAGDHABA AND RAFA

(Turkish figures do not include prisoners of war)

Battle	British KIA	British WIA	Turkish KIA	Turkish WIA
Romani	202	882	1250	4000
	Ratio of British to Turkish: KIA 1:6 WIA 1:5 Total 1:4.6			
Magdhaba	22	124	97	40
	Ratio of British to Turkish: KIA 1:4.5 WIA 3:1 Total 1:1			
Rafa	71	415	200	168
	Ratio of British to Turkish: KIA 1:3 WIA 2.5:1 Total 1.3:1			
	Captured and missing: British 45; Turkish 6644[13]			

The statistics suggest that Romani/Qatya/Bir el Abd represented a major victory for the British, never subsequently to be repeated. While no figures are available for ammunition expenditure, it would be reasonable to assume that, in the defence of Romani, the ease of digging in sand dunes reduced the lethality of Turkish HE fire. The use of shrapnel and HE mix by the RHA and RFA guns was reasonably effective and, in that battle, the ratio of killed to wounded was almost the same for both forces. This may be explained by the accounts of advancing horsemen arriving at a redoubt relatively unscathed despite machine-gun and shellfire, their movement well dispersed to avoid offering a good target. The sabre or bayonet-led rush at a trench often saw the Turkish riflemen shoot inaccurately given the urgency of the movement, an attacking advantage for the troopers' leaders to exploit. The light casualties of the gunners were due to the passably effective Turkish counter-battery fire (given their superiority in heavy ordnance) being absorbed by sand and also due to counter-preparation fire once the Turks had been overrun and/or surrendered.

At Magdhaba the ratio of wounded is a significant statistic, relative to Romani. While the ratio of those killed was similar to Romani, the number of wounded can be explained by the long, open approaches and well-sited machine-guns, rather than the effect of mountain artillery fire. Magdhaba trenches had been filled with sand from a recent *khamsin* and this would have nullified the 13-pound round's lethality. Rafa was the first 'firm ground' battle, and it is statistically similar to Magdhaba. Open approaches and well-sited defences resolutely manned took their toll in wounded. What is of interest is that the attackers found the trenches and redoubts they reached 'thick with dead'. An examination of the ammunition expenditure for the three RHA batteries shows a three to two ratio of shrapnel to HE allied to which was a phased forward movement of batteries (to an 'open sights' situation) to close the redoubts, and would seem to contradict Gullett's comment that 'they [sic] shot without effect all day'.[14]

An interesting aspect of the Rafa battle was the siting of all but one of the batteries at the southern end of the area rather than their dispersal to reap the benefit of the length of the impact area zone. Perhaps being close to the road for ease of ammunition replenishment was a key factor in this decision. But how could they assist the troopers assaulting the northern and eastern redoubts with their flat fire? This has been partly answered by B Battery HAC. The artillery commanders must have been gratified by the low casualty count and the high expenditure and effectiveness of shrapnel over the hard ground (plus and minus of the trench lines) at short times of flight. This was observed direct shooting at its best. Following Romani, accounts of the effects of Turkish artillery fire on the cavalry are few, though there were exceptions. Those gunners may have fled north from Romani and Bir el Abd and lived to fight another day, which they certainly did at the next battle, First Gaza.

The success of the day's proceedings at Rafa pales into insignificance compared to the trials of the withdrawal of B Battery HAC to El Arish. Exhausted from the day's fighting and heat, one water bottle to sustain the men and nothing for the unfortunate horses, they set off on a forced march at 11.00 pm. Men dropped from their horses or fell asleep at halts. This continued until they reached their destination at 8.30 am when their horses were finally able to bury their faces in cool, sweet water. They had been 46 hours without water and covered 70 miles. It was the first of two similar experiences the battery would endure.

After Rafa

In the early months of 1917 operations took second place to reorganisation and logistics. First, the 42nd (East Lancashire) Division was despatched to France. Next, three new infantry brigades were formed from yeomanry units that had returned from Gallipoli but for which there were no horses. These became the 229th, 230th and 231st brigades of the 74th Yeomanry Division. They had no organic artillery, engineer and signals elements. Lieutenant General Chetwode then placed the 1st and 2nd Light Horse brigades, NZMR Brigade and the 22nd Mounted Brigade under Chauvel's command. The 3rd and 4th Light Horse brigades and the 5th and 6th mounted brigades formed the IMD under Major General H.W. Hodgson. The 4th Light Horse Brigade comprised the 4th, 11th and 12th Light Horse regiments.

In terms of logistics, General Murray's main concern was water and the operation of his supply chain by land (railway) and sea to the port of El Arish. The railhead reached Sheikh Zowaiid, 30 miles from Gaza. By 5 February the pipeline had reached El Arish. Already pressure from the War Office was pushing Murray to assault Gaza, and in terms of water supply there was some water available from the Wadi Ghuzze but not sufficient for his force of two corps. Capturing Gaza and its water without the operation stalling was therefore a key consideration in his planning.

Chetwode wrote an 'appreciation of the situation' confronting the EEF on the expulsion of the Turkish Army from Palestine. His 'Notes' have passed into history, not only for their lucid argument and deductions, but also due to the fact that, the following year, General Allenby adopted them 'in toto' in his campaign planning. What was the background of this remarkable cavalryman? Philip Walhouse Chetwode was born on 21 September 1869 in England and entered the army as a militia cavalryman but later gained a regular commission. He won a DSO and was twice Mentioned in Despatches in colonial wars. In World War I he commanded the 19th Lancers (in Allenby's brigade) and was then promoted to brigade command before later commanding XXI Corps. Wavell wrote that 'He had about the best and quickest military brain I have ever known, an extremely good tactical eye for ground and a great gift for expressing a situation clearly and concisely, either by word or on paper. I think he just lacked as a commander the quality of determination and drive, certainly compared to a man like Allenby.'[15]

Chapter 7
The First Battle of Gaza: 26–27 March 1917

Misfortunes never come singly.

Proverb

Following the Battle of Rafa, General von Kressenstein withdrew to a line from Gaza to Beersheba. He was determined to retain the vital town of Gaza as long as he could with all the assets he had. Gaza's location along the line of advance made it an important objective in a strategic sense. The town was a major centre with telegraph and a railway terminus, and a substantial built-up area that spread inland. There were commanding views in all directions and the terrain was ideal for defence. Between the town and coast were sand dunes and the Turkish outpost line lay one mile south of the town. The key tactical features of the town were (from west to east) Bunker Hill, El Arish redoubt, Romani trench, extensive cactus hedges eight feet high known as the Labyrinth, Green Hill, the high peak of Ali el Muntar (Arabic for 'watchtower' and the key to the defence) and Fryer Hill. Other features that were key to the battle were Australia Hill (to the north-east) and Middlesex Hill (south). There were four ridgelines oriented from north-east to south-west: Mansura, Es Shire, Burjabye and Sheikh Abbas. These provided good observation towards the town and held some concealed gun positions as they extended south two to three miles towards the assembly areas south of the Wadi Ghuzze.

The terrain from Gaza south-east to Beersheba was generally flat with few features. The Turks were reported to have two infantry regiments, the *79th* and *125th*, plus a battalion from the *81st Regiment*, two field artillery batteries, two Austrian mountain howitzers and two 100mm German *kannons* to defend the town, a total of some 2000 rifles. In his own area, von Kressenstein's expeditionary force totalled 16,000 rifles, 1500 sabres and 74 guns. On the force's eastern and northern flanks the *3rd Division* and the *31st Regiment*, *53rd Division*, could reinforce Gaza. These were estimated to be 12 miles away at Huj, 10 miles south-east at Abu Hureira and at Tel el Sheria (sometimes Tel esh Sheria), 16 miles to the south-east. Allied planners anticipated that these troops would be too far away to help the defenders, should everything proceed according to plan.[1]

Image 10: The terrain showing the infantry's approach to Gaza prior to First Gaza. The cactus hedges evident here proved a serious obstacle for the infantry. They were eventually obliterated by shellfire (AWM B00969).

General Murray, whose distant command style saw him rarely visit his front-line commanders, had seen a steady flow of materiel bolster his force, and felt optimistic over the looming operation. He reflected this in his messages to the War Office but was unable to influence the battle once joined because of his diffuse command arrangements. However, he now had three heavy (60-pounder) batteries — the 15th, 91st and 10th — instead of only one as in his previous encounters. To save horses, each battery manned only two guns instead of the usual four. Murray was certain that the batteries would make a difference. Attention had also been focused on protecting the assembled forces from German aircraft, and several 3-inch anti-aircraft batteries were sited in defence. No. 1 Squadron AFC, which counted strategic reconnaissance among its roles, spent three days from 15 April attempting to lure German fliers over the anti-aircraft guns. While this proved unsuccessful, the time was used more profitably by the squadron's observer, Lieutenant Ross Smith, to range the heavy artillery.[2]

The operational commander for the first corps operation of the Palestine war was Lieutenant General Sir Charles Dobell, his BGRA Brigadier A.H. Short. In contrast to Murray, then back in Cairo, Dobell made a point of becoming familiar with the country and brought vigour to his command. His presence was clearly visible to all. Murray's battle plan gave Dobell command of the overall attack. The infantry would make a direct assault on Ali el Muntar, while the mounted troops would act as screening and cut-off forces and would have a secondary role to support the infantry. According to this plan, there would be two separate operations: the cavalry deployed east and north of the town, and an infantry/artillery battle south of the town. The War Office had directed that 2000 gas shells be sent to the theatre for the 18-pounders to fire in this assault. This would be the first time chemical warfare would be used away from France.

Unsurprisingly, the introduction of gas warfare generated much correspondence between London and Cairo. The issues ranged from the type of gas, availability of trained operators for its discharge, local meteorology, training of the corps in gas warfare, and ethical issues within Murray's several headquarters. Above all, the gunners questioned where gas would fit in the artillery and infantry tactical plans, and whether it would be of value in the battle given that the desert was typically dry in March with inconsistent winds. The gunners asserted that these factors would reduce its effectiveness. Eventually, the decision was taken not to use the gas shells.[3]

Murray, like Lawrence at Romani, ordered Dobell to direct the attack while Chetwode commanded the Desert Column and the attacking infantry under the 53rd Division, led by Major General G. Dallas. Dobell retained command of the reserve 52nd and 54th divisions. His force amounted to 25,000 rifles (19,000 without the 52nd Division) and 8500 sabres, supported by 94 guns and the 11th and 12th light armoured motor batteries. Chauvel would command the mounted troops under Chetwode. The senior gunner was Major General S.C.U. Smith, MGRA to the forces, but with no command responsibilities, inferring that his input was purely advisory, as decisions on divisional artillery matters were left to his BGRA, Brigadier Short. This proved to be a difficult arrangement during the battle.

The mounted troops, with allotted artillery, comprised:

- Chauvel: A&NZ Mounted Division less the 1st Light Horse Brigade; the 19th RHA Brigade of Ayrshire, Leicester, Inverness and Somerset batteries, each with four 13-pounders.
- Hodgson: IMD less the 4th Light Horse Brigade; the 20th RHA Brigade of Notts and Berkshire batteries, each with four 13-pounders, A and B batteries HAC, each with four 18-pounders.
- ICC Brigade: Hong Kong and Singapore Mountain Battery with four 3.7-inch howitzers.

One feature of the staff's planning for the first corps operation of the desert war was the constantly changing organisations, establishments and affiliations. They also realised that their orders required Gaza to be taken in one day. To this end they organised camel trains by exchanging the mounted division's camels for the infantry divisions' horse-drawn supply columns.

Chauvel's force. Part 1: H Hour to 4.00 pm

Chauvel's and Hodgson's RHA batteries were deployed with their affiliated mounted elements for their supporting role. For the first time since August 1914 the two HAC batteries were brothers-in-arms, and were to spend almost the entire war under the command of Major General H.W. Hodgson. The HAC revelled in Hodgson's command, its war diarist writing, 'No finer soldier or more sympathetic commander and friend was to be found in all the force.' Hodgson's CRA was Lieutenant Colonel the Marquis of Exeter.

The gunners moved from Khan Younis towards Gaza. The town emerged as dawn broke, a picturesque panorama in the distance and a scene of great beauty and peace. It would be much changed by the battle that was soon to ensue. From the Beersheba road the mounted troops moved off at 2.30 am on 26 March in a wide quadrant-shaped screen five miles east of Gaza, via the Wadi Ghuzze, Deir el Belah, the eastern extremity of which was Beit Durdis and which extended north-west to Deir Sineid across the road from Huj, where Chauvel's troopers would be operating. The batteries (without pedrails) moved with their divisions and brigades. There was much congestion as only one cutting had been made in the steep sides of the Wadi Ghuzze. Accordingly, much time was lost. A sea fog unexpectedly rolled inland cloaking the troopers' advance and causing Chetwode to delay the movement of his infantry, all with enormous repercussions. The two mounted divisions in column of march swung north, Chauvel's aim to be positioned north-east and north-west of Gaza once the bombardment began. Hodgson's division was to be sited east of him, on his right, with his 6th Mounted Brigade in the lead destined for Beit Durdis, followed by the 5th Mounted Brigade which would block the Beersheba-Gaza road some five miles away. The ICC Brigade, the slowest to manoeuvre, guarded the area north of the Beersheba road at Khirbet er Reseim. The fortunes of the 6th Mounted Brigade will be described first.

At 9.30 am the brigade crossed the Gaza-Beersheba road and occupied a position some three miles from the Huj track. A mile north, Hill 405 was covered by Ryrie's 3rd Light Horse Brigade, and there the Notts and Berks batteries took their positions closest to Gaza (as the crow flies) in support of the 3rd. The Berks Battery, commanded by Major Mayall, had the longest trek to its position, starting at 10.30 am on the eve of battle and finally reaching its position at 3.00 am, where it dug in. At H Hour the battery opened fire at 4500 yards on the opposing trenches, the battery's observers sited behind the battery in an elevated observation post (OP). Turkish fire cut the telephone line during the battery's five hours of firing, forcing the use of a 'chain of command' for fire orders relayed by orderlies until the line was restored. Much of the fire was sweeping and searching, with useful information signalled by Lieutenant Colonel Scott, commanding officer (CO) of the 9th Australian Light Horse, including the effect of the battery's shooting. At 11.00 am a 'streamer' message was dropped by Lieutenant Turner, RFC which, while being appreciated, was not as useful as wireless communication. At 12.00 noon the brigade adjutant selected new positions a mile away. Again, sweeping and searching were employed at ranges of 4600 to 5300 yards, and the battery's expenditure for the day was 912 rounds. The gunners withdrew at dusk to Charing Cross and 'stood to' all night.[4]

The Hong Kong and Singapore Mountain Battery, arriving mid-afternoon, occupied a position some 3000 yards to the rear of the brigade. Standing patrols were sent out and Hodgson's headquarters enjoyed a commanding view to the east. A Battery HAC lay half a mile behind, its teams at the ready. This area was critical for stemming the movement of Turkish reinforcements to prevent Gaza's capture. As expected, the commander of the Turkish relief force arrived in the afternoon and ordered his troops forward. Ryrie's men noted that they were tired after their long approach march, although their gunners were clearly less exhausted, immediately opening fire on the cavalry. Later, Ryrie repositioned his brigade to conform with Chetwode's other alignments and create a continuous cordon around the town.

The appearance of an enemy observation aircraft was followed by shelling from '5.9s' in Gaza and Hareira, prompting the brigades to disperse. However, soon afterwards, the gunners found their first targets — enemy infantry on Tel esh Sheria, which invited retaliatory counter-battery fire. By late afternoon A Battery HAC was contemplating a night bivouac when Hodgson rode up and ordered the gunners to move to a position facing north to cover the withdrawal of his division. The cavalry had occupied a ridge that was clearly visible from the gun position. Several positions were occupied and, at length, the BC received orders to go to Deir el Belah, which had been the battery's start point. The delayed infantry progress had caused the battle plan to implode.[5]

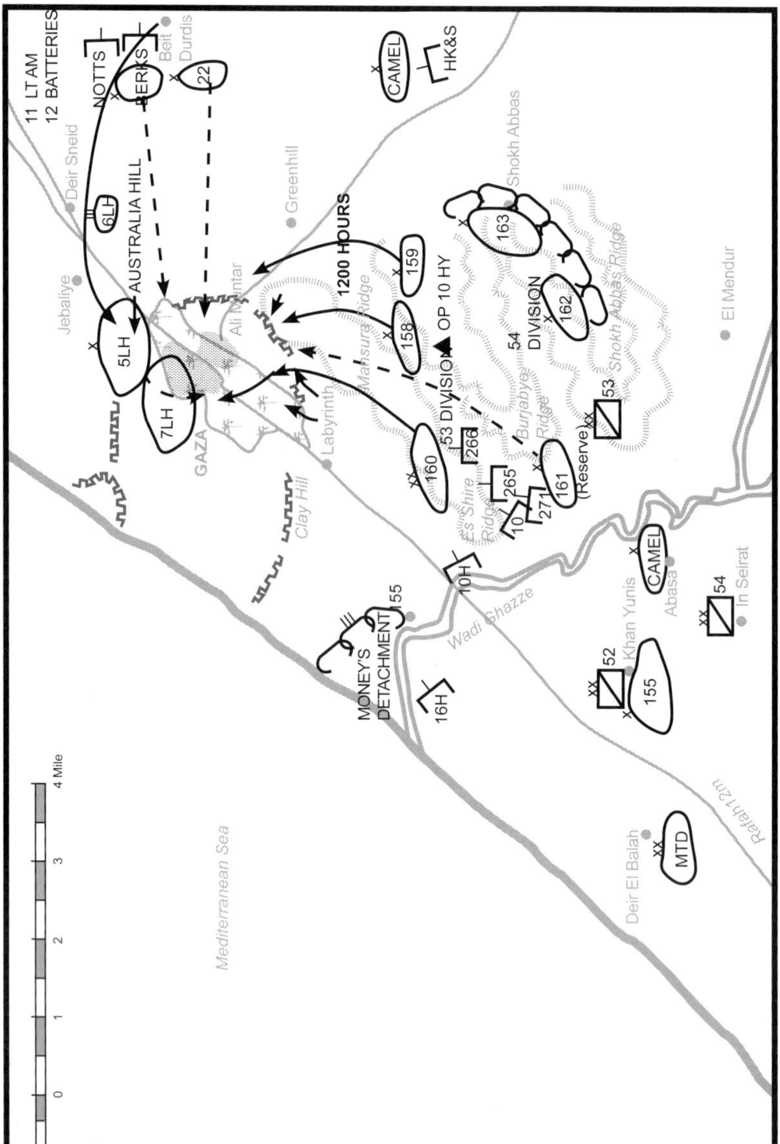

Map 5: The First Battle of Gaza, at dusk on 26 March 1917, showing the dispositions of horse and field batteries east and south of the town when it was surrounded, before the force was recalled to its start line (source: Hill, *Chauvel of the Light Horse*, p. 144).

Chapter 7

Chauvel's force: Part 2

B Battery HAC and the 5th Mounted Brigade endured a tortuous crossing at Wadi Ghuzze. The battery occupied a position adjacent to the Gaza-Beersheba road where Brigadier Wiggin, by virtue of his battery's position on top of a prominent hill, enjoyed good observation towards Huj. However cover was scarce and the position was shelled by a heavy gun from the direction of Hareira redoubt after an enemy aircraft spotted the concentrated brigade. Brigadier Wiggin ordered the guns out of action and they split into sections and withdrew. This set the pattern for the afternoon with heavy enemy attacks from Tel el Nejile and Sheria. Realising he was outnumbered, Wiggin withdrew his troops to the south-west, the battery preparing to respond to fire orders in minutes. However, as the day progressed there was to be no glory for those gunners as the tactical situation deteriorated.[6]

The 2nd and 6th Light Horse regiments had continued the left hook manoeuvre to cut off a Turkish retreat via the Deir Sineid road north of Gaza, while the 7th Light Horse Regiment concluded its advance west of the town. Gaza was now encircled and one part of Murray's plan had been outstandingly successful. On the way the troopers captured a Turkish general who told them that Gaza would be 'no Rafa'. By 10.00 am the 2nd Light Horse Brigade had finally found time to water its horses.[7]

While the day ran smoothly for the mounted troops, the infantry and their commanders were well behind schedule. Where the mounted men were in action, their adversary comprised exhausted reinforcements, their artillery sited to the east. However, it was not until Generals Dobell and Chetwode heard a report of Turkish reinforcements bearing down on Gaza that they decided to involve the mounted men in support of the infantry attack following its late start. Chetwode signalled Chauvel at 1.00 pm, telling him to gather his division to attack Gaza, using Hodgson's men under his command to relieve the A&NZ Mounted Division. Chauvel received the signal at 2.00 pm, and it was 4.00 pm before he could issue his orders to support Dallas' division.[8]

First into the fray were the 2nd Light Horse Brigade, the NZMR and yeomanry brigades on their left which moved close to the town. The New Zealanders captured two 77mm field guns but were held up by machine-guns. The Kiwis turned the guns around, sighted them down the barrel at the offending weapons, and fired two rounds. As a consequence 28 bemused Turks went into captivity. The 5th and 7th Light Horse regiments approached Gaza from the north without artillery support but with the 2nd Machine Gun Squadron as their proxy. The New Zealanders led the rush from the east and, 30 minutes after receiving their orders, had captured 129 Turks and other war materiel in Gaza, having been subjected to ineffective Turkish shrapnel. At the same time the 22nd Yeomanry Brigade on their left joined the 53rd Division's infantry at Ali el Muntar and Gaza. Thus, a short time after their first bloody experience of street fighting, the Antipodean troopers stood in front of the Great Mosque. Gaza, to all intents and purposes, had fallen. This was the cavalry's situation when Dobell issued his first order to withdraw at 6.00 pm.[9]

Infantry operations: Part 1

Dobell's artillery for the infantry battle comprised:

- 52nd Division: 261st, 262nd and 263rd RFA brigades at half strength, i.e. eight 18-pounders and four 4.5-inch howitzers.
- 53rd Division: 265th and 266th RFA brigades, each with eight 18-pounders and four 4.5-inch howitzers.[10]
- 54th Division: 270th and 271st RFA brigades, as above.

Total: seventy-two 18-pounders and twenty-eight 4.5-inch howitzers.

- Heavy artillery: 10th, 15th and 91st heavy batteries, each with two 60-pounders.
- Dallas: 53rd Division and 239th Brigade (of the 74th Division), CRA Brigadier Sir Joseph Laycock; 265th, 266th and 271st brigades RFA of the 53rd Division. Each brigade had eight 18-pounders and four 4.5-inch howitzers, 36 in total (remainder with canal defences).
- Dobell: reserve divisions, 54th Division (protecting the eastern flank) and 74th Division (less 239th Brigade) of XX Corps in reserve.

Colonel Money's cavalry detachment was by the sea at the mouth of the Wadi Ghuzze ready to exploit northwards.[11]

Due to poor staff work and execution there were shortages of ammunition, guns and trained personnel. For the counter-battery tasks Dobell's orders placed artillery fire control in the hands of forward observers (FOOs) and RFC aircraft The counter-battery plan involved a two-gun section of the 15th Heavy Battery deploying to the mouth of the Wadi Ghuzze some 12,000 yards from Gaza. It was to be protected by a three-squadron force under Colonel Money at Tel el Ujul on the other side of the wadi mouth by the sea. Another section of the 91st Heavy Battery was to occupy a position in the wadi on the Rafa-Gaza road and a section of the 10th Heavy Battery was to move with the 160th Infantry Brigade to a position 1000 yards south of the end of Es Shire ridge, some 10,500 yards from Gaza. This artillery was to blast the trenches in the Labyrinth, and a dedicated OP moved up to Mansura ridge in the tracks of the 158th Brigade.

The infantry had to march some 4000 yards in full battle order to engage their foes.[12]

Initial deployment for the infantry attack was assisted by a starless night, but at 5.00 am a sea fog rolled in. By 8.30 two brigades of the 53rd Division had crossed Wadi Ghuzze (the start line) and advanced, the 158th Brigade on Mansura and Es Shire ridges, and the 160th on El Sheluf ridge, an approach march of over two miles, which they reached after some confusion at 8.00 and 8.30 am respectively. Their objective was Ali el Muntar. At 8.00 am two RFA brigades went into action and began a 30-minute bombardment, described by Gullett as 'ineffective shooting'.[13] The attacking brigades, which at this stage had not yet been fired on, awaited Dallas' order to continue. At 9.00 am he conferred with his brigadiers, concerned that artillery support would be problematic if the fog suddenly lifted. As it was, weather conditions made observed shooting difficult, although the fog later cleared.

By 10.00 am the gunners were ready and simply awaiting their orders. Dallas was unaware that his batteries had crossed the wadi and were available at the time of his conference. The 158th and 160th brigades advanced while the 159th, still without firm orders, moved up on their right in reserve. At 11.30 am Chetwode's chief of staff sent a message to Dallas noting that he 'had been out of touch with his HQ for two hours, no gun registration was being undertaken, time was passing and … you must order your attack forthwith.' Dallas' division was five hours behind schedule, including the time he had spent with his brigadiers formulating his orders. Half an hour later, the 161st Infantry Brigade was ordered forward to attack Mansura ridge, but its organic artillery, also ordered ahead a distance of three and a half miles, took almost three hours to move before coming into action.[14] The division, now moving forward and with the benefit of aerial observation of the battlefield, had fire from the 265th and 266th RFA brigades' 18-pounders on Ali el Muntar by 10.10 am, despite their late orders. The CRA 53rd Division, Brigadier R.E.A. Le Mottee, had ordered them forward on his own initiative.[15] At noon the heavy artillery opened fire and the Turks replied. Chetwode ordered the Desert Column artillery remaining in the area to be used to support the infantry. The bombardment was brief due to a limited allocation of ammunition. The shooting was described as 'poor', with rounds falling well plus of the target in the cemetery on the north-eastern outskirts of town, and much time passed before the range was corrected.

Between 12.00 noon and 4.00 pm, both Chetwode and Dallas became aware that Turkish opposition and the long delay would render the capture of Gaza by dusk problematic, particularly with reports of Turkish reinforcements now reaching headquarters. Dallas had resorted to using the 161st Brigade (54th Division) to boost his attack. The effective intervention of the 271st Field Brigade RFA to neutralise machine-guns on Clay Hill during the afternoon represented a turning point in the attack. At 1.45 pm the Somerset Battery was sent across to the 161st Brigade to engage enemy guns and parties of enemy infantry in the Labyrinth. The guns were neutralised. At 3.30 pm orders for the attack arrived at Headquarters Royal Artillery (RA): 'There being no better position available, Ayrshire and Leicester Batteries came into action in the open 100 yards and 1,000 yards away in relation to Ayrshire Battery in the cactus hedge [Labyrinth]. All batteries advanced to support the attack at ranges upward of 2,200 yards. At 1810 orders went to the guns to withdraw to their old bivouac positions, which they reached at 0200 27 March.' There were no gunner casualties. In total, the four batteries fired 257 rounds of shrapnel and 56 HE, a fifth of what they had expended at Rafa for an operation by one mounted division.[16]

It was now clear that the Turks had more artillery and infantry than intelligence and previous reconnaissance had estimated: two field batteries, two Austrian mountain howitzers and two 100mm guns. General Chetwode urged the Mounted Division to attack each with one brigade. Dobell agreed. By 6.30 pm all the brigades were on their objectives and, as Farndale describes, 'the troops were weary but exultant and confident of the surrender at dawn'.[17] At that point, much to the surprise of the commanders, a report was received (false, as it eventuated) that Turkish reinforcements were entering Gaza. The town had been captured and a wireless intercept from the defenders stated that the garrison was on its last legs and would have to surrender at dawn. However, back at Turkish Army headquarters, von Kressenstein urged his Gaza commander Tala Bey to hold out and, if possible, counter-attack. Tala Bey wired back, 'Position lost' — by which he meant Ali el Muntar, which the 53rd Division had captured. Dobell and Chetwode knew that the horses and men would have to be watered and, with all wells destroyed, they ordered a reluctant withdrawal at 6.30 pm, despite the fierce objections of Chauvel. More mortification for the British was to follow. Dobell and Chetwode then made their divisional dispositions and movements on the basis of the false reinforcement report, and based on inaccurate reports of divisional boundaries. Dallas was the victim of this communications blunder and objected strongly to his orders, unhappy that he would have to yield ground dearly won. According to the official historian, 'he would not have abandoned all the captured positions', but nonetheless he did.[18]

Chapter 7

Chauvel's force: Part 3

By late afternoon the commanders of the mobile forces, with Chauvel's latest order in hand, had altered the dispositions of their regiments to meet the Turkish reinforcements coming from the north and east. At 3.00 pm the 3rd Light Horse Brigade was involved in a spirited action supported by the Berkshire and Notts batteries at Beit Durdis north-west of Hill 405. They inflicted heavy casualties on the advancing troops, catching them in enfilade, and the Turks did not press on. The light horse commanders noted that the Turks appeared reluctant to attack which, as it eventuated, increased their dissatisfaction with the order to withdraw when it came later in the day. The cavalry commanders reasoned that they, not the enemy, would occupy Gaza that evening, and they were confident of their ability to prevent the Turks re-entering the town. The veracity of the decision to withdraw was questioned by all the cavalry commanders who had done much to ensure the success of the attack. They vehemently opposed it and obeyed with great reluctance when the orders were passed down; the troops in turn were astonished by the orders, particularly those in the town itself.[19]

The troops were also mystified by the fact that they could not see any tangible evidence of Turkish aggressiveness in those advancing towards their screening positions. This force was estimated at 3000 infantry and two cavalry squadrons from Huj, and 7000 troops from Hareira. As per their orders, the troopers re-formed with their squadron, regiment and brigade commands during the night, a very difficult task. Gullett wrote that, when the cavalry brigade reached Mendur, it passed a tall pole without realising the significance of the pole itself. It was a Turkish artillery ranging marker. When the brigade moved towards the Wadi Ghuzze it came under fire from eight guns firing shrapnel. These guns also targeted the 5th Mounted Brigade, prompting its commander, Brigadier Wiggin, to order his troops to disengage and his batteries to retire when 'bad light stopped play'. The fire caused a number of casualties, the troopers remarking on the dangers of fuses and shrapnel skittering over the hard ground 'faster than cricket balls'. The 7th Light Car Patrol and its machine-guns came to their rescue and inflicted losses while the horsemen cleared the wadi to occupy a defensive position and count the cost.[20]

The difficulties encountered are best described in the words of B Battery HAC while supporting the 5th Mounted Brigade. The battery historian is worth quoting in full as he describes, in some detail, the problems of battery deployment not only for this battle but for many others involving night movement and operations:

Before night fell the gunners could see their RHA colleagues heavily engaged three miles to their north. Night fell. The battery retired in a south westerly direction as previously indicated by the brigadier. The OC fell in with a Warwickshire Yeomanry sergeant carrying a message to brigade ... that indicated it was marching north and would stop for the night at Beit Durdis, about four miles away. However the OC turned the battery around and steering north east by the stars, the first of the files trotted off, followed by the farrier's staff and such details, the Battery Staff, and lastly the detachments. Men disappeared into the night till there were only three men left in the detachments. We were marching alone into a black and silent world. The BSM was the last man and we encountered the Brigade, and fell in on the left flank. The BSM rode off and brought in the connecting files. The OC reported to Brigadier Wiggin — who told him he had no orders — but sent officers to find Div HQ.

Shortly afterwards we encountered a deep, steep sided wadi. The only passage across it was very narrow, with deep holes on either side, a nasty obstacle in the dark. Two regiments crossed first and disappeared once they reached the other side, leaving the battery without an escort, or even so much as a guide. We had a nightmare of a job getting the guns across, and it took an hour to do so. The long delay was caused by five poles breaking. We only carried four spare jointed poles in the Battery, and we had to splice three of the broken ones with handspikes. Wheeler Sergeant Wright worked like a Trojan at this job, and throughout the night rode continually up and down the Battery, tightening the splices and patching broken vehicles. He seemed insensible to fatigue, and it was chiefly due to him that the Battery rejoined the force next morning with all its vehicles.

In the meantime the connecting files had been sent out to keep in touch with brigade . . . and we marched along picking up files as we went. To our surprise we found that we had made a complete half circle to the left and in a quarter of an hour we were back at the same wadi. An orderly from brigade told us to move towards the south and make for the coast at all speed. All the available men were put to work with picks and spades to ramp the banks of the wadi, but the ground was iron-hard and the men dead-beat. After three quarters of an hour's work the Battery was got across the wadi, yet another pole being broken. At this point the GSO1 of the Imperial Division brought them the latest situation report and ordered the battery to continue its retirement until across the

Gaza-Beersheba road, and it would be safer to cross it before daylight. If necessary, wagons could be left out but guns brought in.

Our march resumed at 2230, but in turning another spliced pole broke. It was impossible to repair so the wagon was unlimbered and the body of the limber lashed to the rear of the other two wagons. Then we go wearily on again, the OC leading on foot. An hour later we met the Imperial Camel Brigade, the first troops we had seen since nightfall who had definite orders, although they did not know where they were, but were supposed to patrol the Gaza-Beersheba road to cover the retirement of the two cavalry divisions, then to fall back on Deir Belah. Half an hour later we came across another steep wadi that took half an hour's reconnaissance to find a way down one bank and up the other side. Sergeant Major Stanford had to ride down the line literally hitting the drivers awake. This had to be repeated several times over as they crossed another wadi every mile or so, ramping up the sides, men falling asleep on the ends of their shovels. About 0130 we fell in with the 8th LH Regiment of 3rd LH Brigade. They had had hard fighting, been cut off at nightfall, had no orders and were making their own way back.

At 0245 we crossed the Gaza-Beersheba road and got better going and the OC decided to push on till daylight, alone and without an escort. Just before daylight we crossed the Wadi Ghuzze. He had to rest the Battery as men were beginning to fall off their horses, and the horses could scarcely crawl further. As dawn broke the Battery halted, off-saddled, picketed and fed, and the men turned in. Except for the Stable picket, the men were asleep in 30 seconds after the last nose-bag had been put on. They dropped where they stood. A quarter of an hour later the OC heard heavy rifle and machine gun fire to our north, and immediately afterwards a number of motor cycles and staff cars passed us going south. They were followed by a brigade of cavalry going in fast trot in the same direction. A cavalry officer told the Turks were attacking and close to us. The OC ran back and roused the men, ordering them to saddle up and hook in. Dead beat as they were, the men sprang to work, urged by the speed of enemy shells which then burst around them. In exactly 17 minutes from the time the order was given, the Battery was on the move again, a good example of training in small details. Then Turkish heavy guns joined the fray, shells bursting behind us, but the huge cloud of dust raised by the cavalry obscured us effectively and we suffered no casualties. Crossing some rising ground half an hour later we saw the Wadi Ghuzze

> below us, so were still on the wrong side of it. We crossed the wadi, halted at Deir Belah at 0730, having been marching and fighting for 28 hours. At 1130 we moved on and reached Khan Younis at 1600, having taken five hours to cover seven miles.[21]

Infantry operations

Following the decision to abort the attack, Dallas had ordered his infantry to patrol to and, if possible, take the vital ground of Ali el Muntar ridge, which was eventually captured by the 53rd Division at 11.00 pm. All this time the 54th Division under Dobell's command was guarding the south-eastern flank astride the Beersheba road. The 53rd, under Chetwode's command and in combination with the cavalry, bore the brunt of the battle, the Antipodean troopers fighting magnificently. As the sun was setting the misbegotten command structure began to unravel, mainly because Chetwode was largely ignorant of the gains made, tucked away in his headquarters well behind the fighting. But his cavalry generals, closer to the action, knew and backed their own judgement. Eventually Chetwode decided to abort the assault and the Turks, believing they had a windfall reprieve and urged by their commanders to continue the fight, ejected the British, who fell back.[22] Turkish infantry pressure and artillery fire then forced all the attackers into a defensive posture behind the original start line south of the Wadi Ghuzze, beyond which neither commander had ventured throughout the day.

According to the official historian, had the 'fog of war' not intervened, the outcome would have been vastly different. Little wonder that Chetwode's Antipodean commanders Chauvel, Ryrie and Chaytor believed it was a battle won then lost because of Dallas and Chetwode's generalship. At dawn the Turkish reinforcements made the gleeful discovery that the British had lost their bid for possession of the town.[23]

The failure of the British forces at the First Battle of Gaza heralded the prospect of battles similar in duration to some Western Front epics. This was the first corps-sized operation in Palestine and, based on the events of 26 March, there would have to be a substantial improvement in command arrangements, leadership, staff work and communications before another attack could be mounted against those resolute soldiers, Johnny Turk and his German artillerymen. The defeat was all the more galling because a Turkish commander had earlier signalled that his troops could not face any more artillery fire.[24]

Despite skill shortages all round, at one stage Chetwode and Dallas had 'captured' Gaza. In hindsight, Chetwode may not have grasped the concept that he was fighting two battles — an infantry operation and cavalry battle to first seize and then prevent Gaza's recapture by Turkish reinforcements. His choice of his headquarters site was poor and should perhaps have been at Sheikh Abbas. His use of his infantry was also flawed, exacerbated by poor communications between his headquarters, his generals and their brigades. The infantry battle drills lacked finesse, and these drills had to become ingrained prior to further operations. Another factor can be inferred from the standard of shooting — the inexperience of artillery observers combined with pressures of adjusting fire in the heat of battle.

The use of artillery was not without its problems and it is clear that more field and heavier artillery better employed would have enabled counter-preparation fire plans to maintain the troops' hard-won and costly gains. The official historian commented that 'the enemy positions were invisible, no definite artillery program had been drawn up and it was necessary to trust reports by FOOs, though batteries were ranged by RFC aircraft.' He concluded that 'artillery support was not very effective owing to its unavoidably hurried entry into the attack.' This observation is hardly sustainable in view of the deployment of the 161st Brigade's artillery, which was ready by H Hour.[25] Had he consulted Chetwode's report, Gullett would have noted that 'the infantry were not given the artillery support it should have received … during the whole day batteries were not shooting at all, being unaware of the requirements of the infantry.' Farndale writes that 'the artillery played its part but was not really big enough or concentrated enough'. Brigadiers Laycock and Le Mottee were hostage to Dallas' orders for eight hours. MacMunn and Falls also comment that 'It is not unreasonable to suppose that the attack might have been launched one hour sooner if the conference [of generals] had assembled sooner.' This would have caused a four-hour delay in the execution of the plan, which may have prompted the Turkish high command to temporarily withdraw troops from the front-line trenches and/or despatch reinforcements sooner. The extra hour would have allowed the weakened brigades to occupy the town and move artillery up. However, it is axiomatic that a good general 'reads' the battle and can do so if his headquarters is properly sited. Chetwode and Dallas should have been at Sheikh Abbas, closer to the front.

The last word on the subject is best left to MGRA Sydenham Smith. His status during the battle was, as he described it, 'rather limited'. He noted that the GOC retained command of the artillery and such grouping of artillery and tasks that were made were flawed and he could not properly advise from his location. Had these 'groups' been properly constituted, the OCs of the field brigades would have been with the infantry brigade commanders they were supporting and most of the difficulties could have been avoided or minimised. The failure of the 53rd Division to push on faster with fewer casualties was due to misuse of divisional artillery by the GOC of the division. Indeed MGRA Smith saw 'a whole brigade of field artillery near Kh. El Shire doing nothing for two solid hours while the infantry were in sore need for their assistance.'[26] Gullett's analysis blames 'deplorably weak and chaotic command' between the EEF and the Desert Column as the greatest single factor, while Farndale's comment misses the point completely.

Three differing sets of casualty figures for the combatants were recorded in the aftermath of the battle. One source records British casualties as 3484 (384 killed, 2900 wounded and 200 missing/captured). The official historian reported that the British lost 3967 killed and wounded, with 246 men taken prisoner, while the Turkish losses were 2447 with 837 captured. The 2nd Light Horse Brigade lost one killed and five wounded, the New Zealanders two and 29 respectively.

Enemy strength and casualties were significantly inflated in Murray's and Dobell's reports, their estimates of the former four times the actual number (20,000) and of enemy casualties a factor of three applied (6–7000), while their own losses were ignored. In the A&NZ Mounted Division the troopers believed the British casualties to be much higher than the Turk's and even more than officially stated. They were — by almost 50%. Clearly there was yet another casualty — honesty in official reporting to the War Office. Murray's description of his 'victory' defied events and whitewashed the command structure, while Dobell's report was not much better, glossing over his misjudgements.[27]

Chapter 8
The Second Battle of Gaza: 17–19 April 1917

In Palestine nothing and nobody could have saved the Turk from complete collapse in 1915-16 except our General Staff.

Lloyd George[1]

In the aftermath of the Battle of Romani General Murray asked the War Office for more aircraft squadrons for surveillance of his front, but received nothing until later in 1917. All he had for First Gaza and now Second Gaza was the RFC's 5th Air Wing of 24 aircraft plus Short and Sopwith seaplanes to direct naval gunfire. His heavy artillery now consisted of four heavy/siege batteries, the French warship *Requin* and two RN monitors (floating heavy gun platforms). Another priority was to improve the efficiency of his logistic chain, principally the railway. The line was completed at an astonishing 15 miles a month, running from Kantara to Wadi Ghuzze, six miles south of Gaza. The use of one-inch wire netting (usually for rabbit/vermin control) saw the construction of passable roads six feet wide which now snaked across the desert. Synchronised with the desert advance of the British forces was a pipeline that carried fresh water from the Sweetwater Canal area which reached El Arish in February 1917. One of Murray's next decisions was not a wise one. He moved his headquarters from Ismailia back to Cairo. As Bruce notes, 'he lost direct contact with the officers of his expeditionary forces and his lines of communication were seriously weakened.' Murray was to feel the devastating effects of this move four months later.[2]

Despite the debacle of First Gaza, both Murray and Dobell were convinced that taking the town simply required a superior force. The staff at Eastern Force headquarters began to assemble another division with additional artillery from the canal zone. Murray's brief from the War Cabinet emphasised that he 'was relied on to pursue the enemy with all rapidity compatible … with your communications.'[3] In other words, he was to deliver a *coup de main*. Broadly speaking, his resources comprised 24,000 rifles, 11,000 sabres and 170 guns. Battle command was again delegated to Dobell and, on 16 April 1917, he issued his Eastern Force Order No. 41 for the Second Battle of Gaza. H Hour for the two phases of attack would be advised, and would depend on the weather. The opening shots would comprise a massive bombardment by naval and heavy artillery a day before the first phase, the infantry assault and Desert Column assignments on the left and right flanks. The assault commander was faced with an 11-mile front line. Communication, coordination and timing would be vital.[4]

Following his fortunate reprieve at First Gaza, von Kressenstein had wasted no time strengthening his defences against the next British assault. The Turks moved more troops forward and now deployed their forces in an arc stretching 26 miles from the coast to Sheikh Aljin and Tel el Fara. They were confident of the strength of their defensive dispositions, artillery strength and air support. Von Kressenstein's command now totalled 18,000 rifles, of which an estimated 8500 were in Gaza, with 1500 sabres deployed from east to west to guard his flanks and rear in the *3rd*, *53rd* and *16th divisions*. He brought in another 30 guns, registered targets and dug deeper, siting his extra machine-guns in defilade positions. He was determined to make Gaza impregnable. He was conscious of the vulnerability of his eastern flank where his *53rd Division* now had extra single guns and batteries and where he recognised that the Desert Column could deploy to exploit its capacity for manoeuvre. A series of redoubts was constructed and others strengthened.[5]

Dobell's corps plan would primarily focus on the 53rd, 52nd and 54th divisions (from left to right). The 74th Division and Desert Column were tasked with the protection of the eastern flanks and operations to the north-east. Their battles will be described later. The first preliminary phase of the attack was H Hour at 2.00 am on 18 April, when the Desert Column would move out, and 4.15 am for the artillery bombardment. At 7.00 am a general infantry advance would commence with an approach march across the Wadi Ghuzze of almost three miles to capture their Phase 1 objectives.[6]

The divisional artillery orders were initially straightforward, with H Hour to be decided by the MGRA Eastern Force, Major General Smith. CRAs Laycock and Le Mottee were to draw up their own fire plans while the heavy ordnance was given specific targets. However, at the last minute, having considered the advantages and disadvantages of using gas, General Murray expressed reservations about the plan, particularly the role of the heavy and field guns firing gas shells. Eventually he decided to limit the time for bombardments, hoping the use of 'special shell' — lachrymatory — would devastate the Turks. Meanwhile 'normal' artillery operations were maintained nightly by harassing fire (eight rounds per gun at irregular intervals from 7.00 pm to 3.00 am) from designated batteries.[7]

Chapter 8

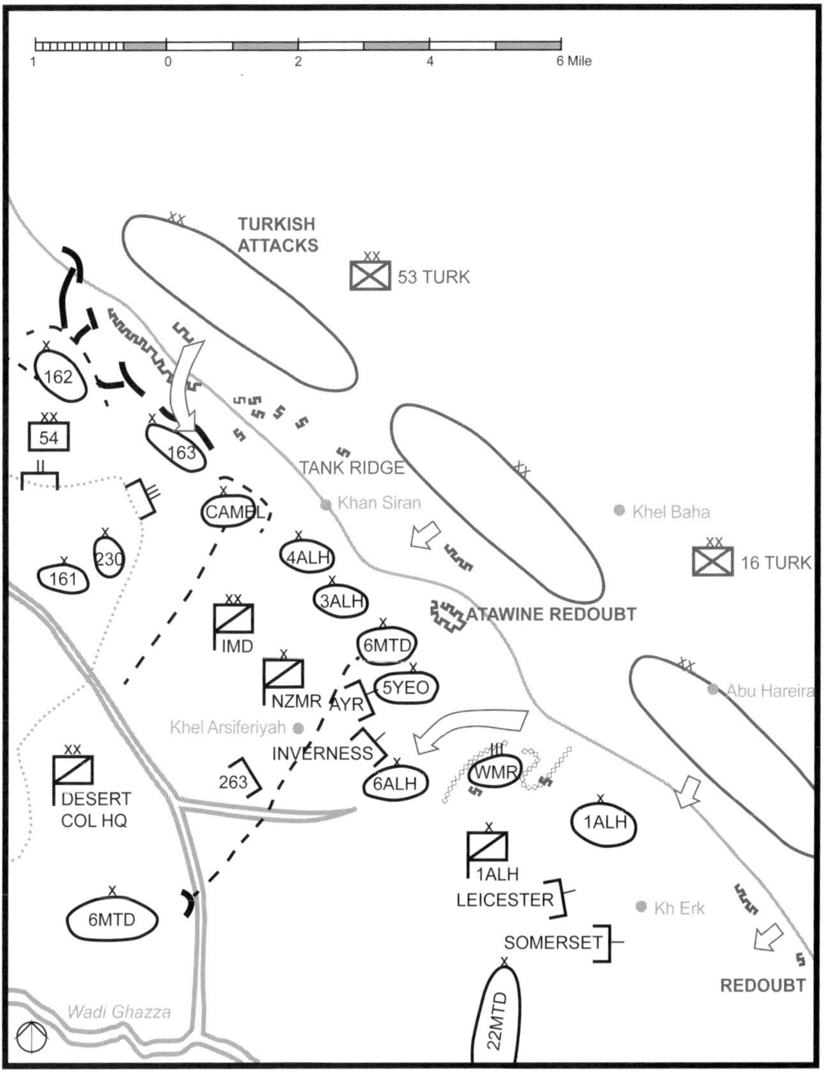

Map 6: Second Battle of GAZA showing the cavalry friendly eastern flank on which the Turkish attack was concentrated and repulsed. The Atawine Redoubt was the most important tactical feature (source: MacMunn and Falls, *Military Operations in Palestine and Egypt*).

The operation of the heavy and naval artillery support had been substantially refined following First Gaza, particularly communications between the FOOs and the guns. The artillery support program was developed by Eastern Force headquarters, with Lieutenant Colonel Niven, RA, as its commander. On 17 April the *Requin* was to pound the Ali el Muntar ridge. Monitor M21 would engage The Warren and Green Hill (an area south of the town) and M31 would bombard the Labyrinth. The 10th Heavy Battery would target guns and trenches in the area around The Quarry and Fryer Hill. The 201st Siege Battery's 6-inch guns would target Middlesex and Outpost hills and its 8-inch section the Labyrinth and Green Hill. The 91st Heavy Battery was allotted the El Arish and Magdhaba redoubts. All these batteries were now at full establishment of four 60-pounders but deployed in sections. Ten minutes prior to H Hour all the field guns engaged their targets and, at 7.30 am, all the heavy ordnance lifted to targets in depth and counter-battery fire. In brief, Dobell's 150 guns were deployed across a shallow arc-shaped front of almost 15 miles. Current Western Front accepted wisdom held that, for frontal attacks, a concentration of one field gun per 10 yards of front and one heavy gun per 25 yards was required. The heavy guns' allocation of 500 rounds per gun was the same as for the 18-pounders and 4.5-inch howitzers. The 53rd Division was also allocated two tanks.

There were two artillery brigade redeployments. First, A and B batteries (18-pounders) of the 53rd Division's 267th Brigade were to support the 52nd Division from 7.30 am on 19 April for Phase 2 while the 273rd Brigade B (field) and C (howitzer) batteries, recently arrived from the canal zone, were allotted to the 74th Division from 6.30 pm on 18 April. For the first time gas shells (4.5-inch howitzers) mixed with HE were to be fired by these units against the Turks in the Ali el Muntar locality for 40 minutes during Phase 1.[8]

The gas bombardment has been well described by Sheffy and, in brief, it was fired by twenty-four 4.5-inch howitzers — six batteries of the 53rd Division — which had been moved forward for the operation. They engaged 12 well-known and frequently shelled targets. The bombardment used 2000 shells and was extended from the planned 40 minutes to 90 minutes until 7.00 am when the infantry moved off on their long approach march.[9]

At 5.30 am on 19 April the Phase 2 bombardment by 130 guns began. The 53rd's objectives were trenches in the dunes west of the town and the entrenchments beyond (Rafa, Zowaiid, El Arish, Magdhaba, Mazar and Romani), between Gaza and the sea and the Labyrinth. The 53rd moved off 45 minutes after the 54th and 52nd. The 54th would clear Es Shire ridge and the Ali el Muntar 'group of works' towards Australia Hill. The 54th Division's objectives lay on the high ground west of Sheikh Abbas. Divisional frontages were 4000 (53rd) and 5000 yards for the other two. The boundary between the 53rd and 52nd was the Rafa road. Eight tanks would accompany the infantry, two with the 53rd and six with the 52nd and the IMD. Coordination by the commanders of these two divisions for the assault on Middlesex Hill was specified in orders. The 74th Division's objective was Sheikh Abbas ridge, its supporting artillery the two RFA brigades, the 272nd and 263rd which, for some reason were not regarded as Eastern Force artillery. The RFA brigades were sited between Sharta and Wadi Nukhabir protecting the 54th Division's flank.[10]

Phase 2 of the plan called for further advances by the 53rd and 52nd infantry to overcome the six trenches and redoubts between Gaza and the sea and the Labyrinth. The capture of this feature, which arced west-south-west some 1000 yards beyond Samson ridge, would require a herculean effort. If successful, Gaza would be threatened from the rear. While Dobell's plan for Phase 2 had specific objectives, implicit in his order was the direction that, if his attack gained sufficient ground, the infantry and tanks would exploit to envelop Gaza itself. The 52nd Division was given all the well-known objectives from First Gaza, south of Gaza on Es Shire ridge. Overcoming these would also require superb gunnery support, and perhaps effective tank-infantry cooperation. On the eve of D Day, German airmen dropped smoke balls over the 52nd Division's gun line south of Mansura ridge. The Turks then strafed the line with shrapnel inflicting a number of casualties.[11]

The infantry, having already fought over the ground, knew it was going to be tougher than First Gaza, when fog had minimised casualties from enemy small arms and artillery fire. They set off, resolute in the face of rifle, machine-gun and artillery fire. At least the Turks did not have tanks. The bulk of the fighting occurred on the right flank where most of the tanks were used. Five of the six remaining British tanks (Marks V and VI) were allocated to the 52nd and 54th and, as Gullett describes, 'they were scattered along the front, and, advancing singly on the naked slopes, became in turn targets for a great number of the enemy's guns.' Some tanks escaped being hit, but the accompanying infantry became casualties from fire aimed at the tanks. On the 52nd's front, when the troops came under heavy artillery fire while digging in a tank, it took three direct hits from artillery fire and 'brewed up'.[12]

Image 11: Australian light horsemen look over a British Mk I female tank prior to the Second Battle of Gaza. This tank from E Battalion, armed with Vickers machine guns, was commanded by Second Lieutenant Roy Ansted Winder, formerly of the Middlesex Regiment and later a captain in the Tank Corps. During the Second Battle of Gaza this tank provided valuable support for the British 155th Brigade with Winder awarded the Military Cross for his actions (AWM P08401.004).

The 52nd Division's role in the plan involved desperate attacks by the 155th Brigade on the well-known features from Outpost Hill and El Shire ridge. The ground was hard to entrench, the brigade's axis of advance taking it along a crest line with numerous nullahs. Earthworks, wire entanglements and cactus bushes (or what was left of them after First Gaza) rendered these infantry objectives impregnable. The artillery plan detailed 18-pounder fire with Fuse 106 as the chief means of cutting wire, but this was neutralised by restrictions on the number of rounds available and the sandy terrain. Gas shelling of targets such as the woods on the El Shire ridge was ineffective. Despite the high hopes held for the gas bombardments, the Turks had made their line impossible to breach.

And so it proved. One particular obstacle, the Lunette, was taken and lost three times during the afternoon. No matter what gains each battalion made, it was unable to hold them. At the *moment critique* for the Scots, the Turks counter-attacked from the Delilah's Neck area. The whole of the divisional artillery was brought to bear, its historian recording that, '... in less than two minutes the whole of the guns ... were pouring a storm of shrapnel onto masses of the enemy. The Turkish infantry was smothered by the shell bursts, broke, scattered and doubled back to the shelter of their trenches.' The divisional artillery FOOs were alert and liaison between them and their batteries was described as 'excellent'.[13]

Chapter 8

The travails of Major General Nott's 53rd Division artillery mirrored the experience of the other two (although not the 74th). The 54th also had responsibility for the FOOs from the 265th FAB who directed naval gunfire, sometimes by moving to better observational positions with the infantry. For their initial move from their opening barrage firing positions, brigades were enjoined to move into action quickly and dig in immediately or, depending on orders, when opportune. On the first night (18 April) preparatory barrages were fired on night lines to secure small but expensive gains made after the long approach march. Both divisions struggled, the 52nd's task more challenging than that of its colleagues close to the sea. Mid-morning the 52nd called for help. The 53rd Division's gun zones for this task were at 20 and 120 degrees (pointing north-east to south-east) to enable them to cover the front of the 52nd, specifically to bombard the expected Turkish counter-attack on Kurd Hill and use the dust raised to some tactical advantage. There were times when the lack of accurate information for the gunners to prevent them firing on their own troops was frustrating for all commands. At one point the 91st Heavy Battery was placed under command of the 160th Brigade to assist in its travails.

All through the day naval artillery had fallen short, and the Turkish guns were firing uninterrupted counter-battery fire. So fraught was the situation that the GOC ordered a FOO to move to Es Shire ridge. Here he engaged Lambeth Wood with 150 rounds of gas shells. While orders specified that shoots would be directed by the RFC, the weather on the day (light cloud) resulted in 'difficult and unsatisfactory shooting'. The 267th FAB moved positions twice, having been advised in orders to 'avoid sand'. The 266th C Battery howitzers fired gas at 5.30 am and 2.30 pm, averaging 250 rounds in each delivery. The one big gas shoot by the brigade on El Arish redoubt totalled 1100 shells over two hours.[14]

By 7.15 am on the morning of 19 April General Nott was able to advise that both Sheikh Aljin and Samson ridge were occupied — taken at bayonet point with 39 prisoners captured. Coincidentally, RFC reconnaissance reported that the enemy positions were still strongly held, but the brigade commander swore that the trenches were empty. This was followed by a bombing attack on the troops and guns by German aircraft. The afternoon descended into stasis — one side watching and suffering, the other waiting and shooting confidently — until Dobell's order arrived at each headquarters. At 10.00 pm barrage fire protected the infantry on the dunes and the CRA's log records that, one hour later, the order came for his guns to return to their original position. His log records only one counter-battery shoot in two days.[15]

To conclude the infantry account, Dobell ordered a general withdrawal after conferring with his commanders. By 2.00 pm the Turks had already counter-attacked but had been repelled by the decimated, weary but determined British infantry. The official historian describes the artillery contribution to the outcome: 'By the 19th it became speedily apparent that the fire of the warships, the heavy artillery and the forward howitzers firing gas ... directed at the trenches had in no way silenced the enemy artillery.'[16]

The Desert Column under Chetwode still comprised the A&NZ Mounted Division and IMD, similar gunner groupings to those of First Gaza. The ICC formed the link with the 74th Division. From north to south, the other IMD brigades were: the 4th Light Horse, the 3rd Light Horse, and the 6th and 5th mounted brigades. The A&NZ Mounted Division south of Sausage ridge fielded the NZMR, the 2nd Light Horse and the 22nd Mounted Brigade with the 6th Light Horse in reserve. Squadrons of the 2nd and 22nd Light Horse brigades had been detached to operate in a skirmishing, intelligence-gathering role south from Khurbet Erk to Tel el Fara. The cavalry front was an arc 12 miles in length from Mansura ridge.

Major General Hodgson's IMD and Chauvel's A&NZ Mounted Division were both under Chetwode's command. Hodgson's front was oriented north-west to south-east, where the Turkish line of redoubts was located right of Wadi Ihan at Ataweineh ridge, Sausage ridge and Hairpin redoubts. His orders were to maintain the utmost pressure on the Turks so that they could not interfere with the infantry attack. Hodgson's force included the 161st Brigade, while the 3rd Battalion of the ICC, manned by Australian troopers, was at the forefront in the fighting on the ridge. The artillery moved out on 18 April and A Battery (with the 6th Mounted Brigade) crossed the wadi at Tel el Jemmi where it found good water. A night occupation followed and the battery's first shots were fired at dawn (5.30 am), the targets engaged until 8.30 am. Half an hour later the battery limbered up and crossed the Wadi Ghuzze at Asyferieh, the gunners arriving at their next position to be greeted by accurate Turkish shellfire.[17]

The mule-drawn Notts Battery under Major Lambert had moved to positions at Wadi Sihan and dug in its guns. The gunners opened fire at 5.30 am at 4500 yards but engaged better infantry targets at 3000 yards with what they described as 'excellent results', expending 513 rounds of shrapnel and HE while supporting the 2nd Light Horse Brigade.[18] The cavalry dismounted and set off towards the enemy trench lines. Initially the troops made good progress and some prisoners were taken. But, as the sun climbed higher in the sky, the combined strength of Turkish entrenched infantry with superior machine-gun numbers and artillery began to tell, and the attackers' casualties soared. As the 5th Light Horse Brigade developed its attack on Ataweineh redoubt, flanking fire from Turkish guns on Sausage ridge began to impede the troopers' progress. The Ayrshire and Somerset batteries combined to neutralise the fire with their steady shooting. Hairpin redoubt withstood every attempt to breach it, and there was no opportunity for the troopers to mount a bayonet charge against the redoubts as their casualties mounted and the Turkish fire intensified. A Battery HAC was kept busy engaging targets on the Gaza-Beersheba road, the Turks retaliating by bombing the battery's wagon lines. The 4th Light Horse Brigade was also taking serious casualties and sent urgent requests for artillery fire. At dusk the battery withdrew, again drawing shellfire, and the infantry took over the brigade's positions. The gunners, having learned of yet another defeat, withdrew disconsolately to Abasam el Kebir.[19]

At Tank redoubt, where the terrain offered no possibility of a covered approach, the advance of the Australian troopers was halted 400 yards from the enemy trenches. Hodgson had been promised artillery support from two of Dobell's RFA brigades in this sector, as they were all in range. However the artillery support offered to the right flank was 'very faulty' and, as the Turks were now sure that the decimated troopers (who had suffered 30% casualties) offered no serious threat, they turned their attention to efficient counter-battery fire. The Notts Battery withdrew to Sharta where it was soon found by enemy aircraft which bombed and machine-gunned the area without inflicting any casualties. The aircraft then dropped smoke markers for the enemy long-range artillery that predictably heralded hostile fire. A heavy shell landed 50 yards in front of C Detachment and another to its rear, both of which failed to explode. As Gullett recorded, 'they [the Turks] had the best of the exchanges'.[20]

On Hodgson's right flank, the 5th Mounted Brigade's B Battery HAC began its deployment at 2.00 am. It reached Munkeilleh at dawn and occupied positions with the other batteries behind the same ridge, opening fire at 8.00 am on targets on Sausage ridge. During the night the BC had reconnoitred and dug in his OP on top of the ridge. Dawn revealed him standing, looking over the ridge giving his fire orders, which he declared a 'one sided form of warfare'. The cavalry had dismounted and the troopers were working their way towards the Turkish entrenchments while the battery registered targets. The gun's responses were described as 'poor' with high shell-burst shrapnel. By comparison the German heavy guns shot well. Throughout the day the enemy machine-gunners caused the troopers much grief as they tried every tactic to move close enough to charge with the bayonet.

At around noon, on B Battery's left flank, a lone tank lumbered into battle. Despite the fact that it was not supported by artillery or infantry, it incited remarkable reactions from enemy soldiers, also causing considerable casualties to the following infantry until it ground to a halt. Williams and his fellow pilots of No. 1 Squadron noted that 'steam' from the tank exhaust was a pinpoint artillery target for German observers, and the machines were punished accordingly. While travelling around his fiefdom, the BC discovered a party from the 3rd Light Horse Regiment withdrawing due to heavy casualties. This left the 5th Mounted Brigade unprotected on both flanks, which the lone OP was forced to manage. The BC gave one of his subalterns '1000 yards of trench to play with' and later reported that 'he directed the fire of the battery with admirable skill and coolness with complete disregard for his own personal safety.' At 3.00 pm the battery was tasked to 'keep firing [a barrage] at all costs' when the Turks counter-attacked. Some 90 minutes later, enemy aircraft attacked and heavy guns harassed the battery, with one gun hit and disabled for a short time:

> When B sub-section was hit and every man of the detachment was knocked out, the regular rate of fire was interrupted. The gun, though damaged, was not put out of action, and in a few minutes men had been sent to it from other guns, and it was firing again. As it was impossible to bring up teams under fire, ammunition was carried by hand. Even Captain Berry, our stout doctor from Queensland, with his coat off and with his shirt open to the waist, was carrying shells under his arms …

Worse was to come. At 5.30 pm, during the battery's withdrawal, a heavy shell stampeded the horses; by the end of the day, all but one had been recaptured before the battery marched to Mendur. The gunners had fired 1042 shrapnel and 353 HE shells.[21]

The Turks mounted a counter-attack along the whole line from the coast to the east. The gap that had opened between the 3rd and 4th Light Horse brigades was plugged by two regiments of the 6th Mounted Brigade, and the 263rd RFA Brigade (74th Division) was ordered to support the AMD. Under Major Daniel it came 'smartly into action … and concentrated on the enemy line of massed infantry.' However, the enemy's superiority was demonstrated by its ability to devote substantial guns to counter-battery fire against the assaulting infantry divisions, 'while he continued to enjoy immunity from our fire'.

Further to the south, both the Ayrshire and Inverness batteries were more than interested spectators in the general Turkish attack, being tasked for whichever IMD unit required the most urgent assistance, which they duly rendered. A screen from the Auckland Regiment guarded them as they served the guns in a patch of barley. To their east was the important feature of Sausage ridge and, at 2.00 pm, a brace of Taubes flew over them and dropped smoke markers. This foretold an impending attack that developed within the hour. The Wellington Regiment was in the thick of it and about to be sorely pressed by the relentless Turks on their right flank. The batteries responded when the Turks opened fire. Kinloch describes the scene:

> Most marvellous exhibition of big gun practice I have ever seen. Shell after shell, as fast almost as one could count, landed on our little battery. They burst like claps of thunder. Bits fell all amongst our horses and the battery … it was covered in dust most of the time. The gunners would flop down as the shells landed. Then up after the burst and at their firing again. Talk about a little Hell! Gee Whiz those Tommy gunners were game, and lucky too, for every shell that actually went under the gun failed to explode.[22]

At 5.15 pm the attack was checked and the enemy retired. The battery had extricated the brigade from a serious predicament, but not before the enemy had put another '5.9' salvo on its right section as it was limbering up, knocking out one of the teams. For its day's travails the battery lost one third of its men as casualties, albeit none fatal, from very accurate counter-battery fire. Major Preston's B Battery HAC fired 1500 rounds during the day. The battery subsequently withdrew in good order and reached Mendur at 8.30 pm. Its valour and contribution were recognised in the accolades it received from Chetwode, Hodgson and FitzGerald, the new brigade commander.[23]

Hodgson's division was ordered to withdraw to and dig in on the outpost line (Meshrefe–Aseiferiyeh–Hill 310 on the Wadi Sheria) at 6.00 pm, on the premise that the attack would be renewed the next day. The troops dug all night 'with eyes like owls' and at dawn only two posts needed realignment. It was the gunners' fourth night without sleep. Next day aerial reconnaissance by No. 1 Squadron AFC discovered a Turkish cavalry force five miles away assembling for a thrust at the division's line. The squadron swiftly sent five aircraft into the air armed with sixty 20-pound bombs. They found their target and caused so many casualties and confusion that the cavalry cancelled its operation and saved the slender force opposing them. It was to be the first of a number of similar examples of the utility of 'air power'.[24]

The A&NZ Mounted Division on the right flank had somewhat less stressful tasks than the IMD. Chauvel's orders forbade a mounted thrust. He positioned (from left to right) the 22nd Mounted Brigade across Wadi el Fara, the 2nd Light Horse Brigade marched towards Hareira, the 1st Light Horse Brigade moved to Baiket el Sana, and his New Zealanders remained in reserve. The Leicester Battery was deployed waiting at the rear of Khurbet Um Adrah behind them until ordered up. To coincide with the other Turkish attacks, some 3000 of their infantry and 1000 cavalry massed and advanced on Baiket el Sana, supported by a mountain battery and a single field piece. Then four armoured cars arrived and began advancing towards the Turkish redoubts. Soon after, the Turkish observers engaged them in a 'cat and mouse' duel, which the Turks won, disabling two, while the other two moved into the Australian lines. The horse commanders asked the cars to charge the Turkish cavalry. Their officers declined.[25]

Having endured an hour of accurate machine-gun and rifle fire from the troopers, the Turks swung left towards the 7th Light Horse Regiment. When the enemy's intentions became clear, 'Fighting Charlie' Cox ordered his battery forward and, under Captain Elwis, the teams and gunners swiftly came into action and exerted a positive influence on the encounter, effectively neutralising the guns and causing casualties. The light horsemen repulsed the Turks who, by now had brought heavier guns to bear on the Leicester Battery. Elwis took his four guns out of action one at a time and redeployed 2000 yards south near Khurbet Erk. They silenced one of their opposition in quick time, and the enemy infantry suffered severely at their hands and retired. At the same time the cavalry battle evolved, this time with the machine-gunners holding the enemy at bay for an hour.

The southernmost brigades of Chauvel's A&NZ Mounted Division, which had no organic artillery, also scored some initial successes south of the Wadi Imleih, but enemy responses soon had the regiments realigning their fronts to leave no gaps for exploitation. Their commanders rode many miles to keep their line intact as the Turks increased their fire from all sources. As dusk fell on the battlefield Dobell was contemplating further action in view of his losses while the men in the line were expecting a counter-attack the next day, 20 April. The enemy had gained the upper tactical and psychological hand, believing his position, as Gullett wrote, to be 'one of which the God of battles favoured their efforts … that could resist all the British could bring against them.'[26]

Gullett's account also described the actions of the enemy artillery: 'All day the enemy artillery was exceedingly accurate, and it was clear that their gunners had carefully studied the ground and registered their ranges. They picked up the positions of the British batteries and led horses with remarkable rapidity, and also made precarious the communications over open ground between the rear and firing line.' For the RHA batteries, it was a painful truth that the 13-pounder 'produced little or no effect upon his trenches'.

To add to the attackers' discomfort, enemy aircraft dominated the skies over the battlefield and frequently bombed batteries and horse lines, the 2nd Light Horse Regiment becoming an early victim, losing 18 men and 30 horses before the advance began. Nor were headquarters ignored in this masterful display of offensive tactical air support.[27]

The lot of the three infantry divisions on the second day can be encapsulated in the military axiom 'no plan survives the first shot'. The modest pre-H hour bombardments and counter-battery fire accounted for a mere fraction of the ammunition expended, and both were singularly unsuccessful. Infantry brigades endured well-directed artillery and machine-gun fire and supporting artillery fire was insufficient to assist the infantry onto their objectives. The only instance of effective massed fires occurred at 3.00 pm, when the whole Turkish line pressed forward. The 52nd Division artillery broke up an attack on its front, only to be stalemated within the hour. As Farndale notes, 'So ended a disastrous day. Casualties have been heavy almost everywhere.' This was also the first time tanks had supported the infantry and a useful *modus operandi* had clearly not been formulated. Despite many displays of individual heroism, cooperation between infantry and artillery merely resulted in the supporting infantry receiving substantial enemy artillery fire directed mainly at them as they moved behind the tanks.[28]

Artillery fire directed at the British wreaked considerable havoc, and British counter-battery work appeared generally ineffective in terms of both damage and ability to neutralise its opponents, suggesting insufficiently developed indirect fire practices. There was yet another factor. It was the first time both corps had worked together without the benefit of rehearsals, much less practised barrages. There is also no record of the effectiveness of gas against the Gaza garrison in official accounts, probably because it was largely ineffectual, evidenced by the continued robustness of the enemy defence. Gullett and other historians' criticism of artillery support at First Gaza was equally applicable to Second Gaza. But they were only partially correct. The MGRA, Sydenham Smith, writing to the official historian after the war, was again scathingly critical of Dobell's infantry general's artillery planning and execution. No heavy guns were allotted to Turkish trenches and redoubts. The naval artillery, particularly from the French battleship *Requin*, with its designated aircraft observer, waited only for the first observation and correction before it 'fired its allotted 50 rounds indiscriminately, and was no further use to us as her expected consignment of ammunition did not turn up.' On the other hand the RFC was very pleased with the fire of the heavy guns. Having spent a wretched day at EEF headquarters listening to reports of the battle's progress, Smith wrote that

> … he took serious objection to plans for the two hour bombardment planned for the second attack and also to the use of gas. This was the most futile thing possible … only in warning the enemy of the point of attack and a gross waste of ammunition. The fire trenches were the object of the bombardment and to think that any intelligent enemy will hold his front trenches in strength when there is no threat of an infantry attack was ridiculous — considering the distance apart of the opposing forces.[29]

Dobell considered renewing his attack the next day, but a casualty count of around 5000 prompted him to postpone it. Despite some good shooting, the quality and planning of artillery support was below par relative to the Turk's, whose artillery decisively dominated the battle. Within Chauvel's command, the Australian commanders' comments on 'artillery practice' were generally uncomplimentary, primarily relating to the 13-pounder's lack of killing effect and inaccuracy, although they acknowledged the moral effect of its presence in support and the conscientiousness of the gunners.

The casualty count for the two assaulting infantry divisions was horrendous at 4336. The 52nd Division lost 1914 killed and wounded, the 53rd Division 584 killed, while the ICC Brigade's toll was 345 killed. The A&NZ Mounted Division suffered 105 casualties and Hodgson's division 547, a total of 4920 including other troops. Coming after First Gaza's 4213, this amounted to approximately 40% of Dobell's 'rifle strength' and, while comparable to some of the worst Western Front battles, was totally unacceptable to the War Cabinet. It sounded the death knell of the careers of the two senior commanders, Dobell and Murray. Indeed Dallas fell on his sword after the first battle.[30]

However some good did follow these two disasters. The War Office and EEF headquarters responded to increased Turkish strength with more guns and a structural change to the force. On 28 June General Allenby took command of the field force, assured by the War Office that more artillery, more ammunition and other materiel would be sent to the theatre. In the event, he received all his divisions, but not all of his artillery.

Gas at Gaza

The use of gas shells in the Mediterranean theatre began in the Gallipoli campaign with the British forces afraid that the Turks would use asphyxiating gas against their amphibious landing on 25 April 1915. 'Gas helmets' were issued, but the British decided against the use of gas primarily on moral grounds, reasoning that, if gas were used to support tactical operations, it could also be used in retaliation. By August 1915, when the battle had stalemated, the issue was raised again and

600 cylinders and a detachment of 'chemical operators' were shipped to the Middle East. It was November before another 3000 cylinders reached Mudros. The vessel returned to Europe after the evacuation and the commanders in the 'new' EEF at GHQ in Cairo decided to maintain the *status quo ante* while the War Office saw fit to equip the troops with gas masks ('defensive gear'). Murray was not keen to use gas. In January 1917 the 'gas mood' at GHQ changed to one of using gas, but in artillery shells rather than cylinders. The reasons given were 'a combination of diminishing ethical restraints and faulty alarming intelligence on Ottoman capability and intentions'. The recognition that the Turks would fight for every inch of territory in well-prepared defensive positions anchored this staff 'rethink'.[31]

On 3 January General Murray officially requested permission from the Chief of the Imperial General Staff (Robertson) for the despatch of 24,000 4.5-inch howitzer shells, half of tear gas (lachrymatory) and half asphyxiating gas. He was keen to use these in his April offensives. He ultimately received 4500 of CBR (phosgene) and another shipment of 6000 CBR and 10,000 SK (tear gas) which arrived after First Gaza. At this time the staff were preparing plans for Second Gaza under General Dobell, now commanding the EEF. He was averse to using gas and also to using tanks for this purpose, 'until the time comes for putting out the whole of our strength'. He planned to use 'chemical agents' in an evening bombardment '… so that the enemy will know what they have to expect'. For Dobell, it was a matter of achieving an effect on morale. He also proposed to use smoke shells and to have his infantry light 'smoke candles', believing that enemy troops would mistake this for gas from cylinders and be frightened. The appearance of tanks from E Company Heavy Section Machine Gun Corps in action for the first time in the campaign would also figure prominently as a factor in Dobell's 'morale effect' strategy. However, rather than being a significant factor, it was instead a 'weak reed' and constituted yet another disaster.[32]

General Murray also expressed reservations when Dobell sought approval for his plans on 10 April. Murray altered Dobell's artillery plan, hoping to achieve surprise with a short bombardment. The DACs delivered shells for six 4.5-inch howitzers and the EEF gas expert gave safety ranges for the advancing infantry (2500 yards from the chemical impact or one hour after impact).[33] The meteorology in the Gaza area was vastly different to that of the Western Front, but in the early hours of the morning, the preferred H Hour for big attacks, wind speeds were low between 5.00 am and 7.00 am, and gas lingered about the point of impact. Over time wind speed and temperature increased and dispersion was also significantly increased. Experience in France had shown that the time gap between the gas and infantry advance was critical. This was the reason that night was the preferred time for gas shelling. It slowed entrenched enemy infantry and the gunners' reactions and minimised risk to the infantry if they attacked in the early hours in still air. This situation did not apply at Gaza as the Turks had no masks at that time. Taking all these factors into account, the chemical bombardment was duly planned, scheduled from the night before H Hour until dawn. It was also shortened to continue for 40 minutes, two hours before the infantry H Hour although, at the eleventh hour, uncertainty over timings plagued headquarters. According to Sheffy, the final gun programs reached the guns just a few hours prior to H Hour.

Twenty-four guns from the infantry's six affiliated batteries fired gas onto 12 targets — isolated redoubts, trenches within larger posts and gun positions. The batteries' programs, planned and actual, involved 70 shells lobbed onto small targets and 350 onto large. The planned time for the bombardment was 40 minutes, with H Hour at 5.30 am. The actual time for the bombardment was 90 minutes and it ceased at 7.00 am. At 7.30 am the infantry advanced towards their objectives, by which time the howitzers had fired HE on the same targets for 30 minutes, followed by the rest of the artillery. CBR ammunition fired totalled 2000 rounds.

The results of this gas (plus HE) assault were regarded as ineffectual by observers from both sides ranging from von Kressenstein down the chain of command to other observers in Gaza. The reasons were obvious. It was normal Turkish practice to withdraw troops from trenches until the bombardment finished, and then reoccupy them as soon as possible afterwards. The gas onslaught seemed to hardly rate a mention in Turkish reports. Experience in France had shown that gas was only effective in neutralising an area if applied in sufficient quantities (6000 rounds per square mile) to achieve 'critical mass'. The number of gas shells fired fell far short of that figure on all targeted areas.[34] Other factors identified included the inefficiency of fuses, dense terrain features and soft/sandy soil.

With all the data available over the next few weeks and its distillation into doctrine, the stage was set for the next attempt to capture Gaza in the near future. Operational post-mortems from Second Gaza dealt harshly with Dobell and Murray, and the MGRA, Sydenham Smith, criticised the 'grouping' concept that broke with artillery doctrine. That Dobell had retained control of his artillery instead of delegating it to the appropriate level of command was a significant factor, as was its misuse by divisional commanders.[35] Smith's position was that of adviser to Murray and Dobell, and his wisdom and authority apparently carried little clout in headquarters. However the main objections may have come from the infantry commanders, still smarting after the First Gaza debacle. This notion is supported by the late arrival of gun programs after several weeks of planning and consultation. These were not the only shortcomings in the artillery staff work.

Both Murray and Dobell stopped just short of saying nothing in their official reports, and the official historian was, in brief, misled. Sheffy also notes that many officers from the brigadier down did not know that gas was used, which is somewhat surprising given the army culture of ever-present 'rumours'.

Chapter 9
Aftermath, artillery reorganisation and interregnum

The ability to innovate is rapidly becoming the primary source of competitive success.
C. Bartlett

At 56, General Sir Archibald Murray was already an old and tired man when he took over from Maxwell. He had performed admirably early in the war on the staff of Sir John French in France as an organiser with an infantry background, and handled the retreat from Mons extremely well. Ironically, his successor handled the cavalry aspects of the retreat equally, if not better. In Ismailia, not only had Murray both the Sinai and Palestine campaigns to manage, but his span of command extended from the Egyptian Western Desert to Sudan and Salonika. In this broad command he was not helped by his betters in Whitehall, Gullett observing that policies forced on Murray and his predecessor 'played from first to last into the hands of Germany ... and accomplished ... very little good for England' without offering his alternative views on how he might have done better. This was the fate of all British generals conducting campaigns in far-off places when the prime focus of Cabinet and the War Office was on the Western Front. Murray had a good grasp of strategy, was politically shrewd, charming and too generous in his confidence in his subordinates. His major achievements were in the field of logistics, a fact acknowledged by his successor who used them to much greater effect in subsequent battles. In Dobell he was given a general who had made his reputation in colonial wars, but was sadly ill-equipped for the complexities of modern corps leadership of an all-arms fighting force, much less a doughty foe — and Murray gave him a second chance. For a generalissimo, Murray involved himself too much in detail. These frailties were greater than his strategic and operational mistakes. The antithesis of Murray's style was required, 'an independent, even selfish, aggressive and persuasive character who had a reasonable chance of success'. The troops did not have to wait long for such a drastic change.

Chapter 9

Another attack on Gaza was out of the question until Murray had a much better equipped and bigger force, and this was recognised by the War Office. However, to give Murray his due, despite an uncooperative government and many other obstacles placed in his path, by the end of February 1917, some 388 miles of railway had been laid, 300 miles of water pipeline, 203 miles of metalled roadway, 86 miles of wire and brushwood road, and 960,000 tons of stone won from quarries — all thanks to the Egyptian Labour Battalion's workforce of thousands. The importance of these worthies was recognised by scaling down bombing raids on enemy positions and airfields in the hope that the Germans would do likewise — which they did. This enabled more civil works to be completed with more 'stable' labour. Without a sure strategic grasp, a lesser commander may have achieved less than Murray, but his legacy was logistics and without logistics, no battles can be won. The irony was that his successor benefitted most from Murray's efforts.[1]

Murray ordained that the commander of the Eastern Force would be Chetwode, while Chauvel was promoted lieutenant general — the first Australian to reach this rank — and given command of the DMC. Brigadier Chaytor of the New Zealand Mounted Rifles Brigade was promoted to Chauvel's previous command, and Major General Hodgson retained the Imperial — now renamed the Australian — Mounted Division (AMD). Murray was fortunate in that these subordinate cavalry commanders would bring him and his successors mostly brilliant victories. Likewise, his infantry commanders grew in confidence with experience and he found stability in his senior gunner, who was there for the duration. In the wake of Second Gaza, Murray undertook yet another reorganisation of his cavalry commands. He secured two cavalry brigades from Salonika and also grouped its organic cavalry with a RHA brigade of two batteries:

A&NZ Mounted Division: Major General E.W.C. Chaytor

1st and 2nd Light Horse brigades, NZMR Brigade, 18th RHA Brigade (1/1st Ayrshire Battery and 1/1st Somersetshire Battery, each with eight 18-pounders)

AMD: Major General H.W. Hodgson

3rd and 4th Light Horse brigades, 5th Mounted Brigade and 19th Brigade RHA (A and B batteries HAC, each with eight 18-pounders, Notts Battery with four 13-pounders)[2]

Yeomanry Mounted Division: Major General G. deS. Barrow

6th and 8th mounted brigades, 22nd Brigade RHA (1/1st Berkshire and 1/1st Hampshire batteries, each with four 13-pounders)[3]

Army troops
7th Mounted Brigade[4]

Infantry division artillery

The field batteries of the 53rd and 74th divisions were increased to eight guns each, and those of the 52nd, 54th and 75th to seven pieces. The 74th's field brigade, the 44th, arrived in July and was upgraded from 12 'lightweight' 13-pounders to two batteries of six 18-pounders. The 13-pounders had a poor reputation for 'killing power'. There were other redistributions of guns and batteries, both field and howitzer, but there was a welcome increase in infantry when the 60th (London) Division arrived from Salonika. By July 1917 the artillery order of battle comprised:

52nd Division: 48 x 18-pounders and 16 x 4.5-inch howitzers in three brigades (216, 262 and 264)

53rd Division: 35 x 18-pounders and 14 x 4.5-inch howitzers in three brigades (265, 266 and 267)

54th Division: 35 x 18-pounders and 14 x 4.5-inch howitzers in three brigades (270, 271 and 272)

60th Division: 48 x 18-pounders and 24 x 4.5-inch howitzers in three brigades (301, 302 and 303)

74th Division: 36 x 18-pounders and 12 x 4.5-inch howitzers in three brigades (44, 117 and 268)

75th Division: 36 x 18-pounders and 12 x 4.5-inch howitzers in three brigades (37, 172 and 1 South African)

Each division also had close to its establishment allocation of medium and heavy trench mortar batteries, conferring an extra level of firepower on the division.[5]

In the aftermath of Second Gaza, the regiment had much hard work to do to reach a state of operational efficiency and make good shortages of various kinds. This took place *in situ* or at special training venues to the rear of divisional and brigade areas. Some activities designed to enhance operational readiness on both sides were beholden to the climate and oppressive heat. Regiments were withdrawn to seaside camps on the Mediterranean to train in more comfort, and their numbers boosted to establishment strength.

The last phase of reorganisation involved the arrival of the new theatre commander, General Edmund Allenby, who took over from General Murray in June. He used the EEF headquarters at Deir Belah and quickly moved to examine the Gaza battle zone to determine the structure of the army he hoped to lead to victory.

Chapter 9

Allenby used estimates of the overall Turkish strength as a basis for assessing the requirement for extra troops and resources — particularly artillery. The Turks had five infantry divisions and one cavalry division in the line, as well as a reserve division. Intelligence overestimated this by around a third, the final figure reaching 33,000 rifles, 1400 sabres, 260 guns and 250 machine-guns. Allenby calculated that he needed eight infantry and extra divisional field artilleries to bring his force to establishment strength — thirty-six 18-pounders and twelve 4.5-inch howitzers. The arithmetic came to an additional thirty 18-pounders and twenty-four 4.5-inch howitzers. In heavy ordnance, he was able to secure for his theatre (where Murray had not) eight additional 60-pounders, thirty-eight 6-inch and twelve 8-inch howitzers and four 6-inch Mark VII guns for counter-battery work. The Mark VII 6-inch guns gave extra capability in terms of range. Ultimately, Allenby did not receive all he wanted, as there were some divisional adjustments. In terms of heavy ordnance, he was denied two batteries each of 6-inch and 8-inch guns. In assuming an allocation of the 'heavies', each division would have four 60-pounders and eight 6-inch howitzers per division. None of this ordnance would reach Palestine before October, and Allenby would have to be satisfied with seven divisions.

Allenby then put his stamp on his macro organisation by adjusting Murray's June initiative. One of his early decisions was to retain Major General S.C.U. Smith as his MGRA.

By October the artillery order of battle for Beersheba and Third Gaza was:

Desert Mounted Corps: Lieutenant General H.C. Chauvel

GOCRA: Brigadier A.d'A. King

A&NZ Mounted Division: CRA Brigadier W.D. Nichol, 18th Brigade RHA of Ayrshire, Inverness and Somerset batteries

AMD: CRA Brigadier Sir J.F. Laycock, 19th Brigade of RHA Nottinghamshire, A and B batteries HAC

Yeomanry Division: CRA Lieutenant Colonel O.L. Eugster

20th Brigade RHA Berkshire, Hampshire and Leicestershire batteries and ICC Brigade[6]

XX Corps: Lieutenant General Sir P.W. Chetwode

GOCRA Brigadier A.H. Short

10th, 53rd, 60th and 74th divisions

XXI Corps: Lieutenant General E.S. Bulfin

GOCRA Brigadier H.A.D. Simpson-Baikie

52nd, 54th and 75th divisions

GHQ troops

8th (10th and 11th batteries) and 9th (A and B and 12th batteries) mounted brigades; RGA 16 x 3.75-inch and 12 x 2.75-inch howitzers

Corps troops: all siege except those with the designation 'H' (heavy)

96th Heavy Artillery Group: four brigades of heavy artillery [15th, 91st, 181st (all H), 378th, 383rd and 440th batteries], 22 guns and howitzers

97th Heavy Artillery Group: three brigades of heavy artillery [189th (H), 195th, 201st, 205th, 300th and 380th batteries], 20 guns and howitzers

100th Heavy Artillery Group: 10th (H), 43rd, 379th, 422nd and 423rd batteries, 20 guns and howitzers

102nd Heavy Artillery Group: 202nd (H), 292nd, 420th, 421st and 424th batteries, 18 guns and howitzers

95th Heavy Artillery Group: 134th, 209th and 304th batteries, 10 guns and howitzers (two-thirds were 6-inch and 8-inch howitzers and one-third 60-pounder guns)

Siege Brigade: two batteries, each with four 6-inch howitzers as illustrated in Table 6 below:

TABLE 6: SIEGE BRIGADE ORDER OF BATTLE FOR BEERSHEBA AND THIRD GAZA

Unit	Officers	Senior NCOS	R/F	Total	Horses/Lorries
Brig HQ	2	3	18	23	11 horses
Att	(2)	(6)	(8)		
Btys(2)	10	36	314	364	206 horses
Ammn Col	3	6	49	58	2 horses
Att	(2)	15	84	101	
Siege Brigade	19	58	470	554	217 horses
Base Det	2	4	123	129	

Lorry-equipped Siege (Power) Brigade comprised 33 lorries, 64 heavy draught animals and 96 carts and wagons. The lorry component included 33% spare.

Heavy Artillery Battery: four 60-pounder guns. The order of battle for Beersheba and Third Gaza is illustrated in Table 7 below:

Chapter 9

TABLE 7: HEAVY ARTILLERY BATTERY ESTABLISHMENT

	Officers	Senior NCOS	R&F	Total	Horses*
Heavy Battery	5	8	149	162	113
Ammn Column	1	1	39	41	47
Total	6	9	188	203	160
The establishment for a heavy artillery battery with heavy draft mules was:					
Battery	6	9	165	178	26 H 116 HDM
Ammn Column	1	1	49	51	62 HDM[7]

*H: heavy; HDM: heavy draught mules

Army troops

7th Mounted Brigade

The Composite Force

Imperial Indian Service Troops, 1st Battalion, British West Indies Regiment, French and Italian contingents

On the other side of the hill, there were interpersonal tensions between senior leaders in the Turko-German camp. Kress von Kressenstein was soon to be removed by General Falkenhayn, who had problems with Mustapha Kemal — he refused to serve under von Kressenstein. While gaining consensus in the enemy command group was very difficult, the strategic aim was clear. Baghdad must be taken, and this depended on weakening Allied forces in Palestine. Defeat along the Gaza–Beersheba line must be avoided as this would open the way for Chauvel's forces to reach Aleppo.

Facing the strife-torn Turko-German high command was new EEF commander Edmund Allenby. Allenby was not the stereotypical British cavalry officer so often portrayed as effete, languid, unscholarly and given to sporting rather than military attainments. Born into a well-to-do country family at Brackenhurst in Nottinghamshire, he was schooled at Haileybury and, as a young man, was very interested in flora and fauna. Allenby passed out of Sandhurst and was commissioned into the 6th Inniskilling Dragoons, an 'unfashionable' regiment, seeing his first active service with them in Bechuanaland (now Botswana) in 1882, and later in the Boer War. His assessment of the British Army's performance in these campaigns was scathing at best. He arrived at Staff College sporting an easy-going manner, was very athletic and of good humour. Staff College turned him into a martinet who displayed a withering temper and an obsession with discipline. Allenby's subsequent promotions to general rank cited his irritability as a brigadier and described him as an 'explosive' general. Gardner, his biographer, writes that 'here was a general who could quote Milton's Comus at length and would break off discussions about strategy to discuss roses, French literature, habits of birds and incredibly, Crusader castles.'[8]

In 1914 Allenby commanded a cavalry force and conducted a masterly retreat south of the Marne, subsequently commanding the Third Army. His temperament was unsuited to static warfare but his arrival in Palestine on 27 June 1917 cheered the Allied troops. He decided to move Eastern Egyptian Force headquarters from the Savoy Hotel in Cairo to Kelab, north of Rafa. In Cairo, Major Andrew 'Banjo' Paterson, then commanding a light horse remount unit in Egypt (and who knew him from South Africa), wrote that 'Things began to move the moment "The Bull" started. The Shepheard's Hotel generals were dispersed with scant ceremony. Then began the weeding out process … He tried out his personnel in little expeditions and raids, giving every commander a chance, but only one chance.' He began a five-day whirlwind tour and Gullett recorded that 'He went through the hot dusty camps in his army like a strong, fresh, reviving wind', but he also observed the terrain over which his battles would be fought and appraised the commanders he met and their standard of turnout with a very critical eye.[9]

Allenby adopted Chetwode's famous 'Notes' — a military 'appreciation of the situation' on the strategic possibilities of conquering Palestine. He also publicly recognised Murray's immense logistic contribution and its utility for future strategic plans.[10] He then proceeded to implement his plans for the taking of Gaza, not 'directly' but by an indirect strategy of first capturing Beersheba. This involved moving water and rail lines east without alerting the enemy to his intentions. The transformation in attitude among the troops was also boosted by the tangible effect of the materiel arriving to support the coming offensives — guns, munitions, aircraft (eventually the excellent Bristol Fighter) and so on. Maintaining this latter advantage was contingent on gaining superiority in the air so as to deny the Germans observation of his eastern flank.[11]

Allenby's Eastern Force was becoming a far stronger and better equipped army for the task his political masters had set him — to capture Jerusalem by Christmas and win the war in Palestine.

Chapter 10
The guns of XX and XXI Corps prior to Third Gaza

Whatever a man soweth, so shall he reap.

Galatians 6:7

This chapter describes the activities of an infantry divisional RFA in the months prior to Third Gaza and Beersheba in October. The activities are described in the form of a letter. The period of structural reorganisation of Allenby's force in Palestine was also a time of consolidation, of training units new to campaigning in the harsh desert environment, and of assessing the fitness of individuals for command and/or staff duties. The letter was written by the field brigade commander of the 271st RFA Brigade to his father, and described life at the infantry division's gun line. A copy was included in the brigade's war diary.[1] The letter begins on 29 June 1917 when his division, the 54th (East Anglian) Infantry, was being brought up to strength, retrained and was fast becoming desert-worthy. It concludes on the eve of Third Gaza (25 October 1917).

From the CO 271st RFA Brigade, Lieutenant Colonel R.M. Laurie, RFA.

Dear Father,
KURD HILL
25 October 1917

As an old gunner I know you would appreciate knowing about how we went about supporting the infantry and tanks these days, so you may compare it with your own service life. I suppose the only commonality is that we still used horses and our gun drills were quite similar. Other things have changed a lot since those days. The above address has been my home on and off for nearly four months, and we have been quite busy. I attach a map to help you follow my doings. We moved into the line on 29 June, and since Second Gaza the Turk has had ample time to conceal his gun positions from our observation — even from the air. He shelled us that day and we retaliated but were unable to stop him, as our sister brigade (270th) and mine had only 12 x 18 pounders and four x 4.5 inch howitzers each. Next day he started again at 0630, and a real duel developed, even involving our 8 inch howitzer searching and sweeping. Next day a FOO spotted a battery from its smoke and dust, so I went up Kurd Hill and soon I had my brigade onto it. We silenced it but after dusk we sent some shrapnel over his position in case he was moving out. It was quieter after that until the CRA (Brigadier H. G. Sandilands — do you know him?) put on a scheme for our division bombarding Umbrella Hill for 20 minutes, again also with the 8 inch howitzers, with a view to retaliating, damaging earthworks, shaking morale and compelling him to rebuild under shrapnel fire.

On 2 July we had a big shake up of officers, six of mine going to the other brigade and DAC. I was pleased that three of the five BCs in the DAC are from my brigade. Then on 4 July my A Battery went over to 53rd Division and occupied Kurd Hill with a section. It moved its Depot Section up to make it a six gun battery. It had been decided that FOPs [forward observation posts] on Kurd Hill would be permanent. Thus I had A/271st on Lees Hill, B/271st on Blazed Hill, B/274th on Heart Hill, and each battalion had a telephone line to the FOO. That night a wiring party from the Essex battalion was hit by MG fire from the SW corner of The Plantation and Umbrella Hill. We kept up the fire intermittently for nearly an hour after the CO telephoned us. Being in a static position meant we had four main phone lines. We had a line between brigade HQ and the batteries, from brigade HQ to an FOP, a line from brigade to each OP and a line from brigade HQ to brigade left (Coastal) and right (Sheikh Abbas) groups. This is a big improvement and means we can bring down fire quickly. A couple of days later General Allenby visited thc brigade HQ and Kurd Hill.

The first two weeks of July were quite busy. We brought a section forward on a wire cutting scheme on Outpost Hill and we had a nightly harassing fire program with pre-arranged bursts of fire on specially selected targets, such as enemy reliefs and communications. Our patrols reported enemy working parties repairing wire, so we fired salvos at them with good results. Being on the left flank put us near the coast, and apart from wire cutting and registering targets, one night we supported an infantry raid with intense fire. His casualties were about 60 KIA. Ours were one KIA, nine WIA and two missing. We also noticed the enemy using shrapnel in his AA guns instead of HE. Either his HAA were in workshops or he was short of HE. On 20 July we were involved in a scheme on Umbrella Hill which I controlled.

My brigade was reinforced with B Battery 18 pounders and C Battery 4.5 inch howitzers of 303rd RFA Brigade gun line. I also had a section of 6 inch howitzers, 201st Siege Brigade and C Battery, 264th Brigade, under my orders

Chapter 10

too. A couple of nights before the guns moved into position registration began. Much study was made of the air photographs in OPs where the ground and the photos could be compared. The enemy shelled us heavily and often, creating an atmosphere of 'jumpiness', so I made a provision to engage HBs [hostile batteries] without waiting for them to unmask. I arranged for all my 18 pounder batteries to engage (using search) the batteries well forward of Plantation feature. We had a warning from EASTFORCE [Allenby's headquarters] that an attack was probable. This caused me to register reinforcing batteries on active defence zones. This enabled me to switch them onto first objective and areas that would otherwise not be possible. So good were our communications that I decided to conduct brigade operations from a dugout adjoining an opening into the brigade telephone exchange. I detailed two officers to take bearings on enemy flashes. The timings were well kept, the artillery scheme provided destruction, demoralization and protection. The work by batteries was admirable, great care being taken with drills. However, during and after the raid the enemy artillery fire was intense on battle HQ on Hereford Ridge and many casualties caused to the returning infantry. It was evident that for such operations some plan should be organised for engaging HB positions with heavy artillery previously registered by aeroplanes. There was some consolation for me — the GOC described the artillery work as 'perfect'. Four days later there was another scheme at Umbrella Hill, with less effect than the previous attempt, the enemy profiting by his previous experience.

By way of difference, the CRA asked me to reconnoitre Happy Valley area for OPs, wagon lines and gun positions. The enemy was trying to find our gun areas, which he did using aeroplane observation and found A and B Batteries of 270th Brigade. They continued to bombard our support trenches. The command of the air was an absolute necessity for the thorough preparation of an artillery scheme. It makes the difference between a haphazard cooperation by artillery and an almost perfectly organised bombardment with effect, neutralization and barrage of communications. The 6 inch howitzers have now reverted to HAG control.

In August Brigadier Le Mottee, CRA 53rd Division came and inspected our positions, OPs etc, preparatory to taking over. This relief was completed over four days, as we had to keep as many guns in action as we could at any one time by scheduling sections to move. My brigade then concentrated at Deir Belah Station. It is a dirty place with flies, fleas and other insects. We are under fig trees. The horses suffer from sand colic. We now came under XXI Corps (Lieutenant General Bulfin) and we stayed there until ordered back to our old positions on 27 August. My brigade was still in the coastal sector and was known as Right Artillery Group. Things were relatively quiet, although it was noticed the Turkish guns were firing at long ranges. On the 29th hostile fire developed which coincided with the infantry digging a new trench line which drew persistent shelling of Queen's Hill, Blaze Hill and Lees Hill areas. We bombarded the El Arish redoubt to get him to unmask his guns, which he did. We passed a fortnight of trench warfare routine, and we had an outbreak of sand-fly fever, causing many casualties.

In mid-September we had visits from RFA officers from 52nd Division, 44th Brigade RFA 74th Division, and 75th Division RA who relieved our divisional group. Many of our personnel including me attended very realistic lethal and lachrymatory gas training school. Brigadier La Mottee gave me the task of an extended reconnaissance for the group on the left hand side of the line in the sand for OPs and battery positions in the Sheikh Aljin area. Good observation of enemy works was difficult to find. Our ammunition pits had to hold 600 rounds and we needed much material from RE stores to be brought up by our horse teams, which were then in good condition, fortunately. On 17 September I experienced my first shower of rain in the desert. We were still in light rig. The rain seemed heavier over enemy lines.

Towards the end of the month I went to a demonstration (a practice attack) behind smoke clouds south of In Seirat. The wind was favourable, ground broken by deep wadis and hills and a position to be attacked prepared with trenches and wire. From an artillery point of view smoke would not give immunity from fire — on the contrary it would attract it — for a barrage put down in front of the advancing smoke would be almost certainly effective. On broken ground intersected by wadis, ravines and small valleys it would draw down and create wide gaps and defenders would get a good view of what was happening behind the smoke cloud. It might be useful to blind.

On 27 September we had a divisional scheme under the CRA that started at 0345, the aim of which was to draw enemy fire by bombarding his trenches and support lines on the coastal sector. To cut the wire on Outpost Hill we used the 44DA Fuse. The day before two 'five nine' batteries heavily shelled my howitzer battery and caused casualties to both men and equipment. One gun was destroyed. Our batteries were in action almost non-stop as we geared up for the next assault on Gaza. The howitzers, field and heavy, were quite busy. Enemy aircraft doing registration shoots ranged their '5.9s' on batteries at Mansura and the aircraft was later seen to crash. Good work by the AA gunners.

During the month a sound bearing section RE was installed in our sector to locate enemy gun positions. I was told that their work with the RFC and heavy guns knocked out a 77 mm battery and a '5.9'. The Turk moved some of his batteries over the next 5 days as a result. September was quite a busy month for my brigade.

I became quite involved in early October 'digesting' operations orders for forthcoming events. My brigade fired on Fig Grove to support patrols of 161st Brigade on Samson's Ridge line. Three bursts of three minutes was our part in it. The enemy artillery went quiet and on one day no enemy shell fell in the brigade's area, a most unusual state of affairs. A few days later I did another recce of the Aljin area, this time to the siting of RAPs, wagon lines, locations of forward HQs and OPs. This took place over a number of days, and it was topped off by a first for me — a reconnaissance in a trawler! Not only that but from a captive balloon. These vessels were 'impressed' by the RN and they worked with a mother ship up and down the coast ranging monitors and other warships on inland targets. It was very interesting to compare the difference behind the lines — ours and theirs. Theirs was the complete absence of any apparent human habitation — a great contrast to the rear of our own lines.

D Day minus six for the operation we have been working hard at was set for 26 October. Our CRA's orders and schedules were very extensive. Guns moved to their new positions at Sheikh Aljin progressively and we then registered targets. We were fired at soon after. So were the roads and wire of our position. This coincided with a terrific thunderstorm and one and a half inches fell in an hour or so. It flooded dugouts, some from floor to roof, and it didn't stop the Turks from shelling us with shrapnel. And for the first time the infantry were told to wear steel helmets. Shooting continued both day and night and was interfered with on one occasion when four enemy planes hovered above our positions for nearly two hours.

I'm afraid I will have to stop now. I will not have time to write during the next few weeks as General Allenby starts his northward drive and I expect to be very busy. Till then,

Yours ever,
RML

Chapter 11
The cavalry's guns prior to Beersheba: May October 1917

Better to be safe than sorry.

Proverb

It was to be six months before the batteries supporting cavalry formations following Second Gaza were to engage in a set-piece battle at Beersheba. That six-month period was probably the most important of the whole campaign, for it revitalised the troops, filling them with optimism after the pessimism of Second Gaza, thanks largely to the influence of General Allenby and his staff and the resolution of his commanders. Strategically, although the Turks were numerically stronger, they were disinclined to attack, which set the scene for 'passive campaigning on active service'. For the troops, gunners and sappers it was still hard work to ensure that the enemy enjoyed no respite from the attention of his foes. This chapter broadly describes the life of the horse gunner through the eyes of HAC historian Goold-Walker in a period that saw structural changes to the cavalry corps under Lieutenant General Sir Harry Chauvel, now the DMC commander:

> On 28 May we returned to the front and, for the next two months, the battery had a hard and comfortless life. We were now in the *khamsin* period, when for about 50 days hot winds and sandstorms occurred at frequent intervals. Once while at El Ferdan, we had a sandstorm that lasted five days and nights on end in an atmosphere of swirling dust that was unbearable. A species of septacaemia attacked the men, probably caused by a lack of fresh food, by the flies and general unsanitary conditions. The slightest cut or abrasion turned septic at once, and in spite of every precaution, in a short while the whole battery was affected. The division had to be withdrawn from the line for a month, and the battery sent to a bivouac at the seashore at Tel el Marakeb, where the men spent most of the day bathing in the sea. Some relief was experienced by

Chapter 11

these measures, but after a week we were back, and the battery was very much 'under the weather'.

After the reorganisation the three cavalry divisions were disposed, one in the front line from El Shellal to Gamli, one in support near Abasan el Kebir, and one in reserve, resting on the seashore at Tel el Makarab, spending a month in each position. The men were accommodated in tents, which were pitched a few yards from the water's edge, so we could tumble out of bed and take a few steps for our morning tub. Indeed, men and horses spent half the day in the sea. The horses and the men were 'groomed and exercised', and after other routine chores were done, and with complete rest, coupled with constant sea bathing, soon restored the battery to health. It was possible to restore the battery canteen, and thus obtain small luxuries, chiefly liquid, without which war is a sad business, and no trade for an honest man.

To test the mobility of the troops (while in the Abasan area) the divisional commander would issue, from time to time, a surprise order for the troops to turn out, ready for operations, and rendezvous by brigades or regiments in stated places, where they were carefully inspected. These orders were generally issued in the early morning. No hints were given. The time taken for each unit was taken and noted by staff officers, and the keenest rivalry sprang up between the divisions, and the different units in each division, to make the best showing. Ration and store wagons were packed each night, nose-bags were filled after the last feed, and tied onto the saddles, and all harnesses and saddlery was laid out in order behind the horses. The saddle wallets were kept permanently packed, the rations for them being renewed from time to time. The 'record' for the whole corps ultimately went to B Battery, which turned out in complete marching order, with all its ammunition, rations and stores correct, in eleven minutes from receipt of the order. About once a fortnight the division that was in the line made a reconnaissance towards Beersheba. Moving out in the afternoon the division would march all night, and occupy a line of posts on the high ground west of Beersheba by dawn next morning. Behind the line of protecting posts the infantry, corps and divisional commanders, and innumerable lesser fry, disported themselves in motor cars and on horseback. The troops would then withdraw that night. The reconnaissance entailed two nights and a day of almost continual movement and watchfulness, without any sleep or rest, during which the troops would cover 70 miles without water, causing the horses considerable hardship.

> The day was made up by a series of petty annoyances. Our scattered units were invariably bombed, generally with effect, and the Turk's light guns added to the general discomfort by their continual, galling fire. Crossing a deep wadi, often in single file, being swept by shrapnel and high explosive shell, tempers were apt to get short. We on our side could rarely spare an aeroplane to observe one of our own batteries, and so we were seldom able to locate the hostile guns. The hostility of the local natives added to general insecurity, and increased the need for watchfulness.
>
> The work and training increased the cohesion and efficiency of the divisions, the feeling of stalemate after Gaza giving way to a new pace of aggression, and a keen desire to move forward. During this time we had seen the dumps of ammunition, rations and stores growing visibly by the day, a sure indication of a big battle to come. On 26 September, Major Preston took promotion to command a field brigade in 54th Division. A month later, command of 19th Brigade, RHA fell vacant, and Preston 'returned to the fold rejoicing'. Major N. M. Elliott, MC, took command of B Battery.[1]

A summary of A Battery HAC operations from 9 October to Beersheba

This summary is taken from the 19th RHA Brigade War Diary and describes the battery's activity in the period from 9 October to 20 October during the early preparations for the attack on Beersheba:

9 Oct. A Battery (Major O.E. Eugster) marched to Khasi at 3.45 am and its Right Section came into action at 5.20 am, Left Section following a short time later. Turkish cavalry aggressively inclined, so both sections withdrew after firing 47 HE and 80 shrapnel.

13–15 Oct. Thick fog while under orders of 5th Mounted Brigade. Sections went to Goz El Bazar near Esani, and during actions there fired 32 shrapnel and 12 HE at Point 630.

20 Oct. Brigaded with 4th Light Horse Brigade for outpost duty, with an approach to Point 630 again. Returned on 26 October.[2]

Chapter 12
The Battle of Beersheba: October 1917

The race is not to the swift, nor battle to the strong, but time and chance happeneth to them all.

Ecclesiastes 9:2

It was not until the end of October that Gaza was assaulted again by XXI Corps. Prior to this, XX Corps was scheduled to attack Beersheba to draw Turkish reinforcements away from Gaza. Success in these two October battles, Beersheba and Third Gaza, would open the road to Jerusalem, and Allenby was confident he would achieve the War Cabinet's objective of capturing the city by Christmas. This chapter describes the measures adopted by Allenby and his staff to ensure Beersheba's capture, chiefly by formulating, then executing a comprehensive deception plan.

The first of these canards was to create a military camp on Cyprus and to spread the word that it was to be the base for an amphibious landing further up the Palestine coast. The second was the use of naval artillery and a flotilla of small landing craft to effect a landing near the coast opposite Deir Sineid prior to the actual assault. At dusk on 30 October a body of infantry advanced along the beach heading north, a feint attack directed at Wadi Hesi on the coast accompanied by a naval bombardment of the Turkish garrison there. Third, the gunships HMS *Raglan*, the French battleship *Requin* and Monitor M21 with its 9.2-inch gun and six other vessels bombarded targets as far inshore as Deir Sineid. All these measures kept the Gaza defences on full alert. Fourth, when XX Corps moved out under cover of darkness heading for Beersheba, the campfires and lights of the corps near Gaza were maintained to simulate preparations for an imminent attack. Dummy horses were erected to represent horse lines which were moved from time to time. Gunners dug gun pits in full view of the enemy and a dummy railway terminal was constructed. Aggressive air patrolling east and south of the Beersheba road combined with reconnaissances of divisional strength kept the enemy ignorant of Chauvel's broad enveloping route march and developments in the XXI Corps area and rear areas. In this Allenby was favoured by good luck. In conditions of low cloud cover 'a German aircraft photographed Allenby's dispositions. It did not carry wireless but on its return to base was shot down within the force area and the airmen, their photos and marked maps were captured.'[1]

Unconvinced by these measures, the Turks sent a division to Beersheba. As part of his deception plan, Allenby had brought a new field intelligence officer to Cairo, Major Meinertzhagen, who would establish a reputation as a brilliant operator. His plan was simple. Leave a haversack in the desert for the patrolling Turks to find, allowing them to discover 'authentic' military documents, money, copies of signals, personal papers, binoculars and a map. After a few 'non-events', on 10 October he rode out into the desert until he met a Turkish cavalry patrol which gave chase. The major simulated a panic, a wounded horse and dropped his rifle, haversack and binoculars, and, before 'escaping', made sure the Turks had found his haversack. Ten days later, von Kressenstein visited Beersheba and discussed this 'intelligence' with Ismet Bey, who set about strengthening defences, priming wells and ammunition dumps for demolition and other measures. Despite Ismet Bey's incredulity and grave doubts over the documents' authenticity, von Kressenstein was convinced that a large cavalry force could not operate south and east of Beersheba, and withdrew the division to Gaza. However this was a minor but important sideshow in the broad scheme of the battle.[2]

Chauvel's mounted troops spared no effort in securing water for their two-stage approach march of 26 miles via Esani, Asluj and Khalasa from their base at Shellal. On 25 October the troopers and engineers rehabilitated a number of wells in which the Turks had dumped concrete and stones. This would guarantee water on 25 October at the halfway mark for both of Chauvel's divisions. The water was not good quality, some horses refusing a drink with all that entailed. However, the horse's instinct to 'smell water' allowed a regiment to water when an animal unearthed an otherwise unknown well-cover. Coincidentally, a thunderstorm broke over Beersheba the following day leaving much surface water lying around. There was an anxious moment when, during the sporadic skirmishing along the outpost line on 25 October, a forward position previously established by the Australians was heavily attacked after being relieved by the Middlesex Yeomanry. It took the intervention of two brigades from the 53rd Division and 3rd Light Horse Brigade to restore the front. This sector was vital to the security of XXI Corps' southern flank, and to the deception measures.[3]

Chapter 12

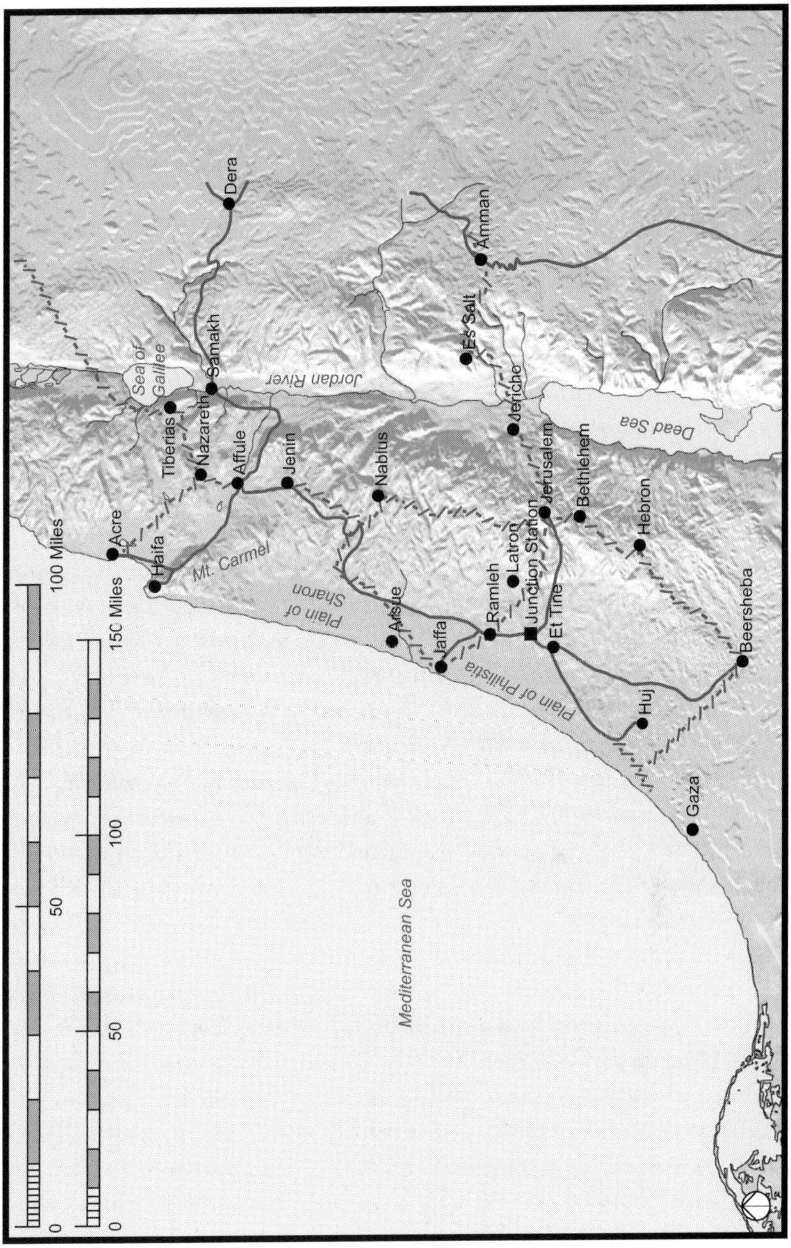

Map B. Map showing the coastal plain and rugged nature of the hinterland, major towns and villages, roads and railways of Palestine where most of Allenby's battles were fought.

The corps staff estimated that Turkish forces on the Gaza–Beersheba front included *III Corps* (*3rd Cavalry*, *27th Division*, *2nd* and *48th regiments* of the *16th* and *24th divisions*) and numbered 40,000 rifles and 1400 sabres. Around a quarter occupied this small but strategically important town, in all some 5000 rifles, four batteries of 28 guns and 60 machine-guns.[4] But all was not well. There were constant desertions across the whole of the Turkish front, ration quantities for men and animals were at about 50% of standard and ammunition was also short. In addition, von Kressenstein and Ismet Bey differed in their interpretation of the intelligence concerning Allenby's plans.

Beersheba's outskirts at the foot of the Judean Hills were bare. The Wadi el Saba ran south of the mosque almost bisecting the town, and was tactically important. The town's eastern approaches were on level ground, unlike the succession of hills that lay to its north, west and south. General Ismet sited his command for all-round defence. These consisted often of a single line of trenches, some of which lay behind barbed-wire entanglements. Following its capture, the troopers considered the Turks to have made poor use of an inherently strong position. These tactical considerations were more a concern for Chauvel than for Chetwode. On the eve of battle Chauvel's DMC consisted of Chaytor's A&NZ Mounted Division at Asluj and Hodgson's AMD at Khalasa. From these water points in the late afternoon of 28 October the horsemen rode out in a column four abreast and 10 miles long via Esani. They carried provisions for their horses and men for three days and full water bottles. They rested the next day and that night set out for Beersheba via Khalasa for the AMD and Asluj for the A&NZ Mounted Division. The last stage was an approach march of 36 miles for the A&NZ Mounted Division and 40 miles for Hodgson's men. Six cavalry brigades would converge from the south-east at dawn on 31 October to assault the town and cut the Hebron road two miles north-east of the town to complete the encirclement.[5] When Beersheba fell, Bulfin's XXI Corps would begin Third Gaza. The wells at Beersheba were an important part of Allenby's plan, for without them a cavalry and infantry 'right hook' to cut the Hebron road and capture Sheria would founder. It was a risky strategy.

The three infantry divisions of XX Corps, having completed their approach march, were deployed (north to south): headquarters 53rd was behind its 159th and 160th brigades in a gully with a depleted 158th Brigade in reserve. The 74th arrived from Khasif, its headquarters close to the Wadi es Sabe west of the town. Headquarters 60th Division was sited between Wadi Mirtaba and Wadi London. The ICC Brigade placed its 4th and 2nd battalions between the 53rd and 74th divisions, with the 3rd in reserve. The 10th (Irish) Division was also in reserve. The infantry front was approximately 5000 yards long, and the enemy front line some

2000 yards from the town. The XX Corps objective was around 1000 yards west of the town. One of the keys to those western Turkish defences was Hill 1070. The infantry plan called for the 60th Division's Londoners to capture this feature and, once it was taken, the 74th Division's infantry would halt on their objective line while Chauvel's force took the town from the east and south.

The XX Corps supporting artillery came primarily from the 60th and 74th divisions: the 310th, 302nd and 303rd RFA brigades' A and B batteries' 18-pounders and B Battery's 4.5-inch howitzers. The 96th Heavy Artillery Group (HAG) and the Berkshire Battery's 13-pounders were on hand, as were the 10th Mountain Battery's 3.7-inch howitzers. This group of five batteries was readied for counter-battery work. So that the heavy artillery in front of Gaza was not weakened unnecessarily, comparatively few guns and howitzers were spared for this operation. Another key consideration was the logistic tail for water (6000 camels) and the distance to be covered by the heavy guns. The artillery plan was a compromise between what was prudent to take from Gaza and divisional resources in terms of logistics, bearing in mind the exploitation phase if and when Beersheba was captured. The route to the gun positions was over difficult country but traversed in bright moonlight. For some deployments there was a special track plan for each major group, facilitated by the exertions of the 521st Field Engineer Company. All guns were in position by 1.30 am and encountering desultory fire from light guns and rifles. By 4.00 am the brigades had all reported ready with telephone lines laid. The grouping of batteries was quite complex, as the provenance of their affiliations took second place to their mission. In the event, total corps artillery support amounted to batteries of:

- 8 x 6-inch howitzers
- 8 x 60-pounders
- 32 x 4.5-inch howitzers
- 4 x 3.7-inch howitzers
- 96 x 18-pounders

The right brigade of the 53rd Division engaged targets to the left of the 74th Division. The 60th Division artillery was also divided into two groups, the right to support the 179th Infantry Brigade (RHA, RFA and RGA), while the left group supported the 181st Infantry Brigade (RFA only). The 74th Division artillery right group supported the 231st Brigade and the left group the 230th Infantry Brigade. Two medium trench mortar batteries (X and Y) made their debut.[6] The gunners could hear the heavy artillery bombarding Gaza, but had to wait for their fire plan to begin at 5.55 am.

In sum, Chauvel and Chetwode had 8500 sabres in their mounted troops, 27,000 rifles in attacking forces plus reserves (of which only 17,000 were engaged) and 180 guns of all types. In terms of ratios, only in cavalry did Allenby have a clear-cut advantage of 8:1. For the infantry it was 2:1, and for the gunners 3:2.[7] Chauvel's supply train was several miles long and, incredibly, its movement at night from its previous positions remained undetected by the enemy. This was due to excellent staff work and the quality of the deceptive measures mounted in front of the Turkish positions at Gaza.

The narrative that follows covers artillery support for the infantry followed by support for Chauvel's mounted troops. H Hour for the bombardment was 5.55 am. The dust rising from the bursting shells obscured the infantry to the extent that fire was suspended at 7.00 am but resumed two and a half hours later. Some 45 minutes after that, the infantry of the 181st Brigade had captured the vital Hill 1070 assisted by 'wire parties' which operated within 30 metres of the line of 18-pounder fire. This enabled the guns of the 60th Division to advance to the main Turkish line, and some came into action again at 10.30 am. They engaged targets of opportunity until the final assault, timed for 12.15 pm. For the first time in the campaign, the generals were able to claim that 'throughout the battle the action of the artillery proceeded smoothly in strict accordance with the artillery plan.' This was reflected in the corps casualty figures of 136 killed and 1010 wounded. As Farndale notes, 'To advance over featureless desert, come into action at night and in great secrecy, and give a highly effective, coordinated and concentrated bombardment at dawn … is no easy task for regular troops, but they [the New Army batteries] had done it in fine style and with great success and accuracy.'[8] The actions of the DMC, on the other hand, differed markedly.

On 11 October Hodgson's 19th RHA Brigade had amalgamated its battery ammunition columns in preparation for the forthcoming offensive. On 25 October the brigade moved first to El Buggar, then Esani and Khalasa, arriving at 10.30 pm the following day, when they fed their horses. They then moved to join the main body where they received their orders for the battle on 31 October. Chauvel rode behind his columns of light horsemen who moved into their attack formation as they approached their start lines. He established his headquarters on a knoll, Kashim Zanna, which provided panoramic views of Beersheba and the approach ground to the north-west. Chauvel knew he had to subdue the two strongest enemy outposts at Tel el Saba and Tel el Sakati, objectives for Ryrie's 2nd Light Horse Brigade, if he were to obey Allenby's instruction to capture the town in one day. The Turkish lines of defence were closer to the town on the south-east side, some 1500 yards outside the settlement and inferior to those on the other side of the town, with the notable exception of Tel el Saba. XX Corps cavalry (with Essex Battery, RHA) filled the gap between XX Corps and the DMC. Chauvel's cavalry was disposed left to right, from south to north:

- 7th Mounted Brigade: three regiments astride Khalasa road to the south, supported by the 20th RHA Brigade, Berks, Hants and Leicester batteries
- 4th Light Horse Brigade: 11th, 12th and 4th Light Horse regiments, supported by the 19th Brigade RHA, A and B batteries, with the HAC and the Notts Battery to the east-south-east
- NZMRB headquarters, AMD headquarters and the 1st Light Horse Brigade, its headquarters to the east
- 3rd Light Horse Brigade and the 18th RHA Brigade, Somerset and Inverness batteries
- Canterbury Mounted Regiment, the 7th and 5th Light Horse regiments to the north-east
- 5th Mounted Brigade in reserve to the south-east

Chauvel's headquarters personnel established themselves around his Rolls Royce and, in so doing, attracted the attention of the Turkish artillery observers. The CRA's staff to one side of the knoll likened the scene to one replicated during 'staff rides' and awaited developments and orders. They did not have long to wait as the Turkish artillery opened up, producing 'a scattering of maps, field glasses and staff officers like chaff before the wind.' It was, according to Preston (BC B Battery HAC), a salutary reminder of their adversary's professionalism.

The British infantry had halted on their objective (short of the town) as per their orders, believing that the DMC had already captured the town or was close to doing so. Ryrie's brigade's objective was to straddle the Hebron road at Tel el Sakati and, at 7.00 am, he advanced on Bir Sale-Abu Igreig, which his two New Zealand regiments took by 9.00 am, the time ordained for the second phase of the attack. However he spied parties of Turks and baggage trains leaving the town with indecent haste, so he sent his 7th Light Horse Regiment after them. On the way they were shelled by an enemy battery deployed near the road but suffered no casualties as they attempted to ride the battery down. The *ahmet* gunners dropped their range to point blank but departed when the troopers sought cover. The brigade remained in this position for the rest of the day.

Tel el Saba proved a hard nut to crack. The feature itself was around 400 yards long and 200 wide, with steep-sided, rocky slopes, particularly in the fork of Wadi Saba and Wadi Khalil. A combined infantry-artillery attack was required for its reduction. Chaytor sent the 1st Light Horse Brigade and the NZMR Brigade to form a semicircle some 1000 yards from the redoubt. They were supported by both the Somerset and Inverness batteries which were 3000 and 2600 yards respectively from their initial targets. As Gullett wrote, 'the faithful little Royal Horse batteries were flinging out their shells, or, gun following gun at the trot and canter, were hurtling over the rough ground into positions nearer the enemy.'[9] The 13-pounder, however, was unequal to the task of assisting the troopers to close with entrenched enemy. Chaytor was stalemated. The stalemate was broken when the AMD signals officer, Lieutenant Hatrick, was able to direct the fire of the Somerset Battery by flag signals with the battery a mere 1300 yards from the wadi. The Somersets had also moved a section to a right flank to better engage two machine-guns. These developments, small though they were, gave their attack momentum. Just before 3.00 pm, the Aucklanders having crawled as close as they dared, rose and dashed forward with the bayonet just as Major Clowes, their BC, ordered the fire lifted. Some 132 Turks were taken prisoner and the rest fled via the wadi, hotly pursued by the Australians on their flank who caught them in crossfire at the junction of the wadis.

At 3.00 pm Chauvel finally received some good news. However dusk fell at 5.00 pm, and there was still much hard work to do before he could rest. It was time to bring in Hodgson's brigades. At that time Brigadiers Grant (4th Light Horse Brigade) and FitzGerald (5th Mounted Yeomanry Brigade) were both with Chauvel. Both sought the honour of charging the town — Grant's suggestion — each believing that a cavalry action was the speediest way to success. Jones catches the moment with his vignette of 'Chauvel the commander' at a critical time of day: 'The remarkable panorama of battle lay below him, its details pinpointed by frequent phone messages. The passing of time was uncomfortably marked by the swing of the sun from behind his left shoulder, to overhead, and then in steady decline towards Beersheba.' Chauvel considered his options. In a phrase for which he is most remembered, he issued his command to Hodgson: 'Put Grant straight at it.'[10]

Hodgson ordered A Battery HAC and the Notts Battery to ride with the 4th Light Horse Brigade and together to go 'straight for the Mosque Beersheba and capture the town'. Gathering both batteries in their wake, the horsemen moved off at 4.30 pm at a trot. The intense Turkish rifle fire and enemy '77' shells that fell close to the batteries precipitated immediate action for both, the Notts first engaging entrenched enemy in the hills on the left flank, neutralising the machine-guns hindering the charge. They advanced in line and, when the light horsemen broke into a gallop, the guns were left behind.

Chapter 12

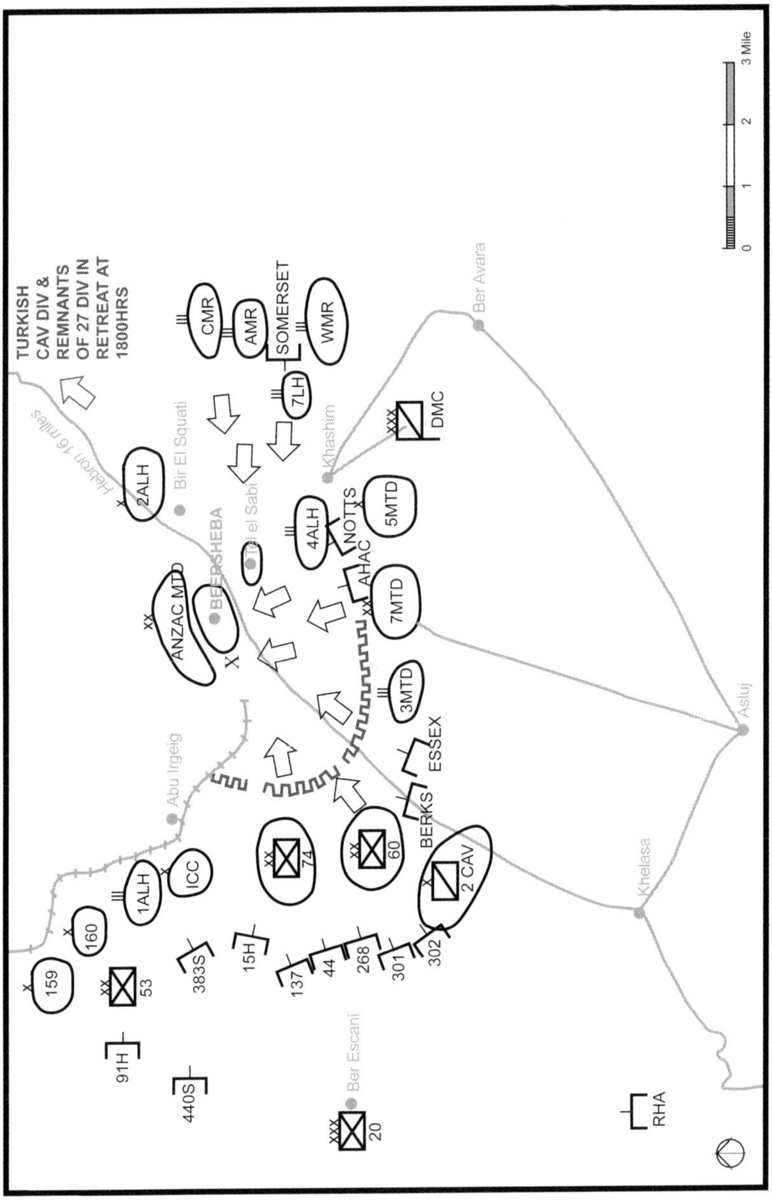

Map 7: The Battle of Beersheba, 31 October 1917, and the assault on the town by XX Corps infantry and cavalry on its western side. The primary assault by Chauvel's cavalry was from the south-east. Two of the three RHA batteries advanced with the light horsemen of the 4th Light Horse Brigade during their famous charge (source: Hill, *Chauvel of the Light Horse*, p. 129).

The charge by the 4th and 12th Light Horse regiments into the setting sun was a classic operation. These two units ran a desperate race against time to gain the wells.[11] It was just 20 minutes before sunset. On the way a squadron of the 12th was fired at from the rear, and veered left to launch a dismounted attack. The Notts Battery hove into view and Grant pointed out the origin of the fire. The Territorials under Major Price-Harrison silenced the enemy fire with their second shot, limbered up and moved off again, bound for Beersheba, A Battery following close behind, their shrapnel 'bursting like a row of red stars over the Turkish positions'. Horses and men fell to enemy 77s air-burst and ground-burst shells until they passed under the range of the Turkish guns and rifles. They gave way to the mayhem of trench and bayonet fighting until the regiments burst into the town at dusk. The success of this unique action considerably heartened the HAC's gunners, their historian noting that, 'though little was heard of it at the time, this was one of the great charges of history, and it was a high privilege for a unit of the HAC to have assisted with it.' The next day the Commander-in-Chief congratulated the battery on its shooting.[12]

The 1st and 3rd Light Horse brigades had continued the battle against the enemy in the eastern sector during the fight for Tel el Saba. Heading west towards the town, they were shelled and one of their detached regiments, the 8th, positioned itself to support the New Zealanders. The Ayrshire, Somerset and B Battery HAC were all thrown into the fight, with B Battery galloping over half a mile of open ground and coming into action in a small tributary of the Wadi Saba. Although sections were pushed up to reduce the range, the 13-pounder shells' main contribution to the engagement was to keep enemy heads down and reduce the casualties from trench fire. Historians have since concluded that Tel el Saba would have been taken more quickly with tank support.[13]

At 5.00 pm the 8th and 9th Light Horse regiments were ordered to advance. The 9th suffered in a very expensive and accurate bombing attack from the air before the pilot turned his attention to the Kiwis. Earlier, at 2.30 pm, the 8th had been bombed and strafed severely and lost its gallant, revered CO, Lieutenant Colonel Maygar, VC, an outstanding leader whose death from wounds the following day was widely mourned.[14]

Probably the most singular event that followed the capture of the town was the action of two Australian troopers (Hudson and Bolton of the 4th Light Horse Regiment) who bailed up the startled German engineer as he was about to detonate a charge and destroy the wells. Some 400,000 litres of water were saved for the very thirsty horses. Nine enemy guns were overrun and there were many skirmishing incidents as the troopers pursued the Turks fleeing the town.

Chapter 12

In Beersheba itself, all the prisoners were gathered by 7.00 pm. A vast phalanx from XXI Corps entered the town from the west, transforming a dusty desert town into a 'military metropolis' before the corps reassembled for its next task.

The British losses totalled 1348, most of these in close-quarter fighting in the trenches after the remaining machine-guns had been silenced by Allied machine-guns and the infantry. The Australian casualties amounted to 31 killed and 36 wounded. Some 70 horses had died, some carrying their riders many yards during the charge before expiring. Gullett wrote that 'nothing but a "forlorn hope" charge could have captured Beersheba that evening, and all Allenby's plan rested on the fall of the town on the first day of battle.'[15] In Australian military 'mythology', Beersheba stands out as 'the last great cavalry charge in 'modern warfare'. It was not. This honour was to go to two Territorial cavalry regiments which charged the little settlement of Huj at great cost, two days' ride away, a week later.

The British success at Beersheba was notable for several reasons, not the least of which was the success of galloping horsemen against entrenchments, and the resurrection of the debate over the value of *arme blanche* cavalry shock tactics against the Turks.[16] Grant later wrote that, 'If we had swords, I am sure we could have ridden on and captured thousands; as it was we stood off and shot hundreds only.'[17] Beersheba also instilled a strong reluctance in the Turkish cavalry to engage Australian and New Zealand horsemen, likewise in the *ahmet* in the trenches and redoubts. It was a heavy blow to Turkish morale and undermined Kress von Kressenstein's standing with his superiors. Interestingly, in the post-mortems that followed, artillery rated one mention which focused on the difficulty of locating enemy guns. Already at Second Gaza there was ample evidence that Turkish artillery and machine-guns inflicted higher ratios of British casualties per Turkish gun. Subsequent battle ratios were far less. The difference lay in the number of heavy pieces needed to neutralise both major sources of casualties. Once that ratio increased, the number of casualties fell.[18]

The use of two tanks against the eastern defences (Tel el Saba and Wadi Saba) raises interesting questions concerning the tactics of their employment. First, would the tanks, had they been available and not become casualties from either artillery fire — as at Second Gaza — or mechanical malfunction — as after the 27-mile cross-country run to Beersheba — have provided more timely offensive clout? Would both have survived a 54-mile return journey in a battleworthy condition? Second, the tanks' utility in cooperation with mounted infantry could be questioned in terms of the relative speed at which tactical situations change when the two arms are launched on a broad frontal attack. Risk analysis by the staff and tank force commander appeared to favour keeping them intact for Third Gaza.

In planning Beersheba, the staff may well have appreciated that the effort required to move the heavy ordnance 50 miles to Beersheba and return for the real prize of Gaza, was unwarranted. They may have noted the parlous state of the defences, which Gullet described as 'poor due to the lack of materiel'. Ismet Bey assisted the Allied planners through his error in dismissing the cavalry attacks from an unexpected direction as 'diversionary'. By mid-afternoon, having realised his mistake, it was too late for him to move his forces to more useful positions. As Hughes writes, the Germans and Turks differed on the *ahmet's* ability to cope with mobile warfare. The Germans argued that, instead of having a strong front line, the defence should have been structured around depth in reserves, such as the Germans used in France. The Turks, however, did not agree.[19]

These disadvantages mattered little to an army indifferently led, armed, clothed and maintained. Once General von Kressenstein was aware of the British strength, he ordered Ismet Bey to fight it out rather than order a tactical withdrawal. This cost him his job and Turkish losses of 1948 prisoners, at least 500 dead and 15 guns. Corps Commander Ismet Bey headed north, narrowly avoiding capture by light horsemen a few minutes after leaving the town. Allenby, having now secured his eastern flank, turned his forces once more against Gaza — for some troops, their third crack at a tough nut.[20]

Chapter 13
The Third Battle of Gaza: 25 October–7 November 1917

If at first you don't succeed, try, try, try again.

Proverb

Allenby used Chetwode's XX Corps, Bulfin's XXI Corps and Chauvel's DMC to finally end the protracted battle for Gaza. The benefits of the capture of Beersheba would not be felt until its precious wells were secure. Some wells had been wired for demolition but were saved by the momentum of the assault. Chauvel's tired troops took two full days to prepare for their part in Allenby's grand design — preparation which was to prove the key to eventual success. He had a balanced force of cavalry and infantry echeloned from east to west consisting of: the DMC, the A&NZ Mounted and Australian Mounted divisions, XX Corps (the 10th, 53rd and 60th infantry divisions), XXI Corps (the 52nd, 54th and 75th infantry divisions with the Yeomanry Mounted Division to protect his right flank) and the 74th Infantry Division and ICC Brigade in reserve.

Allenby's opponents in the Ottoman *Eighth Army* comprised *III Corps* (*3rd Cavalry Division, 27th Infantry Division*), *XX Corps* (*24th* and *16th infantry divisions*) and *XXII Corps* (*26th, 54th* and *53rd infantry divisions*). The *7th Division* was in reserve.[1] The nominal divisional infantry component of the Turkish force in Gaza (*XXII Corps*) comprised three regiments (nine battalions). The estimated number of 'effective' rifles varies considerably depending on the source, ranging from 20,000 to 40,000. The latter figure gives an approximate 500 rifles per regiment or 1500 for the division. One estimate of artillery strength put the number of guns at 300, while the *Official History* noted 116 belonging to *XXII Corps*. Against this arrayed defence, Allenby's gunners despatched 12,105 rounds from all natures of ordnance during October and, it can be assumed, received around the same in return.[2]

On 25 October, even prior to the capture of Beersheba, preliminary bombardments were being fired at Gaza. On the ground, movement by day was restricted to essential traffic until the elements for Beersheba were in place there. At night, campfires were lit in vacated positions. These and other incidental measures completely misled the Turks. The air effort invested in the battle was significant, if not in numerical terms, certainly in effect. RFC and AFC squadrons patrolled aggressively beyond the line to deny enemy observers aloft the opportunity to survey the Allied lines. Lieutenant Colonel Salmond (CO 5th Air Wing) was heavily involved in the staff deception planning. His aircraft also reported on the effectiveness or otherwise of the concealment of troops and particularly of guns. Occupied and dummy gun pits and machine-gun pits were assessed for their camouflage. All hostile aircraft were driven off, a significant feat which blocked all but one or two daring flights by German airmen. No. 1 Squadron processed air photos for the staff in four to five hours. At headquarters 5th Air Wing, 'an enthusiastic officer, Lieutenant Hamshaw-Thomas, undertook all the photographic work, his darkroom being an aircraft packing crate and a tent. Initially he was handicapped by a shortage of chemicals for developing and water.' No. 114 Squadron shot up enemy batteries by moonlight. Fifteen sorties produced reports of 16 hostile batteries, five of which were silenced. The observation balloon occupants registered 61 targets which were also duly bombarded. Over the front, the RFC located 126 enemy guns. Allenby's request for more high performance aircraft had been answered by the War Office, and the redoubtable Bristol Fighter, or 'Brisfit' as it was known, made its welcome debut prior to Third Gaza. In a short time the aircraft, in the hands of their aggressive pilots, established air supremacy over the enemy tactical area of operations, demonstrating their superiority to an enemy that earlier that year had bombed Cairo and outclassed the machines used by the RFC and AFC. The efforts of the pilots and observers to gather intelligence were reflected in a Turkish report 'that no further reconnaissance is done', despite the fact that intelligence assessments estimated that the Germans had 70 aircraft available for operations.[3]

Opposing General Refet Pasha was Lieutenant General Edward S. Bulfin, GOC XXI Corps. Bulfin had enjoyed a varied career. Born at Woodford Park, Co. Dublin in 1862, he was educated at Stonyhurst and partially at Trinity College before entering Sandhurst. He was commissioned into the Prince of Wales (Yorkshire) Green Howards in 1884 and saw service in the Boer War, first as brigade major to the 1st Guards Brigade and later as CO of a mobile column. His biographer (Bourne) notes that 'every career needs a slice of luck', and so it was with both his African service (Belmont, Modder River) and, 13 years later, on the Western Front, where his Territorial brigade of the British Expeditionary Force (BEF) responded to his 'courage and steadfastness' during 1914–15. His first divisional command saw him lead the 28th Division before he was appointed to XXI Corps. Bourne remarks that, in Palestine, it 'was the combination of Bulfin's bludgeon and Chauvel's rapier' that did the work.[4] This allusion recognises the threat to Turkish communications posed by the DMC cavalry beyond Sakati and the road between Hebron and Dhaheriye and the movement of a brigade or more of mounted troops towards Tel el Khuweilfe, with Tel esh Sheria as an objective for an attack on 4 November.

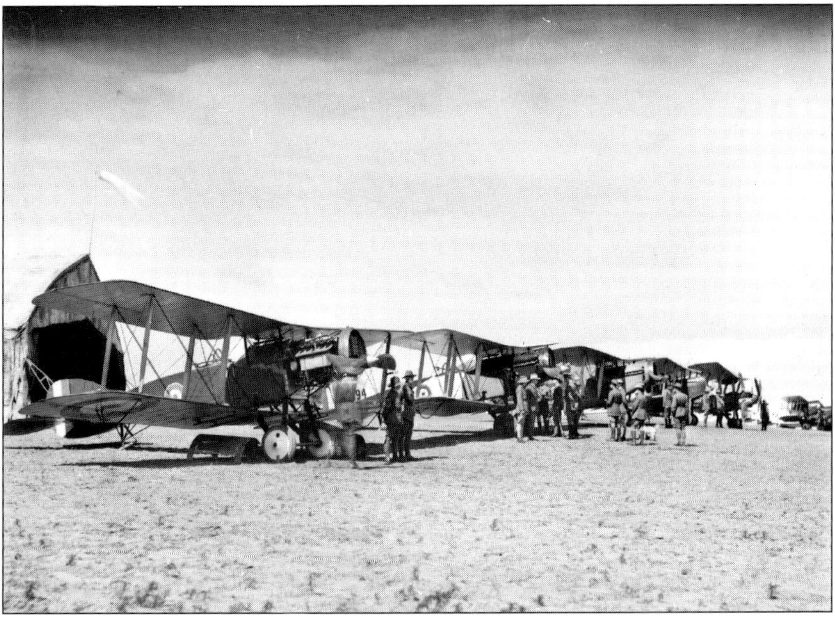

Image 12: The aircraft of No. 1 Squadron, AFC. Left to right: three Bristol Fighters, a Martinsyde and BE2 aircraft (AWM 1663).

When von Kressenstein moved six battalions from Gaza to the east, convinced that Allenby was going to Jerusalem via Beersheba and the Hebron road, Turkish command responded. Allenby's plan was to direct Chetwode's corps north-west. Sometime after D Day, and depending on the progress of the other corps' attacks, XXI Corps was to assault north-east to draw away the Turks opposing Bulfin. Theoretically this would render Bulfin's attack more certain of success.[5] Ryrie's brigade and another three (the 7th Mounted, 8th Light Horse and ICC), moved along the road to threaten Khuweilfe. This left the Turks with troops from the *3rd* and *53rd divisions*, with the *7th Division* in reserve, all supported by 116 guns of all natures. In the period between Second and Third Gaza the enemy had constructed almost 4000 yards of trenches from the sea to the cactus-infested hedges and 'woods' that marked the town's eastern edge.

Unbeknown to British intelligence, almost every skerrick of timber from Gaza's buildings had been taken to strengthen the trenches and redoubts. The Turks also felled palm trees and liberally protected their defensive works with barbed wire. In the centre were the notoriously strong defensive positions in the cactus hedges and woods. On the eastern flank, Umbrella Hill was 2000 yards from the 52nd and 54th divisions' start lines. Thus the night attack over ground offered little if any cover. The other unknown was the number of mines, the sum of which promised a bloody battle for an advance of 1000 to 2000 yards to the enemy forward lines of defence, and a further 4000 yards beyond the town to Fryer's Hill. On the Western Front, these distances would have tested credulity for a corps operation.[6]

Bulfin's rifle strength was approximately 11,000 from the 54th Division and an attached brigade (the 156th) from the 52nd Division. His plan was to strike the western side of the town rather than the eastern side or town centre. He was opposed by 14,000 Turks in the Gaza area (against his 40,000 on the front and in reserves). Thus the grand design of the plan was to concentrate early bombardments and 'stunts' on the eastern flank to persuade the Turkish command that this was where the corps assault would fall. It also inferred a simultaneous cavalry attack to encircle Gaza from the north. Bulfin's force comprised the 52nd Division in the east and the 54th Division in the west, his two strongest. All six tanks would operate with his infantry. Bulfin deputed Major General S.W. Hare (GOC 54th Division) to command the attack. His staff began planning and preparations in mid-September in what was known as 'Scheme M'. They critiqued the data and 'lessons learned' from the previous battles in a systematic fashion. Their critique is worth recording as their successful analysis became the bedrock of planning success for the battle.

Their brief was for the artillery of two divisions to support a division augmented by one brigade. This amounted to 10 batteries of 18-pounders (60) and four batteries of 4.5-inch howitzers (24), with six mountain guns (2.75-inch) added later. The outline plan involved grouping and siting batteries, preparation of OPs and gun positions, establishment of communication (artillery system), and the allocation of zones and tasks during the bombardment and then in the attack. One 6-inch gun target was the Turkish railhead nine miles away for which 300 rounds were allotted. The 8-inch howitzers had 15,000 rounds to expend. Bulfin had 68 pieces across 4000 yards or a ratio of 1:60, compared to 1:25 in France. Ammunition dumping and replenishment concluded the deliberations that determined a 'three-group' configuration based on three assaulting brigades whose objectives were:

Chapter 13

1. The capture of Umbrella Hill by the 156th Infantry Brigade (attached to the 54th Division)
2. The capture of the front-line trenches from El Arish redoubt to Sea Post by the 156th, 161st and 163rd brigades
3. Advance into Gaza by the 163rd and 161st brigades
4. The capture of Sheikh Hasam and Gun Hill by the 162nd Brigade[7]

Bulfin's front ran 5000 yards from Umbrella Hill (east) to the sea (west) where the distance between the protagonists was around 1000 yards. The westernmost objective, Sheikh Hasan (Gaza's port), was 3000 yards from the start line. Moving east, the heavily laden infantry encountered sand dunes up to 150 feet in height which proved very tough going. The assaulting brigades and their artillery comprised three groups:

No. 1. Right Group: Lieutenant Colonel Farquhar — three 18-pounder and one howitzer battery from A, B and C batteries 261st RFA Brigade and B Battery, 262nd RFA Brigade

No. 2. Centre Group: Lieutenant Colonel Dunbar — three 18-pounder and two howitzer batteries from A and C batteries, 270th RFA Brigade, A and C batteries, 264th RFA Brigade and A Battery, 270th RFA Brigade

No. 3. Left Group: Lieutenant Colonel Laurie — four 18-pounder batteries and one howitzer battery from A and B batteries, 271st RFA Brigade, B and C batteries, 272nd RFA Brigade, B Battery, 270th RFA Brigade and B Battery, 9th Mountain Brigade RGA

The gun positions were in sand dune country, adding considerably to the amount of construction materials (corrugated iron sheets, timber, barbed wire and sandbags) required. The labour for this huge effort, in excess of 100,00 man hours, was cheerfully given by the infantry working parties (who were grateful), and the 52nd Division gunners. Ammunition recesses were given priority in terms of material. Even while this construction was in progress, existing and new gun positions were registered by the German airmen and engaged, their fire exploding stored howitzer ammunition and starting fires. Despite this, all was ready by 25 October.

It was impossible to provide every battery with an independent OP as only small portions of the front line could be seen from the safest places. This problem was solved by giving each battery a share in an intermediate OP and a share in a forward OP in trench lines — virtually in only three locations. RE sappers constructed the solidly built OPs, one surviving a direct hit by a '5.9' without casualties and sustaining 'trifling damage'. FOOs used neighbouring trenches. There was a complete divisional artillery line network, the work of Major C.G.

Howes of the 54th Division Signal Company. It was entirely constructed of buried cable, 'metallic returns' for OPs to group headquarters, all connected laterally. All groups were connected to Divisional Artillery headquarters and to Battle Headquarters. It was a vast improvement on the communications 'performance' of Second Gaza.[8]

Zones and tasks were allotted on the principle of one 18-pounder per 90 yards of front (one 4.5-inch howitzer per 350 yards). This precluded the possibility of a simultaneous bombardment and barrage across the whole front. Attacks then focused on definite areas, including Umbrella Hill and Zowaiid-Rafa redoubt among others. These targets were included in the preliminary six-day bombardments. Umbrella Hill was the key feature requiring the bulk of fire after which Nos. 2 and 3 groups reverted to their own priorities. According to the plan, once all the objectives were taken successively — without pause — the divisional artillery would come under command of the CRA 54th Division. Once Sheikh Hasan was taken, Lieutenant Colonel Laurie's 271st RFA Brigade would move forward. Batteries would then advance to a position in which shell trajectory would be a critical factor in engaging defiladed targets.

The preliminary bombardment used every element of the gunners' repertoire. It began on D-6 (27 October) and focused on those earthworks, strongpoints and wire (with wire-cutting Fuse 106) which remained intact following the heavy artillery bombardment. Harassing fire was maintained by day and night on approaches, bivouac areas, stores and headquarters. Periodic intense bombardments and barrage fire on successive positions were applied across the front. Gas shells were lobbed onto bivouac areas.[9]

Orders specified that Bulfin's troops would cross their start lines at 3.00 am on 2 November. As Umbrella Hill was the key to Bulfin's plans, the corps order noted that the 'CRAs of 54th and 75th Divisions should keep in touch for efficient operations'. The 156th Brigade knew the area intimately following Second Gaza, hence the choice of General Hare to effect its capture. Six tanks were available for the attack and corps staff, with the knowledge that their previous use at Gaza had been undistinguished, spread them across the front instead of concentrating their offensive power. Only one was allocated to the 54th Division's main thrust on the seaward flank. Restrictions were placed on the tanks' forward movement. This instruction directed that tanks were not to be north of Rafa redoubt before Z+55 hour, the time set for its capture and, once on their respective objectives, they were to return to Sheikh Aljin.

Some aspects of the artillery plan are worthy of note given the ultimate success of the corps attack. Artillery staff prescribed a daily ammunition expenditure rate for all types of ordnance. If this was exceeded, recalculation would be based on an '18 pounder - 100 rpgpd [rounds per gun per day]'. The overall plan contained a 'deception plan' of sorts which specified that 'the number of guns participating should not disclose the greater concentration of our guns west of the Cairo [main] road.' The HAGs' headquarters was sited at 54th Division headquarters, and five-minute duration calls for SOS fire were stipulated, with the CRA assessing the situation if a repeat was required. Gas shell objectives with both lachrymatory and lethal types were delineated in an area of 100 x 10 yards or 120 x 15 yards on enemy dugouts, firm ground, and thickly wooded areas. The six tanks were to support the infantry from Phase 2 onwards. However, the plan also involved a subsidiary attack by the 233rd Infantry Brigade, 'borrowed' from the 75th Division, to capture Outpost Hill, which was eventually taken by a Gurkha battalion (the 3/3rd), and subsequently regained by the enemy. It was not retaken by the division until 1.00 am on 7 November.[10]

Nine naval vessels acting as a proxy HAG had assembled off the coast north-west of Gaza and began their bombardment on 25 October. By 27 October they had been reinforced by HMS *Grafton*, Monitor M15, RN destroyers HM Ships *Staunch* and *Comet*, the French destroyers *Abbalete*, *Voltigeux*, *Coutlas*, *Frauconnau* and *Hache*, and two river gunboats, HM Ships *Ladybird* and *Aphis*. Land and sea bombardments consumed 15,000 rounds of heavy shells prior to D Day. Allenby's orders stated that on D-1 the *Requin* and HMS *Raglan* would bombard Deir Sineid station, road junctions, railway bridges and camps on the Wadi el Hesi. Arrangements were made with the Senior Naval Officer, Egypt and Red Sea, to provide a seaplane to direct fire. Requests for naval support were to be conveyed from headquarters XXI Corps to the Senior Naval Officer, Marine View. His superior was enjoined to 'meet all demands for co-operation so far as the means at his disposal allow'.[11]

Bulfin was also the beneficiary of Allenby's successful pleas to the War Office for more and heavier guns and gas shells. These were organised in brigades of mixed ordnance, usually in batteries of four pieces. He had eight mountain guns in addition to his 78 heavy pieces, organised into the 97th, 100th and 102nd HAGs. This allowed the allocation of one piece to every 60 yards for a front of 4000 yards, in sum 148 pieces. This collection of 108 x 18-pounders and 36 x 4.5-inch howitzers made an impressive 'Western Front'-sized array of ordnance.[12]

XXI Corps GOCRA Brigadier H.A.D. Simpson-Baikie had served on all four other fronts before coming to Palestine with impressive credentials and was responsible for the overall plan. As the official historian recorded, 'at this time there were no heavy artillery brigades with definite establishments in the EEF.

Instead there were a number of group HQs, to which a number of heavy batteries were attached. Nor was there, until the following December, a brigadier general commanding heavy artillery in either XX or XXI Corps.' This fell to Colonel O.C. Williamson-Oswald, whose 61st HAG was supporting Chetwode. He was in charge of the 'heavies' and acted in a senior capacity, having no batteries attached to his group headquarters. He organised them in two counter-battery groups, right and left, each with four 60-pounders, eight 6-inch howitzers and four 8-inch howitzers. His bombardment group comprised eight 60-pounders, twenty-two 6-inch howitzers, two 6-inch Mark VII guns and four 8-inch howitzers.

With the arrival of daylight, the 6-inch guns were given the rail terminal at Beit Hanum as their target. Ammunition was plentiful. Already 15,000 rounds had been expended prior to D Day and 300 rounds had been allotted to destroy each enemy battery on the fire plan. A snapshot of the preliminary bombardment for 28 October reveals a total of 12,494 rounds, ranging from 2.75-inch howitzers to 8-inch howitzers — 9558 from the RFA brigades alone — compared to a daily average the following week of almost 19,300. Ammunition supply increased as the battle raged with the infantry making sure but steady progress along their advance lines.[13]

For the five days leading to Zero Hour, artillery was firing, non-stop, somewhere along the front. War diaries mention a Turkish ammunition dump falling to a heavy bombardment, and naval gunfire immobilising the railway line at its vulnerable cutting to thwart resupply, which the Turks tried repeatedly to repair until driven from the area. There were temporary changes in brigades' affiliations with their artillery, enemy bombing at night and counter-bombardment shoots based on the data gained by N and V Observation Sections. Rear area targets were not neglected, particularly those where troops congregated. These were engaged with HE and gas. Plans detailed the supply of plenty of tractors to move the guns to ensure that they followed the advance and moved to optimum positions.[14]

Once the infantry battle began, the pressure was on all ranks. A graphic description of an artillery action at Zero Hour was provided by a member of a mountain howitzer battery:

> The battery opened fire with ranging shots registering targets. A field battery behind us opened up, as also did several batteries around … Bullets whistled over the top of the dugout and an occasional shrapnel burst unpleasantly near. At noon, all batteries having registered targets the signal for the bombardment was given. Then we heard the music of the guns.

Air liaison was very important and an Air Liaison Officer (Captain Mutton, RA) was at 75th Division headquarters from the outset when target registration was checked from daylight (6.00 am) on D Day. It is unclear whether he had ever flown as an observer but the record suggests that his expertise was respected.[15]

The progress of the 75th Division on the eastern flank, which faced the *3rd Infantry Division*, is illustrative of the situation of its sister divisions on its left. Tactically, this division's gains had to accord more with those on its left than its right, or it would be enfiladed from either flank. As the 54th gained ground, the Turks responded by 'straightening' their line with gradual withdrawals without surrendering their tactically important high ground, honeycombed with dugouts. The 75th Division's field artillery provides a snapshot of gunner activity for the preliminary D Day-5 (27 October) to D Day +8 (8 November) over 12 days. During the first six-day period, CRA Brigadier H.A. Boyce's 8th South African FAB, 37th and 172nd field brigades, fired 7177 rounds of 18-pounder shrapnel and 2520 of HE shell (approx. 25% HE) and 1980 rounds of 4.5-inch howitzer, D-2 marking the heaviest, at 1700. The 4.5-inch howitzer batteries' contributions comprised 1910 HE and 830 'special shell' rounds. Other batteries had larger allocations of 'special shell' for their tougher engagements. The target lists show wire-cutting with Fuse 106 as vital in the early stages. On the second day (2 November) the 75th Division artillery expended almost 6000 rounds of all types. By now the battle had developed into a slogging match. Ammunition usage was prodigious, not only for the heavies, but also for the infantry divisions' 18-pounders which shot 9600 rounds, and the howitzer batteries which expended 2400 in 28 hours. The first three days of the battle were crucial for the gunners, and the CRA recorded 'a continuous bombardment' as the 234th Brigade beyond Outpost Hill on the eastern flank called for a barrage to support its Indian infantry attack.[16]

The operations of the 52nd and 54th divisions were different in scope and purpose, and it is worth examining some features of their 'slogging match'. Farndale describes an accurate barrage at the El Arish redoubt which appears at odds with events at Rafa redoubt during Phase 4 of the battle for Gun Hill. He describes the 'almost perfect' artillery-infantry cooperation over these assaults for 'only 2,696 casualties'. The remainder of the battle is summarised in just 15 lines. The Scots and the East Anglians benefitted from the 'grand design' by virtue of their vast allocation and array of artillery, the tanks' contribution comprising support for the 163rd Brigade.[17] The 4th Royal Scots and 7th Cameronians bore the brunt of the fighting for the El Arish redoubt and Umbrella Hill respectively, as their casualty figures indicate. Umbrella Hill was the key feature for the 54th Division's attack and it was the attached brigade (the 156th) that was given this task. The Turks here could dominate the El Arish redoubt so it was vital that the hill be captured first.

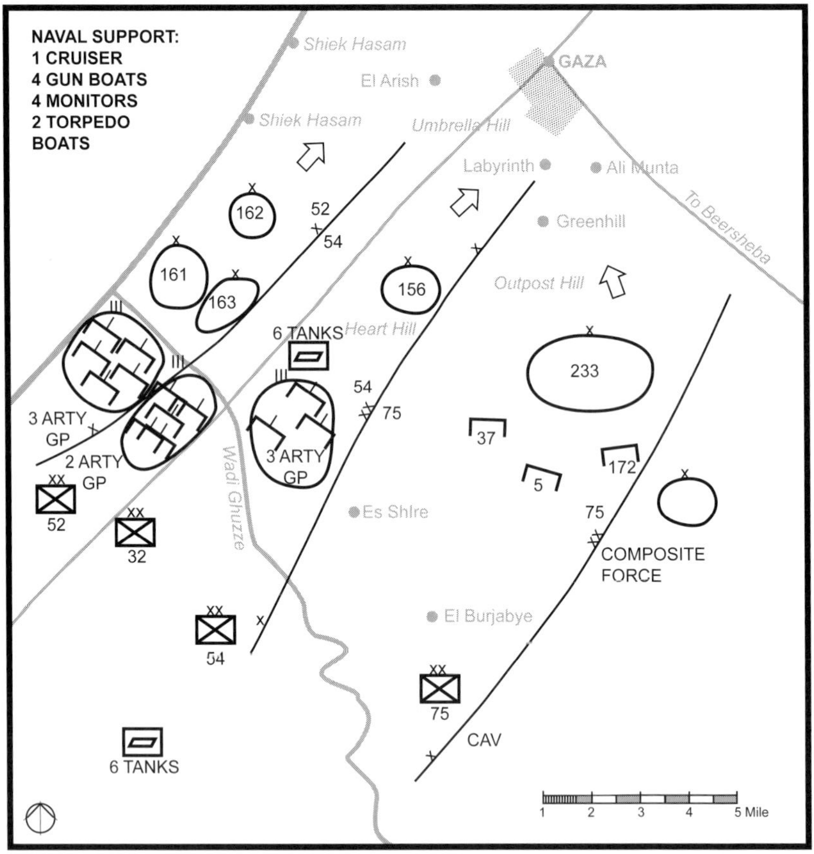

Map 8: The Third (and decisive) Battle of Gaza, 27 October–7 November 1917. This map shows the 15-mile front from the coast to the 96th RGA Brigade at a crucial time — 6.00 pm on 31 October. The field and heavy artillery was concentrated on the four-mile front south of Gaza (source: Gullett, *Official History*, Vol. VII, *Sinai and Palestine*, Map 16).

Chapter 13

Another aspect of the battle is also described by Farndale, who writes that 'a heavy defensive barrage and the dark night caused the infantry loss of direction. Another battalion lost the barrage and ... another keeping close to an accurate barrage did well.' The Turkish counter-attack came from the north-east just before 9.00 am the next day. This was anticipated by Simpson-Baikie, who had registered his batteries. He fired the entire corps artillery on the advance which 'completely destroyed and scattered the attack'. The suspected enemy forming-up place had been registered by aerial observation. This was just one of the many counter-attacks the enemy launched against the 54th Division and, ultimately, its 161st, 162nd and 163rd brigades were all involved. Using the biblical dictum that 'it is better to give than receive', Turkish artillery fired tear gas at the western divisions on 3 November to little effect, and this remained its only contribution.

On the eastern ridges leading to the town of Ali Muntar, the Labyrinth, Maze and Magdhaba Trench, the *ahmets* of the *3rd* and *53rd divisions* continued to hold out. On 5 November the RFA gunners fired 2025 rounds of 'special shell' on communication trenches and supply routes for water, rations and ammunition in a three-hour bombardment. It was still not enough. Phase 2 H Hour was then scheduled for 3.00 am the following day. Positions on either side of the ridge somehow survived this weight of shell and the infantry still had a hard fight on their hands. One infanteer described the artillery contribution: 'Our bombardment continued night and day, sometimes bursting forth in great volume and at other times dying down to a steady pounding ... every part of the enemy's defences seemed to be systematically pounded; bursting shells from the big guns threw up great clouds of sand and smoke.'[18]

Overall, it had not been all plain sailing for Bulfin's command. The 266th RFA and other battery positions had been bombed and there are frequent references in the corps war diary to the effectiveness of Turkish shelling and the casualties inflicted on the infantry. Light relief for those below was afforded on one occasion when a kite balloon came adrift from its mooring and floated north over the battle zone. Its fate was not recorded.[19] There were many calls for fire by Very light and, from time to time, 'Three Greens' to signal that (for example) the East Anglians were on their objective. At headquarters all was not 'sweetness and light' and, on 5 November, General Hare had an angry corps commander on the line demanding the reason for the delay in responding to calls for artillery fire.[20]

Ali el Muntar, a key feature of the Gaza defences, was subjected to an enormous bombardment, certainly the largest display of artillery strength in the Palestine campaign, and 'had been almost shelled away'. To borrow a phrase from Bidwell, 'the bombardment would hardly have been a distraction for Haig', a rough comparison between the two fronts of the artillery scene in 1917. However, the bombardment had achieved one important objective — that of cutting the barbed wire, which rendered the infantry task easier, albeit only in that sector.

There were two more instances in which the fire order for massed artillery was given by Simpson-Baikie and, until the Turkish front collapsed, Bulfin's infantry suffered substantial losses during Turkish rearguard actions against the Phase 3 and 4 objectives. Where artillery support was problematic, some battalions were forced to adapt to street fighting in the ruined town. General Hare, writing after the war, remarked that 'the pounding the Turks had suffered for six days had effectively cut their wire and so the enemy positions fell "without difficulty".' This was a patent overstatement of the facts, as the Turks resisted strenuously despite the weight of shell thrown at them and despite the destruction of the wire entanglements. That said, in the context of Western Front casualties, it may have been an accurate statement.

The attack on Turtle Hill, Belah and Younis at 1.00 am on 7 November found empty trenches. The last shots were fired by the 271st RFA's C Battery on stragglers heading north. The wreckage and desolation of Gaza threw into sharp relief the ability of the Turkish infanteer when well led to fight to the bitter end, albeit in the most indescribably squalid conditions imaginable. He had taken every piece of removable timber from Gaza's buildings to fortify his redoubts and construct overhead cover for his guns. As a consequence, the buildings quickly crumbled under the weight of shell and aerial observers experienced considerable difficulty locating the Turkish guns. This also partly explains the Turk's ability to resist strongly to the bitter end.[21]

The artillery staff examined the battlefield as soon as possible so as to observe, measure and critique — quantitatively and qualitatively — the artillery's contribution. The Phase 1 barrage appeared to have been well directed, the infantry maintaining its pace. Enemy retaliatory fire was very heavy on the first night, and more violent than any during the six-day period of preliminary bombardment. During Phase 2 the batteries had to resort to enfilade fire, sometimes requiring a switch of 25 degrees. Otherwise enemy fire was spasmodic, paying most attention to Sheikh Aljin and Samson's Ridge once these features were occupied and, despite much shellfire, 'neither casualties or material damage were serious'. The attack on Belah on 3 November made the enemy 'uncomfortable', and B Battery, 270th RFA Brigade, moved to a new position with the help of working parties from the 155th Brigade.

Chapter 13

Subsequent inspection of the battlefield revealed that the batteries' fire had been 'accurate and effective' while the howitzer fire caused the trenches in some places to be 'much knocked about and in some cases obliterated'. Field gun barrages were effectively placed. Gas shells seemed to have had little effect overall — some Turks were affected, but no firm conclusion could be drawn. The staff's conclusion was that the work of the telephonists and FOOs deserved recognition. They had moved forward early, maintained contact during incessant fire, and their reports were of considerable value and always confirmed by the (infantry) brigades. One of the big surprises the staff reported was the excellent camouflage of the Turkish gun positions. They remarked that it was a wonder that the aerial observers could locate them at all, so efficiently had they been prepared.[22]

Patrols across the Turkish front late on 6 November (11.00 pm) by the 42nd Division found empty trenches, as did the other formations. Ali Muntar was a pile of rubble. Trenches had become pulverised depressions, even those recently constructed, as their perimeter shrank; the town was a pile of smouldering ruins. The Turks had had enough.[23]

Farndale's gloss on the gunners' efficiency appears to conceal shortcomings in infantry-tank-artillery cooperation, and the minimal effects of gas shells on the fighting efficiency of the Turk. The fact that Outpost Hill, the Labyrinth, Sheikh Redwan and Green Hill did not fall until the early hours of the morning of 7 November speaks volumes for the *ahmets* in defence against infantry compared to their comparative timidity against the cavalry charge. Patrols found Ali el Muntar almost blown away with thousands of shell holes inflicted by the 8-inch howitzer. The effects of the bombardment were everywhere to be seen. Farndale is lavish in his praise of the aerial observers — 'without them there would have been no victory at all.' However, it is worth asking what this meant in terms of the neutralising and destructive effects of HE (not gas) artillery fire.[24]

One can only speculate that many of the other company and battalion attacks required concentrations and barrages to enable their infantry to move into favourable attacking positions. The distance from the initial start line to beyond Gaza was around three miles, a substantial distance by Western Front standards. It suggests that this was an infantry 'slogging match', unfolding incrementally as brigade after brigade fought its way forward behind barrages or concentrations. The battle for Gaza town continued over six days, culminating in its capture. The capture of the ground north of Gaza and later Sheria and Khuweilfe by cavalry and infantry took another four. This throws into focus Allenby's good fortune with the results of the famous cavalry charge and the XX

Corps performance at Beersheba, rather than the protracted battle that could have lasted another two days.

Analysis of the use of gas at Third Gaza is far more instructive if compared to Second Gaza. The failure of Second Gaza compelled the staff to drastically improve their planning and methodology for Third Gaza, reaching for gas clouds from cylinders and 'special shells'. The War Office responded with a new range of chemical fillings even more lethal than those of early 1917 and more specialists in gas handling. When General Allenby took command in June there were 20,000 4.5-inch howitzer shells in stock and a further 30,000 in transit. This included 60-pounder chemical shells. Allenby favoured the use of gas, Sheffy noting that 'he intended to stock 2,000 gas shells for each of the EEF's 82 howitzer batteries and heavy guns, that is 164,000 shells, one third in Egypt and the rest on the way.' He wanted 60% of his chemical ammunition to consist of lachrymators and the rest lethal substances. For the forthcoming battle he had two new lethal gases, PS and VN. Further experience in France had confirmed that, in order to neutralise enemy troops wearing gas masks, HE plus gas in short bombardments worked best, both as a means to surprise and to adversely affect a soldier.[25]

The infantry thrust was to occur on the coastal sector, and this and its accompanying gas attack were anticipated by the Turks. Bulfin planned, as Sheffy notes, 'for XXI Corps to use chemical weapons to achieve the operational level mission but also to effect its own tactical action.'[26] The artillery groupings of three heavy batteries and four howitzer batteries of both assaulting divisions were aimed at drawing the defenders east/south-east from the coast. Firing began in the evening and continued until dawn, designed to catch reserves, supplies and reinforcements on the move, with 'stationary' targets to be engaged late at night and at dawn. An analysis of target lists reveals that 90% of the 35 chemical shell targets were applied away from the beach area. On the evening of 30 November, 4000 gas shells were fired, with another 2000 the following night. As a result, 60% of the chemical shell allotted was expended prior to the infantry H Hour. When the western attack developed, another 4000 were despatched, most for area targets away from the beach or for impromptu fire missions. In sum, 9400 of the 10,600 chemical shells allotted had been fired over five nights against 30 targets, as summarised in the table below. The objectives of the barrages and concentrations were counter-battery, crossroads, bivouacs and defended localities (including redoubts). The use of gas at Gaza is illustrated in Table 8 below:

TABLE 8: GAS AT GAZA[27]

Date	Guns	Shells Type	Main Targets
30–31Oct	Heavy 1709	VN+PS	Xroads N 2 btys N of Gaza
	Field 2310	CBR	Labyrinth, El Arish, bivouacs W of Gaza
31-1Nov	Heavy 899	VN+PS	Same Xroads, Wof Kh. Sihan 2 trenches
	Field 1200	CBR	Labyrinth, El Arish
1–2 Nov	Heavy 2245	VN+PS	Roman Hill
	Field 600	CBR+SK	trench W of Labyrinth
2–3 Nov	Field 600	SK	Labyrinth
3–4 Nov	Field 600	SK	Labyrinth
TOTAL [28]	**Heavy 4853** **Field 5310**		

On a 'gunner to gunner basis', an Austro-Hungarian battery officer reported that the fire was light and ineffective, causing no casualties to his gas-masked crews. Another report noted that a single battery had been neutralised for a short time by the heavy artillery bombardment. Other reports varied and it took post-war interviews to obtain more facts from the participants on both sides.

Despite being adequately forewarned of the EEF's use of gas, Sheffy also recorded that the Turkish army facing Bulfin was indifferently prepared for gas warfare. Senior commanders were dismissive of reports of its effectiveness, and the *ahmets* deeply suspicious and sceptical of training and gas discipline. Nonetheless, they stocked tear gas shells which they expended on the East Anglians. The same comment could be applied equally to their opponents, except perhaps for the Turkish notions of 'evil spirits' associated with wearing gas masks. Within the EEF the cavalry were the most sceptical, probably reasoning that their *modus operandi* in daylight hours would prevent the effective use of gas against them and their horses.[29]

When it came to the 'official version', both sides wrote it out of their reports, although first-hand accounts were available at the time and subsequently. Sheffy notes in his exhaustive research that 'no British first-hand testimony on the lethal results have emerged so far.' The Turks admitted to a casualty count of 500 to 1000 at Gaza. Australia's official historian provides the *obiter dicta* on the matter:

> Gas was used in front of 52nd Division at Gaza, and scores of dead found in the enemy trenches. In one ambulance station an enemy doctor was

> found with bandage half on a wounded man. Wounded and orderlies all dead. At one Bn. HQ a CO and staff were found dead about their table and maps. The sea breeze at Gaza made the use of gas difficult. The air was too clear and volatile for gas to be very effective and never stable enough for a good barrage.

Gullett also referred to the use of gas shells at Second Gaza, but did not describe the results. In his account of Third Gaza gas did not rate a mention.[30]

Thus, by transferring the hard lessons of German army counter-bombardment from the Western Front to Palestine, the Turkish artillery was effectively stiffened by the presence of German and Austrian officers and men. This combined artillery force was clearly a more efficient instrument of war than the cavalry and infantry, and a trial to the British at that point in time. After Third Gaza, once the Allied divisional and heavy artilleries and their infantry had gained one another's confidence, the Turks were never able to deploy artillery resources that exceeded the potential firepower of the EEF. Gas became a 'dead letter' until mid-1918, when Allenby became alarmed at reports of Turkish interest in gas. In the event, this interest lay in training rather than aggressive intent. Nonetheless, he had 100,000 gas shells stockpiled for the Battle of Megiddo.[31]

The *Official History* data ('Attack on Gaza Defences') for the battle is at odds with several other accounts of the Gaza campaign.[32] These accounts placed Refet Pasha's force strength at 8000 rifles supported by 116 guns. He had 14,000 across his front. His opponent Bulfin had 17,000 rifles (2.1:1 ratio) and 148 guns from the 97th, 100th and 102nd HAGs and divisional artillery. The official historian allotted only three days (1–3 November) to the battle and noted that the British lost 2696 from all causes. The casualty toll was certainly much higher than that. The Lowlanders on their front buried 201 at Umbrella Hill and 169 at El Arish. The 54th Division buried 709 dead and took 104 prisoners. The Turks yielded a total of 446 prisoners. The RE field companies (410th and 412th) supporting the 156th Brigade lost 27 killed and wounded. From 1 to 7 November, the 52nd Division's 156th Brigade had a total casualty count of 650: 30 officers and 620 other ranks. Some 400 fell at the El Arish redoubt alone. Of that 650, two battalions accounted for 19 officers and 388 other ranks. Applying a rough 'rule of thumb' to the other infantry divisions' brigades gives a total of 400 per brigade. The Scots' 'rule of thumb' was that they inflicted three to one.[33]

The narrative now moves to General Allenby's grand design to use the mounted troops and infantry of Chetwode's XX Corps as they swept north-west from Beersheba to the coast and ultimately to Jerusalem. Bulfin's XXI Corps battles as part of that design are also described in detail.

Narrative Two

November 1917 to May 1918

Narrative Two
November 1917 to May 1918

General Murray's initial strategic plan involved a northern thrust to Junction Station and coordinated coastal advances and territorial gains to force the Turko-German command on the defensive. Following Beersheba the Allied thrust aimed to interdict the Hejaz railway — the route to Mecca and southern Arabia — while General Allenby astutely directed his forces to exploit their gains and deliver the British War Cabinet the prize of Jerusalem for Christmas. This coincided with the move by Russian rulers to sue for peace following the revolution of October 1917 and signalled a surge of confidence within the Central Powers. It released troops for the Western and Central fronts and, in March 1918, for the German spring offensive — a dramatic thrust on the Western Front that severely strained Allied relations and armies. One consequence was the War Office plan to move more troops from Palestine to France and Belgium.

The blockading of German trade and ports by the RN and the entry of the United States of America on the Allied side changed the whole European strategic and political balance. The Central Powers now began to realise that victory may be beyond their resources.

But in November 1917 the fight was far from over. When Allenby attempted to seize the Hejaz railway he badly misjudged the strength of Turkish forces at Amman and failed dismally. This failure had the unintended outcome of misleading the Turko-German command as to the location of Allenby's next major thrust. Against the backdrop of the ongoing campaign, the War Office continued to leach more troops to the Western Front and it was left to Indian Army reinforcements to make good these losses.

Allenby, realising he had to do more with less, continued to focus the Turk on his eastern flank during the summer. Through a series of masterly deceptions he succeeded brilliantly, assisted by a highly competent staff and abetted by Lawrence of Arabia and his newly won Arab allies. He planned to use his infantry to break the Turkish front on the coast so that mounted troops could manoeuvre behind the Turkish front line while also avoiding the mountainous hinterland.

Chapter 14
The Great Northern Drive

The rule is jam tomorrow and jam yesterday, but never jam today.
Lewis Carroll
Through the Looking Glass

According to the official historian, the Third Battle of Gaza lasted from 27 October to 16 November 1917, although Allenby's troops had, by that later date, advanced 16 miles and begun manoeuvre warfare once again over markedly different terrain as they approached the formidable Judean Hills. The previous chapter outlined Allenby's force structure for Third Gaza. Once Gaza was taken and a salient formed around it by XXI Corps, he employed Chauvel's DMC and Chetwode's XX Corps on his eastern flank driving north-east and north-west to try to bottle up the Turks retreating from Gaza and Beersheba. However the Turks' stubborn resistance across the front and the dislocation caused by water supply problems disrupted Allenby's plans. Allenby was keen for Chetwode, the 60th Division and its mounted troops to reach Sheria on 4 November rather than 7 November as it transpired. Had this been possible the destruction of the Turkish *Eighth Army* would have been complete. The plan involved Allenby's Eastern Force pivoting on Gaza by sending Chauvel's force, less the Yeomanry Division, ICC brigades and NZMR Brigade under Hodgson, across the Judean Hills.

In preparation for the cavalry advance the gunners made several regroupings that would cover the approaching phase of operations, some commencing prior to Beersheba. These regroupings were aimed to ensure a balance, for example, in trading mobility for firepower, and for ease of command. Brigadier d'Arcy King amalgamated the ammunition columns of the 19th and 20th RHA brigades under Lieutenant Colonel Eugster. Captain N.M. Elliott of the Hants Battery was promoted to BC B Battery HAC and Captain A. Smith of the Ayrshire Battery was appointed OC of the amalgamated ammunition column. Draught teams were increased from six to eight and baggage wagons reduced from four to one, presumably by drastically reducing the number of items designed to provide 'comfort'. Within the DMC the Leicester, Hants and Berks batteries had earlier left their 18-pounders with the 19th RHA Brigade and taken their 13-pounders.[1]

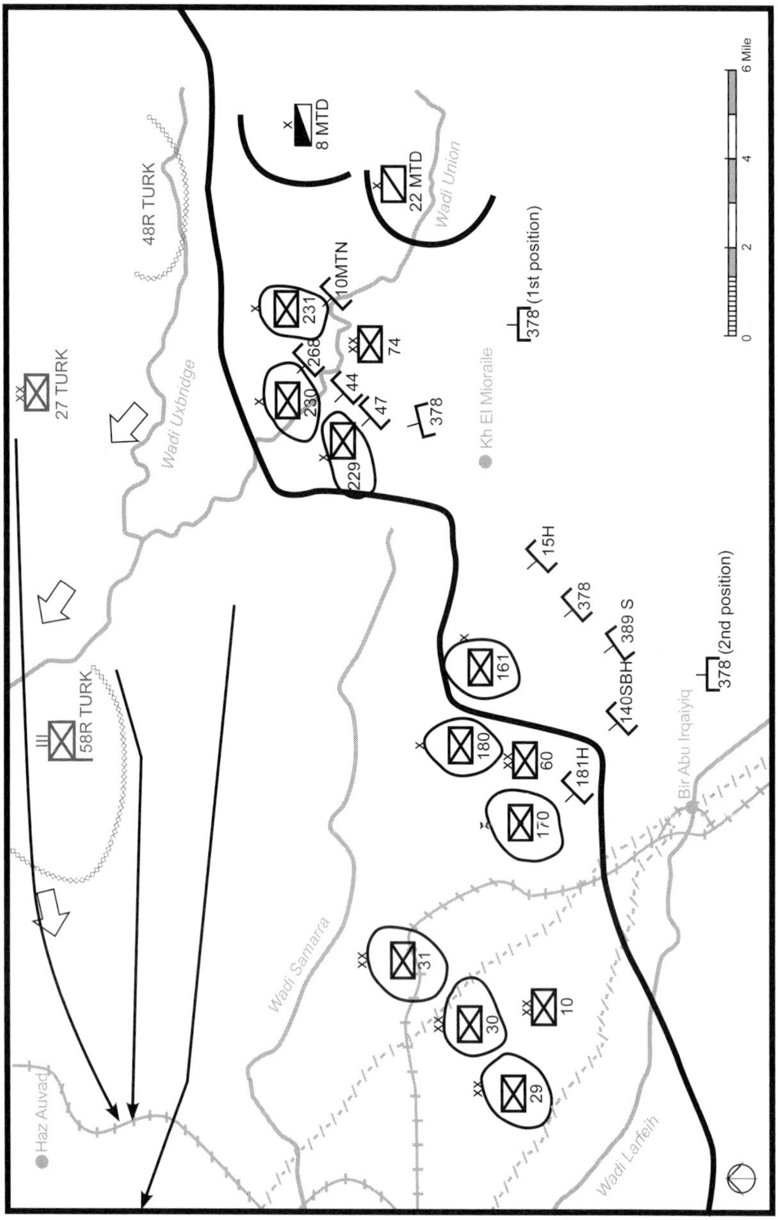

Map 9: The beginning of the Great Northern Drive to secure the coastal plain. The combined infantry-cavalry force pivoted on the Sheria position on its drive to capture Junction Station (source: Hill, *Chauvel of the Light Horse*, p. 131).

Chapter 14

The preparatory phase of Chauvel's advance represented a trying period for him and his staff who were keen to fulfil their orders from Allenby. Chauvel had to juggle resting his weary and depleted regiments, British, Australian and New Zealand, following their tiring march to Beersheba, while also maintaining pressure on the Turks. The enemy constantly reinforced his left flank — which was good news for Allenby. The more troops von Kressenstein moved east, the easier the task for Bulfin's XXI Corps on the coastal front and for Chauvel's mounted men as they veered north-west with the infantry for the set-piece engagements. In their path were the Judean Hills. A west to east track linked Hareira and Khuweilfe and the Hebron road, enabling the enemy to move reserves when and if required across the two corps' lines of advance. Chauvel had to deploy his cavalry between the coast and the escarpment in a way that best utilised their mobility and preserved the element of surprise. Following Beersheba, half the foot soldiers (10th and 60th divisions) advanced to El Faluje to the north, pushing towards Sheria astride the railway line, their boundary with the 74th and 53rd divisions. The 53rd Division's objective was south of Tel Khuweilfe. To their east were the camels of the Yeomanry Division. The speed of advance for the entire force was predicated on the physical capacity of the artillery teams which were losing condition, and that of the marching infantry. To the north-west were Chauvel's two divisions, less those regiments being rested, provisioned or watered. A few days after Beersheba, regiments from Chauvel's A&NZ Mounted Division reached a point three miles beyond Bir es Sqati, the northern limit at that time. During the advance the mounted New Zealanders had a stiff fight with Turks who crossed their line of advance and took 179 prisoners and captured four machine-guns.[2]

There was no rest for the horses of the AMD's RHA brigades. On 7 November both Berks and Leicesters came under heavy machine-gun fire but avoided casualties. The Hants and Leicesters supporting both the yeomanry and the 8th Mounted brigades had 'many grand targets' as they moved towards Khuweilfe. Nonetheless, as 'spectators' to the withdrawing Turkish force, they were able to capture the view eloquently:

> We were privileged to see a sight few mortals eyes will ever look upon again — the great force of cavalry pursuing a retreating army over wide and open country. The fighting was all of small units, a regiment here, a squadron there, meeting a party of the enemy in position, and going for them instantly, ruthlessly, the whole line eating its way forward like the rising tide that swirls and eddies a little while round rocks and stones here and there, and then submerges them.[3]

On the Gaza front, the 54th and 75th divisions were based around the town, screened by a composite force while the 52nd Division paused near Deir Sineid on the coast, its flank protected by the Imperial Service Cavalry. By this time the plight of the Turks north of Gaza had become desperate. Gullett noted that their communications were disorganised, supplies were short, dysentery rife and discipline was breaking down, the survivors' only thoughts to escape capture.[4]

On 3 November the advance of the 2nd Light Horse Brigade in the eastern sector of the front was held up at Deir Saide, the forerunner of many contested actions. On this occasion the enemy guns could be seen quite clearly, prompting the Ayrshire Battery to unlimber and neutralise them. Those Turks who had escaped from Beersheba were holding three trench systems protecting the important features of Tel Khuweilfe, Tel esh Sheria and Hareira. Allenby needed Khuweilfe for water, and he needed to capture it quickly or deny it to the enemy to maintain his momentum. He chose the former course of action. Chetwode grouped the 53rd Division with the ICC Brigade as its cavalry component on its right flank in the vicinity of the Hebron-Beersheba road. To its left were the 7th Mounted Brigade (South Notts Hussars and Sherwood Foresters) and the 8th Light Horse Regiment (attached) as the formation advanced through Muweileh and Towal el Jekwal. The division marched in two columns with two RFA brigades (the 266th and 267th) with the right column and one (the 265th) with the left. XX Corps Headquarters RA duly despatched the 91st Heavy Battery and the 440th Siege Battery in readiness for yet another assault on a well-defended position.

Khuweilfe was in reality three features: Ain Kolah, Ras el Nagb and el Jabry — bare, flat hills with commanding views and good defensive positions. During the early skirmishing the South Notts Hussars captured two guns and bagged 11 prisoners. Given the tactical situation and approaching darkness, they tipped the guns into deep gullies, only to find themselves immersed in a *khamsin* (not normally associated with that time of year) which blew for three days, causing delays and discomfort to man and beast. All the troops and their teams were suffering from exhaustion and the lack of good water, food and ammunition. The horses had been without water for upwards of 48 hours and their watering put a brake on the speed of the advance. No planning or preparation could have foreseen the scarcity of water. There was added gall in the form of accurate enemy artillery directed by German airmen, and 'the manner in which the enemy artillery discovered and re-discovered the horses of the brigade, as they shifted from shelter to shelter … strongly suggested Arab informers.'[5]

Chapter 14

The 53rd Division was to capture Khuweilfe on 4 November to coincide with an attack on Qawuqa by the 60th and 74th divisions. This proved an optimistic staff assessment of the situation. On an extended front that was alive with Turkish machine-guns and artillery, and with the cavalry taking significant casualties, H Hour was set for 4.20 am with the 158th Brigade to advance on a 1500-yard front after a night march over rough country. It involved the biggest artillery demonstration since Gaza, and included one heavy and siege battery, laboriously moved forward to add weight of shell to the fire plan, and 16 machine-guns. Farndale notes that the 53rd's divisional artillery 'got 6th Royal Welsh Fusiliers onto their objective and they captured nine field guns and their detachments ... but were then vigorously counter-attacked and lost the captured guns. They were then shelled by their own guns.'[6]

Gullet describes operational planning deficiencies (lack of preparation and resolution, command and control), linking these to the fact that one of the assaulting battalions advanced at 90 degrees to its intended line of march. When the barrage fire ceased, the infantry was to rise and charge the Turkish trenches. However the Tommies arrived late, missed the barrage, and an order for the 158th Brigade infantry to fill the gap was not actioned. This isolated the Australian battalion from the ICC Brigade which was then attacked strongly. In desperation the 2nd Light Horse Brigade Machine Gun Squadron (led by Captain J.R. Cain) was ordered forward and both Australian units paid dearly despite heroic enterprise for no gain. Late in the afternoon a night barrage was laid using divisional and heavy guns. Finally, by 3.00 pm on 7 November, having moved to a new position, the guns were able to offer the cameleers some degree of support. The Welsh infantry eventually succeeded in capturing the tel with effective artillery cooperation. Following a brief firefight, the enemy fled and the division resumed its march. It split its two artillery brigades, moving them to Sakati and Ras el Nagb. A Turkish position on the eastern flank at Dhareriyeh was effectively engaged by all the batteries in range, including the 'heavies', observers reporting seeing the 'town in flames'.[7]

The Judean Hills introduced another variation to campaigning in Palestine as the soft sand, cactus hedges, cultivation and undulating country now gave way to rough terrain which challenged the brigades and their artillery. Quite apart from the effect on cavalry deployment which aimed to move it within striking distance of an enemy, it also drastically changed the way that horse artillery could move in support of its cavalry. The Judean Hills were extremely rugged, a trial to man and beast to ascend or descend to gain some tactical advantage. With the arrival of the winter rains, the clay turned to vile, sticky mud that hindered movement. Good gun positions were not as plentiful as previously; there were crest clearance problems and dilemmas over where best to site the OPs and command the guns. Ammunition supply from the BAC was difficult and the resolution of such difficulties brought out the best in the officers in command and their drivers. Other unexpected problems also occurred which tested the ingenuity of the Allied soldier. One of the Light Armoured Battery cars broke down embarrassingly close to the enemy trenches at Burj el Beiyara. Rather than have the car fall into enemy hands the cavalry ordered all available artillery in range to 'fire a barrage beyond it'. This they did, keeping the marauding Turk at bay until the car was able to proceed to safety under its own power.[8]

Once the Turkish line from Khuweilfe to Sheria fell, Chauvel had to be ready to exploit towards Ameidat, some 10 miles from Sheria, and then to a line Jemmameh–Huj in a broad sweeping movement. Despite some dislocations to their front, the Turkish artillery was still intact and remained a force to be reckoned with. For the advance to Ameidat, where intelligence sources indicated the presence of a substantial depot, Chauvel chose the 1st and 2nd Light Horse brigades. Within three miles of the settlement and with the 60th Division's flank guard on their left, the regiments of Brigadier Cox's 1st Light Horse Brigade picked up the pace following a delayed early morning start. This delay was due to their supporting batteries' problems with the poor roads and tracks they were forced to traverse to join their brigades. Despite experiencing some perfunctory artillery fire en route, the troopers dashed over the distance and into the depots, which they reached at 10.45 am. Without the assistance of supporting artillery fire, the light horsemen captured 31 officers and 360 soldiers, 27 ammunition wagons, 250 artillery rounds and 200,000 rounds of small arms ammunition, and a complete field hospital.[9]

At the same time, XX Corps (60th and 74th divisions plus the 31st Brigade from the 10th Division and the 10th Division's artillery, in all 17,000 rifles and 168 guns) had a second objective — Sheria — and Chetwode took pains to ensure there was adequate ammunition for his artillery. Most of the heavy guns and howitzers had been underemployed, primarily because of insufficient logistic support since the logistic trains had to come via Beersheba. This operation was to be a divisional artillery show, and so they secured the lion's share of the resources. On 4 and 5 November the batteries received a generous 7000 rounds of 18-pounder and 1500 4.5-inch howitzer ammunition. This was augmented by 700 20-pound bombs dropped on bridges and enemy formations by the aircraft of the 5th Air Brigade. However, while this appeared to be an impressive quantity of ammunition, it was to prove barely adequate for the operation. This ordnance was destined for the trench lines between Tel esh Sheria and Hareira, the former reported to have water. Chetwode's opponent was Ali Faud Pasha, GOC *XX Corps*, which included the *16th* and elements of both the *26th* and *27th divisions*, in all some 4000 rifles and 40 guns.[10]

The Turkish *16th Division* positions at Sheria faced south in an arc from east to west. They were extensive and well constructed, and had interconnecting communication trenches — in a word, they were formidable. They extended some eight miles east from the Wadi esh Sheria at Hareira and the water supply two miles north at the centre, known as the Qawuqa system. For the attack on Sheria, a small dump containing 7000 rounds of 18-pounder ammunition was augmented by 1500 rounds of 4.5-inch. The eastern flank was Khuweilfe, which was held by the enemy. Most of the heavy artillery, which had hardly fired a shot since Beersheba, was still under command of GOCRA XX Corps, Brigadier Short, who grouped the Yeomanry Mounted Division guns under command of the CRA 53rd Division. All 10th Division artillery was to support just one of its brigades, the other two remaining in reserve. Short's planning recognised that he would have to move his artillery earlier in the battle rather than later, to clear advanced positions for the main attack. Short's armoury comprised the 158th and 181st heavy batteries (60-pounders), and the 378th, 383rd and 440th siege batteries.[11]

The assaulting brigade (the 229th) from Major General Girdwood's 74th Division had no preliminary bombardment, Chetwode preferring to rely on surprise. His confidence in this arrangement was based on the arduous summer training completed by these new divisions. Girdwood's CRA, Brigadier General L.J. Hext, committed his 268th Brigade RFA to support the 230th Brigade, while the 44th and 117th brigades RFA supported the 229th Infantry Brigade. The 10th Mountain Battery was also attached. The enemy had ample time to prepare trenches and redoubts and wire entanglements which they constructed with great vigour. The Sheria objective was in fact two positions — the town and the tel north of the town. From H Hour the division's attack met with mixed success and poor visibility hindered observed shooting. Nevertheless a Turkish battery was overrun, only to be retaken in a counter-attack by a determined enemy. The official historian noted that 'the advance was now carried out at extraordinary speed ... Close support by the artillery had so far been impossible owing to bad visibility, but now batteries were moved up to positions close to the line reached by the foremost troops.'

By 8.30 am the battle was all but over, its end marked by an unusual turn of events. The official historian wrote that 'A company of the 16/Sussex, seeing a battery at the head of Wadi Uxbridge firing at the troops of 229th Brigade attacked it with a Lewis gun and two rifle sections. After one drum had been fired at short range … the battery, with a personnel of 3 officers and 25 men, surrendered.' The enemy then counter-attacked, but at the *moment critique* a forward observer from the 268th Brigade 'galloped up and ranged his batteries and sent the enemy flying with shrapnel.'[12] The Black Watch captured another battery which was about to limber up and, by 1.15 pm, Sheria township had fallen. The brigades of the 10th and 60th divisions crushed the Qawuqa position and took possession of the railway station late that afternoon, while the 18-pounder brigades assisted by cutting 10-yard gaps in the wire. This left the infantry positioned for a night attack on the impressive and easily defended Tel esh Sheria (north of the station). Whether by accident or design the Turks set fire to a huge dump at night that illuminated their front. This destroyed the 60th Division's plans to attack under cover of darkness. The enemy's machine-guns played havoc with the assembled troops and no attack eventuated.[13]

For the next phase, the batteries of the 303rd RFA Brigade advanced under shellfire to support the 180th and 181st brigades on the heights, covering a zone of 180 degrees. During this encounter the CO of the 2/22nd London won a Victoria Cross leading a party of volunteers against a Turkish battery firing at point blank range, capturing both weapon and crew. The Turks counter-attacked twice and were driven back by shellfire both times, allowing the infantry to occupy the heights. XX Corps casualties totalled 1750 with 11 guns and 600 prisoners taken.[14]

Notwithstanding many of the obstacles that had come between a plan and its execution since Beersheba, XX and XXI Corps had advanced 10 miles and, with the fall of Hareira, the way was open for Chauvel to direct his cavalry towards Huj and Wadi Hesi. Coincidentally, the 60th Division, having ejected the *ahmets* from Hareira, discovered that the enemy had retired to defensive positions a mile or so to the rear with their artillery. When the Londoners made contact they were unable to continue the advance, the soldiers dropping with fatigue and, in General Shea's opinion, lacking sufficient and timely artillery support. Turkish artillery and machine-guns were dug in, skillfully used and again compelled a change of plan, effectively delaying the infantry and cavalry part of the operation. What followed then was a tragic misinterpretation of orders to General Hodgson's AMD to clear the front of the 60th Division. No artillery support was asked for or given, and in the end it was the Londoners' bayonets that won the day. The 10th Division, which was advancing west towards Hareira, had a far easier task. Its 31st Brigade, supported by the 68th RFA Brigade and C (howitzer) Battery, 268th RFA Brigade, provided a heavy bombardment as the infantry advanced, one battalion taking an encircling route. The position soon fell.[15] The gunner casualties amounted to 13 killed, 26 wounded and 29 mules and horses either killed or wounded. This engagement had an immediate effect on Turkish strategy. With the fall of Sheria and Hareira, both British corps made a joint boundary at Ataweina. In the east, Khuweilfe was ceded to the cavalry, the enemy making off, yet again taking their guns with them.[16]

Chapter 15
The drive north to Junction Station

That but this blow might be the be-all and end-all here.

Macbeth, Act I, scene v, line 7

This chapter begins with what the official historian refers to as the 'Affair of Huj' and an account of the 'Action at El Mughar' in the all-embracing context of a successful Third Gaza. This is followed by a description of the eventual occupation of Junction Station (north of the line Beersheba–Gaza and west of the Beersheba–Jerusalem road) from 8 to 18 November 1917. It ends with the capture of Jaffa. Like the previous chapter, it involves both cavalry (A&NZ Mounted Division, AMD and ICC) and the infantry of XX and XXI Corps, actions that tactically complemented one another during this broad-fronted advance.

By this stage of the prosecution of Allenby's strategy, the organisation of formations had progressed from primarily static in nature to more 'tailor made' for each aspect of his drive north to suit its different flanks. On the coastal western flank there were more brigade-sized operations by the infantry divisions in open country, and more regimental than brigade by Chauvel's corps in the more easily defended Judean Hills. The mounted corps advances resembled two arcs starting at Beersheba and curving north — the A&NZ Mounted Division on the coast and the AMD in the hills. The former followed the road from Deir Sineid to Ramleh, and the latter moved astride the railway through Sheria to Junction Station. When both formations reached the northing of Huj and Jemmameh they guarded each other's flanks and conformed to the prescribed infantry dispositions all the way to Junction Station. Possession of a workable railway system from the Suez Canal to the forthcoming operations to capture Jerusalem was vital.

This operation saw two types of artillery battles fought. The first involved RFA brigades supporting the set-piece affairs, with added weight of shell from the heavy and siege batteries. The second comprised cavalry brigades using shock tactics with fewer opportunities for supporting artillery. Both pursued with the aim of cutting off the enemy escape route or forcing him to constantly retreat, remaining at a tactical disadvantage. These operations occurred during a particular

Chapter 15

time-frame from the capture of Huj to the taking of Junction Station. The latter is an important milestone as it was the logistic centre for both Turkish armies. Strategically, control of the rail network conferred many advantages on Allenby's EEF. From here a clear run — albeit a stiff fight — to Jerusalem was on offer.

The two Australian brigades (3rd and 4th, with the 5th Mounted Brigade) of Hodgson's AMD, with the 19th RHA Brigade in tow, continued the pursuit to Huj to forestall destruction of the wells, which they were unable to prevent. The Notts Battery rattled along with the 3rd Light Horse Brigade until they approached Tel Abu Dilkah, where a brisk assault ejected the Turks and their advance continued. The gunners, experiencing the same privations as the troopers, were unable to assist them, and the initiative shifted to the cavalry as they scouted ahead.[1] Using superb bushcraft, they stalked enemy guns during the day, then attacked them from the rear, killing and capturing the detachment. Preston notes that 'it became commonplace to find a 5.9 howitzer in a hollow with the detachment dead, and the words "captured by 3 LH Brigade" written on the shield.'[2]

A Battery HAC had moved out of Beersheba and, on 5 November, had exchanged its 13-pounders for the Leicester Battery's 18-pounders, before following the 4th Light Horse Brigade to Girheir and on to Irgeig. On 7 November the battery had its first big fight of the northern drive with Grant's brigade objective the enemy position at Khirbet Buteihah. However, it was very well defended and spread over too broad an area to justify yet another charge, and its commander contemplated an attack. The only position for the battery was north of Wadi Sheria and east of the railway line. A Battery was the only artillery unit available with observation for support. Unfortunately the position was in full view of several enemy OPs, and the battery was on the receiving end of harassing fire all day. At times sections were firing 35 degrees apart, such was the plentiful choice of targets from 10.00 am to 4.00 pm. At ranges varying from 3000 to 5400 yards, their principal targets were Turkish cavalry on which they expended 274 rounds. Brigadier Grant praised the battery lavishly for its support under trying conditions. He was, as usual, leading from the front and, on occasions, pointing out targets.

By 8 November, the gunners' horses had reached their limits. They had endured 76 hours without water and were partly relieved on the evening of 9 November, unable to keep pace with Grant's men. It took eight hours to water the battery. Later they caught up with the Australians and were rested four days later. This was the price paid by the attackers in pursuit of their Turkish foe. By this stage the Turks had become a rabble and could easily have been taken prisoner but for two factors: water and German machine-gunners and artillerymen.

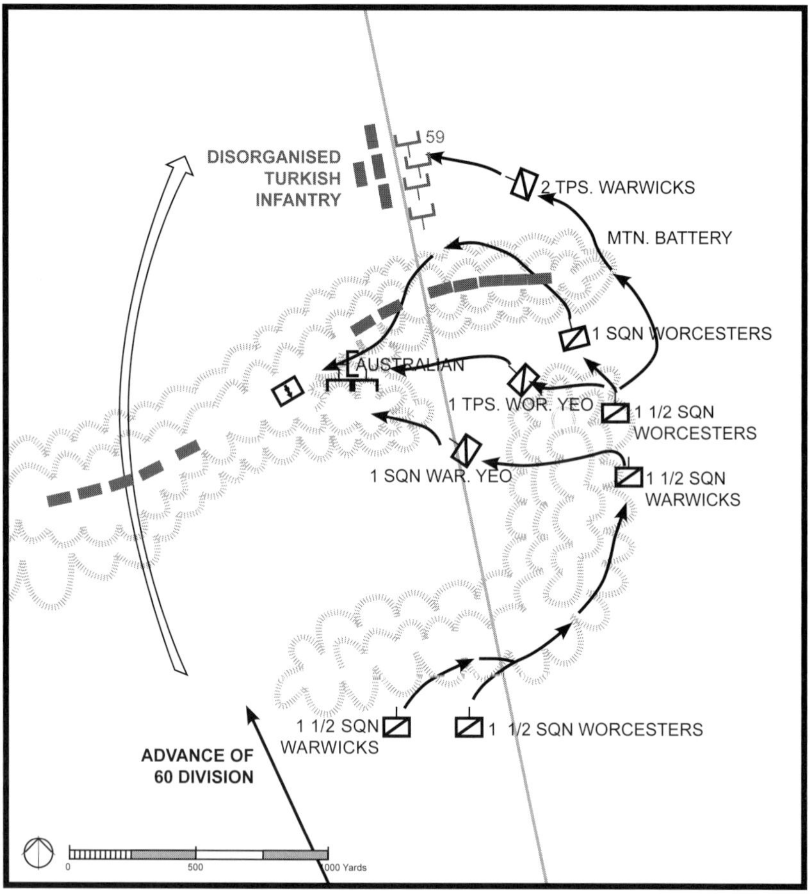

Map 10: The famous charge of the Bucks Hussars, Worcestershire and Warwickshire Yeomanrys at Huj on 8 November 1917 in which they were supported by both RGA and RFA batteries in a very economical operation. The 60th Division's Major General Shea noted that a brigade attack would have cost him 600 casualties, instead of the cavalry's 70 (source: Keogh, *Suez to Aleppo*, Map 17).

Chapter 15

A significant cavalry action by the 5th Mounted Brigade at Huj, again without artillery support, took the form of a charge initiated by Major General Shea, the 60th Division's energetic and unconventional leader.[3] The action was led by the Warwickshire and Worcestershire Yeomanrys, in all 190 sabres who, on Shea's direction to the cavalry commander, charged wielding sabres, and captured some 600 Turkish infantry, machine-gun crews and gunners who were holding up the advance. Shea believed that it would have cost his division more casualties employing a staged/set-piece assault. Such was the impromptu nature of the engagement that B Battery HAC arrived too late to assist, but noted the enormous impact of the charge on the enemy. Later the battery came under desultory fire from enemy guns and the OC went forward to investigate, but there was no action. On this occasion the Australian troopers were spectators at this spectacular demolition of the Turkish rearguard. The cavalry's booty was 11 guns (one escaped), three machine-guns and 93 prisoners amid scenes of great carnage. Other Turkish losses amounted to 110. The British cavalry charge at Huj was the last significant action of its kind in modern warfare.[4]

On 8 November the AMD reached Jemmameh and the 60th Division arrived at Huj. When the troopers reached Arak el Menshiye they found the results of several successful attacks by Salmond's airmen in the form of wrecked and burned out aircraft, and a prize of one aircraft still in its German packing crates. The next day the 5th and 7th Light Horse regiments, moving forward aggressively to Bureir with the A&NZ Mounted Division, surprised the Turks and captured 390 prisoners, two guns and 110 wagons, losses the Turks could ill afford but whose wretched condition explained it all. This force then had to endure three hours of Turkish shellfire and took some casualties of its own. The 3rd Light Horse Brigade (8th, 9th and 10th Light Horse regiments) was tasked with capturing Jemmameh on 9 November with the infantry of the 60th Division available if the Turks became troublesome. The regiment had already been 33 hours without water. Following the Zuheillah Wadi they met stiff opposition and their accompanying Notts Battery provided enfilade fire from Wadi Saleh. They closed the distance, unlimbered and engaged targets at close range, earning the praise of Brigadier Wilson. At Kustine the following day the Australians rounded up another 300 prisoners and 100 wagons. In their enterprising way, their leaders were never confounded by their situation. A squadron commander from the 7th Light Horse Regiment captured a party of Turks using a simple deception. He yelled: 'You are surrounded' in Turkish following a 'parley' with their senior officer. An enterprising Lieutenant Owen Tooth also singlehandedly captured a gun at Jemah.[5]

B Battery HAC rejoined the advance in support of the 5th Mounted Brigade near Hareira, its commander ordering the battery to split into sections for several minor engagements. Turkish artillery was active and, on 9 November, the battery engaged the enemy over open sights with Lieutenant Barney as OPO while the Gloucester Yeomanry was harassing its opponents. The Essex Battery joined the brigade to relieve the Londoners, who retired to water their horses which had been 76 hours without a drink. This was not entirely unusual at this stage of the drive (13 November), as the gunners themselves had been without rations for two days. Lieutenant Jones had been in charge of watering and lost his way when seeking to return to his guns. He finally arrived at their Junction Station gun area at 3.00 am on 18 November, such were the hazards of coping with new terrain in the dark. The next day the battery reached Burej before being attached to the 5th Mounted Brigade and moving on to Latron for a well-earned rest.

At times there was little scope for RHA and RFA batteries to engage the Turkish gunners. On occasion the campaign devolved into a cavalry show, in which against all doctrinal teaching, the sabre was re-emerging as a 'shock weapon' rather than remaining in scabbards in the dustbin of history. The Turks feared the Australian light horsemen without swords and the British cavalry with them. The Turkish rearguards were always supported by their artillery and, at Ebdis and Biet Duras, the troopers were a proxy for counter-battery artillery. On 8 November, for example, Lieutenant G.L.H. Mueller of the 9th Light Horse Regiment was instrumental in his troop's immobilisation of Turkish gun teams through the simple expedient of shooting the animals. In this manner, Lieutenants W.H. Lilley and F.J. McGregor captured a 5.9-inch howitzer and 'despatched' its motive power before moving on. The 9th added yet another scalp when, as Gullett described, 'Lieutenant L. M. S. Hargraves' troop together with that of P. T. Smith had a similar fight for a 15 cm [150mm] gun. The Turks advanced to save the piece but were held up by fire from the troopers, while Hargraves and Smith charged them with a small party, and destroyed the team.' Lieutenant Borbridge and his troop from the 8th Light Horse Regiment pursued two guns while under fire. He dismounted his troop, shot the team of one and forced the other to overturn, capturing both guns. On 9 November four howitzers, 100 wagons and 300 prisoners were captured at Ebdis. They were in action when the 7th Light Horse Regiment rode them down. The 6th Light Horse Regiment also captured guns at Jemah, and the chalked words '10th LH' adorned the shield of a captured Turkish gun.[6]

The 52nd Division, moving via Hamame, and the 75th Division, pushing through Deir Sineid, slowly pushed north with their infantry, the former along the coast. With the 1st Light Horse Brigade in the vanguard, the Scots gunners, shooting from a ridge, put two 77mm guns out of action at Summeil. At this time A Battery HAC was tagging along with the 4th Light Horse Brigade. Its destination was Wadi Hesi, known for its watering places. The battery teams were 'poorly', having last watered at a muddy, worm-infested pool 40 hours before. The delight of the drivers soon turned to dismay and astonishment when the horses were led to running water — and refused to drink it. 'After two years and seven months of continuous active service … it was necessary to have experienced, in order to realize the feelings running water produces, to reach this spot. But the irony of it.' This situation was all the more ironic as, two days previously, a thunderstorm had drenched the division, rendering the going 'abominable' for double teams on the one hand, but enlivening the horses and refreshing the troops who had not washed for days, on the other.[7]

While the Turks had lost another four howitzers at Kustine, they still had plenty of fight. On 11 November they retired to Burkusie, registering known watering spots along the way as productive targets for their artillery. Water could only be secured from deep wells, which meant that watering a squadron took many hours and one regiment as much as 17 hours. There were two sites of major encounters in this area. The first was at Summeil where Hodgson, guided by his orders from Chauvel, was keen to concentrate his division to attack on the morning of 11 November. However this was impossible in terms of 'time and space' — moving 7500 horses with their supply train during the night — and new orders were issued. Chauvel was man enough to admit that he had underestimated the difficulties, not the least of which was the substantial enemy force opposing him. For the next battle at Balin and Burkusie on 12 November, Hodgson faced some 4000 Turks. A Battery HAC had temporarily deployed to provide essential support, sending its horses to water at Faluje, four miles to the rear, before it moved forward. When the battle opened for Burkusie the only way the battery could increase range to reach its targets was to dig pits for the trails. This enabled the gunners to reach 8400 yards with their HE. Faluje was discovered to have no suitable water and food supply, and only water found in an obscure little village enabled the battery to water its horses over the period of a day. The Inverness and Notts batteries at Esdud and Burkusie respectively on 9 and 12 November engaged the Turks on Berkusie ridge 'with good effect'.[8]

While the cavalry was thrusting ahead in the hinterland, Bulfin set about wresting the coastal sector from the Turks. North of Gaza, three miles in from the coastline at Wadi Hesi, the Turks had constructed a fortified line along Sausage ridge (three miles long, oriented north-south), the northern end of which was anchored at Burbera. This protected their withdrawal route through Ashkelon and Nalia. The 157th Brigade with a reinforced 264th RFA Brigade (three A batteries — one from the 262nd RFA Brigade) in support was ordered to lay up in front of the village of Herbie. Two-thirds of the guns were north of the wadi and the remainder south of it, where the 6th Highland Light Infantry was in position. The 157th's brigadier sneaked one of his battalions undetected to the mouth of the water's edge of the wadi. This part of the plan went well. Another brigade (the 155th) with its artillery support then attacked up the ridge and was over the top by 12.30 pm. Its infantry gained and lost ground four times in hard fighting, until the issue was resolved by a battalion flank attack from the 6th Highland Light Infantry at 9.00 pm that finally succeeded, again after a stiff fight. While the infantry were embroiled the gunners were duelling with four field batteries of the *7th Division*, two howitzers and one heavy ('5.9') howitzer, as well as two 100mm high velocity guns. The guns were well concealed and observers had difficulty locating them with any degree of accuracy.[9] After the battle the enemy realised his flank had been turned and withdrew in good order, again thwarting any encirclement.

Allenby proposed to turn the Turkish line at that point if his troopers could take the line Et Tinah–Beit Duras. The A&NZ Mounted Division, acting as a screen for the infantry, advanced to El Mejdel, 13 miles north-east of Gaza, and had entered these two settlements by evening. On 10 November it was joined by the 52nd and 75th divisions. The next defended line was the river Nahr Sukherier, 15 miles north; however, as Bulfin's corps drive lost momentum, the Turks reorganised and constructed defences. Allenby's objective was Junction Station. This lay behind another 20-mile defensive line along the Wadi Surar and Nahr Rubin occupied by some 20,000 rifles in good defensive positions at Qatra and El Mughar. The line brought the two armies face to face. This flank was defended by von Kressenstein's *Eighth Army* (*XX* and *XXII corps* — six divisions, including one in reserve), in total some 9000 rifles and 60 guns. Allenby's plan would see the DMC advance north to work the coastal plain and turn the Turk's right flank from El Kubeibe to Beit Jibrin. Slightly to the rear of the cavalry came the marching infantry with brigades well forward to tackle any enemy in a set-piece attack, such as at Burka. Once the flank was turned it would open the way to Junction Station. A feature of the execution of this plan was the way Chauvel used Chaytor's A&NZ Mounted Division brigades responding to the various fighting abilities of his opponents, from strong and determined to willing surrenders. On 14 November he also strengthened Hodgson's AMD, increasing it to five mounted brigades, the 2nd, 3rd and 4th Light Horse, and the 5th and 7th Yeomanry. While at this time the Turks under Refet Pasha (*XXII Corps*) were withdrawing along interior lines and some of their formations were in poor shape, a reading of Gullett and Farndale confirms that they still had much artillery that was well handled, as were their machine-guns. Their rearguards continued to shell the 54th Division deployed around the town. Their infantry, thus stiffened, was resolute in retreat and ruined Allenby's plan of encirclement and destruction of the enemy corps as a fighting force. Turkish resilience and the impact of the EEF's water supply problems were probably the most significant factors in the demise of Allenby's plan. Interestingly, interrogation of enemy prisoners revealed that they feared attack from the air at this time more than field operations.

Close to the coast on 12 November the 1st Light Horse Brigade's regiments, along with the Ayrshire Battery, prepared for an advance north from Esdud, the 1st and 2nd Light Horse regiments advancing while the 3rd faced enemy cavalry east at El Butani el Charibye in the foothills. The 1st's advance came to a sudden halt as the troopers attempted to cross the Wadi el Khubb.[10] The wadi and the bridge across the Wadi Sukereir, which the 2nd Light Horse Regiment was crossing, had been registered by Turkish artillery and both groups of horsemen were heavily and accurately shelled, causing delays and inflicting casualties. However, the 2nd Light Horse Regiment had the Scots gunners behind it and, after a keen firefight in the dunes, the light horsemen occupied the heights, providing the brigade a bridgehead from Jisr Esdud to Burqa. Burqa was the objective of the 156th Brigade, with the 264th RFA Brigade in support on the Australians' right flank. The Lowlanders and Gurkhas had a very tough fight to take the town. Their attack began at 7.00 am on 13 November and some of the 75th Division's field and corps heavy artillery was detached in support. Included was the South African Field Artillery Brigade, contributing with the 189th and 380th Heavy and Siege batteries in a 60-minute softening-up bombardment. The infantry plan was a two-pronged, three-phase attack, with the Yeomanry Division as flank protection with the 75th Division's 232nd, 233rd and 224th RFA brigades and B Battery, 9th Mountain Brigade. The Berks Battery also supported the 5th Mounted Brigade during another cavalry action by neutralising enemy fire.[11]

The 5th was relieved by the 7th Mounted Brigade whose Essex Battery horses were in better condition than B Battery HAC's teams then at Ijseir. The 7th's commander altered these arrangements and the B Battery guns were then forced to push on to El Kustine. A young subaltern, 'Lieutenant Barney was given the unenviable task of finding the Divisional Train [for relief teams] and then leading the horses in darkness across 10 miles of unknown country to the battery position. Starting at dusk, he carried out this difficult task successfully, picked up the guns and detachments, and brought them safely back to Div. HQ at El Kustine.'[12]

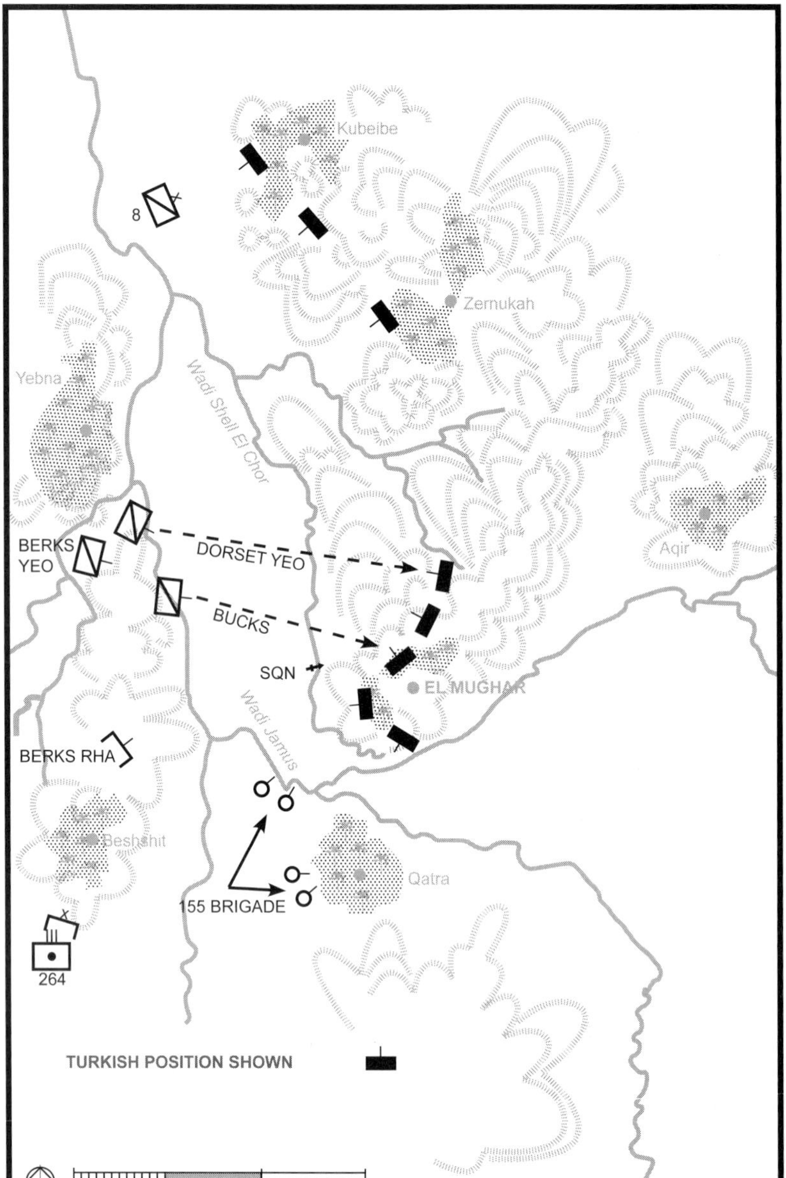

Map 11: The action at El Mughar by the 5th Mounted Brigade's Dorset Yeomanry and Bucks Yeomanry on 13 November 1917, supported by the Berkshire Battery RHA and the 18-pounder guns of the 155th Infantry Brigade's artillery (source: Keogh, *Suez to Aleppo*, Map 21).

Chapter 15

The advance continued with the capture of Tel el Turmus.[13] The 155th Brigade, supported by the 261st and 264th RFA brigades and the mountain gunners, took Beshshit and reached Qatra and El Mughar. Burqa was a key centre of Turkish transportation, as the line from Ramleh (to the north) went east to Jerusalem. Jerusalem was the 52nd Division's objective, its attached yeomanry tasked with opening up the route. In the attack on the tel, approved by the GOC of the yeomanry (Barrow) and the GOC infantry (Hill), the Dorset Yeomanry and Bucks Hussars were to envelop the right Turkish flank from Yebna, deciding that this offered the better option for crossing 3000 yards of open country.[14] This they did, but not before the reserve cavalry of the Berkshire Yeomanry joined the fray and completed the action. All this (inflicting severe Turkish losses and taking 1100 prisoners) was accomplished without a round of artillery fire, as if to demonstrate that against rifle and machine-gun fire, the cavalry were supreme. The cavalry lost one officer and 15 soldiers killed and six and 106 wounded, while the horses suffered most — 265 killed or wounded at a time when good horse stocks were precious. This allowed the 52nd Division to close on Junction Station.[15]

The Turks were pressing forward, urged on by their leaders despite their privations. Having interior lines allowed their reinforcements to detrain and arrive fresh for an attack. This occurred at Et Tine and, with cavalry support, the enemy moved quickly south to embarrass the 5th Yeomanry Brigade and the 9th Light Horse Regiment, which were forced to withdraw. The night passed with the AMD commanders expecting an early morning assault. At dawn the brigade commander ordered the Notts Battery to shell the enemy positions and the Turks retreated north. On 18 November the 3rd and 4th Light Horse brigades and their artillery withdrew to the Wadi Sukerier for a rest. The gunners were located in an orange grove with abundant water. The brigade had left its logistic support behind, so the men rested for four days. They had not washed since 28 October and the horses had not been unsaddled for 48 hours. B Battery HAC at Abu Sushe had endured similar privations en route, and was fortunate that its men were masters of horse handling. In nine days and 100 miles they lost only nine horses to exhaustion.[16]

On 14 November Chaytor continued his northerly march from Nahr Rubin. The 1st Light Horse Brigade made for Ramleh and the NZMR Brigade for Jaffa, the Aucklanders' orders to 'demonstrate'. However their CO was far more adventurous than his general, and pitted his regiment against the defences. The Turks uncharacteristically defended by attacking with grenades and fixed bayonets. This rendered artillery support problematic, even though the Berks and Somerset batteries were on hand. In the resulting hand-to-hand fighting Jaffa was taken with Turkish casualties of 162 killed and a large number wounded. The Kiwis lost one officer and 20 soldiers killed and nine officers and 78 soldiers wounded.[17] The CO of the Aucklanders had interpreted his orders more liberally than his GOC had intended, having been told not to occupy the town if there was any resistance. It was not until later in the day that Chauvel ventured to tell Allenby how far he had advanced.

These battles signified that the route to Jerusalem would now be open, as Junction Station had been taken by two armoured cars. Its capture was a godsend for the thirsty horses and troops, the site equipped with a steam pumping plant for delivering welcome water supplies. The capture of Junction Station cut the railway to Jerusalem, but it was also necessary to cut the road north of the line to isolate the city leaving only the route to Ramleh in the north.[18] Accordingly, the cavalry and Ryrie's 1st Light Horse Brigade, with the Inverness Battery in support, advanced to the orange groves of Ramleh and continued to Ludd. In both places they received a demonstrative welcome from the Jewish locals. During the brigade's pursuit east along the road to Wilhemnia, a German settlement, they rounded up more Turkish stragglers while enemy artillery shelled the settlement.[19] The next night the Light Horse brigades occupied the heights from Hill 265 to the sea at Summeil, and looked down on the Wadi Auja along a line Turmus–Tel el Safi–Kezaz.

The official historian's casualty count during this period was:

	KIA + WIA	MIA/POWs	Total[20]
British Forces:	1339	N/A	c. 1500
Turkish Forces:	500-1000	1469	2–2500

The loss of Ramleh and El Mughar was a serious blow to the Turks, particularly as Ramleh was connected by rail to Jerusalem. It also saw the Turkish front divided, and this was exploited vigorously by the AMD and yeomanry formations. Allenby now ordered his two infantry divisions to push on to Jerusalem. The valley that eventually led to the rail terminus there was well served with defensive positions, a fact known only to biblical scholars and historians (including Allenby).

Chapter 16
Allenby takes Jerusalem

And when strife is fierce and warfare long, steals on the air a distant triumph song, and hearts are brave again and arms strong.

W.W. How (1823–1897)

The 'seed' event that led to the eventual capture of Jerusalem began at Jaffa, its seaport, on 16 November where the RN landed supplies on the beaches at night within range of the Turkish guns. By this time the Turkish *Seventh Army* had retreated to another defensive line north of the Nahr Auja, and Hodgson's AMD was given the task of maintaining pressure on the enemy. The AMD now comprised three light horse brigades (the 2nd, 3rd and 4th) and the 5th and 7th mountain brigades, plus two armoured cars to watch over the line Turmus–Tel el Safi–Kezaz. The Turkish formations were forced to move their supplies from Nablus, 40 miles from Jerusalem, as the loss of Ramleh had cut their railway link with Jerusalem. The possession of the railway network and consolidation of a firm front line were vital to Allenby's thrust towards the Holy City in the last weeks of November. The War Office enjoined him to 'exploit his success to the utmost' and he wasted no time in doing so.

Allenby abandoned his first plan of capturing the 'two Aujas' — the Nahr Auja on the coast and the Wadi Auja eastwards — and the high country. He had four alternatives. First was to strike up the north coast to draw Turkish forces away from Jerusalem, similar to his Beersheba strategy only in reverse. The second was to use his cavalry (Chauvel's Yeomanry Mounted Division) to cut the Nablus–Jerusalem road at Bireh, 10 miles north of Jerusalem. The third was to capture Nebi Samwil and Latron with an eastern push by his cavalry and infantry across a broad (20-mile) front such as the topography would allow. Finally, he could sneak up the Hebron road, take the Mount of Olives behind Jerusalem, and cut the Jericho road. There he had 'Mott's Detachment' — the 53rd Division less a brigade and the Westminster Dragoons. The latter was at Dhaheriye, 30 miles away. Eventually, Allenby's corps commanders employed all three options, with the weight of arms pointing north-east and east.

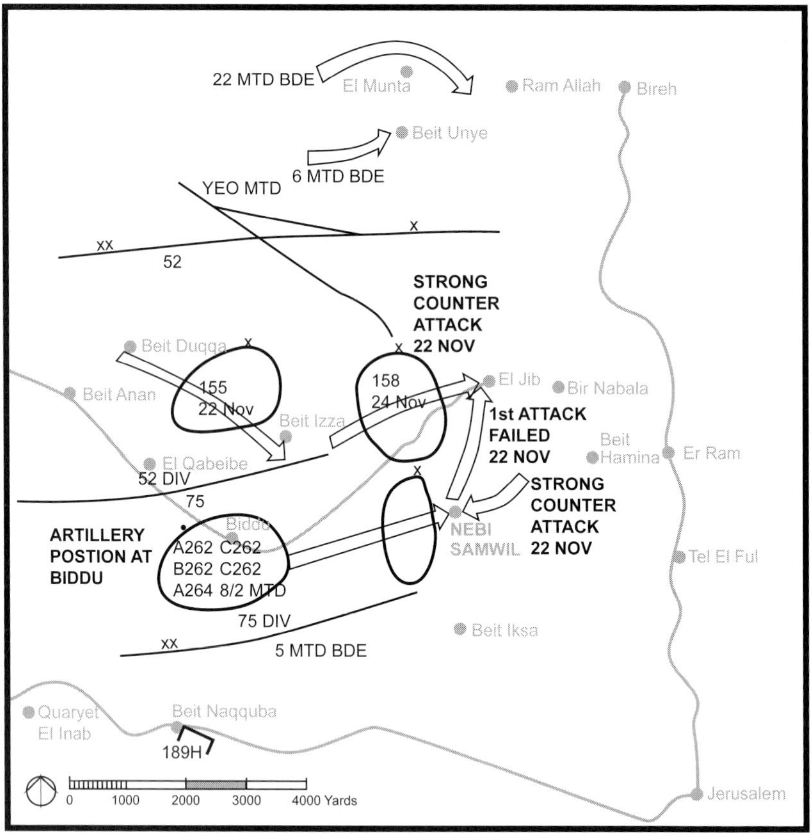

Map 12. The front at Jerusalem in the November attacks involving the infantry divisions and the artillery brigaded at Biddu.

Chapter 16

Any thrust towards Jerusalem other than the more direct eastern push involved a much bigger logistic tail and was best served by using the Junction Station area as a base. Allenby had an important caveat to his plans — there must be no destruction of holy places. He assiduously sought to avoid any collateral damage to Jerusalem. The Judean Hills had been fought over for centuries and had a history of being good defensive country. Thus his tactics would resemble those used in ancient biblical history to isolate Jerusalem, approaching the city from the Judean road via Bireh where it crosses the Judean range between Nablus and the Holy City.

The period from 18 November until the capture of Jerusalem on 9 December was characterised by three main thrusts, all presenting different problems for the deployment of field and heavy artillery and for observation. The first thrust originated from the western end of the 40-mile front line on the Nahr Auja north of Jaffa. The second would see forces move along the Nablus road via the Kereina–Biddu track through rugged country to isolate Jerusalem from the hills (notably the high ground around Nebi Samwil). The third comprised the eastern thrust along the El Qastal–Lifta track. From the northern coast inland Allenby's forces stretched along a 32-mile arc from Jaffa to Beit Jibrin. Mott's detachment kept the Turkish left flank under surveillance. The north-east approach featured poor roads and logistic difficulties that appeared almost prohibitive. Gullett noted that 'Allenby's plan was simple in design but extremely difficult in execution' and aimed to divide the Turkish *Seventh* and *Eighth armies* of nine infantry divisions and one cavalry. The Yeomanry Division from Ludd was to advance rapidly towards Birein. The AMD would lead two infantry divisions along the Jerusalem road to Kuret el Enab, then continue north-east until they intersected the Nablus road, protected by the 5th Mountain Brigade. The 53rd Division to the south would dominate the Jericho road and cut off Jerusalem from the east.[1]

Allenby's GHQ was still on the coast at Um el Kelab (north of Gaza and close to the 5th Air Wing). At the beginning of the first phase his dispositions were:

- DMC (A&NZ Mounted Division): Jaffa and Nahr Auja opposed by the *7th Corps*
- XXI Corps: 54th Division, with the 75th Division in reserve; 52nd Division, 7th Mounted Brigade and yeomanry divisions (both opposed by the *3rd Corps*), the 60th and 74th divisions and Mott's Force (53rd Division less one brigade and Westminster Dragoons)

Allenby planned to use his numerical and logistical superiority to maintain momentum across his broad front, notwithstanding the poor lateral linkages between his divisions.[2]

Bulfin and Chauvel were appointed 'joint commanders' for this operation, a sensible arrangement considering the complexity of his plan. While this force possessed impressive field artillery assets it was unable to deploy them with the same ease it had enjoyed over the previous month. Only a handful of batteries could provide the infantry the support they had come to expect and only at significant times and places. Weather, terrain and the courage and resilience of the Turkish infantry had to be overcome before tactical victories could be claimed. The road from Junction Station through the Judean Hills presented excellent opportunities for defence. During the wet winter season the roads became impassable and the rugged, hilly terrain was barely able to support wildlife. The Jaffa–Jerusalem road was the only one available to Bulfin's XXI Corps for logistic support as it wound east through the valleys and passes. Even this route soon deteriorated from heavy use which made for very slow movement in either direction and created severe logistic problems requiring drastic solutions from all of Allenby's three corps. But this was good artillery and infantry country for the enemy defence, and Chauvel's troopers met accurate, hostile fire every step of the way once they turned their attention to the east and Jerusalem. Allenby's timetable was ambitious and, in less than a month, the Turkish forces with their German advisers 'were slowly but surely forced back from one position to another'.[3]

On 18 November Chauvel ordered the AMD to capture Bireh on the Nablus road, 12 miles north of Latron and five miles from Jerusalem. The force first struck the enemy at Amwas, a key centre on the track. The AMD's RHA batteries and a battery from the 75th Division opened fire on the Turks while the 3rd Light Horse Brigade attempted an encircling manoeuvre around the Turkish right flank. The AMD advanced four miles in eight hours despite the effectiveness of the artillery, frustrating the commanders who considered such an effort more typical of the infantry. However the Australian brigade's action prompted the Turks to evacuate their position overnight, abandoning four guns, their teams killed by the 13-pounders. The next day the 75th Division resumed the advance.

The 8th and 22nd mounted brigades had been tasked to advance, their aim to divide the *Eighth Army*. By this time support from the RHA brigade's animal-drawn guns on wheels had become problematic. Manhandling them forward was the only way and, to their credit, the herculean efforts of the gunners saw the guns moved several thousand yards, keeping pace with the cavalry. The mounted brigades occupied six miles of track, their movement and tactical deployment restricted, as was logistic support in ammunition, supplies, medical and other necessities. At the end of the day the 8th Mounted Brigade reached Beit Ur el Tahta and, by the evening, the 22nd Mounted Brigade had reached Shilta. At times the movement of the guns was beyond the capability of the horse teams. As Preston noted, it sometimes required half an hour's reconnaissance to move forward just half a mile.[4] The Hants Battery reported that it was unable to proceed along its axis, such was the wretched state of the 'going'. The Hong Kong and Singapore Mountain Battery also advanced on a parallel axis and, being camel mounted and requiring 600 animals to sustain it, made better progress. The RHA brigade was desperately short of ammunition of both types and, at that point, received its first reinforcements, who 'were very welcome as old hands were showing signs of wear'.[5] That night (19 November) heavy rains began to fall and added enormously to the difficulties of moving wheeled vehicles. Horses stumbled and fell down ravines or died from exposure, and camels did likewise, their Egyptian drivers occasionally electing to expire alongside them in pools of icy water.

To their west the Turks chose two features, Abu Sushe and Tel Jezar, en route to Jerusalem, to mount their defence. This route lent itself to continual rearguard actions, a technique the Turk had honed to a fine art, and one that suited his temperament as an infantryman. It also ensured that the advancing troops could always guarantee Turkish shelling, which for the most part remained unanswered, the siege and heavy guns out of range given the lack of firing platforms.[6] On 18 November Bulfin directed XX Corps' 75th Division and the Yeomanry Division to press towards Latron, requiring Brigadier Godwin's 6th Mountain Brigade to cross the three miles of open country that led to Abu Sushe and its defenders. This time the Berks Battery had several batteries of the 52nd Division's field artillery to assist in what was a repeat performance of Mughar where the combined artilleries 'made great execution. The support given by the guns was of critical importance and saved many casualties.'[7] Gullett wrote that 'the Yeomanry was led with fine judgment by their regimental officers.' This action resulted in 37 casualties — the Turks suffered 400 to 500 casualties with 360 prisoners taken.

In the centre of the front Bulfin prepared to attack Latron with extra support for the 75th Division. The division's infantry were still in summer dress when the rains began, but 'soldiered on' in shivering silence. They were veterans of 'campaigns in the Indian frontier hills and familiar with mountain fighting', so they were undoubtedly better off than their less experienced colleagues. Bulfin ordered Hodgson's AMD to force the Turks from Latron using the 3rd and 4th Light Horse brigades which had been involved in protecting the flanks.

The village ramparts were formidable, to the extent that the troopers had to lead their mounts. To their rear was the Notts Battery, which was moved forward 'with some difficulty' in preparation. The battery's observer spotted a Turkish gun position of four guns close to Amwas (further east) and, as Gullett described, 'these the Gunners silenced at a range of 5,000 yards, and when they attempted to withdraw with their guns, the Notts gunners opened "rapid fire" on them.' Their expenditure totalled 189 rounds.[8] Hodgson nonetheless ordered a temporary withdrawal.

It was the enemy's stubbornness that forced the two cavalry brigades into the next fight. One brigade was to envelop Latron from the north, the other to mount a direct assault. On 18 November, in a left hook manoeuvre, the 3rd Light Horse Brigade reached a village called Yalo, 4000 yards east of Latron. The Turkish commander feared envelopment and withdrew his screening force from the village. Hodgson's 75th Division's plans for the attack were then cancelled.[9] The guns were found abandoned the next day by the British infantry. At this time B Battery HAC, 9th Mountain Brigade RGA, and the 12th Light Armoured Battery protected the right flank of the 75th Division which had captured Saris. Probing the Turkish flanks relentlessly, their advance was incremental, often costly. The gunners, advancing laboriously, were delayed by clever route destruction and their full support was sorely missed, sections having to do the work of batteries. Good targets and gun positions were scarce in this infantry war, but casualties were not. Bulfin ordered the 52nd Division to relieve the 75th, and later the 60th Division was moved from reserve.[10]

The 52nd Division had two objectives, Burka and Brown Hill, requiring Brigadier Massy to split his guns and utilise a section of 60-pounders and a battery from the 264th RFA Brigade for the assault on Burka. For the attack on Brown Hill, two batteries of the 264th and the ubiquitous Hong Kong and Singapore Mountain Battery were escorted by the 4th Royal Scots Fusiliers and a company of the 8th Cameronians. However their ammunition supplies were insufficient for such an important mission. The start line was Esdud. The Scots artillery was ineffective and the Turks retaliated with shrapnel, much of it too high. In the event, both attacks evolved into rifle and machine-gun firefights. By 20 November the roads had deteriorated to such an extent that two brigades of the division had to forgo fighting to become road-builders so that the heavy artillery could reach Biddu by 23 November for the attacks on Nebi Samwil.[11]

From 21 November the 52nd Division became hostage to the rains. The infantry advanced regardless, aware that their guns had been left behind. However, the Scots gunners were given their route and, with their gun teams often doubled, and against all that Mother Nature could place in their path, moved their guns — sometimes with 100 men on drag ropes — eventually hauling them up the hills (2500 feet) to their gun positions. The first to arrive was a howitzer from C Battery, 273rd RFA, which came into action at Biddu. The infantry's route took them along the Roman road to Kubeibeh at Dukka. Turkish interference was minimal and, by the time the division reached Beit Anan, it had suffered only 17 casualties from shellfire. Its security rested with the cavalry, and a patrol of the Hyderabad Lancers from the 75th Division reached the 157th Brigade to report that the front was clear and that Kuryet el Enab was theirs.[12]

Given the terrain, the artillery staff decided to concentrate guns that could cover the wide northern sector of the front. A gun position was found at Biddu which would accommodate as many of the guns as could be moved there. From this area they could concentrate their artillery to cover the Turkish front from El Jib (northern) to Nebi Samwil (southern). The route was via Beit Anan through Beit Izza. It required 'superhuman efforts, and the use of every horse available … to make 10 horse teams … to push forward four 4.5 inch howitzers and six 18 pounders of 264th RFA Brigade.' Later they were joined by C Battery, 37th Brigade howitzers and a section of the 189th Heavy Battery. This broke the cardinal rule of dispersion, but that mattered less than the support they could provide. Eventually seven positions were occupied by:

B Battery, 9th Mountain Brigade RFA
C Battery, 37th Brigade RFA
one section each of A and B batteries, 262nd Brigade RFA
one section, A Battery, 264th Brigade RFA
one section A and B batteries, 262nd Brigade RFA
C batteries from the 261st and 264th brigades RFA

Biddu was some 3000 yards from Nebi Samwil and 4000 yards from El Jib. The section of the 189th Heavy Battery (60-pounders) fired from the Jaffa–Jerusalem road at Beit Naqquba. However, the honour of firing the first rounds at Jerusalem went to a Glasgow howitzer battery.[13]

The artillery's concentration in reserve at Ramleh had been noticed by German airmen whose subsequent bombing attack killed 32 horses. Its position at the end of an ammunition supply chain that extended for 45 miles over shocking tracks meant that this setback and the effects of the bad weather took their toll on the artillery. The Hants Horse Gunners supporting the mounted division required 3000 rounds of 13-pounder ammunition and a section of the

BAC under Lieutenant Worthington was ambushed by two machine-guns while bringing it forward. He was killed, as were three gunners and three were wounded (four were missing). Fifty horses were killed in this action. With ammunition resupply a critical factor, the cavalry and infantry could ill afford such losses.[14]

At this point of the campaign Headquarters RA was at Kuryet el Nab and an observation balloon section at Saris. Support became a cooperative exercise. Batteries handed over guns and wagons to other formations, reduced manning to a minimum, and attached and detached the heavy and siege gun sections in range almost on a daily basis. Guns were placed under command of infantry brigade commanders (Thatcher's under the 180th Brigade and the 302nd Battery to the 179th Brigade). While positions for 18-pounders were at a premium, there was ample room for the 4.5-inch howitzers. However an observation balloon at Sakia was soon shot down, to the disappointment of the artillery staff.[15]

Nebi Samwil, where the Turks were strongly entrenched, was also a key to Jerusalem. The battle began on 21 November with an action by the Yeomanry Division a few miles north of where it set off to capture Beituniye and El Muntar (with the 6th and 8th mounted brigades), both on the approaches to Ramallah (the objective of the 22nd Mounted Brigade) and half a mile short of Bireh on the north road. Its supporting artillery was the Hong Kong and Singapore Mountain Battery. Farndale describes the division's travails that day: 'One section … by sheer determination got their little guns as far as El Muntar where they engaged Turkish batteries over open sights at some 2,000 yards. Their camels' feet were bleeding as they almost lifted the animals laden with ammunition over boulders and rock. Each time they fired they drew fire of many guns onto them — yet they fired away to great effect that day.' The yeomanry mounted brigades were unable to reach their objectives, their horses used to 'pack' supplies to them. The fiercest fighting of the campaign involving the Yeomanry Division took place on this front.[16]

Bulfin then ordered the 75th Division to lead the advance and capture Nebi Samwil, the 52nd allocated a reserve position until its turn came to defend the vital feature following its capture by the 75th. The 234th Brigade's attack on 21 November was far more profitable given the successful registration of targets by its artillery support. The Turks made repeated counter-attacks to recapture the feature, but were driven back by a steadfast defence and such artillery as could be brought to bear.[17] The next day the brigade attempted to take El Jib, but failed given a lack of coordinated support and the mettle of the desperate Turkish infantry. During the advance and attack phases, both the 75th and 52nd were under constant, if sporadic shellfire which added to an already grim casualty count.[18] The task of capturing El Jib was given to the 156th Brigade, and its attack was launched on 24 November from Beit Izza (captured by the 155th Brigade on 22 November), its success largely due to the combined fire of the guns at Biddu. However there were anxious moments, both at 157th Brigade headquarters when the Turks fired 120 rounds at the position and when the Turkish infantry assaulted a battery of the Lowlanders, but were repelled.[19] Weather conditions at the time were atrocious, and it says much for the stamina and resolution of the Scots and Indian infantry and gunners to have survived, much less triumphed in such conditions. No further progress could be made. The Turks were not going to give up Jerusalem and, as Gullett wrote, 'The Turks had succeeded in fighting the 75th and 52nd Divisions to a standstill.' Unable to bring the full weight of their establishment artilleries to bear, and appreciating the now desperate plight of the Turks, Allenby moved the 60th and 74th divisions forward, and their firepower, assisted by the return of fine weather, tipped the scales. Allenby relieved XXI Corps with XX Corps a week later.[20]

At this time the British front still extended from the mouth of the Auja through the Nebi Samwil salient to the west of Jerusalem. The 4th Light Horse and the 7th Mounted Brigade, now much reduced in strength, then moved into the line and the AMD came under Bulfin's XXI Corps orders to cover a four-mile front — dominated by hills, ridges and narrow gorges — east to Beit el Tatha. They achieved this with the use of patrols. To their left was the 75th Division, with the 10th Division on its right. Between them was the Kereina track. Should the Turk make a central thrust south, Allenby's plans would be in tatters. It was vital that the Turks be permitted no respite lest they reinforce Jerusalem and make Allenby's objective unnecessarily difficult and costly. The Turks invested a great deal of offensive effort in their artillery north of the Wadi Auja and attempts by the force to hold a line north of the Auja from Tel Abu Zeitun to the sea at Nalin were unsuccessful. In response, a like-minded Allenby deployed the Canterbury and Auckland Mounted Rifles, 2nd Light Horse Regiment, 4th Company of the Camel Brigade, and two battalions of the 54th Division with the 161st Brigade in reserve to cover the Wadi Auja. The cavalry and infantry were supported by the guns of the Somerset Battery, the guns of A Battery, 271st RFA Brigade and C Battery, 272nd RFA Brigade. On 25 November bridges crossing the Nahr were accurately shelled and assaulted by 1000 Turkish infantry who occupied the tactically important Bald Hill on the southern bank of the Nahr. The highly respected Major Bryant, BC of the Ayrshire RHA Battery, was killed during this assault. A battalion of the 54th Division was also ejected from Wilhelmia on 27 November by a well-executed attack. At this point the commanders surmised that the *Eighth Army* was uninterested in territorial gain for its own sake.

Brigadier Ryrie planned an attack to retake Bald Hill — now occupied by around 500 Turks — and advance to the Nahr. The next day he ordered Brigadier Smith of the Cameleers to reclaim it, using a barrage as cover for their dash. Some 730 Cameleers found the Turks on the southern slopes, dispersing them with a bayonet charge in which they were assisted by the 6th Light Horse Regiment. Unfortunate mistimings saw 22 light horsemen wounded and one killed by the time the action concluded. At nearby Wilhelmia the 54th Division faced a similar situation, and this part of the front was stabilised. Allenby's plan to use the Nahr Auja as a 'magnet' to prevent the Turkish *Eighth Army* reinforcing the Jerusalem front was vindicated, and he was able to use his 60th and 74th divisions in their intended role. As Gullett noted, Allenby's plan had been 'richly rewarded'.

Following the successful 157th Brigade attack on Nebi Samwil, the division was ordered to rest. Now considerably under strength, the 155th Brigade led it to the coast and much-needed respite. The brigade historian noted that, as they moved, ragged, footsore and in other stages of dishevelment, they passed a light horse encampment. Learning of the much reduced strength of their 'lusty battalions', the Australians 'cheered as only brave, strong men can cheer when their feelings are deeply stirred.' Such adulation was, unfortunately, short-lived for, instead of a well-deserved period of rest, recuperation and reorganisation, a serious Turkish attack erupted on Beit Ur el Tahta, another obstacle on the route to Jerusalem. For the Scots, it was back to the battle.[21]

On 23 November the Turks attacked and two brigades of the 52nd Division (the 156th and 155th) which had rejoined the line held them off over the next four days. The most critical day was 28 November when the 7th Yeomanry Division, light horse units and the 74th Division were rushed to bolster this front. As their historian noted, 'the sound of British guns was heartening to the defenders after the grilling they had endured without effective artillery support.' The CRAs of both the 52nd and 60th divisions had to spread their resources, and the former took over the latter's guns at Amwas. Their orders were to move to Beit Likia which they reached on 29 November following a forced march — they had now returned to the position they had occupied the previous week.

From an artillery perspective, it is a truism that observation, the key to any effective intervention on the battlefield, is crucial to the provision of support. Given the unrelenting Turkish attacks, observers were forced to change position frequently. Major Campbell's (52nd Division) battery was awaiting its next orders and 'he was looking for a good position when he was confronted by an armed Turk. At that moment he possessed nothing more deadly than his slide rule. He pulled it out, pointed it at the Turk — who surrendered and was brought in.' The 157th Brigade arrived just in time for the final Turkish assault on 29 November. Pressed with vigour, the *ahmets* assaulted as close as 250 yards from the 5th Royal Scots. They were dispersed by the battalion's Stokes mortars. That night the 3rd Light Horse Brigade relieved the Scots who, despite their privations, 'had displayed boldness, determination and spirit'.[22]

On 29/30 November, the now much reduced troopers of the 4th Light Horse Brigade were defending El Burj supported by two weakened squadrons and companies from the Gloucester Yeomanry and Royal Scots Fusiliers. A strong Turkish attack materialised from the north-north-east. Allied artillery support, summoned by a message to brigade headquarters and red flares (Very lights), comprised the 268th Brigade RFA and the Hong Kong and Singapore Mountain Battery, which fired concentrations that provided crucial assistance to the light horsemen. The gunners doubled their teams, moved their guns into action and shelled the enemy. This was reciprocated by the Turks, who inflicted numerous casualties. The action enabled the Scots to surround the Turks, who had fought splendidly against the odds, and capture six officers (including a battalion commander) and 112 soldiers, wound 60 and slay over 100. The loss of El Burj exposed the Turk's left flank. The road to Berfilya and the Beit Nuba and Sira valley was close to untenable.[23]

On 1 December, while the Turks were engaging the Australian troopers on El Burj, they also struck Bulfin's 52nd Division at Tahta and almost succeeded in regaining Nebi Samwil. However their high casualty count, to which the artillery contributed significantly, cost them victory. Bulfin's gamble saw the 52nd Division separated from the next formation, the AMD, by a gap of some miles. An enemy thrust into this gap would have caused considerable concern, but fortunately the Turks were focused elsewhere. The Scots were eventually relieved and garrisoned the coast near Jaffa with their XXI Corps brethren.[24]

Allenby's objective of capturing the Holy City was both political and military. Entering Jerusalem by Christmas would deliver a significant political prize, while driving the Turkish armies north and securing the Esdraelon Plain and its vital ports would constitute a military feat with clear logistic ramifications. Chetwode's was the largest of Allenby's forces and was to have the lion's share of the action in capturing Jerusalem which would be a three-day operation. His force's artillery comprised:

- the 53rd and 60th divisions: 301st, 302nd and 303rd RFA brigades — three A and three B 18-pounder batteries, four C howitzer batteries (6:4)
- 74th Division: 268th RFA Brigade — three A batteries and two B batteries

of 18-pounders, two C and two D batteries of 4.5-inch howitzers (2:1); Hong Kong and Singapore Mountain Battery RGA
- 10th Division: 263rd RFA Brigade — two A and two B 18-pounder batteries; two C howitzer batteries (4:2)
- XX Corps Cavalry Division's batteries: 20th Brigade RHA, Berks and Hants batteries 96th Heavy Brigade RGA[25]

In the Jerusalem tactical area of operations, the main roads and tracks ran east-west, making it difficult to redeploy artillery north or south should the situation require. There was easier going in the 53rd Division's sector, or on the south-western approaches to Jerusalem on the Latron and Hebron–Bethlehem roads. The main enemy forces close to Jerusalem were (north to south) the *24th*, *53rd* and *26th divisions.* The latter was the weakest in *III Corps*, its headquarters at Ramallah. The enemy front extended from (north to south) Beit ur el Foka, Et Tireh, El Jib and Nebi Samwil to Beit Iksa, the last the 60th Division's objective.

XX Corps planned and controlled the attack on the night of 7 December with Zero Hour at 5.15 am the next morning. The attack was planned in four phases: to the north, a right hook (60th), and from the south, a second right hook (53rd) to surround Jerusalem. Coordinating these simultaneous attacks required first-class staff work from corps and divisional headquarters which, by this stage of the campaign, had reached an impressive standard. As much of the organic artillery as could be supported logistically was on hand, except that of the 74th Division. To the north, moving the guns into position meant overcoming the hostile terrain and coping with torrential rain. Gunners worked all night to manhandle their pieces into position, ready for H Hour. The infantry attack would be concentrated along a corridor five miles wide, the left flank of which was roughly defined by the eminence of Nebi Samwil and the right by Jerusalem road. As Gullett wrote, 'there are perhaps fifty great defensive positions in the Judean hill country, but for adaptability to measures of resistance the neighbourhood of Jerusalem overshadows them all.' Such was the lot of the infantry and their supporting artillery. The plan envisaged the 74th Division using its 230th and 231st brigades whose guns were at Biddu and Beit Surik. There was no preparatory bombardment, as their approach march was completed in rain, mist and darkness. Both HAGs bombarded El Burj. Some of the 96th HAG's weapons were moved forward to Qalonye for the counter-bombardment plan, coinciding with the advance.

Chapter 16

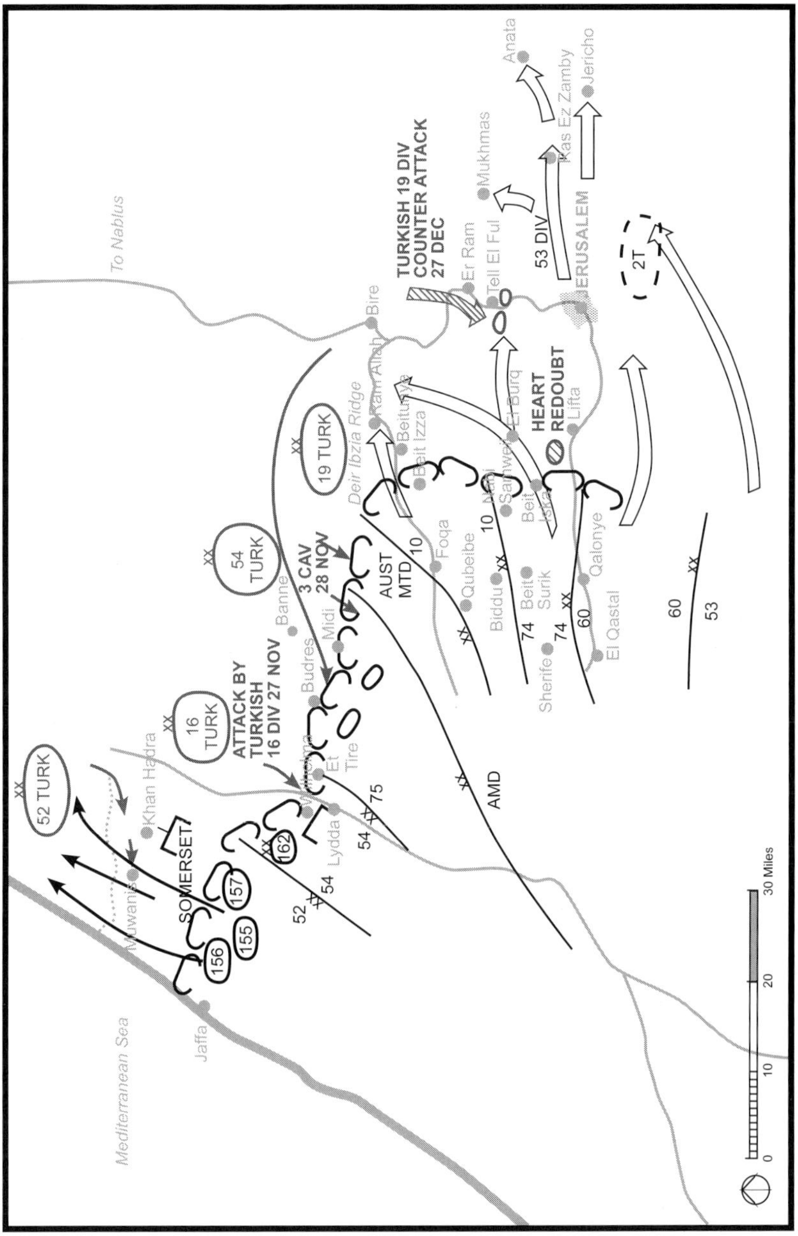

Map 13. This map shows the main battles fought from the northern coastal flank of the Auja to the high ground of the Jerusalem plateau, and major time lines therewith.

The enemy was well prepared in trenches and redoubts with interlocking fields of fire for his machine-guns, but vulnerable to accurate artillery fire. Farndale describes how the enemy on the higher ground at Lifta was 'swept away by gun and machine gun fire' as were the redoubts of 'Heart' and 'Liver', their capture by the 60th Division signifying the end of Phase 1. These redoubts were the prime opportunity targets for the 18-pounder batteries. Other phases followed, the 53rd checked in the morning and the 74th in the afternoon. Both howitzer batteries of the 301st and 302nd RFA brigades suffered casualties from counter-battery fire.[26] It was far from a one-sided affair, however, and the British attack paused that evening to allow the line to be strengthened. In brief, heavy fighting delayed the XX Corps timetable for the advance, and the cavalry had to deploy to cover the 74th Division's flanks with the 10th Division.[27] Possession of the high ground next day gave the attackers an advantage, although machine-gun fire from the Mount of Olives was an unforeseen annoyance, albeit soon neutralised. The Turks began to withdraw, although their artillery remained active with heavy bombardments of Allied infantry positions. Before Mott's detachment could round up the Turkish gunners, enemy artillery astride the Jericho road began to harass XX Corps troops with effective fire. This feature of the Turkish defence 'bluffed' the British force and concealed the Turks' completed evacuation. On the morning of 9 December the enemy withdrew from one part of the front, as the attackers later discovered. On 10 December the 74th Division captured Midie and Budrus and the next day the Turks counter-attacked, again without success. The contribution of the artillery to the capture peaked during the week ending 9 December at 15,098 rounds of the smaller calibre ammunition, around half of which was shrapnel and HE.

The elated infantry of the 60th and 53rd divisions shared the honour of being first into the city. En route, Mott's detachment was joined by the 10th Australian Light Horse Regiment, as it was Chauvel's wish that, should Jerusalem fall, his light horse be represented at any ceremony that attended its capture. In the event, it was Major Dunckley's squadron that was present. The circumstances of Jerusalem's capture and freedom from Ottoman rule form an important chapter in the history of the RA given the part the gunners played. Gullett wrote,

> The governor fled shortly before dawn [9 December] and handed the mayor a formal letter of surrender. Soon after sunrise the mayor, supported by Turkish police bearing white flags walked out towards the British on the Lifta road. Here he met Sergeant Hurcomb and Sergeant Sedgewick of the Londoners, who escorted him to two officers of the 302nd RFA Brigade; Izzet's [the mayor] letter was passed on to General Shea [GOC 60th Division]. After communications between Shea, Chetwode and Allenby, Shea was authorized by the Commander in Chief to enter and take the surrender of the city.[28]

Chapter 16

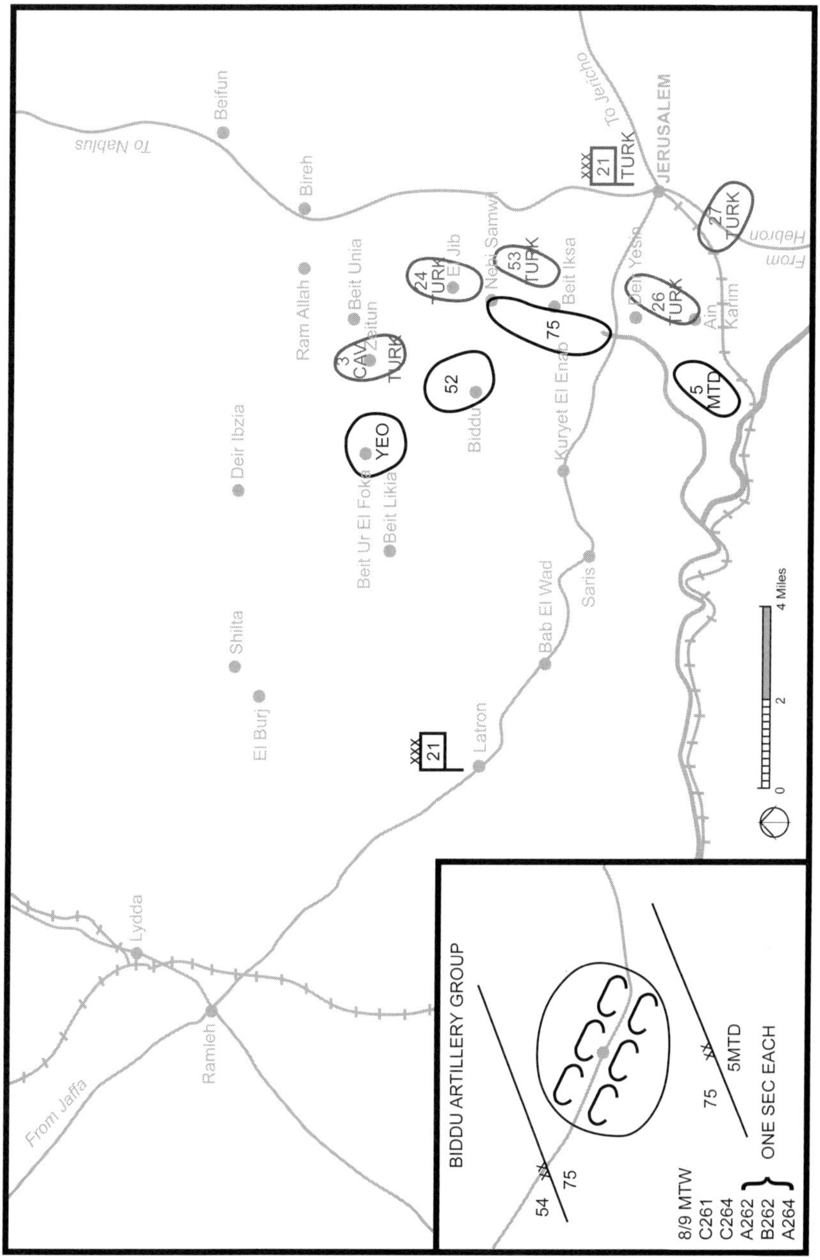

Map 14. The front line just prior to the taking of Jerusalem. Note the detail of the Biddu artillery position.

There was another dimension to this campaign. Brigadier Salmond's air brigade had continually refined its operational practices and, now equipped with more advanced aircraft, was able to dominate the skies over the front. The airmen's bombing and strafing skills were already apparent, and now another skill had also been utilised. They had been linked to XXI Corps Counter Battery Staff Office and their locating and photographing of enemy gun positions meant that the heavy artillery assets were more effectively employed. The airmen reported enemy dispositions, took photographs of gun areas and supplied images for map-making. The prints reached divisional and brigade headquarters promptly each evening. Without realising it, they had become pioneers of depth target acquisition and neutralisation — harassing fire by proxy. The advancing troops noted with jubilation the wreckage of German aeroplanes at Arak el Menshe, damaged railway junctions and dumps and the carnage of bombed men and animals.[29] All the way to Jerusalem the gunners had to use every element of operations to 'keep the faith' with their infantry battalions. Their lot was unenviable, but they triumphed in the end.

This chapter concludes with Gullett's overview of the Jerusalem operation and the capture of the city:

> Jerusalem was won and was due to a very rare combination of military qualities in the British Army at that time. An admirable tactical scheme, impelled by a leader of tremendous and infectious driving power; wholehearted and capable co-operation by corps, division, and brigade commanders; brilliant and self-sacrificing regimental leadership; dogged insistence by the infantry rank and file — these won Jerusalem for Britain.[30]

Chapter 17

The Northern Front and the defence of Jerusalem

If a man begin with certainties he shall end in doubt; but if he will be content to begin with doubts, he shall end in certainties.

Francis Bacon

However satisfying it was for Allenby's legions to capture Jerusalem with the political capital this generated, the Turks and their German masters were far from a vanquished force. They were not prepared to relinquish the city without a fight, and planning began immediately for its recapture. On 27 December Allenby's front line extended in a crescent 40 miles from Arsuf on the coast, through Tahta and Bireh north to Jerusalem and on to Bethlehem. Chetwode had moved his artillery forward and, planning an advance in a two-phase attack, organised his force and artillery into three groups facing their front:

- Right Group: 229th Brigade, 74th Division. Five 4-gun batteries (A/117, C/117 and A/44) near Beit Iksa; C/268 Battery between Biddu and Qubeibe, and a battery comprising sections from A/117 and B/117 batteries at Biddu. The 96th HAG was employed for counter-battery tasks.
- Centre Group: 31st Brigade, 10th Division, 68th RFA Brigade. The 67th RFA Brigade would support both Right and Centre groups.
- Left Group: 29th and 30th brigades of the 10th Division, B Battery, 9th and 10th Mountain Brigade, to which was added Hodgson's three batteries of his organic RHA brigade.

The 96th HAG could produce a counter-bombardment program with inbuilt flexibility if its fire was required by either of the two divisional CRAs. That was the plan.[1]

However, the Turks had made their own plans. They attacked the 169th Brigade in heavy rain at 1.30 am on 27 December but were beaten back by artillery fire, with Very light signals used to call in defensive fire tasks. Further south on the 53rd Division's front, the 158th Brigade also felt the fury of the Turks. However, Chetwode decided that the time had come to maintain the pressure and sustained infantry and artillery battles followed over the next two days. This was only possible with the herculean efforts of the engineers and pioneers who kept tracks open for supplies and batteries to leapfrog forward. It enabled the 96th HAG to eventually move its tractor-drawn guns to Foka.[2]

The terrain was well suited to defence, comprising ridges, a 2200-foot hill (Hog's Back), and gullies in which stone sangars concealed machine-guns. The artillery plan was predicated on the use of the Kereina Track along a ridge top as a single route to bring artillery support forward to assist the infantry's advance. The plan also envisaged the use of other tracks as the secondary means of advance. Foul weather delayed D Day for two days until 27 December. H Hour was set for 5.00 am and the Turkish artillery was particularly active, inflicting casualties on gunner and infanteer alike. The 229th Brigade made good progress and moved ahead of its flank body, all forces achieving their objectives. The Hog's Back feature was crucial and Chetwode's artillery could not move until it was taken, the Royal Inniskilling Fusiliers obliging with its occupation. Artillery support was sometimes fraught because Turkish shellfire cut telephone wires, often at the *moment critique*. As Chetwode's men advanced they left behind the ruined villages that spoke eloquently of previous battles — Beit Izza, Deir Ibizia Ridge, Beituyne and Bireh, the latter taken by the 181st Brigade. Farndale records that '3,170 18 pounder and 791 4.5 inch rounds were expended by 60th Division'. Ammunition usage peaked in the week of 3 January, when the 18-pounders and 4.5-inch howitzers fired a total of 24,106 rounds.[3]

The value of the air arm, not only to the artillery, but to the army as a whole, should also be emphasised. In the autumn, the 40th Army Wing had advanced to aerodromes at Julis and later Mejdel. Here No. 1 Squadron AFC exchanged its 'Harry Tates' for the renowned Bristol Fighter. This guaranteed Allenby continued air supremacy across the front in the hands of the aggressive Australians and Britons of No. 111 Squadron RFC.[4]

The Turks retreated north up the Nablus road, pursued by leapfrogging batteries and by the aircraft of the RFC, which bombed and machine-gunned the departing columns. Across the front they left over 1000 dead and lost 558 men captured. Yet they withdrew once again with their artillery intact, notwithstanding the fact that both types of heavy ordnance had fired 5955 rounds in the last week of December and the first week in January. Two-thirds of this was HE and was fired in the second week. This suggests extraordinary efforts by the ammunition columns and supply organisation. The official historian recorded British casualty figures for the 'Defence of Jerusalem and Battle of Jaffa' for the fortnight as 1890:

	KIA	WIA	POW/Missing
Officers	31	87	3
Other ranks	297	1348	124
	328	**1435**	**12**

Chapter 17

Total EEF casualties for the week ending 29 December amounted to 1360. MacMunn and Falls also recorded the 'Battle from the Turkish side', enumerating the strengths of various Turkish formations, with *Seventh Army* ration strength at approximately 22,000, while Allenby could field 33,000. Gullett drew the conclusion that 'the counter-offensive was a desperate venture'.[5]

During these 30 days the EEF advanced 60 miles on the right flank and 40 miles on the left and fought half a dozen stiff battles. The balance sheet was not always a one-sided affair with Bruce writing that British casualties were around 6000. The enemy lost 10,000 men captured, 80 guns and more than 100 machine-guns, with many more men diseased and others killed. Farndale notes that 'it was a brilliant all arms action, guns, cavalry and infantry cooperating together with great skill and together paralysing enemy resistance.'[6]

Chapter 18
The capture of Jericho: 19–21 February 1918

Softly, softly catchee monkey.

Lancashire Constabulary Training School motto

Following the failure of Turkish attempts to recapture Jerusalem, Allenby's A and Q staffs at GHQ and subsidiary commands used the lull across the front to advance the broad gauge railway, repair captured Turkish lines and begin landing stores over the beach at Sukereir and Jaffa. The Corps Commander RE arranged the metalling and grading of tracks using indentured labour and infanteers to ease and speed supply to the front line. Among these were the Great North road, an 18-foot-wide metalled road built by the 10th Division from Beit Sira to Abu Shukheidin, and the South Circular road that eventually extended to Bir ez Zeit. The troops' amenities improved, reinforcements made good some losses and the wounded and sick returned to units. His EEF reinvigorated, as Gullett wrote, 'Allenby could contemplate without misgiving the maintenance of a substantial force in the Jordan Valley.'[1]

The Judean Hills were more formidable and stark than those west of Jerusalem. Finger-like spurs gave way to deep gorges plunging several hundreds of feet, the sides of which offered scant cover and in some cases no footholds for horses, mules and camels. The wilderness supported sheep and goats, solitary shepherds watching over them. In springtime the desert bloomed with colourful flowers that shielded its ruggedness from the eye. When the flora withered and the mercury rose to abnormal heights it 'gave the strong impression of savage and melancholy grandeur'. During summer it was a place of fierce heat, strong winds and blinding dust storms.[2]

With the capture of Jerusalem, Allenby's strategy was to advance on Jericho and interdict the Turkish supply route to their southern operations supported by the Hejaz railway. He would use his cavalry to head east to Jericho and Amman, south of the 53rd and 60th divisions, to enter the gorge cut by the River Jordan between Jericho and the Dead Sea. The A&NZ Mounted Division (less the 2nd Light Horse Brigade) would outflank the left flank of the enemy which held up

Chapter 18

the advance along the Jericho road. Jericho lay between two road junctions, one (north) at Jebel Kuruntul and Talat ed Dumm and the most southerly the road from Jerusalem via Nabi Musa. The Dead Sea flank would be the province of the New Zealand troopers from the A&NZ Mounted Division.

After a brief and welcome pause from the heavy fighting north and east of Jerusalem, XX Corps pointed the 60th and 74th divisions towards Ramallah and the Nablus road, and the 53rd Division towards Jericho. The weather turned from bad to atrocious over three consecutive days. The Turks, who had arrested several thousand deserters (both officers and men) in Jerusalem during the city's occupation, now decided to counter-attack to reclaim their prize. Their artillery had withdrawn eastwards, still had plenty of ammunition and was only too ready to use it to good effect.

On 14 February the XXI Corps infantry divisions (53rd and 60th) moved east towards Jericho. There was insufficient space for all the 60th's artillery brigades to move in columns towards the town and, after some checks, they advanced around three miles. The 180th Brigade made the best time, using the metalled road that German engineers had built from Talat ed Dumm to Jericho. The 10th Heavy Battery (60-pounders) and the only 6-inch howitzer from the 383rd Siege Battery were able to follow close enough to engage targets. The gunners and infantry approach marches of the other brigades took them down steep-sided escarpments and deployment was much slower with gun positions available only for the howitzers. Farndale records that '60 men from 2/20th London Battalion helped manhandle the guns to support 2/18th London Battalion at Talat ed Dumm.' An hour-long bombardment by the 303rd RFA Brigade was laid on to help the 2/19th London Battalion in its attack. One battery of 18-pounders took 36 hours to advance eight miles, and this was to be the fate of all the gunners and supporting troops. Subsequently, on 20 February, there was hard fighting as the infantry, supported by artillery, stormed the enemy positions at dawn and advanced towards the high ground of Jebel Ekteif.[3]

The A&NZ Mounted Division was ordered to patrol and probe eastwards in the hills between Jericho and the Dead Sea, its boundary the River Jordan which flowed north-south. The Turks had an outpost line on both banks. In the south Chaytor ordered Brigadier Meldrum's NZMR Brigade to launch a dismounted attack on two dominant features, Jebel el Kahmum and Tubl el Keuneitrah. Five Turkish guns and machine-guns slowed the Kiwis, who were unable to summon support from their organic battery. The staff had sent the division's artillery down the Jericho road with the infantry. Plans were made for a dawn attack on Kheir Kakun the next day but the Turks made good their escape overnight. Brigadier

Cox's 1st Light Horse Brigade was ordered to pursue and patrol and his men were soon in Jericho.

By 23 February most of the enemy's *53rd Division* and *163rd Regiment* (some 3000 rifles) were back on the eastern bank of the Jordan, but their artillery was still inflicting casualties on Allenby's troopers. The next day the horse gunners were reunited with their brigades and worked to bring the Ghoraniye bridge under fire. This meant manhandling the guns over extraordinarily difficult country. Chaytor fully appreciated the tactical importance of this bridge over the Jordan on the road to Amman.[4]

On 26 February the Turks launched themselves at the 60th Division and were met by equally resolute Londoners with high morale and an appetite for victory. The enemy retreated, leaving more than 1000 dead and 750 taken prisoner. Allenby's line was now 12 miles north of Jaffa and Jerusalem and bent south down the River Jordan to the Dead Sea. Bulfin's XXI Corps in the coastal sector maintained pressure on the Turk's right (coastal) flank while covering the flanks of its XXI Corps neighbours with cavalry brigades.

The sector was soon to become a critical tactical point for the spring and summer campaigns of the mounted troops. The A&NZ Mounted Division's casualties for this segment of operations totalled just three killed and 14 wounded, although the infantry of the 60th Division sustained significant casualties (309 of 510). The enemy lost 144 taken as prisoners and eight machine-guns.[5] Despite privations shared with the infantry, the gunners' contribution to the battle was generally too little and/or too late.

Chapter 19
The Amman raid and the first Es Salt affair

How sleep the brave, who suit to rest, by all their country's wishes blest.

W. Collins
Ode, 1746

The 'raid' to Amman — an advance over 17 miles of rugged country to a high plateau followed by a fierce fight against a formidable foe — was one of the most heroic feats of mounted troops and London infanteers during the war. The advance began on 20 March and the action concluded on 2 April, the entire operation an unsuccessful gamble by Allenby to dislocate the Turkish lines of communication to the south which passed through Amman. The root cause of failure was a major lapse in security which provided the Turks ample warning of his planned attack, allowing them to organise their defences accordingly. Allenby had decided on a dash — in fact a raid — on Amman to destroy the railway tunnel and viaduct south of the town. This, he hoped, would disrupt Turkish logistical support for its forces in the south and the Jordan Valley which depended on the railway for vital stores and reinforcements. Allenby also hoped that the raid would mislead the Turks over his future intentions. As Gullett observed, 'Success at Es Salt and Amman was desirable but something less would serve the Commander-in-Chief's purpose.'[1] The DMC was to be his striking force once the weather cleared and, along with the 60th Division, formed 'Shea's Force'. The enemy was working on interior lines and comprised the *Fourth Army*, *150th Regiment* and part of the *153rd Regiment*. The German *703rd Battalion* was included to help stiffen the spine of the *ahmets*.

Shea's Force comprised:

- A&NZ Mounted Division (less the 2nd Light Horse Brigade), Light Armoured Car Brigade; 18th RHA Brigade (Ayr, Somerset and Inverness batteries)
- the 60th Division artillery [301st RFA Brigade A, B and C (H) batteries; 302nd RFA Brigade A, 413th and C (H) batteries and 303rd RFA Brigade A, B and C (H) batteries]
- the 10th Heavy Battery
- the 9th Mountain Brigade RGA (A, B and 12th batteries)

In sum, Shea had some 7000 rifles, 2600 sabres and 82 guns. The Turkish *Fourth Army* would total 5000 rifles, 500 sabres and 26 guns.[2] Allenby's planning also included the Beni Sakr irregular Arab force of several thousand horsemen whose task was to make life difficult for the Amman garrison. In orders its coordination was left to the commanders on the spot, a source of misgivings for any commander familiar with the Arabs' ways.[3]

Image 13: An Australian soldier from the Australian Mounted Division, wearing headphones, operates a wireless set at a field station during the first Amman stunt in March 1918 (AWM P02952.003).

Once the orders were issued the force concentrated east of Jericho, the cavalry staging via Latron and the cameleers moving forward from Bethlehem. The infantry was already in place and, like the cavalry, had endured heavy rain and cold winds. This affected the whole enterprise as the river level rose and roads and tracks turned to slush and mud. In military operations opposed river crossings are hazardous tactical enterprises at best. On 20 March, as the horsemen approached, the River Jordan was still in flood, although conditions were easing. Care and concealment were practised but, as Gullett commented, 'These precautions were thrown away. The Turks were aware of British intentions as GHQ's plans were "the talk of Cairo".'[4] The force had to cross to the east bank of the river to begin the ascent to the Gilead (Jilid) plateau. While Shea's Force was concentrating the Turks moved another 600 infantry to the Ghoraniye crossing and a force of cavalry further south. The Turks had destroyed the bridge at Ghoraniye, but the 60th Division advance guard had made a thorough reconnaissance of likely crossing places. Shea selected two sites — Ghoraniye and Makhadet, four miles to the south. The river was around 30 paces across (25 yards) and when the crossing details reached it, the Jordan was running at seven knots.

Image 14: Cavalry crossing the Jordan River at Ghoraniye by pontoon bridge, one of which was erected by a Canadian engineer bridging unit (AWM B02735).

At the appropriate time both infantry and artillery staged 'demonstrations' at several river crossing sites and a crossing was finally secured at Makhadet. The Auckland Mounted Rifles crossed and, moving north on the eastern bank, swooped on the defenders of Ghoraniye from the rear, prompting them to withdraw. The Aucklanders took 68 Turks prisoner for the loss of four troopers. The DMC Bridging Train then swung into action, its 13th Pontoon Park coming to the fore. Getting ropes across the river was the task of the strongest swimmers from the 1st Field Squadron, Australian Engineers, one of whom swam naked but armed with a rifle and managed, despite the current, to cross and help establish a modest bridgehead. The enemy delayed the engineers with well-directed machine-gun fire, causing casualties, but the engineers prevailed and a pontoon bridge was eventually launched. At 1.20 am the first Londoners of the 179th Brigade reached the opposite bank. By 6.30 am on 23 March two battalions of Londoners (the 2/19th and 2/18th) had crossed at Ghoraniye and continued the advance. By dusk four bridges had been constructed at the two crossings. An RFA brigade took an hour to cross the river, as did an infantry brigade, while the enemy withdrew to prepared positions at Shunet Nimrin.[5]

Shea's plan was to advance on four axes, cavalry leading:

- North: 3rd Light Horse Brigade followed by the 179th Brigade with the mountain battery to rendezvous at Cairn Hill, four miles from Es Salt.
- Centre: 181st Brigade to advance to El Huwej, four miles south of Es Salt and bivouac.
- Centre South: NZMR Brigade to advance to Ain es Sir, seven miles west of Amman, with the Somerset Battery.
- South: 2nd Light Horse Brigade to advance via Wadi el Kuffrein, bivouac two miles from Naur, advance to near Ain es Sir then turn north to meet the 'flying columns' from the northern routes.

Heavy rains rendered the road useless for guns except for two batteries which remained in the vicinity of Shunet Nimrin. The impassable tracks prompted Brigadier Ryrie to note that, even for the light horsemen's Walers it was 'hard going', and he doubted that his brigade would reach its objective.[6] When his troops reached the high plateau country, now 3000 feet above sea level, the going became somewhat easier. Heavy rain drenched the troops but it was the cold that distressed the Australians and New Zealanders more, some relief felt when they captured a German convoy stuck in the mud. The converging forces bivouacked during the nights of 26/27/28 March, the infantry brigades arriving ready for battle on 28 March. They concentrated in a semicircle west of the town.[7]

The nine enemy positions west of the town resembled a shallow crescent configuration, their machine-guns alone capable of repelling attacking infantry. The cameleers were supported by their mountain battery, although its 11.5-pound shells were unlikely to make an impression on any of the 5000 Turks in range in Amman. The key to Amman's capture was the occupation of Hill 3039. The gunners were outshot by 15 heavier pieces and many machine-guns. The Turkish artillery had registered every possible approach route the attackers could choose and their machine-guns had wide, sweeping vistas across the plateau. When the Australians attacked, as Gullett described, 'as if in response to a single order guns and machine guns opened fire together.' Seeking to salvage something from the wreckage of his plan, Chaytor, the general on the spot, ordered the 4th Battalion of the ICC and the 5th Light Horse Regiment to demolish the two-span bridge and railway line, temporarily isolating the garrison in Amman. By 27/28 March the attackers had recorded heavy casualties in officers and men. Nevertheless Chaytor, after consulting Shea, ordered another attack the next day, with an RFA battery and the Somersets ordered up to support the new attack.

Chapter 19

The weather reduced the amount of cooperation the RFC could provide over the misty uplands and rain continued to fall. The night of 29 March was 'dark, wet and intensely cold' and, at 2.00 am, the advance began. Everywhere the enemy defences were superior to the heroism of the troops. Despite some noteworthy martial feats, dawn revealed an indecisive result. The artillery, when it did arrive, was ineffective and, when the Turks counter-attacked from their positions of natural strength, they achieved a convincing victory. If any battle in the entire Palestine campaign suffered from the lack of artillery firepower, it was emphatically Amman. The cameleers lost 40 killed and 280 wounded. But the battle was not yet over. A force of 1000 enemy with two guns marched from Damieh towards Es Salt hoping to ambush the northern column. Another 500 were troubling Brigadier Cox's 1st and 2nd Light Horse regiments' troopers during their withdrawal, the Australians constantly harassed by enemy moving west from Damieh, and shelled by their guns from Jozele. The CRA sent his three RHA batteries and the Light Armoured Car squadron to Cox's assistance.

However, of more concern was the effect of the torrential rain on the Jordan which rose nine feet and washed away the pontoon bridges. To add insult to injury, during the withdrawal German airmen harried the cameleers and bombed them repeatedly, inflicting many casualties and increasing their despondency. However great the suffering of the wounded after the Gaza attacks a year before, it paled in comparison with the ordeals of the wounded in camel cacolets, bumping their way down the narrow defiles to the field ambulance post. Many men died of exposure. By 2 April the whole sorry affair was over and Shea left the 180th Brigade to guard the Ghoraniye bridgehead. The dual pontoon bridge there carried 30,000 animals across to the western bank from which Shea's Force had originally come.[8] Casualties for the Amman raid and first Es Salt are shown in Table 9 below:

TABLE 9: CASUALTIES FOR THE AMMAN RAID AND FIRST ES SALT

	KIA	WIA	MIA
A&NZ Mounted Division and Cameleers:			
Officers:	11	42	2
Other ranks:	107	511	53
60th Division:			
Officers:	4	23	2
Other ranks:	55	324	68
	177	**900**	**125**

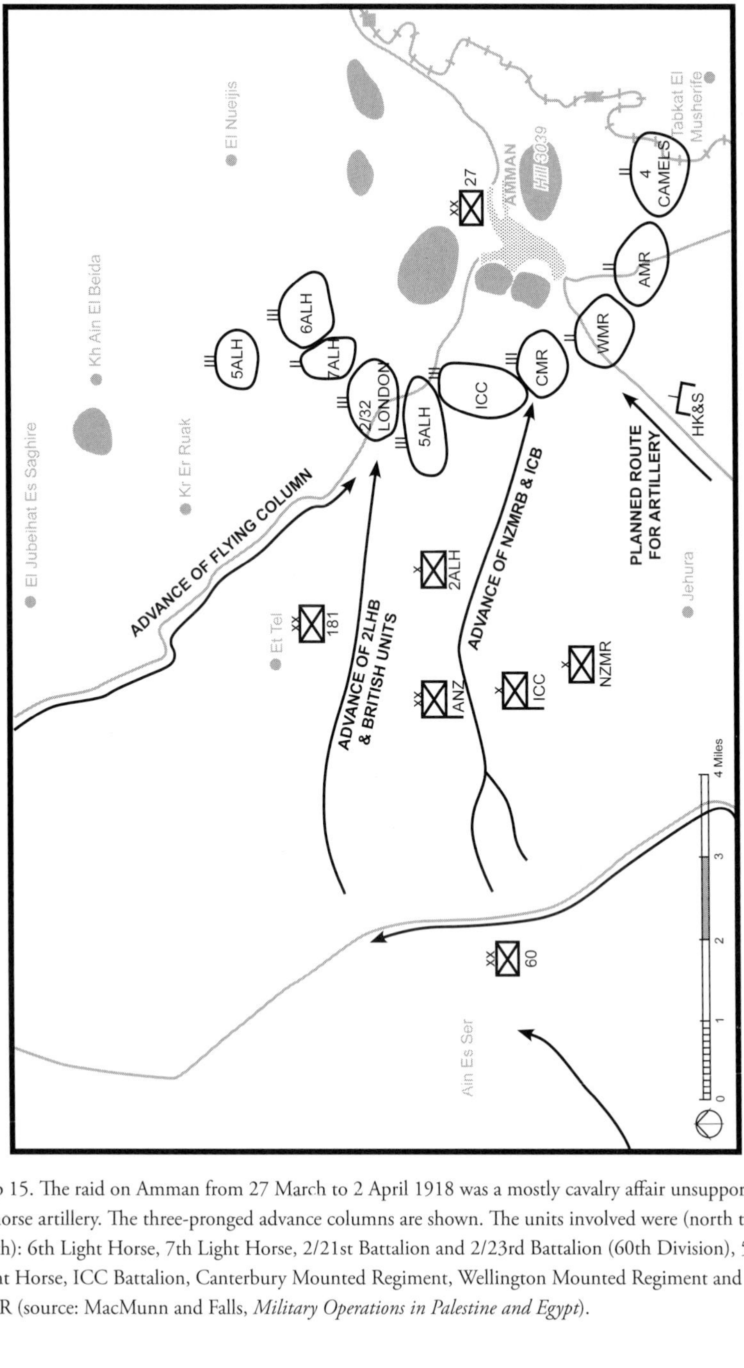

Map 15. The raid on Amman from 27 March to 2 April 1918 was a mostly cavalry affair unsupported by horse artillery. The three-pronged advance columns are shown. The units involved were (north to south): 6th Light Horse, 7th Light Horse, 2/21st Battalion and 2/23rd Battalion (60th Division), 5th Light Horse, ICC Battalion, Canterbury Mounted Regiment, Wellington Mounted Regiment and AMR (source: MacMunn and Falls, *Military Operations in Palestine and Egypt*).

The official historian's enemy tally is 1348 with 986 taken prisoner and four guns captured.

There can be no doubt that this was a gamble by Allenby. To his credit he was astute enough to adopt stern measures regarding the security of his plans, convinced that a lack of security played a major part in the failure of this operation. Another factor may have been the non-appearance of the Beni Sakr horsemen who had failed to arrive to discharge their part in the operation. The pendulum-like swings of Arab loyalty were not an unknown factor in any staff dealings with them. On the night of 30 March, as the operation unfolded, the Beni Sakr leadership probably deduced that Shea could not win and decided against becoming involved.

Logistical planning may have been another factor in the operation's failure. Allenby's staff may not have considered the logistics of supporting a force 17 miles from its own bases over four days without significant artillery and other service support over routes that were nigh on impassable. While the loss of 1202 men and as many animals would hardly have been a distraction to a Western Front divisional commander if one of his 'stunts' had failed, Allenby was not so well endowed. He had been pressured to despatch more troops to bolster the Western Front following the German successes of Operation Michael in March and could ill afford to waste any of his finite resources, particularly since he was poised to embark on a summer campaign in the Jordan Valley, something hitherto never contemplated in ancient or modern history. Allenby had also learnt a valuable lesson and, following the raid on Amman and the first raid on Es Salt, headquarters security for subsequent operations was tightened considerably — with remarkable results.

Chapter 20
The April 1918 battles of XX Corps and XXI Corps

Oh come thou wisdom from on high,
And order all things far and nigh;
To us the path of knowledge show,
And cause us in her ways to go.

O Come Emmanuel
Isaiah 7:14

Part 1. Operations in the Jordan Valley

Major General Chaytor's AMD was charged with the defence of the Jordan Valley. In the northern segment of the front on the western bank of the Jordan, the Turks had a crescent-shaped front that menaced the DMC and the 60th Division from the north-west. Chaytor sent the 5th Light Horse Regiment to relieve Shea's Londoners guarding the Ghoraniye bridgehead. The bridgehead was roughly semi-circular in shape, two miles long and about half as wide and the scrub on the clay hills offered covered approaches to attackers. The 18th RHA Brigade, Ayr, Somerset and Inverness batteries were joined by two 4.5-inch howitzer batteries and a section of the Siege Battery's 60-pounders. On the eastern river bank, water from Wadi Nimrin flowed through the 2nd Light Horse Regiment positions, one flank on swampy ground, with a mobile defence covering gaps in the northern side. A key feature was a knoll known as 'The Pimple' that stood 54 yards above the banks of the wadi. Including all this in his appreciation, Chaytor considered his position safe from attack. One of the factors in that appreciation was his view that the enemy artillery east of the Jordan was weak, the presence of the 60-pounders on the west bank having kept the Turkish guns at a safe distance. Chaytor had three weeks of hard work ahead to complete his comprehensive defence plan.

At 4.30 am on 11 April Chaytor's dispositions were contested when one of his mounted patrols collided with around 100 Turks. This was the enemy advance guard, as another 1000 Turks spread across 600 yards were visible behind it on either side of the wadi. The duty OPO on The Pimple ordered the batteries to 'take post' at 6.00 am and adjusted their fire to great effect. He was killed when he stood in the open to adjust fire but another man immediately took his place. A firefight developed as another 400 Turks moved forward. A German officer leading the assault deployed the Turkish machine-guns, singling out the observers on The Pimple as the replacement OPO 'exposed himself fearlessly directing the fire'. Close to the outposts, the troopers of the 3rd Light Horse Regiment brought a section of their Hotchkiss machine-guns into action and, with battery fire adjusted to within 100 yards of their posts, made any attempt by the Turks to reach the clear water in a nearby wadi suicidal. It was a hot day and the Turks' water bottles ran dry. When they broke cover to refill them they were easily shot down.

An encircling movement by Brigadier Cox's horsemen of the 1st and 3rd Light Horse regiments could not make significant progress due to the strength of the Turkish reserve force which had been their blocking force at Shunet Nimrin. By 4.00 am on 12 April the enemy had withdrawn, leaving 151 dead and 500 wounded. The horsemen had lost six killed and 17 wounded. A post-battle analysis noted 'the prompt and effective cooperation of the artillery. An examination of the ground in and about the wadi disclosed the effectiveness of the light and heavy artillery. The fine shooting [musketry] of the troopers of Lieut. Colonel Bourne's Queenslanders was also significant.'[1]

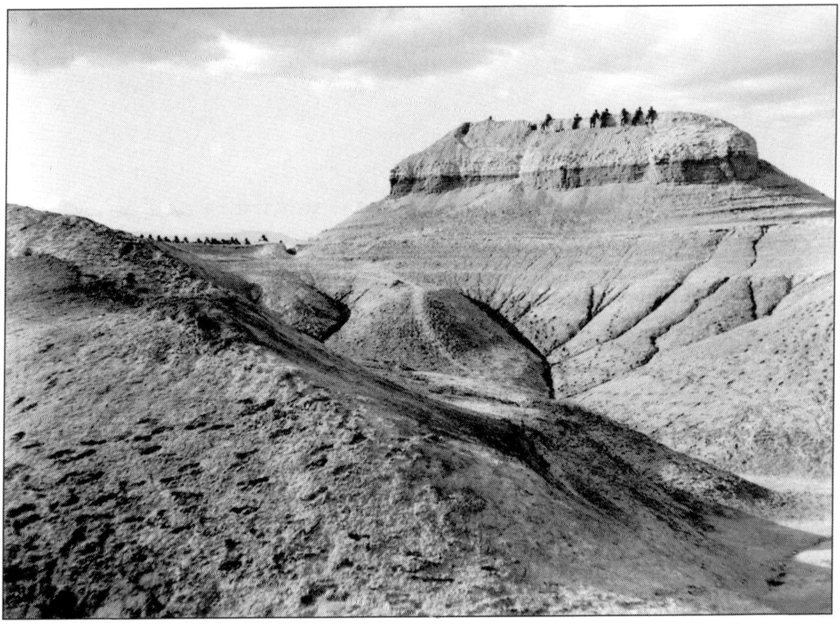

Image 15: The topography of the Jordan Valley and the Musallabeh feature (AWM B00009).

South of Abu Tellul was Musallabeh, a prominent feature with commanding all-round views situated 10 miles north-west of Ghoraniye. The enemy, if he attacked, would approach from the north-north-west. This sector was occupied by two Australian battalions of the ICC and the 6th and 7th Light Horse regiments, attached to Brigadier Smith's formation. The regiments dug well-sited entrenchments and wired the many covered approaches. In support were two 18-pounder batteries (A and B), a howitzer battery (C) from the 301st RFA Brigade and a section of the 10th Heavy Battery's 60-pounders. The howitzer battery line of fire covered the right flank. Other battery lines extended to the north-west, the main axis of the enemy infantry attack. The guns were echeloned some 3–5000 yards from the front line, and howitzer fire could reach an enveloping cavalry force if it passed across the front along a wadi (running north-west to south-east) in front of the 6th Light Horse Regiment. Brigadier Smith's force amounted to 2000 rifles, 2500 sabres and 33 guns.[2]

On the same day (11 April) that the *ahmets* and Germans attacked Ghoraniye, the Turkish command hurled a cavalry and infantry force at Musallabeh. The feature's isolation made it an ideal artillery target. The Turks were fully cognisant of this and, at 4.00 am, fired concentrations on the hill for an hour while their infantry crept up the wadis towards the cameleers. The cameleers had a very hard fight on their hands until 8.00 am. Once the attack eased, the rest of the day was marked by continuous sniping and occasional artillery fire. As at Ghoraniye, it was a combination of accurate and timely artillery fire and musketry that forced the enemy to withdraw at nightfall. They left 170 dead on the slopes. The cameleers lost one officer and 17 men killed, and three officers and 24 men wounded. Despite the casualty count Gullett wrote that these two successes lifted morale in the DMC.[3]

While the Ghoraniye and Musallabeh affairs finished with morale-boosting victories, Allenby was still looking for a way to isolate the Turkish force in the Jordan Valley at Shunet Nimrin as a deceptive stratagem. To that end, on 25 April he appointed Chauvel commander of a force comprising the DMC headquarters, A&NZ Mounted Division and AMD, a composite brigade of yeomanry, Shea's 60th Division (less a brigade), an Indian Imperial Service brigade, and an extra RHA brigade (the 19th RHA), a siege battery (the 383rd), two mountain batteries (the 9th and 10th) and two batteries of light armoured cars. Smith's cameleers were to work with Chauvel. The AMD had to come from Sharon, where it had been rebuilding. While this was happening the Turks were lying low, although Turkish attacks continued on the bridgeheads during the week.

Chapter 20

On 18 April Chauvel launched a strong demonstration in front of Shunet Nimrin, which included the 180th Brigade marching across the plain in broad daylight. The heavy artillery on the west bank engaged its opposition from close to Ghoraniye. During the night the A&NZ Mounted Division protected the gunners but the Turks did not yield. The armoured cars pushed forward, the cavalry hovered and looked menacing, but all along the front the enemy stoutly resisted, with no real battle joined by either side. With the onset of dusk and having received their orders the troops returned to their bivouacs. As Gullett observed, 'the wisdom of this day's work … was afterwards keenly debated.' In short, instead of drawing Turkish troops from Maan, they had improved their defences, making Shunet Nimrin an even stronger position than before. The consequences of this turn of events were to make General Chauvel's task — the second Es Salt raid at the end of the month — well nigh impossible.[4]

Part 2. XXI Corps battle at Berukin, 18 April 1918

The XXI Corps action at Berukin is included in this narrative because at this time it formed a key part of Allenby's strategy of the indirect approach, evolving in stages until the climactic battles at Nablus/Megiddo in September. To Bulfin's XXI Corps fell the task of maintaining pressure on the Turk's right flank arising from the failure of the XX Corps cavalry and infantry to take Amman. Berukin lies south of Mogg Hill, an early objective on the right flank of the corps front. The 54th, 7th Indian and 60th divisions were deployed between Berukin and the coast. The 75th Division's ambitious objective was to extend its front north almost to Qalqile, seven miles to the north-east. Allenby's orders envisaged a number of phases, and Bulfin enumerated three for this battle, including the capture of Berukin, three miles north of his front. Phase 1 was a preliminary operation to capture Mogg Hill, Phase 2 the capture of the Turkish first line positions further north, and Phase 3, consolidation. Bulfin's opposite number was Refet Pasha's *XXII Corps*, recently reorganised as two infantry divisions on the right flank (*19th* and *20th*) and the *Asia Corps*, Colonel von Falkenburg's Turko-German formation (*7th*, *16th Pasha* and *46th*). By coincidence, von Falkenburg's inter-corps boundary was almost opposite Bulfin's. Turko-German artillery had been strengthened since the loss of Jericho. Brigadier Simpson-Baikie, GOCRA XXI Corps, estimated that his adversary had:

4 x mountain guns

11 x 100mm guns

48 x 77mm guns

12 x 105mm howitzers

10 x 150mm howitzers

XXI Corps artillery fielded:

12 x mountain guns/howitzers

84 x 18-pounders

36 x 4.5-inch howitzers

12 x 60-pounders

16 x 6-inch howitzers

2 x 6-inch guns

This gave Bulfin an arithmetical advantage of more than 2:1 (7:3).[5]

The corps plan of attack extended for seven days. As the official historian noted, 'The plans may be considered … if the operation had been carried through to its conclusion, but [they] are of interest … in their similarity to the great final offensive five months later.'

The seven-day countdown comprised:

Z-6: 75th Division advances its right flank to threaten *XXII Corps* left flank.

Z-5: 7th Division takes over left flank of 54th Division.

Z-3: 7th Division advances its line 2000 yards.

Z-2: Overnight artillery moves to its forward positions and ammunition supply is complete.

Z-2: 7th Division and left flank HAG register from their new position. If undiscovered, to shell from their new positions.

Z-1: 75th and 54th divisions advance to Bidya–Kufra Qasim. The 7th and 54th Artillery and HAG advance to suitable positions for Z Day. Cavalry divisions move to Mulebbis.

Z-1: Artillery on left flank to commence bombardment of Qaliye and Tabsor system paying special attention to back areas.

Z+1: Dawn bombardment of Byar Adas and Tabsor. Royal Navy to appear off Nahr Faliq to prevent enemy withdrawing north by ford and bridge at Zerqiye by shelling. Another crossing will be shelled by the RN and left flank HAGs using aircraft observation.[6]

The rationale for the attack was to close off the enemy line of retreat by having the cavalry drive through the centre of the front to Et Tireh. Bulfin emphasised to Hodgson the importance of the AMD capturing as many guns as possible. Its success was predicated on initial surprise and the achievement of the cavalry operation. It was an ambitious plan that was to fail because of three factors.

Chapter 20

The infantry objectives were from one to two miles north-west of Berukin, those of the 75th Division Mogg Ridge and Sheikh Subi and the villages of Ra'fat and Avara. The 7th Indian Division on the coastal sector was to advance 2000 yards and expand its front to around five miles. Naval gunfire close to the mouth of the Nahr Faliq was to 'close the crossings over the marsh by fire'. Once this was achieved the cavalry would push through and 'the attackers might hope for a big haul of prisoners and booty, especially guns from the area north of the marshes. Also, the line at the village of Tabsor to the railway at Jaljulye could be bombarded.' The 53rd Division's brigade group (the 159th), lent to bolster the 75th Division's right flank, would enhance the full offensive power of the corps. That objective achieved, the 54th Division would roll up the Turko-German flank from the east. Once these objectives had been taken, Major General Hodgson's AMD would exploit north to Et Tireh.[7]

H Hour was 5.10 am on 9 April. Bulfin's orders were somewhat unusual in that attacking brigades would have artillery units 'under command' — requiring full logistic support. For example, the 75th Division would have the 8th Mountain Brigade RGA and one section of the 134th Siege Battery RGA under command of three brigade commanders. Of the division's brigades, the 233rd and 234th fared well in their attack. The South African Field Artillery Brigade came to the assistance of the 233rd Brigade with accurate observed shooting at rifle flashes from Three Bushes Hill. The 232nd Brigade came under intense fire from its right from units of the *16th Division* and the 10th Division objective (Kufr Ain Hill) was not taken until dusk. This setback to the 232nd Brigade's advance was due to the fact that it ran head-on into the *Pasha II* positions. The Germans' resistance delayed the entire division; they used a trench mortar barrage against the 233rd Brigade to compel it to withdraw. The divisions could not move ahead until 4.00 pm when Berukin was captured. It was a day of desperate fighting — bayonet, musket, mortars and artillery — with frequent calls for artillery defensive fire tasks at night by Very lights. When dawn broke on 10 April the battle resumed with the same intensity, the resolution of the Asian *Pasha* German troops again a significant factor. Artillery ammunition ran low as expenditure exceeded staff estimates. Strenuous efforts were required to replenish batteries on Z+1, particularly with shrapnel.[8]

The Turko-German artillerymen enjoyed excellent observation, but their commanders' task was helped immeasurably by loose security at headquarters. Indeed, Gullett wrote that the plan was 'the talk of Cairo'. The capture of marked maps and orders early in the battle was also a significant factor in its failure. Another important artillery factor was the policy adopted by the enemy to avoid counter-bombardment. Their adoption of a 'silent' policy meant that many guns had not been located and, despite Bulfin's possession of an efficient sound-ranging base and aerial observation, many pieces went undetected, including a German battery which fired 734 rounds unobserved by aircraft, notwithstanding the fact that its ammunition stock was 16 miles away at Et Tireh. Bulfin's drawing on ammunition stocks on the first day also curtailed expenditure by the heavy guns. In short, the counter-bombardment staff had been misled — this was confirmed by the casualty count. The failure of the 10th Division to draw off reserves and firepower from *Pasha II* on Tin Hat Hill also contributed to the 75th Division's inability to advance its line. Turkish post-war records reveal that the German battery commander (Hauptmann Simon-Eberhardt) observed that, 'had the British artillery given more support and used more brigades, they would have made a catastrophic breakthrough.'[9] In the event, the weekly ammunition returns revealed that this was a 'gun and HE' battle rather than a 'howitzer/shrapnel' battle and, as will be related, expenditure was far in excess of that of Megiddo.[10] Casualty statistics for Berukin are illustrated in Table 10 below:

TABLE 10: CASUALTIES AT BERUKIN[11]

		KIA	WIA	MIA/POW	TOTAL
232nd and 233rd					
brigades:					
	Officers	13	46	6	65
	Other ranks	96	792	131	1019
234th Brigade:	All ranks				414
75th Division (incl. artillery):					1498
		109	**838**	**137**	**2996**
Enemy casualties:		27			c.700
46th Division:	All ranks				202

Chapter 21
The second Es Salt raid: 30 April–4 May 1918

Tout est perdu fors l'honneur.

Francis I, 1547

On 1 April after rest, recuperation and reinforcement, A Battery HAC married up with the 4th Light Horse Brigade once again and moved to Selmeh. The 4th had experienced a change in command at Belah, when Major A. Smith, MC, formerly of Ayrshire Battery, succeeded Major Bamford Smith, who took command of the 19th RHA Brigade. At Selmeh further training was completed and, three weeks later, the battery trekked through famous sites in the Holy Land to a position between Jericho and the Ghoraniye bridge.[1] General Chauvel prepared to implement General Allenby's ambitious plans to deny the May harvest to the Turks in the Es Salt area. Only 6–7000 enemy soldiers were estimated to be ranged in opposition. Once the Amman-Es Salt front collapsed, Allenby's coastal thrust would destabilise the Turkish forces and indirectly assist Allied strategy in France. Implicit in his thinking was that 'considerable help may be counted on from the Arabs, the closest touch being maintained with them.'[2] Chauvel ordered General Hodgson's division to take part in the assault on Es Salt using a night crossing of the River Jordan to secure Jisr el Damieh. General Shea's Londoners would attack Shunet Nimrin head-on. As Turkish forces north-east of Jericho could threaten the division from the north-west, Chauvel decided to seize the Damieh crossing using Grant's 4th Light Horse Brigade. His flank would be protected by the cameleers. Two cavalry brigades would then attack Es Salt.

The topography for this particular operation is important to the narrative given what ensued over the next three days. The Jordan Valley was some 14 miles long north of Wadi Nimrin and around five miles wide. As the map shows, there was a clear run for cavalry (through low scrub or over clay hills) until they reached the foothills that ran east-west on both sides of the river, intersected by steep wadis. The main tracks were east-west. A north-south track in the foothills ran west of the eastern escarpment, affording some cover from an approach from the north and west. A dominating feature, Red Hill, lay on the east bank of the river with clay hills between it and the escarpment. It had commanding views in all directions. Red Hill was the key to any turning movement should the Turks attack from the north-west. The River Jordan had several known crossing places: at Ghoraniye and Mafid Jozele there were pontoon bridges with another at Jisr ed Damieh. Thus the troopers and the gunners would be fighting with their backs to their likely withdrawal route, the Umm esh Shert track. Any withdrawal route the cavalry or gunners would take was across the lie the land. This was not appreciated at the time because of the staff's faulty estimates of Turkish strength and dispositions.[3] Earlier, Lieutenant Colonel Granville's 1st Light Horse Regiment had overpowered the Turks on Red Hill and those holding the Umm esh Shert crossing. The cameleers had also attacked and demonstrated strongly to offer indirect support to Grant, although their brigaded artillery had little effect on the Turks then holding Red Hill given the strength of the Turkish entrenchments and the minimal effect of the 13-pounder lightweight shells.

The 19th RHA Brigade positioned itself as per orders and, with the 7th Light Horse Regiment and attached cavalry under Brigadier Onslow, they attacked Kabr Mujahid at 2.00 am on 30 April in an attempt to draw out the enemy infantry. The Turks did not oblige. A paucity of usable tracks delayed the momentum of the 4th Light Horse Brigade advance, with one regiment taking upwards of three hours to pass. But nonetheless Grant and his three batteries moved north despite artillery fire from the *48th Division*. This loss of momentum meant that surprise, a key element in cavalry warfare, had been lost. The brigade's first contact was with the Turkish outposts extended across the clay hills at El Haud to thc ford.

As the brigade advanced it came under enemy observation and fire from Red Hill, and soon shrapnel was bursting around the 4th Light Horse Regiment as its mounts picked up speed and forced their way through the low scrub.[4] The horsemen took some casualties from shellfire (six killed and 17 wounded) before they reached a turning point where the troopers were regrouped in their squadrons and the batteries came into action. Further progress by the screens was minimal and, at length, Grant was joined by Brigadier Wilson and his 3rd Light Horse Brigade. His brigade had been shelled as it followed Grant, and his objective was to move behind the Turks at Shunet Nimrin while the 60th Division attacked their front. His three batteries had been forced to cover Grant's frontage of around eight miles with both flanks exposed. Gullett recorded that 'they were pushed forward until they could cover the bridge at Damieh and the track leading down on the west side; but the range was extreme, the targets indefinite and the defensive power of the guns small.' Wilson turned right and set out for Es Salt, supported by the Hong Kong and Singapore Mountain Battery RGA and its long ammunition train of 360 camels.[5]

The occupation of Red Hill by a squadron of the 1st Light Horse Regiment was important, but the worrying aspect of the brigade's positioning was that there was a gap of around three miles between Grant's right and Wilson's left. The afternoon disclosed evident signs of a Turkish counter-attack and, accordingly, Chauvel took personal command of the cavalry, fully aware of the looming dangers to his force. He withdrew his regiments and batteries to a position close to the eastern escarpment. The regiments could withdraw into the hills, but the gunners were restricted to passable country to their south. During the night the batteries were withdrawn closer to the escarpment. For Chauvel 30 April was a day of mixed fortunes as he faced the unsettling realisation that he could not reinforce his front. For the Londoners of General Shea's division, it was a profitless slog on perfect defensive terrain that produced many casualties. And, as Gullett wrote, there was 'no news from the Arabs'. The good news was that Wilson's brigade had captured Es Salt. Supported by his Indian gunners and their camels, the 8th, 9th and 10th Light Horse regiments had been ordered to take Es Salt at dusk, which they did in a brilliant feat of arms, the Indian gunners using their guns singly at times to support the widely dispersed regiments. Their best shooting was a three-gun bombardment for five minutes enhanced by 12 machine-guns. It was completely successful.[6]

The first day of May dawned with Grant and his artillery adviser, Major Allen, contemplating the unwelcome fact that the Turks (*145th Regiment*) had built another crossing of the Jordan behind Red Hill, and the news that the enemy was massing for an attack, their guns unconcealed on features and with superb observation — a mark of their confidence. Grant's regiments (the 4th on the right, the 12th in the centre and the 11th on the left and also providing a reserve) could muster some 800 rifles and six Hotchkiss guns along with the brigade's machine-gun squadron. The enemy numbered 3000 and comprised cavalry, infantry and a German stormtrooper battalion. The batteries were echeloned in a diagonal across the line of the Turk's advance, and their headquarters was around two miles to the south. Notts was the most northern, then A Battery HAC and B Battery HAC. A Battery 'chose the least inaccessible wadi' in its given area. At 6.00 am when battle was joined, B Battery was in a reserve position close to brigade headquarters, and was quickly moved north. The batteries engaged the enemy with rapid fire and broke their centre. The Turks then swung south to cut the road (by which the brigade had deployed) and isolate the 3rd and 4th Light Horse brigades, while the Turkish mixed force pressured from the north. The situation facing the Australians was increasingly fraught.

Several hours later Major Allen, in temporary command of the brigade, ordered his batteries to retire by sections to a new position two miles to the south. A Battery's historian noted that,

> … the Left Section remained in action covering the retirement of the Right Section. By this time it was impossible to use the 'road' for retreat, and retirement would be effected through the hills. For this the six-horse teams were found to be useless and wagons had to be temporarily abandoned while the gun teams were doubled ... ammunition wagons were abandoned and orders given to save the guns using two fourteen and two sixteen horse teams. Ironically, the line of retreat chosen provided more cover than the open ground between.
>
> The position of the three guns of the Left Section soon became desperate. The enemy was within 400 yards and the leading gun teams were completely knocked out. With few other alternatives, personnel and horses were withdrawn to cover as quickly as possible. During this phase the section commander, Captain C.L. Harris, removed a breech block and rode off with it, only to be mortally wounded later. While it was small consolation, a signal, never received at RHA headquarters, enjoined its commander to 'dispose your batteries so as to be certain of being able to withdraw them if necessary.'[7]

B Battery HAC moved off on 30 April with the 4th Light Horse and the 5th Mounted brigades. Having pushed some reluctant mules over the bridge at Ghoraniye, they reached their (first) gun area, supporting the 5th Mounted Brigade and, in their usual fashion, opened up on the enemy, clearing the Turks from the ridges opposing them. The cavalry brigades (the 5th and 2nd Light Horse) then pushed forward to El Haud and Es Salt respectively. That night the battery was ordered to move to join the others in the AMD at Jisr ed Dameih in new positions, still on the eastern side of the river, in the foothills of the eastern escarpment. It did not reach its position until 9.00 pm to the sound of sporadic rifle and machine-gun fire. It was initially in a reserve position around a mile south of its colleagues, abeam of Red Hill, some three miles away, now held by a squadron from each of the 1st and 11th Light Horse regiments. Before dawn the battery was ordered up and recorded zero lines at dawn. Each battery had different zero lines to cover 180 degrees of front. Notts had a northern quadrant and A Battery an eastern quadrant. Their sole support was one armoured car, the other one having been wrecked by a shell the previous day.[8]

Chapter 21

When the Turks launched their assault, A Battery HAC and the Notts Battery engaged them at 2000 yards over a frontage of 60 degrees. At 7.00 am Major Allen ordered B Battery HAC to join its colleagues. So rough and steep was the terrain that it was impossible to select a position with any cover, even had there been ample time to do so. Zero lines were ordered so that the combined battery fire engaged the Turks on their most threatening axis of advance. Fortunately, while much musket and machine-gun fire was unleashed at the battery, the gunners' ability to bring the guns into action quickly reduced casualties. By 9.00 am the Turkish advance had slowed, largely as a result of the combined batteries' fire. Major Allen then ordered the batteries to withdraw by sections to a position some 1000 yards south. From this position the battery could cover the cavalry withdrawal to its prearranged line. At 10.00 am both Red Hill light horse squadrons were swept aside by superior forces, reckoned by now at five to one. Allen moved his headquarters to Grant's (brigade) headquarters, and every available man joined the fray.[9] Some hope was held that a relief force of two New Zealand regiments and a cavalry brigade (the 4th) would arrive to stem the attack, but they were too far away.

General Grant now ordered a retirement, despite the fact that the Turkish forces were arrayed across his intended line of withdrawal from west to south. The 4th Light Horse Regiment made a determined attempt to cover the retirement of the guns, holding on until the enemy closed to within 200 yards. While B Battery's fire checked the attackers, the gunners now only had some 20 rounds left: 'Each time a Turk attack closed and melted away before their fire, the enemy dead lay a little closer to our guns.' Eventually the gun teams fell victim to machine-gun fire. Three gun numbers were shot as they tried to remove the breeches from their guns, the guns ultimately abandoned. Once their ammunition was exhausted, the gunners prepared other demolitions before the force withdrew, firing as it retired up the slope to the location of the troopers' horses. Allen had ordered them to go further south, occupy a position and fire their remaining rounds before securing an ammunition resupply. B Battery HAC had the shortest distance to cover and was ordered to return via Wadi Retem. Major Elliott used the ground effectively and retired by sub-sections under heavy and machine-gun fire. The remaining armoured car attached to the brigade was sited to give excellent covering fire. The gunners worked hard to save whatever they could from this disaster. During the withdrawal across the steep, rugged hills, a wagon and gun fell into a ravine. When a party scrambled down to retrieve it, the men were caught by rifle and machine-gun fire, most aimed at the animals. The battery lost most of these horses, and the brigade field ambulance at the rear went into captivity.[10]

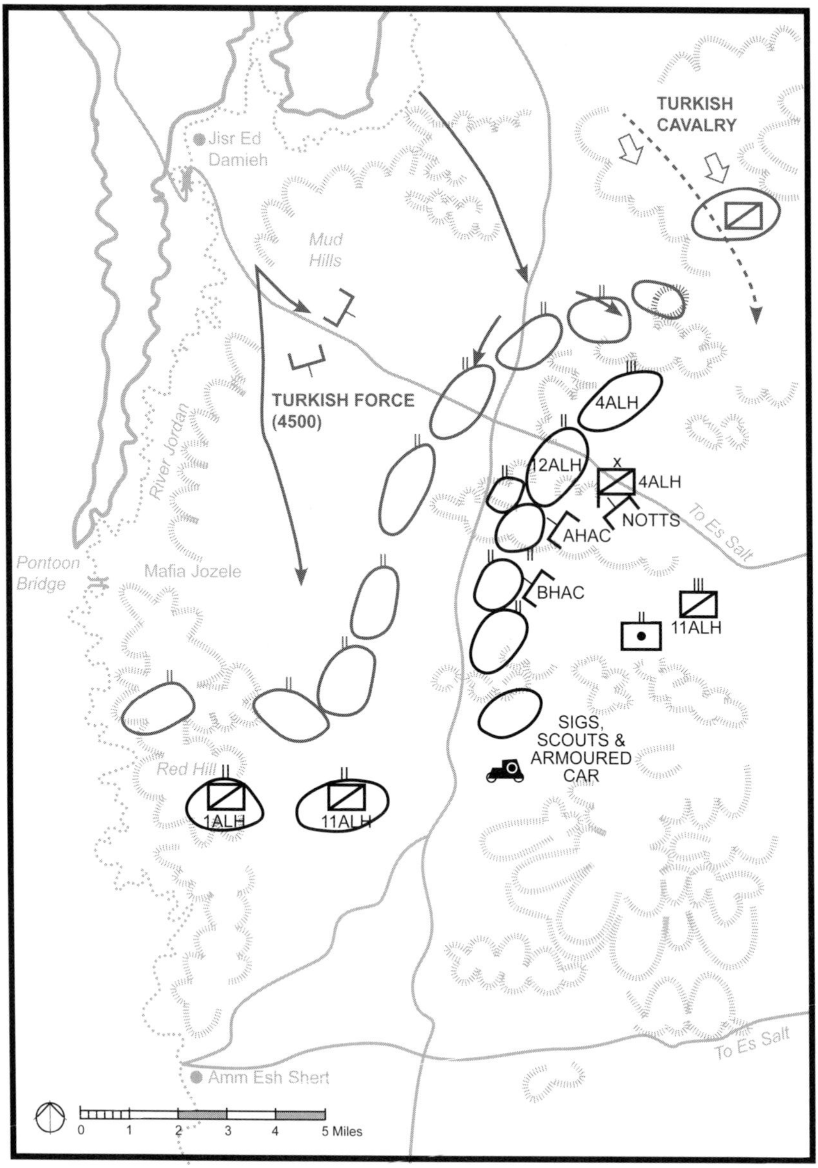

Map 17: The 4th Light Horse Brigade's Jordan Valley debacle of 1 May 1918. The Turks mustered superior forces and drove the brigade from the valley. They also captured nine guns of the Notts Battery RHA and A and B batteries HAC, the worst calamity that befell the horse gunners in the Middle East theatre (source: Gullett, *Official History*, Vol. VII, *Sinai and Palestine*, Map 33).

Chapter 21

By 12.00 the affair was mercifully over and General Chaytor had arrived, assessed the situation, and ordered a retirement to the Umm esh Shert track. At the same time Grant had ordered his 4th and 12th regiments south as fast as possible, and it became a race between the light horsemen, leading their mounts over the rough escarpment, and the Turks racing on foot, to reach the Umm esh Shert track. The light horsemen were desperate to win this race and keep open the withdrawal route for the cavalry stretched out between the Jordan and Es Salt. At length a firing line was constructed on the lower hills and entrenchments dug. This was the limit of the Turks' advance and marked the positions occupied by the Turkish *2nd*, *58th* and *143rd infantry regiments.*

When B Battery HAC arrived back at the impromptu line it immediately brought its three guns into action, this time under cover. Chauvel, grimly monitoring his troopers' situation, ordered Chaytor, who had lost communication with Headquarters DMC during the action due to a break in the telephone line, to take over the defence of the valley. Fortunately, the ground a mile north of the Umm esh Shert track afforded a good defensive line. He ordered this to be held 'at all costs', his only reserve a regiment of New Zealanders. Despite this, Chaytor managed to establish a series of posts on the slopes of the foothills. As the day lengthened, incessant attacks continued, targeting the New Zealanders and the light horsemen in their new positions. The Turks then swung south to cut the Umm esh Shert road by which the brigade had deployed, in an attempt to isolate the light horsemen and New Zealanders. Grant's brigade and attached squadrons made a tactical withdrawal in good order. From its concealed positions in the scrub, B Battery HAC provided crucial support, using its three guns against the enemy artillery, thus reducing casualties from the Turkish guns.

At the recently captured Es Salt, another force from Amman was closing on the town from the east, while two other prongs from the north and north-west were threatening the cavalry force and its Indian gunners with encirclement. Cox and Wilson's brigades were withdrawn to Es Salt, covering the approach from the Damieh track. Troops from the 60th Division were still engaged at Shunet Nimrin, having failed to gain their objective, and Chauvel ordered Shea to continue the attacks to keep the Turks occupied while the cavalry withdrew down the Umm esh Shert track. But the Londoners could not break the Turkish defences and, by the late afternoon of 1 May, as the commanders discussed how best to coordinate their deployments, the situation for the cavalry force was becoming increasingly desperate. The commanders had little option but to cancel the operation and save the force before it fell into Turkish hands. However

Chauvel remained determined not to accept defeat, and ordered Hodgson to attack the rear of the Turkish positions at Shunet Nimrin. The configuration of the DMC force prior to its withdrawal on 2 May resembled a large thumb, the base of which was the Jordan River, protruding from Umm esh Shert east of north, to Es Salt and three miles beyond it, curving south-west to south of Shunet Nimrin.

In the general withdrawal from Es Salt there were several spirited actions in which the troopers' losses were far fewer than those of their enemy. With Allenby's consent Chauvel ordered a withdrawal at 4.00 pm on 3 May. It was not until 4 May that the Turks discovered that their enemy had departed Es Salt. The cavalry made a crucial contribution to the withdrawal. Brigadier Godwin, GOC 6th Mountain Brigade, sent the Dorset Yeomanry to bring in the Leicester and Berks batteries and the three remaining guns of B Battery HAC. The Turks harried the withdrawal with their customary aggression, willing to sustain casualties to gain ground, and consistently employing their artillery to maintain pressure. Allenby's troops finally withdrew across the Ghoraniye bridge along the road they had originally taken.[11]

Only three guns of 12 survived that dismal day. A Battery and Notts Battery, the furthest north in both positions, fared worst, losing all their guns in similar circumstances. B Battery HAC lost one gun and five men wounded, one fatally.[12] In the Royal and Royal Horse artilleries, losing one's guns was historically the equivalent of a battalion losing its colours, and was viewed by some as the equivalent of regicide. An enquiry was held and the commander of the 19th RHA Brigade, Major Allen, took full responsibility for the orders he had issued on the day, insisting that they had been obeyed implicitly by his battery commanders. General Allenby sent a letter to the brigade in which he told the 19th:

> After making a full inquiry into the operations of 1 May, the Commander-in-Chief wishes to congratulate the 19th Brigade RHA ('A' Battery HAC, 'B' Battery HAC and the Notts Battery RHA) on their conspicuous gallantry and devotion to duty. The Commander-in-Chief is convinced that the RHA were not to blame for the loss of guns, or failure, in part, to destroy them.

B Battery's Major Elliott was awarded the DSO, Second Lieutenant P.D. Smith the Military Cross and Sergeant A.J. Clarke the Distinguished Conduct Medal.[13] Gullett provides an overview of the casualty statistics, itemising British losses (1849) and recording other casualties as illustrated in Table 11 below:

Chapter 21

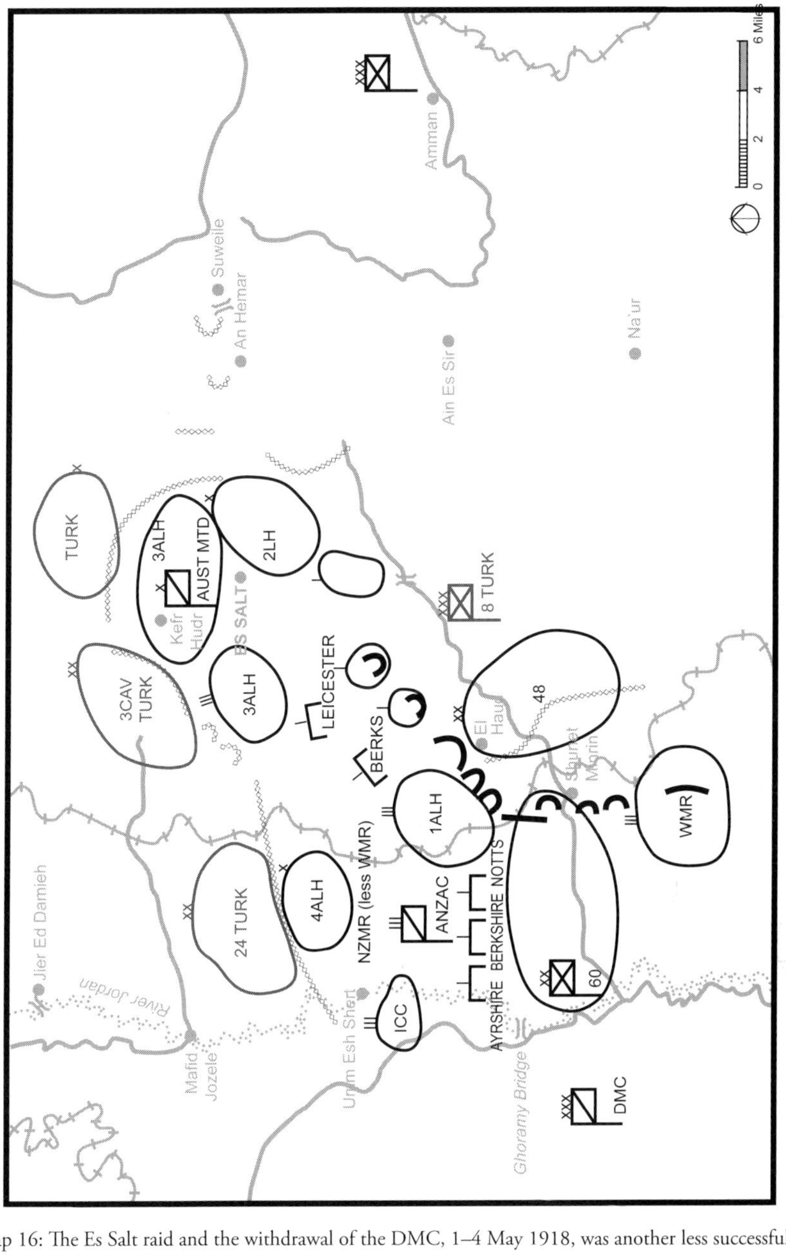

Map 16: The Es Salt raid and the withdrawal of the DMC, 1–4 May 1918, was another less successful operation for both the DMC and the 60th (London) Division against the Turkish *VIII Corps* (source: Hill, *Chauvel of the Light Horse*, p. 150).

TABLE 11: CASUALTIES FOR THE SECOND ES SALT RAID

	KIA	WIA	MIA
British casualties:			
Officers:	16	84	3
Other ranks:	198	1214	134
Total	**214**	**1298**	**137**
AMD			
Officers:	6	32	
Other ranks:	44	278	37*
Total	**50**	**310**	**37**
60th Division:			
All ranks	1116 (roughly two-thirds)[14]		

*most at Damieh

Turkish losses were upwards of 1000 men taken prisoner and approximately the same number killed and wounded.

The entire strategy of the infantry and the A&NZ Mounted Division for penetrating through to Amman and Es Salt had failed and their commanders had then worked hard to rescue those forces to the east of the River Jordan. Enemy forces had reinforced Shunet Nimrin and the infantry attacks supported by artillery had not succeeded, with the Turks threatening a large proportion of Allenby's offensive power. Turkish staff work proved superior and, following their thrust to isolate Grant's 4th Light Horse Brigade, placed Chauvel's forces at a continuing disadvantage. Enemy artillery made its presence felt at every opportunity, and the rough country yet again proved a formidable obstacle to manoeuvre plans and timings. Following their long string of defeats, the Turks' morale now soared. What the Allies failed to appreciate at the time was that losing nine guns dislocated the allocation of RHA batteries for subsequent operations and they were unable to support their comrades-in-arms once the order of battle for Megiddo was decided. For the horse artillerymen it meant severing well-established cavalry relationships and starting the process of rebuilding, albeit for just a brief period.

The attacking troops had been in action for almost four days without relief and their dogged determination was extraordinary. They had minimal support apart from their organic batteries, and the 60th Division could certainly have performed better had more heavy artillery and ammunition been available. For its part, the Turkish high command had been shaken by the ease with which the

Allied cavalry could menace and 'raid at will the mountain fastness'. It reacted by deploying more troops in the 'mountain fastness' to oppose Allenby's anticipated next thrust in the autumn. One significant factor was the non-appearance of the Arab irregular force (the Beni Sakr) which had been tasked to tie down the enemy around Amman. Had it kept its part of the bargain, events may have taken a better turn — for the short term at any rate. But at what cost to future strategy? Where Allenby's staff erred was to believe the reports of the success of Lawrence of Arabia's attacks on the Hejaz railway line in disrupting supplies to the southern front. These were highly exaggerated for political purposes. Hughes notes that Lawrence's irregular forces' disruptions were soon remedied by 'task forces' of labourers and engineers such that there were few consequences of note to show for their demolitions.[15]

However, some long-term benefit did emerge from this failure, which was very deeply felt by all ranks. Their first defeat since Second Gaza was bitter medicine. In the words of Goold-Walker, the HAC's historian, 'the raid finally convinced the enemy that, in our next general advance, our cavalry would be directed on Amman and Deraa Junction (on the Hejaz railway). He was led to place practically the whole of his *Fourth Army* east of the Jordan. The country would separate this army from the remainder of his forces in the Judean Hills.' This set the scene for the apocalyptic Battle of Megiddo in September.[16]

Chapter 22
The Northern Front
1. Wadi Auja:
18 March 1918

Then steadily, shoulder to shoulder,
Steadily, blade by blade,
Ready and strong, marching along,
Like the boys of the old brigade.

'The Old Brigade'
F.E. Weatherly, 1848–1929

Allenby planned an advance to the heights of Abu Tellul through which ran the waters of the (western-flowing) Wadi Auja, a significant asset during summer campaigning. By denying the Turks access to Wadi Auja, he hoped to produce despair in enemy forces on the plateau, significantly affecting their fighting spirit. Allenby's front extended north along the River Jordan at Ghoraniye for three miles then arced north-west for another 50 miles west to end at the coast. The primary man-made routes influencing XX Corps operations comprised the track from Musallabeh north to Baissan on the west bank of the Jordan, a track from Jisr ed Damieh to Nablus, the road to Nablus from Jerusalem that roughly bisected the front, and the railway and road from Ludd to Tul Keram on the coastal sector. The enemy command centres were the recaptured Es Salt (*Fourth Army*) to the east, Nablus (*Central* and *Seventh Army*) and Tul Keram (*Eighth Army*). The terrain in this area was more suited to artillery operations, and Generals Chetwode and Bulfin had almost all the heavy and siege batteries in their area of operations on which to base their planning. This involved a great deal of reconnaissance and cooperation, as both corps sought better areas for their guns. The first of the forward moves began on 2 March. The 53rd Division, for example, advanced three miles to a position west of the Nablus road, and even further three nights later to the village of Taibiye.[1] These movements would not have been possible without the physical labour of the engineers and infantry working parties, as the staff was chiefly concerned with artillery support. Both corps artillery staff and observation groups were keen to further develop their tactics and expertise, and these measures left the gunners feeling particularly buoyant.

Image 16: The Abu Tellul feature was regarded by both the Allies and Turks as tactically important and was contested by both sides. It was the site of a combined German-Turkish defeat (AWM B00035).

The Turkish command covered both the *Eighth (Jevad) Army* with its *3rd* and *7th divisions* and the *Seventh (Ismet) Army* with its *III Corps*, *1st* and *24th divisions* and *XX Corps* (*Ali Faud*) including its *26th* and *53rd divisions*. Their offensive power totalled some 8000 rifles and 800 sabres, bolstered by 150 guns.

Bulfin's XXI Corps went into its attack on 12 March with:

- 52nd (Lowland), 54th (East Anglian) and 75th divisions and XXI Corps Cavalry
- XXI Corps artillery had been organised into groups under the newly promoted Brigadier Williamson-Oswald:
    - 100th Heavy Group — 15th and 181st batteries, one section of the 43rd Siege Battery
    - 102nd Heavy Group — 189th and 202nd, 380th siege batteries, one section each of the 43rd and 304th siege batteries
    - 95th Heavy Group –– 209th Siege Battery, one section each of the 134th and 304th siege batteries

- Under command 75th Division — one section of the 134th Siege Battery (tractor drawn)

Chetwode's XX Corps prepared for its attack on 8 March with the 10th (Irish) Division, 53rd (Welsh) Division, 74th (Yeomanry) Division and the 181st Brigade of the 60th (London) Division. Its objectives were Kheir el Beiyudat and Abu Tellul north of the Wadi Auja. The 53rd and 74th divisions each had a section of the 91st Heavy Battery while the 10th Division had the 195th Heavy Battery attached. The big guns consisted of seven siege and heavy batteries under the command of Brigadier P.deS. Burney.[2] The attached Londoners' brigade had a light trench mortar battery allotted in support, the Aucklanders had the 302nd RFA Brigade (less one battery), a field company of engineers (522nd) and a field ambulance (2/6th London).

The attached brigade (181st) anchored the corps' right flank on the Wadi Auja, while the 158th Brigade was sent to capture the strategic height of Tel Asur (3340 feet above sea level). The artillery line comprised a battery and an RFA brigade from the 60th Division, a battery of the 74th Division Artillery and the 10th Mountain Battery. The 91st Heavy Battery, 527th RFA Brigade, saw the 5th Royal Welsh Fusiliers onto its objective following a heavy bombardment. The Welshmen tried stoutly to defend it but failed and the feature was later recaptured by its sister battalion, the 6th Royal Welsh Fusiliers. Elsewhere, Major General Mott's 53rd Division was denied the heights of Chipp Hill by its dogged defenders.

A simultaneous assault by the 230th Brigade on Burg Bardawil was supported by A and B batteries, 44th RFA Brigade, B and C batteries of the 117th RFA Brigade and 527th Battery, which were sited 4000 yards behind the front at Juffna. The 10th Division on the left flank put its three brigades in line to extend their front, supported by the 67th, 68th and 263rd RFA brigades and the 195th Heavy Battery 2000 yards to the rear. The latter was given purely counter-battery tasks, and contributed to the division's success in achieving its objectives.

The infantry's objective was the line of Wadi Deir Ballut. Farndale notes that 'there were good positions for the artillery', recognising also the impressive road-building efforts of the RE field companies and infantry working parties to move the guns forward. On one such road to Abud, the 172nd Brigade RFA advanced by leapfrogging batteries.[3] On this occasion the 234th Brigade (75th Division) made good progress and was on its objective by 2.40 pm. The division's sector was poorly served by roads. Prompt and effective support from the South African Field Artillery Brigade enabled the infantry to hold their ground. The Springbok gunners were in the centre of the divisional front some 2000 yards behind their affiliated battalions.

On the left flank of the division, right of the north-south railway, were the heavy guns and the 270th RFA Brigade (two 18-pounder batteries only) at Qule and Nabi Tari. They were sited to cover Muzeir'a ridge and Majdal Yaba. H Hour for the 162nd Brigade's operation was 6.00 am for a bombardment of one hour and 45 minutes for the first feature and 12.00 for Majdal Yaba. This second bombardment lasted only 15 minutes, and it took only those 15 minutes to subdue the enemy. The Turks yielded 40 prisoners and the infantry sustained 15 casualties, a fine example of artillery-infantry cooperation and fire planning. By afternoon all the Turks had withdrawn north of the Wadi Deir Ballut.[4]

The official historian observed of both corps' artillery work: 'If known British preponderance in both field and heavy artillery had been anything approaching equality, the British field batteries would not have been able to move forward as they did.' The inference was that far higher infantry casualties would have been sustained had this not been the case.[5]

Gullet recorded casualties for the action at a total of 1415, with enemy prisoners at 281, although he provides no figures for Turkish fatalities. Casualty figures for the 53rd and 60th divisions were:

	KIA	WIA	MIA
Officers:	13	81	3
Other ranks:	168	975	73
Total	**181**	**1056**	**76**

This amounts to 1313, or 93% of the gross count.[6]

Chapter 23
Summer in the Jordan Valley: May–July 1918

Flies die in July, men in August and we shall bury you in September.

Turkish military proverb

The recorded history of military operations in the Jordan Valley during the summer months was non-existent, and the area was well known to be 'depopulated' for several months at that time of the year. The oppressive heat and epidemics of reptiles and insects prompted the Arabs to move out of the hills, particularly given the plague proportions of mosquitoes which spread a particularly malignant form of malaria. It was generally believed that a white (Caucasian) man could not survive the summer season. Allenby, however, was faced with little in the way of choice. While he could evacuate his forces from the valley, the Turks would immediately return. This would make any future operations to reach Amman or the Hejaz railway far more difficult even than the recent failed operations of April–May. Alternatively, he could maintain a force in the hills over summer and simply accept the accompanying wastage of man and beast as the lesser of the two evils. Ultimately, Allenby left the decision to Chauvel, whose DMC was to be the garrisoning force. Chauvel decided to stay and established his headquarters on the new Jericho road, east of Talat ed Dumm.[1]

Chauvel divided his tactical area of operations into the left (northern) sector and right (eastern) sector. The left sector extended from the foot of the Judean Hills west for 10 miles towards the XX Corps area of operations. It crossed some of the most rugged country, 'so rough as to be practically impassable to an enemy force', the task of patrolling the gap given to the cavalry. The area included the northern bank of the Wadi Auja to where it joined the River Jordan, including the bridge at that point. The high ground features were Abu Tellul and the Musallabeh bluff. The heights overlooked the scrub, swamp and rocky plain riven by smaller wadis. This area was given to Brigadier Hodgson, whose force comprised the AMD, 20th Indian Brigade, 22nd Mounted Brigade and 383rd Siege Battery. The right sector, extending from the mouth of the Wadi Auja on the right bank of the Jordan and the vital bridge at Ghoraniye south to the Dead Sea, became the responsibility of Chaytor's A&NZ Mounted Division. His force comprised the cameleers and the 181st Infantry Brigade (60th Division) and their artillery. The staff had recognised that the use of camels in this terrain was problematic, and at length Brigadier Smith's force changed to horses and became the 5th Light Horse Brigade, 14th and 15th Light Horse regiments, commanded by Lieutenant Colonel George Onslow.[2] This arrangement allowed the brigades to be rotated between active duty and rest camps near Jerusalem's higher and cooler climate (2500 feet above sea level). It was Allenby's stated policy 'to subject as few as possible to the evil conditions'. For gunners this was a luxury they had to forego as few could be spared at any one time. A small rest centre was established for gunners for the horse, mountain and siege/heavy artillerymen at Kolonieh, operated by the HAC B Battery's Captain Rushbrooke.[3]

The troops came to 'know the valley climate' intimately and were soon all too familiar with its terrain. The valley floor comprised marl, a loose soil rich in clay, almost a foot deep and as fine as flour. Men and horses kicked up dust clouds with the slightest movement. The winds varied with almost clockwork timing. In the morning, after a still night, a hot (katabatic) wind blew strongly from the north until around 11.00 am. Once it abated, the intense heat — up to 130º Fahrenheit (55º Celsius) — lasted until the wind reversed direction (anabatic) with similar strength until 8.00 pm. Dust rose in clouds from nose height to hundreds of feet, known as 'dust devils'. The dust was no respecter of tentage or belongings when it came to penetration. This enervating climate produced a sick rate of around 1% per day, and the gunners' horses, with little work to do and unwilling to walk to watering places, quickly lost condition. While flies disappeared, mosquitoes thrived and spread the dreaded malaria. Scorpions and snakes also contributed to the troops' discomfort, with no fewer than 32 varieties with which to contend. It was a sad but true fact of life that many a veteran trooper or gunner who survived Turkish shot, shell, accidents and hard campaigning would succumb to malaria, despite the latest medical and prophylactic practices. It was particularly hard on older men.[4]

The eastern sector of the front had a different topography to its north and dictated the dispersion of Chauvel's front line and administrative areas. The A&NZ Mounted Division provided part of his cavalry, with its organic RHA brigade and an assortment of mixed ordnance. The DMC at this time (May) included the 4th and 5th Indian cavalry divisions. This allowed the horsemen to be rotated monthly to rest areas close to Jerusalem. As indicated, however, this was not the gunners' lot. On 26 May Colonel Preston returned to command his brigade (19th RHA) of both A and B batteries HAC and the Notts Battery. They occupied positions on the valley floor of the Wadi Auja east of the Abu Tellul ridge where the Notts Battery endured the same privations as the HAC's personnel. Preston also had a section of 60-pounders and mountain battery howitzers at his disposal. The only concealed positions for his 13-pounders and mountain guns were in different areas of the wadi. The gunnery advantage clearly rested with the Turks in terms of both concealment and screening, chiefly from the north-east. Thus the British gunners could expect 'searching fire' on a regular basis. The enemy maintained this fire both day and night prompting the troops' chief gripe of having to wear a 'shrapnel helmet' (tin hat) for long periods in searing heat.

Image 17: A wagon brings supplies to a detachment — note the tracks (foreground) and dust. Troops were rotated for duty during summer in the Jordan Valley which was noted for its vile climate, sickness, mosquitoes, dust and heat (AWM H02984).

On the gun line, A Battery HAC had to wait a few days before re-equipping with guns and absorbing reinforcements. In the interim, battery personnel were employed on the supply train for the Amman raiding force until 6 May. They escorted donkey transport bringing men, guns, rations and ammunition up and down the withdrawal routes. The battery then repaired to a camp seven miles north of Jericho and completed its rehabilitation and partial re-equipping. It waited another week for its 13-pounder guns and, on 21 May, moved back to the front but with only five guns. The battery was in the line until July, having taken over from a battery of the 302nd RFA Brigade, and for the next week registered targets, fired at opportunity targets and worked itself back into a cohesive sub-unit of the brigade while supporting (up to) a light horse squadron 'on rotation'.

The gunners settled into a routine involving a static front (or trench warfare) enhanced by a selection of OPs over the Jordan that provided superior observation of the Turk's front line. The battery also took possession of a Krupp 75mm gun, the type that had caused much grief on the road to Jerusalem. It was superior to the 13-pounder, 'lighter, more mobile, solid platform, longer range and a lesser flash profile during night shoots.' As Goold-Walker writes, 'it gave forth the smallest of flashes, a most important point in avoiding drawing enemy counter battery fire.' However its biggest drawback was the quality of ammunition. By now the battery had dug in its guns, camouflaged them well and watered the gun position twice daily to lay the tell-tale dust during firing, thus enjoying high immunity from counter-battery fire.[5]

Yet another feature of operations was the use of Australian Light Horse officers as proxy OPOs. With a front of a mile and only five guns it was almost impossible for the OPOs to cover the zone while Turkish troops were moving their front line forward under cover of the scrub. A pattern of operations developed which saw 'stand to' marked by the teams assembling in the wagon lines until 'stand down'. One gun was deployed forward by night to retaliate when enemy artillery fire was unusually heavy. In the afternoon, between 2.00 and 4.00 pm, both sides maintained their presence with fire on registered targets. The A Battery diarist noted that, 'in one case the light horsemen pushed forward under cover of artillery fire and captured a considerable number of the enemy, which resulted in the enemy resuming their original line.'[6]

When B Battery HAC was in the line, Colonel Preston visited his OPs, at one point attracting the attention of a sniping gun which fired shrapnel at him. The fuse finished at his horse's feet. It was a 13-pounder round. Like his opposite number, he too applied for a Turk 7.7cm gun, and duly received it. Manned very early in the morning by volunteer detachments from all batteries, it was connected by phone to the OP on the top of Abu Tellul. The duty OPO returned the 'annoyance' compliment by inflicting casualties on the Turks, 'who never ventured to show themselves in daytime. It was the only real entertainment we had, and was mightily diverting for the first few weeks.' However, the Turks' initiative was not restricted to light guns. They sited a 15cm gun north-west of Chauvel's line that could range out to 20,000 yards. Dubbed 'Jericho Jane', the piece was augmented by two more guns and was reported in the daily Headquarters RA report as 'Jericho Jane and her two Wicked Sisters'.[7]

Enemy fire was referred to as 'galling' insofar as the soldiers of the service and medical corps (to single out two) felt frustrated by the absence of any real counter-battery fire because there was no reduction in the attention they received from the enemy gunners. The field ambulance, ordnance and ammunition columns, and headquarters personnel were located on the east side of the Tel el Sultan–Abu Tellul ridge. This lay 7000 yards from the Jordan and in clear view of the Red Hill OPs. The Turks moved more guns and howitzers south to harass the headquarters echelon. Camps and horse lines had to be moved with monotonous regularity every few days to reduce their impact. B Battery HAC's wagon lines were co-located and, during a 'hate', 'a G.S wagon full of HE shell was set on fire in the camp of the Divisional Ammunition Column. Second Lieutenant Jones, with Sergeants Mott and Davis at once rushed to the burning wagon, and succeeded in unloading all the cases of shells, some of which were actually on fire.'[8]

Watering parties were shelled daily and decoy measures adopted to beat the Turk who took advantage of the clear early morning air to move a small sniping light gun to harass the first working parties on Abu Tellul. This attracted a heavy shelling program that targeted his artillery in retaliation. Despite this, there were losses of men and beasts and much material damage to tentage and sandbagged revetments. The only benefit to raising dust clouds was that it neutralised observation. There were relatively fewer casualties to personnel in the static locations. Furthermore, enemy long-range guns could easily reach the administrative areas whereas the 60-pounders lacked accurate target fixation to retaliate effectively. Clearly the Turks' aggressive approach to Chauvel's force kept them 'on their toes', despite the enervating climate, and was effective for all that. Their superior observation meant little rest for the men. This was not the first, nor was it to be the last time the troops were critical of Brigadier Salmond's air force's inability to locate and neutralise enemy artillery. The airmen protested that they were 'unable to see gun flashes in the broken ground, dust, scrub and the damp atmosphere', the latter a reference to the effect of water vapour rising from the Dead Sea. If Chauvel's command enjoyed any advantage it lay in the skill and audacity of the light horsemen and the Indian soldiers whose patrolling and scouting were 'second to none'.

The infantry developed the position into a defensive stronghold, digging miles of trenches on the flat clay and sangars in the rocky slopes, wiring their positions and clearing many miles of tracks for vehicle movement. Their camps were constructed on the tributaries of wadis and the engineers worked hard to drain the swamps to defeat the mosquito and malaria menace. Their efforts were complemented by precautions suggested by the medical corps which saw a drop in cases of infection. Serious cases were sent to the 14th Australian General Hospital close to Jerusalem. The soldiers' chief recreation was swimming and bathing their horses. However, they continued to succumb to sandfly fever and 'five day fever'. Their patrolling regimes, which took them some distance from their trench lines, were undertaken on horseback at night and in the early morning and, by the time the Indian lancers joined them for 'training', the Turkish *ahmet*'s appetite for a fight was waning and desertions to the patrols were common. As was recorded, 'nearly all the Intelligence reports during the summer months made cheery reading for the British.'[9]

Despite this, the Turkish command pursued its aggressive plans to eject the British from the Jordan Valley. With the April raid on Musallabeh behind them, the Turks were eager to take the bluff as part of a plan to gain the Abu Tellul feature. If Chauvel was uneasy about the soundness of any part of his defence structure, it was the force he maintained at Abu Tellul to defend it from a Turkish attack from the west.

The Abu Tellul defences covered several thousand yards in a triangular shape, the apex of which was the high ground of Musallabeh, the sides some 4000 yards long. The 1st Light Horse Brigade held the north salient and the 2nd Light Horse Brigade was sited to the east, with the Wellington Mounted Rifles to the right. The 1st Light Horse Brigade's 2nd Light Horse Regiment held around 2000 yards either side of the triangle. East to west the localities and features were:

- The Bluff — 1600 yards south and reached by a track from El Madhbeh further south.
- Vyse post, extending south-west and divided by sharp ravines with the posts Vale, View, Vaux, Zoo and Zeiss some 100 to 400 yards apart. Zeiss lay 3000 yards from Vyse.
- El Madhbeh and Wadi Nueiame, the location of the reserves, formed the base of the triangle. The Wadi Mellahah lay 4000 yards to the east. A series of defended localities, some 20 scattered posts including Star, Scrap and Shell, covered these eastern approaches.

The NZMR Brigade acted as the divisional reserve with the 4th Light Horse Brigade in corps reserve, ready to react to any tactical crisis. Chauvel's other tactical responsibilities included the Ghoraniye and El Hinu bridgeheads. These were the province of the 2nd Mounted Division (Imperial Infantry Brigade, Imperial Cavalry brigades and 7th Mounted Brigade, all Indian troops). Total troop numbers for the Abu Tellul affair amounted to 4200 sabres, of which 2500 participated, with 1500 rifles in reserve and 36 guns. The Abu Tellul ridge was the key as it commanded the waters of the wadi.

By previous standards in Jordan Valley 'affairs', the artillery strength was considerable and Colonel Prescott's command comprised:

- Notts Battery, A and B batteries HAC with 13-pounders
- C/301st and C/303rd 4.5-inch howitzer batteries (detached from the 60th Division's CRA)
- 11th Mountain Battery RFA
- Hong Kong and Singapore Mountain Battery RGA[10]

The light horsemen had dug in and wired their positions, built sangars in the refractory ground and pegged out fields of fire. Their posts were sited and constructed to allow a tactical withdrawal if necessary, the troopers aware that their posts were susceptible to encirclement. Never did an area of tactically important ground receive so much scrutiny in finalising the defensive layout. The problem attracted the wisdom of the collective minds of every general officer from Allenby down: operations staff officers, brigade, regimental and squadron commanders, and probably individual troopers. The gunners' major problems concerned the hard, rocky ground in which they were unable to bury their telephone cable and the location of suitable positions in the El Madhbeh locality.

On14 July at 2.30 am, four battalions (two German, two Turkish) attacked Musallabeh and Abu Tellul, while the Turkish elements of the *10th* and *3/43rd infantry battalions* attacked across the Wadi Mellahah. Their combined rifle strength was 5000 (engaged) and 1200 sabres (800 engaged). The Germans and Turks attacked at the point anticipated by Chauvel, launching their assault from the north-west, and following it several hours later at Wadi Mellahah and El Hinu with a subsidiary 'diversion' cavalry attack close to the river. All their attacks were well supported by around 150 artillery pieces and machine-guns. In essence, water and guns meant that the defence of Abu Tellul could have just one outcome — it must be held at all costs. The Turko-German assault was hardly a secret or a surprising venture. The troops all along the front were shelled frequently and heavily by the German batteries of 77mm, 4.2-inch guns and the '5.9s' of the *702nd* and *703rd batteries* from the north-west causing considerable casualties. This fire was well directed, not only on the forward posts, but also on reserve regiments. Nor were they at pains to conceal their reconnaissance, and the *Yilderim battalions* had an excellent picture of Chauvel's defence plan. Elsewhere a battalion of the *146th Regiment* and a company of the *11th Jaeger Regiment* associated with the *Turkish Caucasus Brigade* (*32nd*, *58th* and *163rd regiments*) comprised the attacking force in two other locations.[11]

Chapter 23

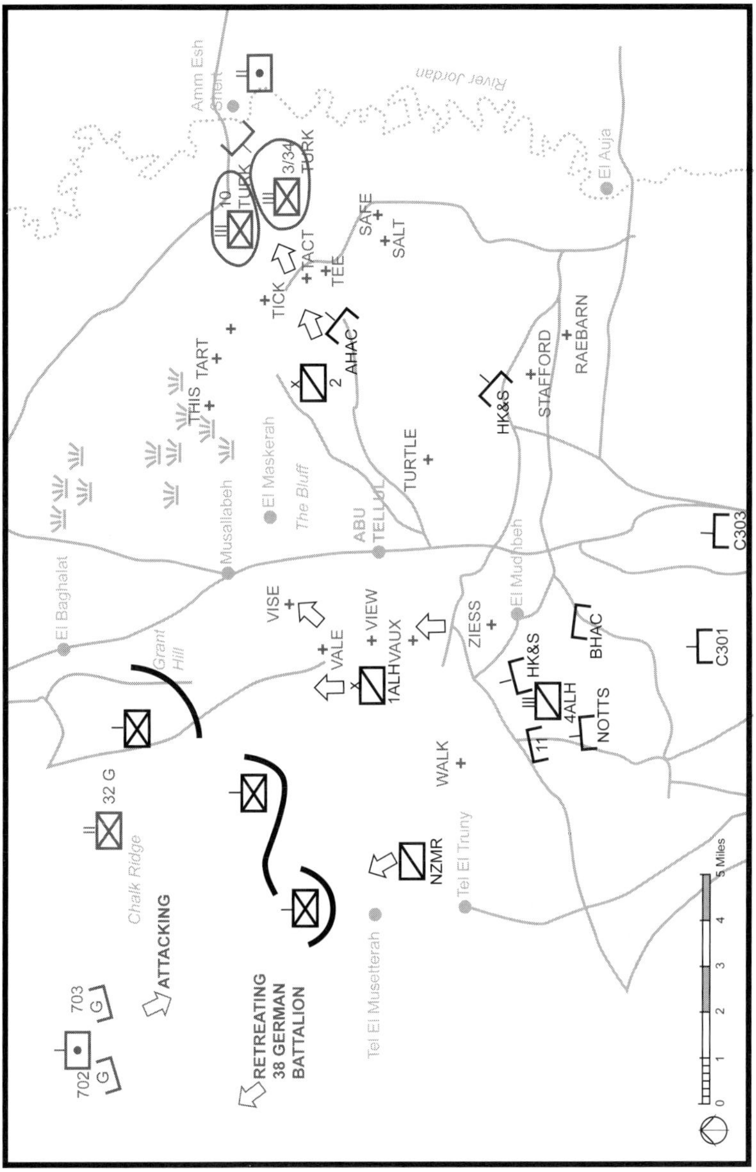

Map 18: The Abu Tellul defence and counter-attack of 14 July 1918. This was primarily a defensive battle for the light horsemen (2nd Light Horse Brigade) who were used as infantry and dug in on this dominating feature (343 feet high). A strong artillery presence was deployed. The German/Turks attacked strongly using artillery from the west, north-west, north and north-east. They were soundly defeated (source: Gullett, *Official History*, Vol. VII, *Sinai and Palestine,* Map 36).

Chauvel had no way of efficiently utilising counter-battery fire, as he lacked heavy or siege guns. The gunners were acutely aware that the enemy could bring a wider range of ordnance to support their attack compared to Cox's relatively light field pieces. Nonetheless, the Australian troopers' morale was high and, should the enemy penetrate their posts or move in behind them, they were determined to continue the fight. While they were short of machine-guns to cover all possible approaches, preparation of the defences had given all ranks an intimate knowledge of the terrain. Despite this, the hard, stony ground prevented the gunners preparing alternative positions and digging in their communications.

The 2nd Light Horse Brigade was in the line when the enemy attacked. H Hour at 2.30 am on 14 July was marked by heavy counter-battery fire which fell on Prescott's gun positions. They responded by firing their defensive fire tasks in front of View and Vale posts, the most likely line of approach as assessed by Chauvel. During the bombardment telephone lines between the OPs and guns were cut and the gunners were unable to respond as effectively as they had planned. The observers shared their OPs with the troopers and, as rehearsed, planned to withdraw if they did. The German troops swept through the troopers' positions between Vale and View and, at one stage, were only 200 yards from some of the guns. They continued eastwards, turned north and attacked the outposts on The Bluff (which withdrew) and also occupied the ridge where brisk firefights ensued, one at 3.30 am prompting the CO of the 2nd Light Horse Regiment to hastily move his headquarters to safety. The Turkish infantry had been given the most difficult approaches and a combination of slope and barbed wire delayed their forward momentum. This left the Germans to do extra work.

At 3.40 am Brigadier Cox ordered Lieutenant Colonel Granville's squadrons of the 1st Light Horse Brigade to eject the enemy. Their élan cleared the Germans from the right sector, but not from The Bluff. Fire from the Notts Battery and A and B batteries HAC helped clear that feature, which the Australians seized with the bayonet, taking 100 prisoners. The Wellington Mounted Rifles had been ordered forward and cleared Vaux post. By 9.00 am the original line had been restored and a significant quantity of small arms (machine-guns, rifles and ammunition) captured. The Antipodeans had shown perfect discipline. At 7.00 am, at the height of the battle, the temperature reached 100°F, and continued to rise as the enemy withdrew, many shot down as they moved into the killing zones of the superbly sited machine-guns. As with the Turks at Romani, a contributory cause of the German defeat was the enemy's empty water bottles. The survivors, now retreating, were demented by thirst and eventually surrendered. Of the performance of the 2nd Light Horse Brigade, Gullett wrote, 'The resolution of the Queenslanders was never excelled in the career of the Light Horse.'[12]

To the east, another German force (the *10th* and *3/43rd battalions*) attacked the 2nd Light Horse Brigade positions on Wadi Mellahah some 1000 yards from the battle raging close to The Bluff. Following a night of shellfire, the enemy attacked at 5.30 am, the assault broken up by well-directed fire from the three posts Star, Shell and Scrap. Effective fire from these posts prevented the Germans withdrawing. The gunner OPs shared posts on the front line with the troopers. A Battery HAC's guns were busy, and its OPO spotted two machine-guns which he engaged promptly. He destroyed one and the other withdrew. The enemy's discomfort was heightened by an audacious raid by a troop leader who surrounded a German company. With bayonet and bombs the troop despatched 25, wounded 30 and captured 30. The remainder fled.[13]

Yet another Turkish attack, this time on the river at the El Hinu ford, involved the Imperial Cavalry Brigade Indian lancers for the first time. The aggressive action and mettle of the lancers 'was reassuring to the Commander-in-Chief' given their short period on operations. Two batteries provided artillery support, the Hong Kong and Singapore and the RFA Mountain, their high trajectory necessary to clear the clay hills that rose on the western bank of the Jordan where the 5th Light Horse was positioned. During the day, the Turks manoeuvred large bodies of troops towards the Umm esh Shert track and Shunet Nimrin. However, despite pounding Chauvel's positions with shellfire, they did not attack. General accounts of this battle provide little detail of the contribution of Chauvel's various batteries and their valuable close support, particularly their effect on attacking troops and counter-battery fire given the enemy's numerical superiority on both eastern and western fronts. The Abu Tellul casualty count is outlined in Table 12:

TABLE 12: ABU TELLUL CASUALTY COUNT

	KIA	WIA	POW/MIA
AMD Officers:	2	7	nil
Other ranks:	21	39	
Total	**105**	**45**	**630**
Turko-German all ranks:			

The official historian recorded the British casualties for these three actions as 189. The enemy yielded 540 prisoners and 'well nigh a thousand dead all told'.[14]

While this victory was ostensibly similar to others across the front during the campaign, Gullett emphasised its significance in terms of its value for analysis of the Allied performance. This was the last set-piece attack on the DMC in Palestine. It was also the first attack by German stormtroopers whose attack planning was meticulous. The performance of their Turkish brethren was poor in comparison. Gullet makes an indirect reference to the quite different nature or exhibition of 'martial virtues' between the Turkish and German infantry. Visiting staff officers from France had made unflattering comparisons between the Western Front and Palestine, the officers implying that the British were fortunate in only having the Turk opposing them. This was certainly not the case early in the campaign, as defeats at Katia, Amman, Gaza and the Jordan Valley amply demonstrate.

The Australian soldier rated the German superior to the Turk as an offensive fighter. However, when it came to 'rifle work', the Turk was more feared as a marksman than his Teutonic ally. By July the *ahmet* was less resilient than 12 months earlier, perhaps some indication of the effect of the merciless summer weather on his morale. While it was well known that there was tension within the Turko-German command hierarchy, mistrust and chagrin between the two allies was also present at foot soldier level. Yet the Palestine campaign was marked by an element of chivalrous behaviour not seen between the protagonists since the opening shots in Belgium in 1914. For example, the Australian troopers opened their water bottles to alleviate the raging thirst of the captured stormtroopers after Abu Tellul. Later, as the Germans were lorried off to the prisoner-of-war cage, they cheered their captors.[15]

Significantly, Chauvel's victory thwarted Turkish plans to reoccupy the Jordan Valley. Their plan had envisaged the *24th Division* recapturing Jericho, providing a significant boost for Turkish logistics. This accomplished, the *53rd Division* would then attack the rear of the bridgeheads at Auja and Ghoraniye simultaneously in an attack supported by a heavy artillery bombardment.

Following Abu Tellul the sparring between the forces in the valley continued. They were unaware that greater plans were being formulated which would involve most of the troops. Sub-units and units were withdrawn as Allenby assembled his striking force for his schedule of autumn operations. On 28 July, for example, A Battery HAC was relieved by the 270th RFA Brigade and returned to GHQ at Bir Salem where 'it began training with the greatest diligence in a much more congenial coastal climate'. B Battery HAC was relieved on 31 July and moved out of the valley with the AMD, reaching Selmeh by moving at night and hiding in olive groves by day. There, 'the blessed coolness of the nights, and the clear and comparatively bracing air of the plain, soon began to have a good effect on the jaded troops and horses, worn out by their long period in the dismal Valley of Desolation.'

Their Jordan Valley ordeal was over.[16]

Narrative Three

May 1918 to November 1918

Narrative Three
May 1918 to November 1918

While the Salonika campaign dragged on, the Russian capitulation saw an influx of German troops into the Balkans where they inflicted massive defeats on their opponents. On the Western Front the arrival of American troops lifted Allied morale. The RN blockade was beginning to bite and the populations of the Central Powers chafed at the widespread shortages which provoked increasing civil unrest as militarism was replaced by communist sympathies and a spike in revolutionary zeal. France still had one million men under arms, and the national cry was '*Revanche*!'

May saw Haig's British command introduce enhanced tactical methodology — more efficient artillery tactics, mechanised armour, gas and enhanced battalion firepower —and the casualty rate fell by almost half. Some of these benefits flowed through to Allenby's command. The Turkish Army was impregnable beyond the Jordan River where it had concentrated, leaving the coastal plain underdeveloped in terms of defensive works and lacking quality troops. Turkish morale was low and Turkish soldiers poorly fed and badly trained.

Allenby replaced some British infantry and cavalry with Indian Army troops. The onset of summer campaigning in the desert saw his troops and animals subjected to extremes of heat, dietary and insect-borne diseases and illnesses. Nonetheless, the men's morale was high following a period of much-needed recuperation on the coast.

The Turkish Army was now a shadow of its former self. It was enfeebled by a lack of supplies, divided and distracted by the need to maintain civil order against the depredations of the Bedouin, and riven by tensions with its German advisers. Allenby, for his part, had three significant advantages — tight security, an array of deceptions and a superb air arm that was worth a division to him. His aim to knock Turkey out of the war would be achieved in less than two months.

Chapter 24
A summer of contemplation and creativity

The whole art of war consists in getting at what is on the other side of the hill.
Arthur Wellesley, Duke of Wellington

This chapter covers two important military activities, both cerebral. These relate to artillery 'state of the art' tactics and employment, the use of cavalry given the shape of future operations, and the creation and employment of a highly efficient military force that would utilise all the elements of deception, organisation and planning. If successful, both activities would have a significant strategic and political impact on the outcome of the war. Many lessons had been learned by the cavalry and infantry whose minor tactics and materiel support in 1918 were enormously improved compared to the experience of 1916. Of all those factors the most important was security. The staff, now a tried and true cohort, could pool their experiences and draft a plan that would astonish the world — without committing it to paper.

During the Palestine spring and summer the tempo of operations diminished in all sectors. Despite the weather, both sides 'faced off' across the Nahr Auja from the coast over an expanse of 35 miles. During this period commanders rotated divisions and cavalry brigades and regiments, the latter as flank guards albeit with an offensive agenda as directed by the staff. The overriding aim was to husband their resources for the autumn battles and, in the case of the EEF, maintain an offensive spirit in preparation for the coming months.

1. Cavalry tactics and mobile firepower considerations

This part of the narrative covers the Battle of Megiddo, in which cavalry would assume a far more prominent role and use a broader range of their martial arts. Similarly, the use of the Light Armoured Motor Battery would also provide an opportunity to demonstrate its flexibility in working with cavalry formations or infantry operations.

A. The Light Armoured Motor Battery

The Light Armoured Motor Battery was not strictly a battery in an artillery sense. Instead it was a collection of Vickers machine-guns mounted in armoured cars and deployed with the horse artillery and cavalry. Initially these were primarily used as individual vehicles attached to a mobile brigade or regiment to augment its machine-gun section, troop or squadron. In later operations they operated as a battery, numbers of cars being 'detached' or 'attached' to cavalry regiments or brigades. This allotment also depended on the terrain, as the vehicles required solid ground to reduce the risk of their becoming bogged in sand, bottoming on rough ground or breaking down for mechanical reasons. Following Megiddo more references appear in narratives describing these vehicles' utility over the ground covered from the Nahr Auja to Damascus. However, they were not impervious to shellfire, with several destroyed by direct hits during the war.

A battery comprised 12 Rolls Royce cars powered by six cylinder 80 horsepower (60 kilowatt) motors with a top speed of 45 miles per hour (60 km/hr). The car's half-inch armour plating increased its weight to five tons. It mounted a Vickers water-cooled machine-gun and the car, with commander, driver and two gun numbers, had a radius of action of 150 miles. The battery was originally designed for use by the RFC in France, where its poor performance in wet conditions undermined its utility. On hard, flat desert surfaces it allowed mounted troop commanders to increase their firepower and rapidly alter the direction of attack or defence. The 'killing range' of the Vickers was 700 to 800 yards and its 'suppressive range' upwards of 1000 yards.[1]

B. Mounted rifles or cavalry?

As the long, hot summer of 1918 occupied the troops on the Auja or on the River Jordan, commanders and staff were discussing the relative merits of the use of cavalry based on several actions since the famous charge of the 4th Light Horse Brigade at Beersheba. When the Light Horse and Yeomanry joined battle with the Turks in 1916, the charge with sword or lance was regarded as having little future against machine-guns, barbed wire and trenches. The cavalry-mounted rifle dichotomy (but not mounted infantry) was almost as one on all other doctrinal concepts. The experienced professionals in command or on the staff were aware that cavalry sword/lance-wielding charges required a much higher level of training than those undertaken with mounted rifles. That is to say, regular soldiers would do a better job than former Militia/Territorial mounted soldiers, even when they both held the rank of trooper. In 1914 an instruction was issued directing that yeomanry regiments that carried swords into battle — which the Antipodeans did not — be trained as cavalry. During the campaign the armourers who supported these troopers kept their bayonets sharpened for any eventuality.

Topography and the type of terrain on which horses and camels travelled comprised another major factor in operations planning and analysis. On the sands and dunes of the Sinai and the Mediterranean littoral, horses were inferior to camels in several respects, primarily load-carrying, mobility and dependence on water. When the topography 'reversed', the horse was superior. In many of the actions after the Sinai, the terrain was relatively benign and better suited to defence given the absence of cover. Any approach across exposed terrain would be difficult for either trooper or infantryman. This precept also held true once operations began to reach up into the gorges and chasms of the Judean Hills. Sometimes it took more enemy troops to cover all approaches, sometimes fewer. However, for the cavalry to engage with the enemy, speed over the ground was the key factor in neutralising enemy rifle and machine-gun power. Whether a charge was ordered depended on the cavalry commander's appreciation of the suitability of the ground ahead. It was here that the mounted trooper wielding a sword or bayonet had a better chance of success than a mounted rifleman's dismounted attack, no matter how well the latter's fire and movement drills were executed. In Chauvel's attack on Beersheba, for example, Bou writes that 'only mounted troops could have made the approach the plan called for.' This approach crossed more than 3000 yards of open desert. The approach taken also factored in support from the organic horse artillery, two batteries of which kept pace with the light horsemen in this (and other) assaults on prepared positions. Doctrine had to be all-encompassing. Prior to Beersheba, the troopers had been trained in basic (new) infantry skills such as grenade throwing and use of the Stokes mortar. They may well have been bemused at their conversion to mobile infantry.[2]

The 4th Light Horse Brigade provided the two best examples of the relative success of the cavalry. At Beersheba, the 4th suffered a fraction of the casualties an infantry assault would have sustained in similar circumstances. Its commander, Brigadier Grant, was firmly of the opinion that opportunities to inflict further casualties on the Turks after the taking of the town had been missed because his troops were not armed with swords. At Second Gaza, 'this brigade made a long advance on foot, with two regiments (4th and 12th) and the Machine Gun Squadron and had 187 casualties without any satisfactory result being obtained.'[3] Prior to that, A&NZ Mounted Division charges at Qatya and Bir el Abd had not succeeded, whereas at Magdhaba speed of closing was crucial and successful.

At Huj, the yeomanry charged a well-defended position without artillery or machine-gun support incurring somewhere between 70 and 90 casualties. Nonetheless they triumphed in this remarkable cameo action, a fact recognised by the GOC 60th Division (Shea) who had been spared many more casualties than if his division had organised a set-piece cavalry attack on the position.[4]

Major General Hodgson was the driving force behind the move to use cavalry alongside light horsemen and mounted rifles at Megiddo. In his detailed orders he directed that sharpened bayonets were not to be used attached to a rifle (as it affected horse control), but used in 'pointing' rather than striking. He stressed that in the moral effect, the bayonet was as good as a sword. In Chauvel's DMC, the doctrine of 'speed and moving quickly in extended order carried through in successive waves at the gallop' was promulgated in January 1918. The deployment of troops or squadrons to attack the left, centre and right of the enemy line was an adaptation of the age-old 'one point two sides' tactic, in which the momentum of the attack would be sustained through the weakest part of the position to 'roll up' the remainder. The adoption of this amended doctrine affected the horse artillerymen's method of supporting mounted attacks. In early engagements the horse battery would move to a flank so as not to block the troopers in their approach and from where the BC/forward observer could coordinate fire (its application and stoppage), particularly during the final stages of the action. The new doctrine rendered observed fire in those circumstances more crucial, requiring greater finesse and judgement. On the threshold of Megiddo the gunners were not to know that cavalry would be used to great effect — and without the crucial assistance of artillery fire support.

The staff also correctly reasoned that the enemy (both Turk and German) had no 'spirit for a mounted fight … and thus risks could be taken.' Their operations analysis thus far had revealed that the troopers had little to fear from enemy shellfire when dispersed and at the gallop. The horse had a far greater chance of becoming a casualty than the horse and rider, from both shell and machine-gun fire, from front or flank.[5]

Out of the line the DMC practised against cavalry, infantry and guns in anticipation of the nature of offensive operations which General Allenby planned for his projected advance towards Damascus some months in the future. The terrain on the Esdraelon Plain, Moab Heights and Gilead and for the thrust towards Deraa would favour cavalry operations. In July Chauvel agreed to Hodgson's proposals and, in August 1918, the light horse began sword training. There were arguments against this training, ranging from objections to the weight of the sword (7 lbs) and protests that the training would simply produce 'badly trained cavalry'. However, by the time Allenby's force was ready to launch its attack in September, the Australians and New Zealanders in the AMD had been won over and convinced of the need for an alternative weapon. The success of this weapon was later demonstrated at Jenin, near Nablus, at Semakh and by the 4th Light Horse Brigade en route to Damascus.[6] However Major General Chaytor, GOC A&NZ Mounted Division, was unimpressed by these developments, arguing that the terrain in which he operated reduced opportunities for direct action. Hodgson was to have the last say, and subsequently wrote:

> The experience of the division throughout operations from 19 September to 2 October 1918 was that our force had its value practically doubled by the issue of the sword. They retained all their old value as mounted rifles, with exactly the same firepower, and added to this was the power of shock action — a power [whose lack] had been keenly felt on previous occasions since leaving the desert of Sinai.[7]

Preparations for Allenby's grand design

Lessons learned at the seminal battle of Berukin formed the basis of Allenby's plans for a victorious conclusion to the war in Palestine. These included lessons relearned and, in several instances, relearned and/or forgotten. Chief among these was security in an environment where 'words travelled'. The ability of his commanders to innovate and revisit history — in the case of the use of the sword — and many minor 'tinkerings' with other facets of desert operations all contributed to the final form of his operations orders. Communications and logistics would define his vision of a magnificent army advancing and attacking and sweeping all before it.

The lead-up to Allenby's operation to drive the Turk and German from Palestine with his DMC's three mounted divisions and his eight infantry divisions of XX and XXI Corps represents a significant element of the campaign. His enemy was less formidable given its lack of materiel and administrative support, and the Turks' poor relations with their German allies also weakened their fighting power. Allenby's campaign to push north from Gaza had been preceded by a series of engagements of varying degrees of intensity. Jerusalem had been captured on 29 December 1917. Since he issued his first order in July he had kept the Turks on the defensive, using his mounted troops to achieve surprise and his dispositions to mislead and confound Turkish intelligence, supported by an efficient logistics system that kept his army in good shape. His cavalry/light horse had taken many prisoners and captured many guns over the previous months. Allenby held the initiative.

At Sarona, just north of Jaffa, Allenby spent the summer plotting his next moves.[8] Nine months after Jerusalem his breadth of front was 150 miles, some 10 to 15 times the Western Front 'span of control'. It ran from Sarona on the coast (15 miles north of Jaffa) to the River Jordan. His cavalry under Chauvel was sited close to the coast, Chetwode's XX Corps guarded his eastern flank and his XXI Corps under Bulfin was also located on the coast. His eastern flank under Chaytor lay astride the Jericho road and Jordan. GHQ was established close to Lydda/Ramleh.

Allenby's grand plan to knock the Turks out of the war was strongly influenced by the topography of the country held by his enemy. With the exception of relatively small areas such as Mount Carmel and the rugged uplands further north, this comprised rolling country eminently suited to cavalry operations by his DMC's five divisions. It was also an area that promised to provide natural forage for his mounted troops. To reach the Plain of Esdraelon with wheeled traffic, however, his force would have to use the Musmus Pass. This led through narrow defiles with steep, rocky and unforgiving slopes. It was excellent defensive country. A metalled road ran from Jiljulieh via Tul Keram to Nablus. Nearby was the village of Megiddo, the scene of an Egyptian Army victory in 1479 BC, synonymous with its now biblical name of Armageddon. To the east was the River Jordan, dividing the enemy's lateral connection between the east and the coast. The towns of Afule, Beisan and Deraa were critical centres for Allenby's communications. Seizing these would also cut off a retreat route for the Turkish forces. Allenby, cognisant of the fact that poor security prior to his thrust at Amman had contributed to its failure, determined that security for his coming offensive would be 'watertight'. As Keogh notes, he undertook, often at some risk, to personally survey the terrain in great detail, from the front line, from the air and mounted, determined to assess which option offered the greatest success. His GHQ subsequently produced possibly the most comprehensive plan ever devised and probably only exceeded by that of the 21st Army Group's invasion of Normandy in 1944.

Some of these measures are worth describing given that, in sum, they embraced the most potent of the principles of war — surprise. Allenby proposed to persuade the Turks that he would attack eastwards towards Amman and wheel left towards Damascus. According to his grand design, his forces would advance by the coastal route and cut off his opponent's withdrawal routes to the north and east. To achieve that simple feat he would mislead the Turkish high command as to where and when he would unleash his 120,000 men against Liman von Sanders' 90,000. In gunnery terms, Allenby would pit his 540 guns against the Turk's 400. In formulating his deception plan, Preston notes that, for Allenby, 'No detail was too small, no dodge too insignificant to engage his full attention' in his attempts to focus his enemy on the eastern flank. Camps in the Jordan Valley were left standing, and other camps and tracks were created, with visible movement between them indicating they were 'inhabited'. At the same time, two cavalry divisions were quietly removed westwards. The British West Indian battalions marched and counter-marched to raise dust. Horses dragged a shrub behind them to raise bigger dust clouds indicating 'troop movements'. To the troops it all appeared a pointless exercise. To gull the natives in his own territory, Allenby made 'elaborate bogus preparations for the removal of GHQ to Jerusalem. One of the hotels there was cleared of its occupants, much to their disgust, and staff officers busied themselves installing office furniture and telephone equipment, and painting the names of a multitude of departments on the doors.'[9]

In a more entertaining ruse, the army conducted a widely publicised horse race meeting at Jaffa on the eve of battle (19 September). Even the troops were told they were going to the Valley of Desolation. They could not believe they would be sent there again.[10] Decauville railway track was laid towards crossing places and new bridges now spanned the River Jordan. Several bridges were built on the Auja by the RE to train its sappers. A few days later they were dismantled. When new bridges were built they aroused no suspicion. In this way heavy pile bridges were constructed for the 60-pounder RGA guns, two pontoon types for the 18-pounders and one trestle type for the heavy lorries and Holt tractors. Dummy horse lines such as those constructed prior to Third Gaza were erected. No written plans were drafted and commanders submitted plans verbally at conferences. This was surely a first for commanders and their staff who found themselves conjuring a battle plan without a paper record until the very last minute. Once the plan had been settled the gunners could begin their detailed planning and decide how best to distribute 60,000 rounds against their hapless opponents.[11]

By this time Allenby also had a superb air arm in the 40th Wing RFC (which included No. 1 Squadron AFC and three RFC squadrons, 111, 144 and 145) which multiplied his offensive strength. Air officers such as Brigadier Salmond, who had returned from six months in Britain, were at the forefront in formulating new tactics and deceptions along the Allied front. These had driven the German air force from the skies. Its aerodrome at Jenin was patrolled ceaselessly by a section of SE5As, which also dropped 104 bombs to good effect just prior to the battle and from Z Hour. So effective were the Allied airmen's methods prior to and during the battle that the German air force was utterly demoralised and the aerodrome easily captured. This was another instance of tactical air power expertly applied. The AFC squadron continued its allotted strategic reconnaissance, photography and bombing. A squadron was dedicated to each corps and another to the DMC. Two weeks before the attack the air arm applied some of the successful practices that had been developed in France and improved since Third Gaza. Gun positions and machine-gun posts were dug, temporarily occupied and then photographed. Changes were made to their camouflage to conform to the deception plan. If unsatisfactory this was remediated or the position re-sited. Digging and camouflaging began in July, ready for occupation on 18 September.

The RAF historian noted that, had one German reconnaissance aircraft crossed Allenby's lines, the whole concealment and battle plan would have been compromised. The 5th Air Wing 'made it impossible'. By this time aircraft were able to create smokescreens and one squadron (No. 113 RFC) was to do so at two chosen points on the morning of the assault. Ultimately, only one was required. The photographs taken by the Australian pilots were studied for possible Turkish lines of retreat. Every defile with a straight stretch that made gun deployment possible was noted and registered for the artillery plan. The air plan placed high priority on the bombing of enemy headquarters areas and telephone exchanges at El Affule, Tul Keram and Nablus. A Handley-Page bomber had arrived in theatre and was tasked for the role. From No. 1 Squadron AFC Signals Section, there were 10 wireless operators and sets paired in (RFA) artillery field and anti-aircraft unit headquarters for artillery observation and liaison tasks.[12]

The artillery stockpiled a considerable quantity of ammunition and other necessities in its A Echelons for the opening concentrations and barrages. While the number of rounds was not overwhelming, the movement of this ammunition represented a level of efficiency in the logistic system of the Army Service Corps hitherto absent in the campaign. The gunners had no choice — the ammunition supply had to be mobile to help maintain the momentum of the advance. A total of 450 rounds per gun was carried by the corps ammunition column while another 150 rounds were available on lorries. A further 500 rounds per gun were stockpiled in dumps. Back on the gun line, now functioning far more smoothly than before, ammunition was delivered on the following scale (rounds per gun):

60-pounder gun	500
6-inch Mk VII gun	250
6-inch howitzer	500

8-inch howitzer	400
105/150mm (Turkish)	250
French artillery	250[13]

In addition to the divisional artillery allocations, two RN destroyers, HM Ships *Druid* and *Forester*, were also included in the fire plan. In typical Allenby fashion, there was a deception plan to conceal the regrouping and concentration of batteries. The survey sections established their sound ranging and observation detachments and Bulfin's corps counter-bombardment officer located almost every hostile battery opposing him. Preparations by the RE bridging parties, including one Canadian Army bridging train, were vital to the movement of the 60th Division's artillery across Nahr Auja. Ten bridges had to be constructed across the Auja from its mouth to Ferrikhiye, seven miles inland.[14] Two pontoon bridges were suitable for the 18-pounders, the other bridges for the 60-pounders built using heavy piles, while another bridge was constructed for the gun tractors. Other engineer stores were stockpiled for crossing the swampy ground that lay a few miles behind the front. Water and its availability for the advancing cavalry and infantry was a priority to which the engineers devoted much attention. Behind the front, material for a seven-mile pipeline had been moved forward. The pipeline would extend as far as Jiljulieh, seven miles away, and would be laid in around eight hours, providing 17,500 gallons of water an hour. Further inland two camel water companies of 2400 beasts would cater for the 7th Division infantry and gunners.

Another raft of problems anticipated in the advance involved the signals network so vital to the artillery headquarters at ascending levels of command. This was particularly true of Chauvel's corps and, as it eventuated during its rapid advance, the Chief Signals Officer's plans involved using, wherever possible, 'air lines' (existing telephone poles/lines) instead of employing line-laying parties which would hamper cavalry and infantry deployment. The plan for the security of interior communications involved wireless messages broadcast from the previous GHQ location. The three balloon sections observing over the front would contact formations direct by phone and heliograph. Allenby pressured General Chauvel, against his serious misgivings, to release his Chief of Staff, Brigadier Howard-Vyse, to command the 10th Mountain Brigade.[15]

By this time the senior staff officers of GHQ, corps and divisions had, after just over a year, become very familiar with one another's *modus operandi*. As the front line was extensive (by European standards) and covered terrain of varying types, arrangements that suited one division might not suit any other. So it was a triumph of staff work to flesh out Allenby's grand design in a way that suited every general officer. The official historian cites the concentration of Chauvel's cavalry divisions in their assembly areas behind the 60th and 7th divisions on the coast as the source of greatest concern. Here they were concealed in the numerous orange groves that provided shelter, a less stressful lifestyle and a chance for man and beast to reinvigorate. The most significant cause for concern was the forward movement of the guns to support the cavalry.

According to Allenby's plan, the cavalry and its horse artillery had to be just behind the infantry once the enemy's line was broken. The assembly areas extended south for three miles. General Barrow, 4th Cavalry Division, stressed that the opportunity for a complete victory at Cambrai two years earlier had been lost because the cavalry had been late in exploiting the gap in the German lines. He did not want this to happen in front of XXI Corps. General Macandrew, 5th Cavalry Division, presumably agreed. The nub of the problem concerned cavalry units interfering with Bulfin's infantry and/or cavalry masking guns. Bulfin, for his part, was concerned that, if the Turks counter-attacked, this would create a frightful muddle in his lines if the cavalry was close. He was also concerned that the DMC units should not pass north and east of the line of the artillery's wagons until the artillery moved forward. Chauvel had the choice of a short or long route north. The short route utilised a track running past Tabsor to the Zerquiye crossing which would save time. Allenby considered this better suited to the infantry, and was keen that no cavalry should move to mask the artillery fire or movement. The problem was eventually solved by having the GOC (or senior staff officer) of both cavalry divisions co-located at the headquarters of the 60th and 7th divisions. Allenby's orders specified that 'DMC [supply] trains and parks would have precedence over those of XXI Corps on all roads on "Z Day".'[16]

While General Chaytor's role involved the lesser of the corps frontal attacks, he had the highest workload to ensure that the deception plan was strictly maintained. It was also a measure of Allenby's confidence in him that Chaytor was entrusted with the subsidiary operation of crossing the Jordan. On the day of the assault the tight security measures that had now become crucial to his plans bore fruit in the achievements of his troops. As the official historian wrote, 'the long experience of most commanders and senior staff officers and their knowledge of the country made it possible to keep the preparation of orders in such few hands.'[17]

Chapter 25
The Battle of Megiddo: the first three days

The military axiom of 'knowing your enemy' was never forgotten by Allenby's intelligence staff. Assiduous collectors of the obvious and distillers of minor factors allowed him to gauge the strength and the state of morale of his opponents. Allied patrols and the rate of prisoner of war captures in the preceding months, and the use of small raids to discomfort the Turks had ensured that enemy morale was low. The Turks' bitter hatred of their German superiors who treated them dreadfully and the appalling state of Turkish troops who were diseased for want of medical attention, poorly fed and clothed, combined to make these illiterate townsmen and peasantry war weary and eager for the conflict to end. These factors were critical to Allenby's overall appreciation of the mettle of his enemy, and were embodied in his ultimate plan. While there were enemy units whose performance defied these generalisations, overall, Allenby's men had their measure.

The attack — the first three days (19–21 September 1918)

The topography of this operation played a crucial role in Allenby's plans and extended from north-west clockwise to north and then to the east. XXI Corps and the DMC would manoeuvre across the Sharon and Dotham Plains once the dunes, the extensive Tabsor trench system and rugged country was behind them. XX Corps would drive up the Nablus road through the defiles. Chaytor's force would re-cross at the now-familiar Ghoraniye bridge and the new bridges and move east for Amman via the Jericho road, hopefully meeting Lawrence's irregulars, coming from the south, at Deraa. Allenby's four-phase plan involved:

XXI Corps Operations

Phase 1: XXI Corps (60th, 7th, 75th and 3rd Indian divisions), 5th Light Horse Brigade and a French cavalry force attack to gain objectives from Bidya to Et Tireh and the mouth of the Nahr el Faliq on the coast. The force was then to advance to Tul Keram and Sebustiye.

Artillery component:

60th Division: 301st, 302nd and 303rd RFA brigades

7th Indian Division: 422nd and 423rd RFA brigades

75th Division: 37th and 172nd RFA brigades and 1st South African Field Brigade

3rd Indian Division: 372nd, 373rd and 374th RFA brigades

Corps artillery: 102nd Brigade RGA — 91st Heavy Battery (horse drawn) and 380th Siege Battery (motor drawn)

Phase 2: DMC: AMD (less 5th Light Horse Brigade), 4th and 5th cavalry divisions, with which were brigaded 19th RHA Brigade (A and B batteries HAC, Notts Battery). The mounted troops were to pass through XXI Corps and advance quickly to El Affule and Beisan and cut off enemy retreating to Nablus.
Artillery component:

18th and 20th RHA brigades; Berkshire, Hampshire and Leicestershire batteries; Essex Battery (unbrigaded)

Phase 3: XX Corps [54th Division, French cavalry (FDFA), Watson's Force and 53rd Division] attack astride the Nablus road conforming with XXI Corps on its left once the 53rd and 10th division launched their attacks prior to the main 'block'.
Artillery component:

54th Division: 270th, 271st, 272nd and 440th (H) RFA brigades

10th Division: 67th and 68th 263rd RFA brigades

53rd Division: 265th, 266th, 267th RFA brigades and 439th (H) Battery

Corps artillery: 103rd Brigade RGA — 10th Heavy Battery and 205th Siege Battery

Phase 4: Chaytor's force was a depleted A&NZ Mounted Division — 1st and 2nd Light Horse brigades, NZMR Brigade; 20th Indian Imperial Service Brigade, two battalions of British West Indians and two Jewish battalions
Artillery component:

18th Brigade, RHA (Inverness, Ayrshire and Somerset batteries)

75th Battery RFA (ex 10th Division)

195th Heavy Battery

11th, 13th and 16th mountain batteries RGA; 29th Indian Mountain Battery[1]

Chaytor's force was to protect the right flank and conduct offensive operations to prevent the enemy withdrawing troops from his left to reinforce his right. It was in this area that some of the most comprehensive deceptions were implemented to mislead Turkish intelligence as to the major thrust of Allenby's army. Corps artillery comprised four brigades of 18 heavy and siege batteries, the 95th, 96th, 100th, 102nd, the 8th and 9th mountain brigades with 2.75-inch guns and three anti-aircraft sections (38th, 55th and 102nd).[2]

XXI Corps GOCRA, Brigadier General H.A.D. Simpson-Baikie, arranged for the 6-inch Mk VII howitzers of his three siege and the 60-pounders of his two heavy batteries to cover their tasks without having to move. Their gun positions were sited forward to reach the Turkish heavy artillery at their maximum elevation but well able to engage the Tabsor trench system should this be required. One of each could achieve this (for counter-preparation tasks) two hours after Z Hour. A group comprising one tractor-drawn siege battery and a horse-drawn heavy battery was to move to Tul Karm at four miles per hour to support the 60th Division's attack on Anebta once the corps had achieved its objectives. Seven captured Turkish guns and howitzers were included in the GOCRA's plan. XXI Corps situation reports to flank divisions would be copied to the Heavy Artillery Brigade headquarters. It is illustrative to note the measures that this division undertook in the preparation phase. First, the 10th Division artillery took responsibility for its place in the line on 14 September. The next day the 20th RHA Brigade marched in from Ramleh and was concealed in a bivouac in Mulebbis with divisional headquarters, while the 37th RFA Brigade remained in hides at Nabala. Three days before Zero Hour, the horse artillery batteries (Hants, Berkshire, Leicester, Notts RHA, all HAC) of the 18th, 19th and 20th brigades, now regrouped and re-equipped following the previous loss of nine guns, moved into their positions. Orders directed that a senior gunner from each brigade be stationed at both cavalry division headquarters. Once the fire plan was complete, batteries were to 'marry up' with their divisions after consulting GOCRA headquarters. Over the next three days the guns moved to their firing positions around Mulebbis while the Notts and Hants batteries provided artillery protection. The division's fully laden ammunition column had a long march through sand and 'it was doubtful the wheels of the GS wagons would stand it'. They did.[3]

Three and a half hours before the army Zero Hour, airmen in a newly arrived Handley-Page bomber dropped half a ton of bombs and those from No. 1 Squadron AFC dropped almost a ton of bombs on the railway junction at Tel Afule. Later, one and a half tons were dropped on the German aircraft lined up at Jenin aerodrome, over which the RFC's SE5As had established standing daylight patrols from 19 September. Following a refuelling and loading stop they attacked the two Turkish Army headquarters (*Eighth* and *Seventh armies*) whose troops were opposing XX and XXI Corps. They specifically targeted the enemy armies' telephone exchanges to destroy Turkish communications between their divisional headquarters. When all was ready, the troops moved into their attacking formations for their various Zero Hours. The 53rd Division artillery opened at 10.00 pm on 18 September and Major General Longley's 10th Division at 7.45 pm on the 19th. This stratagem was designed to focus the Turk's attention on the 'inland' and eastern sector of the front line.

At 4.30 am the next morning the artillery opened fire on the remaining fronts with a deafening roar. Bulfin's XXI Corps 5th Division's guns were at maximum strength. Between Rafat and the British 6.5-mile front line of Chetwode's XX Corps of two divisions and a corps cavalry regiment there would be five 60-pounder and 13 siege/heavy batteries for both counter-battery and infantry support. The latter could also count on 258 guns of the divisional artillery which, with trench mortars, numbered almost 400 in total. In the period leading to D Day, a deliberate but varied artillery program was implemented. It was based on what the artillery staff deduced the Turks and Germans would equate to an artillery strength of 70 guns on their front. When the artillery program began with almost 400 guns the Turks were taken by surprise, although their artillery replied instantly. However, their fire soon became less intense and its accuracy diminished; indeed, opposite Major General Hare's 54th Division, the enemy fire 'became wild'. Guns ceased to fire, were destroyed or detachments were withdrawn from them.[4]

A feature of the XXI Corps artillery plan was that the 18-pounders engaged on barrage tasks were to fire up to their extreme range. The howitzers were tasked on targets beyond barrage limits. As noted, two RN destroyers were on hand for opportunity target engagement after the breakout, the infantry provided with large, distinctive red and yellow flags for signalling their forward lines. The 'shoot down to' line was from the sea to Et Tireh. There was no preliminary bombardment; the heavy batteries were tasked for counter battery so that at least a 4:1 ratio was maintained over the enemy. RHA batteries also fired at their extreme range. Their barrage participation lasted 74 minutes and A Battery HAC fired 735 rounds, the most it had ever fired in such a short time during the entire war.[5]

Bulfin's XXI Corps headquarters was sited on Bulfin Hill on Sarona ridge, his formations ranged from left to right. In the corps area and enemy territory natural features had been assigned 'Anglo' names, by which they were known in orders except where local Arabic names were used in the cartographer's notations. By evening the next day most of Bulfin and Chetwode's infantry were beyond the ridgeline and the DMC well beyond that. Major General Shea's 60th Division (Headquarters Arsuf) front extended a mile from the coast and echeloned south to the cavalry assembly areas. Major General Sir V.B. Fane's 7th Indian Division front was a mile wide facing the Et Tireh road. The front shared by Major General Palin's 75th Division and Major General Hoskin's 3rd Division was five and a quarter miles wide from Seaforth Hill to the Tul Karm road. On their right flank XX Corps' 54th Division occupied a four-mile-wide front with a French cavalry detachment (DFPS) on its right, extending from Ras el Ain to Rafat on the railway.

On the left flank, the 60th Division's 180th Brigade led the assault behind the artillery barrage and concentrations, its sister brigades' orders prescribing their subsequent objectives from supporting and reserve areas. After firing their barrage allocations, the 303rd RFA moved at 6.05 am, the 301st moving 15 minutes later, followed finally by the 302nd. At 9.25 am the 302nd was in touch with the 179th Brigade providing much-needed support. The leading battalions had to cover some distance across open ground to close with the enemy, just as they had at First Gaza. This they did but at a heavy cost until the survivors reached the intricate network that was the Tabsor trenches where they found a demoralised enemy. Despite the fact that the bombardment had a minimal effect on machine-gun posts, the artillery fire 'lifted' this brigade onto its objective and, by 7.20 am, it had reached Wadi Faliq, a key reporting point for the cavalry to advance.[6] The push continued with no serious opposition. Next day the division's artillery reached Anebta, the 102nd HAG arriving at 5.00 am, its 60-pounders drawn by horse and its 6-inch howitzers by tractor.

At 7.00 am the 5th Light Horse Brigade and its horse gunners passed through the 180th on their way to create mayhem further north. The 181st Brigade passed through the 180th and was ordered to push on to Tul Keram. This brigade swung east on the road to Nablus and took Tul Keram by late afternoon after a march of 10 miles. Its 301st RFA Brigade pushed two 18-pounders further forward at Nahr el Faliq. The brigade's allocated big guns, the siege horse-drawn 380th and mechanised 91st brigades RGA, had little work to do, and the 179th Brigade reached Tul Keram at 3.30 am and Anebta at 9.00 pm the next day, having covered a distance of 28 miles.

While in general Megiddo was representative of earlier battles, it encompassed all the elements of success that had been absent earlier. The final RGA preparations began a fortnight before D Day, the forward battery positions filled with ammunition. Prior to D Day, full echelon ammunition for the 60-pounders (640 rounds) and for the 6-inch howitzers (360 rounds) plus an extra 60 and 160 rounds respectively, spare gun parts, petrol, oil and grease were loaded onto trucks and wagons. This was followed a few days later by the guns themselves which were pulled into position, all carefully concealed from view. The guns were kept quiet and practically no registration was completed, although hostile battery shoots continued. Prior to and during this period, exchanges in personnel were made at intervals to equalise the work. This kept men fit and ensured that all had a share in continuing the destruction of hostile artillery. When the final positions were adopted, all men had been trained by actual firing and were full of confidence both in themselves and those above them, accustomed to shooting with aero-observation and thoroughly fit for any emergency. Some batteries were given a shoot on hostile batteries in order to ensure that the guns were calibrated together as, owing to wear, it was necessary to redistribute the guns among batteries, the staff reasoning that those batteries detailed to move forward should be armed with the best weapons. Almost all the shooting in the RGA barrage was consequently done from the map. A margin of 500 yards between the infantry's advance 'profile' and the RGA targets was mandatory. This was difficult to estimate, the worst case scenario that the infantry would be held up by friendly fire. The accuracy of the shooting was confirmed on subsequent examination. After 6.30 am any ammunition remaining once the gunners had fired their gun programs was left to be collected by the salvage parties.

At 4.30 am on 19 September every gun on the front opened fire. The tasks allotted to the heavy artillery were twofold. A large proportion was designated to neutralise every known enemy battery that seemed likely to be active. The remainder was laid on to trenches, strongpoints and headquarters to the rear. No heavy artillery fire was directed at points that could be within 500 yards of friendly infantry at any point in their advance. Given the long advance planned, this was very difficult to estimate and necessitated the lifting of the fire somewhat early in the latter parts of the advance so as to ensure the infantry was not held up by friendly fire. The RFA put down its barrage and the infantry advanced at 4.30 am. The XX Corps' 60th Division was on the left of the line and, with the 7th Indian and 75th divisions in that order from left to right, attacked the Tabsor defences with the 3rd Indian Division on their right. The RGA brigades from left to right comprised the 96th (which remained stationary and did not advance), the 102nd and 95th with the 100th on their right.

Chapter 25

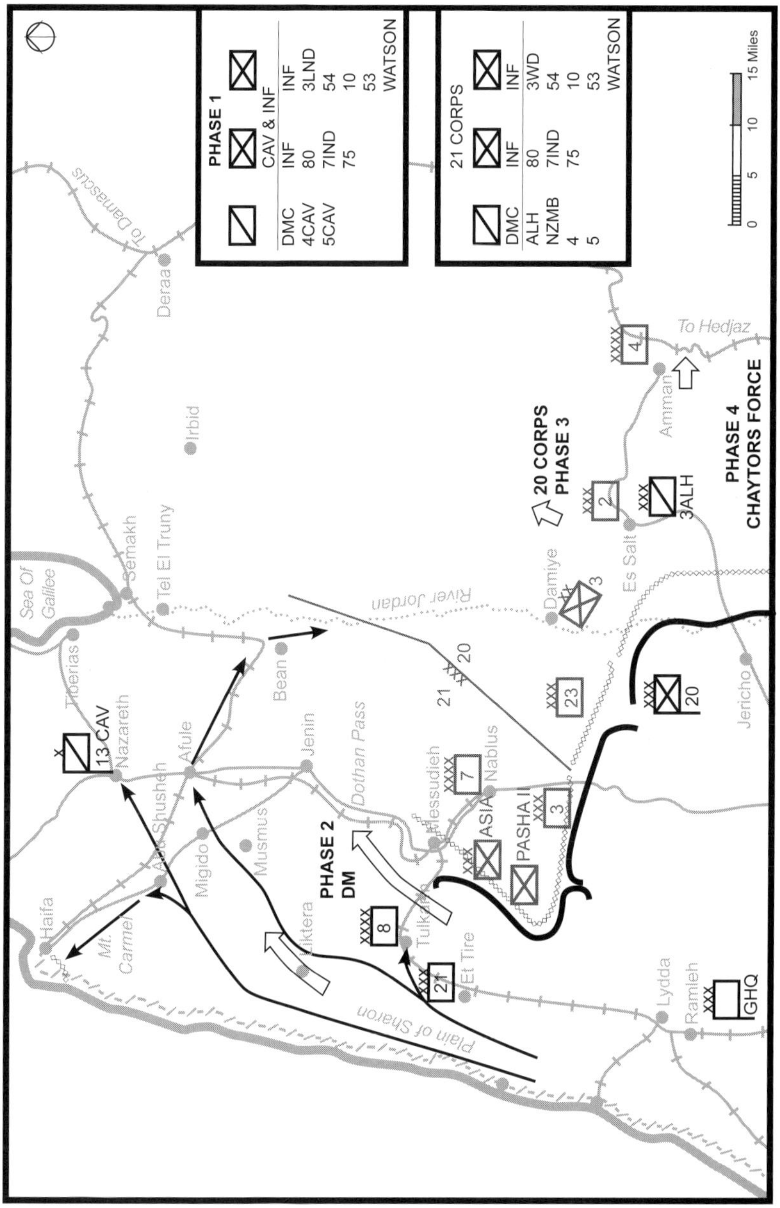

Map 19: The Battle of Megiddo evolved as General Allenby planned, with the DMC bearing north-east to encircle the Turkish *Twentieth Army* while the XX Corps infantry and Chaytor's cavalry pinned down the Turks' western front prior to the capture of Amman (source: Hill, *Chauvel of the Light Horse*, p. 170).

The 60th Division pushed at once for the Nahr el Falik so as to allow the cavalry to cross the Falik and make for Tul Keram, as well as to mop up any enemy escaping from the line of defence, Et Tireh to the sea. The whole attack from the right front of the 3rd Indian Division on the sea carried the first line of defence in approximately scheduled time, and the cavalry went through at Nahr el Falik and captured Tul Keram, pushing north and north-east into Turkish territory. The 102nd Brigade RGA with its signal section, 91st Heavy Battery (horse drawn) and 308th Siege Battery (tractor drawn) were ordered to advance as soon as the 75th Division had secured the line Et Tireh to the sea, provide assistance to the 75th Division and then advance to a position just east of Miskeh and there await a cavalry escort for safe conduct to Tul Keram. Moving the heavy artillery proved a trial throughout, as the following description of the 95th Brigade RGA illustrates. This doubtless applied equally to the other two brigades to varying degrees as they sought to support their divisions and adhere to the timings and objectives required:

> At around 9.00 am, the brigade received orders to advance. Two officers were sent forward by horseback, and the motor transport officer attached to brigade and his counterpart in a car made a hasty reconnaissance of their rendezvous while the batteries prepared to move. By 10.30 am it was clear that their assistance would not be required and the advance to Miskeh was ordered. The route selected as a result of the reconnaissance was along the old front line to Brown Hill striking the Hadrah road with the 91st Heavy Battery (horse drawn) leading, the 380th Siege Battery (tractor drawn) following, and the headquarters retained in its battle position to maintain contact with the division. The composition of the 380th Siege Battery's order of march was:
>
> - A pioneer tractor with a general service wagon containing spades, picks, etc., and a party of one sergeant and 20 other ranks to make practicable all difficult places. This activity proved invaluable throughout, although after Miskeh it had to be utilised for other purposes.
> - Four tractors each drawing a gun with a general service or buck wagon attached carrying 30 rounds.
> - Two tractors with caterpillar tracks carrying ammunition.
> - Two tractors with trucks and section stores.
> - Two tractors with petrol, oil and grease and carrying 3000 gallons of petrol.

Chapter 25

- Two tractors with spare wagons and motor transport workshops.

Colonel Hutchinson noted that the heavy sand along the old no man's land taxed the horses of the 60-pounder battery rather heavily, and they had frequent short halts before reaching the Hadrah road, keeping back the tractors, which seemed to revel in the going. This was unavoidable and the correctness of the 'order of march' was proven later in the day. From the Hadrah road to Miskeh the march was uneventful except for a tractor behind the guns slipping its track. Miskeh was reached at around 2.00 pm and the horses were watered immediately. Most of the horses received around half a canvas bucket of indifferent water. The BC pushed forward at once through Et Tireh to assess the situation, and found fighting still in progress some three miles beyond, conjecturing that the road to Tul Keram was not likely to be open for some time. While they were halted, some of the officers examined several excellently camouflaged (Turkish) 4.2-inch howitzer positions and a hastily abandoned divisional headquarters close to the halting place. The men received a meal of tea, bully beef and biscuits at 6.00 pm. The tactical situation had settled and a liaison officer arrived with orders for the brigade to proceed to Tul Keram. It was 6.30 pm before the column was on the move again with instructions to arrive before daylight. The advance began with an amended order of march given the presence of a difficult wadi around half a mile ahead. The Pilot Tractor was put in front of the 91st Battery. The horse-drawn Headquarters 102nd Brigade and its signal section followed the 91st Battery, the 380th Siege Battery bringing up the rear.

Trouble soon began, with an ammunition tractor shedding its track, detours, misfortunes immediately after and to follow the next morning. The workshops and some petrol remained with the stricken tractor as the brigade moved on. The horses, showing signs of fatigue in the heavy sand, were double teamed. By this time the column was short four tractors, one assisting with the horse transport, two with tracks off and one back with the workshops. It was 9.00 pm by the time the back of the column cleared Et Tireh. The horses were so 'dead beat' they could barely move the guns through the sandy stretches. The tractor loads were then readjusted, freeing the gun teams to help with the ammunition wagons and to pull the guns behind the howitzers, a tractor taking a gun, a howitzer and a general service wagon in some cases and, in one case, a tractor pulling a truck with 180 rounds of 60-inch ammunition and a 60-pounder gun. The tractor loads varied as it was necessary to increase their loads in the manner most economical in time. Even so it was 11.00 pm before the last tractor pulled away from the far side of the village.

Further trouble befell the column — mechanical and electrical problems occurred with the workshop far away and the brigade was forced to leave several tractors behind. Yet one more misfortune befell the struggling column as a tractor became jammed in a cutting going into a wadi. After this conditions improved so that, by 3.30 am, four howitzers, three 60-pounders, full echelon and 60 extra rounds of 60-pounder and 320 rounds of 6-inch howitzer ammunition arrived at Tul Keram. The horses were sent at once to water. By evening the brigade's elements were all on site, including the large stock of petrol and oil. The tractor breakdowns were primarily caused by the narrowness of the Turkish roads, particularly in the wadis. This caused the sides of the (caterpillar) tracks to bite and pulled them off the rollers. The sand at various points was extremely heavy and pushed the horses to exhaustion. Despite this, orders to arrive before daylight with full echelons were accomplished (with the exception of 40 rounds of 6-inch howitzer) after an eventual trek of 20 miles over tortuous tracks. The two 'heavies' were the only artillery pieces to arrive complete.

All the way from Et Tireh the brigade's troops could see the lights of the front line. At the halting place the batteries came within 1.5 miles of the front. On the morning of 20 September, one section of the 380th Siege Battery advanced with the 179th Brigade, while the 91st Heavy Battery came into action east of Tul Keram. That afternoon the 91st Heavy Battery and the remaining section of the 380th Siege Battery again advanced and both batteries came into action one mile west of Anebta, the 60-pounders shelling the road running north from Samaria at odd intervals during the night. The route from Anebta was strewn with dead horses, mules and bullocks and abandoned transport, including lorries, motor cars, carts and wagons of all kinds.

The 7th Indian Division attack was entrusted to the 21st Brigade on the left and the 19th on the right. Their supporting barrage moved at 100 yards per minute and was provided by the big guns, although there was provision for calling up field guns if required. The division enjoyed marked success, overrunning the Tabsor trench lines and, after capturing some guns that were just about to withdraw, turned east towards Et Taiyibe, which was occupied at 6.00 pm with the support of the 264th Brigade, RFA. It reached Beit Lid, 18 miles from its start line, by late afternoon.[7]

Chapter 25

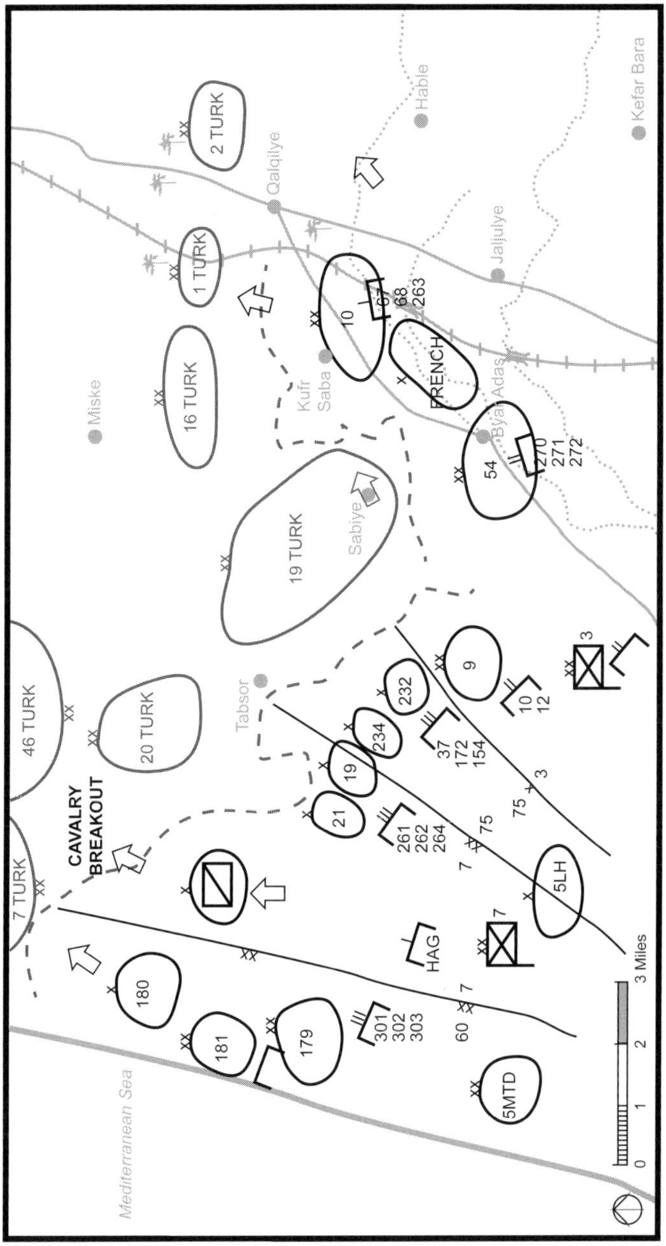

Map 20: The Megiddo left flank showing the preponderance of artillery and infantry tasked with blasting a passage for Chauvel's cavalry to exploit.

The 75th Division's distant objective (after the Tabsor trenches) was Et Tireh, the headquarters of the Turkish *XXII Corps*, the settlement of Miskeh marking the halfway point to this objective. Its three brigades (the 232nd and 234th assaulting and the 233rd in reserve) made good progress capturing the trench lines. On its dash to Miskeh, the division's affiliated 1st South African FAB came into action to assist in its capture. By 7.10 am, the South African gunners reported that they were at Miskeh and their batteries were engaging targets at Et Tireh, the infantry having only to cope with rifle and machine-gun fire. A highlight of their mission was the capture of a Turkish battery (three 150mm and seven 77mm guns) in a wadi south-west of Miskeh, which was still active despite the barrage. It was captured by an Indian brigade (the 152nd) at bayonet point. The division also captured the enemy headquarters, complete with its records, a great bonus for the intelligence staff. The division's progress was hostage to poor observation conditions as well as line communications which were continually broken by traffic. Nonetheless a divisional artillery casualty count of 18 was offset by the expenditure of 7585 rounds of 18-pounder and 4.5-inch howitzer ammunition. The accurate gunnery of the corps heavy brigades in putting down their barrage where the troops could close to within 40 yards of their shells also ensured success. These guns were Colonel Hutchinson's six 6-inch howitzers, which had 18 designated counter-battery tasks. In total, from Z to Z+55, his siege batteries despatched 625 rounds of HE.[8]

Casualties for Bulfin's corps totalled 3378, of whom 446 were killed. The other side of the balance sheet saw the enemy concede 12,000 prisoners and 149 field guns. 'Careful CB study which had preceded the battle was now indeed repaid and British artillery by its neutralising fire gave full value for its superiority.' Many of the batteries had been located by aerial reconnaissance and, according to a later report, 'by listening' — an oblique reference to V Section Sound Rangers under Captain Cockburn, Royal Canadian Engineers.[9]

XX Corps occupied an 18-mile front with the 54th and 10th divisions, French FDFA, Watson's Force and the 53rd Division, each with some five miles of front. This corps was faced with more formidable terrain characterised by rocky ridges that clearly rendered any concerted attack impossible, the centre line of which was the Bireh–Nablus road. There the enemy had well-developed and selected positions dug in (sangars) and XX Corps had to use a greater proportion of heavy and siege artillery. A cavalry component, the Corps Cavalry Regiment, acted as Chetwode's reserve and a mobile tactical resource until the Wadi Fara was reached.

XX Corps' 54th Division, old desert hands, was sited on the left of the line and included a French cavalry force that formed a boundary with XXI Corps. They advanced on a four-mile front, the axis to the north-east. They gained their primary objectives largely because, when the Turkish artillery replied to the barrage, the Allied infantry discovered 'lanes' — ground where fewer shells fell. The terrain was also sandy, and this reduced the lethality of the counter fire. By the evening of 20 September, the brigades were spread between Kufr Qasim and Bidya. To this point the division had enjoyed remarkable success to which the French had contributed handsomely. The 54th's brigades (162nd, 163rd and 164th) captured all their objectives with moderate losses. When held up at the railway viaduct, a brief but intense bombardment lasting a mere five minutes soon had the attacking infantry rounding up prisoners and counting the booty. A similar episode occurred at Jiljulieh where a column of pack mules and their loads were put to flight. The division's success cost it 525 casualties, and it captured nine guns, 20 machine-guns and 700 prisoners. The division suffered just a single casualty from the barrage. At the end of the day both the 7th and 3rd divisions were threatening Nablus.[10]

Allenby had set the 10th Division Zero Hour at 7.45 pm on 19 September. The division launched a three-phase attack on a five-mile front with the 29th Brigade tasked to capture Furqa ridge over the same ground as the previous action at Berukin in April. The Singapore and Hong Kong Mountain Battery was affiliated with this brigade. The infantry had a very tough fight and paid dearly for ground won. It was supported by the 67th and 68th RFA brigades whose barrage on Furqa was effectively modified to suit the advance of the brigade. Farndale notes this as 'indicating effective and smoothly operating fire control' by the infantry and the OP parties. Support was also provided by the 387th Siege Battery. Farndale glosses over the difficulties this attack faced. Moving slowly north and approaching Qusra (Quza) at 5.30 am on 21 September, the 29th Brigade, whose platoons had already reached Huwara, saw its sister brigade (30th) pass through it to the plain leading to Nablus. General Longley reached Quza at 8.00 am in time to see the Indian Army's 38th Dogras and 1st Royal Irish, closely followed by the Singapore and Hong Kong Mountain Battery, making for Azmut. The 266th Brigade RFA was south of Huwara and opened fire at 6000 yards to help neutralise 'the considerable but erratic plunging machine gun fire' aimed at the Dogras. The 30th Brigade marched on Nabi Belan, four miles north-east of Nablus, looking for a position from which to control and block the Wadi el Fara road. South from Huwara came an 18-pounder battery (A) of the supporting RFA brigade, as did the remainder of the brigade and the 10th Heavy Battery RGA. They came into action south-west of Balata, targeting the road. At 5.00 pm the Dogras occupied Nabi Belan, covered by the guns of the 103rd Brigade RFA. The 29th Brigade then moved to Balata to join the 53rd Division at 1.00 pm. In 48 hours the division had fought and laboured unceasingly (the Royal Irish were almost asleep on their feet), a reflection of high quality leadership. Later, the Corps Cavalry Regiment would cooperate with the DMC advance elements in clearing the ground between Nablus and Beisan. Occupation of this area allowed the division to interdict the Wadi Fara road already crowded with Turkish transport.[11]

The 10th Division suffered some 800 casualties in its various affrays. It took 1223 prisoners and, in the opinion of the official historian, 'Its final effort had been magnificent, and in particular the march on Nablus deserves an honorable place in our military records.'[12]

The night before the XXI Corps Zero Hour, Chetwode had ordered the 53rd Division to advance its right front flank to conform with the 10th Division. On the night of 19 September, the XXI Corps attack with two brigades up and one in reserve on the right of the corps front progressed well in the early stages. Both divisions met stiff opposition from the Turks in well-prepared positions on the Furqa and Berukin ridges. The 158th Brigade stormed Kheir Jibert at 4.40 am following a 10-minute bombardment by the 103rd Brigade RGA. Two battalions of South Africans who were about to consolidate on the feature were fiercely counter-attacked at 8.00 am and suffered heavy losses. A fresh attack with artillery support (a 20-minute bombardment) at 12.25 pm was quickly laid on but was not decisive. Despite this, 'both divisions, although indifferently supported by artillery and paying dearly for their ground, made steady progress'. The progress of the 158th Brigade was slow due to the condition of the road and the work required by the infantry both to fight and to make the route passable. By 11.00 am on 21 September it was halfway to its objective. These setbacks had also delayed the RFA brigades while the infantry, facing a stern Turkish rearguard (unaware that its withdrawal route had been cut) had outranged their guns. Ultimately, all the divisional artillery less the 263rd Brigade moved forward. The 159th Brigade had better luck, achieving its objective (Ras et Tawil) by 3.00 pm. XX Corps lost 225 killed, 1062 wounded and 18 missing (a total of 1505) but took 6851 prisoners, 140 guns and 1345 machine-guns (and automatic rifles).[13]

A group known as Watson's Force was positioned astride the road that led to Damascus through Beisan, 40 miles distant 'as the crow flies', although the twisting, turning wadis made it almost double the distance. Chetwode ordered the Worcestershire Yeomanry of the corps regiment to be ready to move if the enemy retired, presumably on the strength of the opening artillery bombardment. The force covered the three and a half miles beyond the old front line before encountering opposition which was swiftly overcome. Patrolling had revealed that the road north to Beisan was densely mined. However the Turks had left 78 unexploded mines in their hasty evacuation and, as a result, delays to the artillery were minimal. By nightfall the force was at Es Sawiye. Both the 10th Heavy and 205th Siege batteries were 'mechanised', each piece drawn by a four-wheel drive lorry, while the crew and ammunition stores occupied two-wheel drive lorries. These were capable of six miles per hour, and thus had the satisfaction of being ahead of the field and mountain batteries when they reached El Lubban, south of Es Sawiye.[14]

At 6.00 pm on 20 September, Allenby's forces stretched from Nazareth (13th Cavalry Brigade) and Abu Shushe (15th Cavalry Brigade) south to Tel Affule and Jenin (14th Cavalry and 5th Light Horse brigades) in the north. Chauvel had established his tactical headquarters at Megiddo. The infantry division's fronts were arced from astride Samaria (60th and 7th) to the extremity of their advance, as per their orders, some positioned five miles or more from their start lines. From this point, it was a cavalry show, the focal point at Beisan. Turks retreating from Chaytor's force had the choice of heading north up the Jisr ed Damieh–Beisan track or further east, along the railway and road from the south leading to Deraa.

The ammunition expenditure for the battle and the week that followed totalled 71,361 rounds. The 18-pounders whose ratio of shrapnel to HE was 2:1, expended almost half the total fired. The 4.5-inch and 6-inch howitzers fired HE, and the 60-pounders equal amounts of both ammunition types.[15]

The DMC attack and advance

With the din of the bombardment at 4.30 am assailing their ears and covering their movement to the 'exit gates' close to the 60th and 7th divisions' reserve brigades, Chauvel's cavalry generals waited for clearance to begin their advance. This would come once the second line of Turkish defences had been overwhelmed. The objectives set by Chauvel for Barrow's 4th and Macandrew's 5th Light Horse brigades had been carefully selected. They were aimed at rapidly overcoming Turkish command centres and other vulnerable points, particularly as withdrawal routes north and east had limited capacity for traffic flow of guns, wagons and men. With the help of the airmen, the gunners had already planned their interdiction using their 60-pounders. These routes were also on the task lists of Salmond's 5th Air Wing, whose aircraft were waiting to be despatched at first light to report on army progress and harass the enemy. Once the cavalry was on its way, the stout resistance that had characterised the Turkish infantry earlier in the campaign was expected to dissipate. Thus the more speedily and economically the cavalry could bypass or reduce strongpoints, the fewer the casualties, and the higher the numbers of men, guns and machine-guns (and new German automatic rifles) that would be captured. As it eventuated there was very spirited resistance to Allenby's troops in many localised actions when set-piece attacks had to be employed, and to which, as Farndale notes, artillery support of all kinds was on hand to maintain the momentum of the attack.

Chauvel's task was to plan and balance his formations as they ranged widely over the plains of Sharon, Galilee and Esdraelon, sometimes down to tasking regiments for specific missions based on the latest intelligence, including reports from aircraft. He had a special group of liaison officers from light horse and yeomanry regiments that rode from the headquarters of brigades and divisions to Headquarters DMC. Such was the speed of the advance that these officers rode their mounts to exhaustion. The irony of this arrangement was that the faster the advance the less useful these liaison officers became. Having left Sarona on 19 September, Chauvel established his tactical headquarters at Megiddo early the next day. His headquarters and other senior staffs formed a convoy of 60 cars and lorries — Chauvel used a Rolls Royce — which followed the troopers.

Image 18: A scene in the dust at Megiddo (Lejjun) during the advance on Damascus, showing the Australian Light Horse advancing and prisoners by the wayside (AWM B00256).

This was Chauvel's shining hour and, as Gullett wrote at the time:

> Chauvel's bearing during these two momentous days indicated his greatest qualities as a leader. A master of organisation, his plans were laid with a degree of thoroughness which was shown at every stage as the operation smoothly unfolded. Then, satisfied with his work, he awaited the issue with a remarkable absence of anxiety ... All through the long advance, which was to be carried up to Aleppo, nearly 400 miles away, his complete calm, his old-fashioned courtesy to all ranks, and the quiet, even almost languid tone in which his rapid decisions were expressed in orders, gave his staff and fighting commanders a steadying touch of inestimable value in that sustained test of endurance, where, from first to last, so much of the mounted enterprise was sheer gamble ... During operations he enjoyed a measure of trust rarely given

> by a composite force to its leader. All ranks believed implicitly that each task he set was one which could be done, and done without excessive cost.[16]

While both cavalry formations moved forward as one, the 5th leading the 4th, the 5th Light Horse Brigade was attached to XXI Corps to make an 'oblique blow' at Tul Keram once the enemy second line was passed. Then the brigade was to cut the railway leading to Jenin. The main cavalry force's ultimate destination was Tel Afule, a distance of 50 miles. Beisan on the Jordan was 80 miles from the coast. The cavalry was 'to risk their rear' and leave the Plain of Sharon to the infantry. The Turkish line had been sundered so completely that Allenby could not believe his good fortune. To the north, 12,000 horsemen, lances and sabres glinting in the morning sun, were soon across the Nahr Iskanderuneh. At last light Barrow's vanguard was at Wadi Arah leading to Musmus, and Macandrew's near the coast at Abu Shushe.

Thus far, some of the allotted field artillery had been content to follow their brigades, but they soon struggled to keep pace. Their guns had been refitted with pedrails for the first time since the Sinai and it was believed that these would make the going over the sandy hinterland easier for the teams. But the reverse proved to be the case when the horses' condition indicated that the weight of the pedrail was problematic. At Musmus they were removed and the guns regained their mobility. At 4.00 pm on 20 September, A Battery HAC, now affiliated with the 3rd Light Horse Brigade, received an urgent message to join the brigade to advance on Jenin. It covered the 10 miles in just under two hours at the trot and deployed facing south covering the Nablus road.[17] Once the cavalry collected and disposed of all its prisoners, it concentrated at Afule and remained there until 24 September.

The cavalry everywhere generally met minimal resistance, certainly much less than anticipated, and this at times posed problems in terms of food and water for widely separated units and headquarters. It was also an endurance test for the cavalrymen and their horses, some of the latter remaining saddled for more than 48 hours and over 50 miles. On all axes and tracks the cavalry units swept on with their logistic tail never far from their rear, thanks to brilliant staff work. The airmen reported progress regularly, and Chauvel at his headquarters heard of minor actions, none of which required his attention. For example, the Turkish command ordered a battalion of infantry with machine-guns from El Afule to Musmus, the 2nd Lancers arriving at this village at the same time as the enemy was deploying, whereupon the CO ordered a charge. The Turks lost 46 killed and 470 captured after the lancers had twice crashed through them. At Nazareth the 13th Cavalry Brigade encountered a column of 70 German lorries fleeing north. They 'rode' them over the edge of a deep gorge. The Haifa garrison was withdrawing to Nazareth but the 18th Lancers rounded them up, took 300 prisoners and sent the remainder flying north.

Image 19: Two RA officers stand with a captured German coastal artillery piece (150mm) used against the attackers during the cavalry fight for Haifa (AWM J06145).

Probably the boldest of all actions to this point were those of the 9th and 10th Light Horse regiments, ordered by Chauvel to capture Jenin, an important town, aerodrome, railway and stores depot, housing German and Turkish troops and German aviators. It was late afternoon when the 10th Light Horse Regiment, approaching Jenin with the Notts Battery jangling along beside it, having brushed aside an outpost, spotted a Turkish encampment in olive groves. A troop galloped with swords drawn and surprised the enemy who surrendered. Some 1800 prisoners and 400 horses and mules were taken. Leslie Wilson, the brigade commander, closed each escape route out of town with a troop and the main body entered the town, to be met by machine-gun fire. The machine-gun squadron came into action as darkness fell and neutralised the fire, discovering the guns to be manned — somewhat unsurprisingly — by German troops. The troop guarding the southern road into town met a strong force withdrawing in its direction. The machine-gunners again came into action, firing withering bursts over the heads of the enemy to some effect. The troop commander parleyed with an English-speaking German nurse at the head of the column, and the enemy surrendered. As Goold-Walker wrote,

> … the Australians acting with great resolution which suggested a much stronger force, proceeded briskly and confidently with the collection of their prisoners. The captain's bluff succeeded, and 2700 prisoners and four guns were yielded to 23 Australians. This left 300 light horsemen in the midst of 3000 of their enemy. The night passed uneasily without fighting (or sleep), but on the morning of 21 September Brigadier Wilson had 8000 prisoners, two aircraft (the remainder were destroyed

> by bombs), five guns, gold and silver, an ammunition dump and much other booty. A Battery HAC, which had made a fast pace to assist Wilson, was not required.[18]

The initial operation orders for the assault specified those times when the air force would conduct its reconnaissance sorties to update commanders and staff. This fell to No. 1 Squadron AFC which, on its first sortie just after dawn, spied the Turkish columns scrambling up the old Roman road (Balata, Ferweh, Shibleh and the Jordan road) via Wadi Fara towards Beisan. Captain Brown (AFC), who had a special radio fitted to his machine, sent this 'situation report' at 6.00 am. The topography of the wadi made it ideal for an ambush and the pilots, recognising this, at once dropped their bombs at the start of the column and head of the wadi so effectively that it made egress to the plain and the side route to Beisan nigh on impossible. Having blocked the entrance, and flying to and fro along the five-mile wadi, they wasted no time summoning their RFC colleagues to join the execution. To this the airmen added machine-gun 'strafing' of the hapless enemy who were trapped at this stage of their retreat. Some troops tried to escape cross-country only to be followed by the airmen and shot down.[19]

The speed of the rout of this enemy force was a signal event in the annals of air warfare. It was the second clear and palpable application of tactical air power of great consequence. On this scene of slaughter the effects of artillery fire were nowhere to be seen. In a few hours the airmen's blocking tactic resulted in the abandonment and destruction of two armies achieved with three tons of bombs and 44,000 rounds of machine-gun ammunition. General Barrow's force collected the prisoners and 87 guns, 55 lorries, four cars, 75 carts and 837 four-wheel wagons, water carts and kitchens — the destruction of the *Seventh Army* was complete. Nor was there a possibility of escape on the eastern front. Chaytor's force captured the bridge at Jisr ed Damieh and, on 23 September, the 11th Cavalry Brigade destroyed an enemy force trying to cross the Jordan at Makhadet Abu Naj, from which very few escaped. As Gullett wrote of this development on the eastern sector, 'Allenby's victory was almost without parallel in its thoroughness.'[20]

Contributing handsomely to this achievement was the maintenance of secrecy. So successful were these measures that a captured German map still showed the AMD in the Jordan Valley as well as other misleading evidence of aggressive intent. In the Amman area, Arabs financed by British gold bought the substantial amounts of horse feed required to sustain Chaytor's division and deprive the Turk. All the signs of normality on the Allied coastal side were maintained but the right Jordan flank measures 'suggested vast energy'.[21]

Chapter 26
Chaytor's thrust to Amman and Deraa

De l'audace, encore de l'audace et toujours l'audace.

Georges Danton, 1792

XX Corps operations

As described earlier, most of the deception plan activities took place in Major General Chaytor's sector and, at H Hour, there was no massive bombardment to launch his 'thin red line' against the Turks. His orders were to defend the Jordan Valley and to be sufficiently aggressive to convince the Turkish high command that the eastern flank was where Allenby was planning to strike hard. He was assisted in this by a German airman's report on 17 September that confirmed no change to the Turkish estimate of Allenby's order of battle and dispositions. This coincided with the day Allenby first informed his commanders below the rank of brigadier of his grand plan. The Turks, for their part, were content to continue applying 'heavy pressure' against Chaytor's calculated aggression, replying with field and heavy artillery fire. One heavy gun in Wadi Nimrin (known as 'Jericho Jane' or 'Nimrin Nellie') had been shelling Chaytor's headquarters for some weeks. However, after the brilliant success of the attack in the west on 21 September, the Turkish high command realised that their lines of retreat to Deraa and Damascus were threatened, not the least by Colonel Lawrence's irregular Arab legions.

General Chaytor had disposed his force (whose front line formed a 'shoulder' arcing to the River Jordan from Abu Tellul–Jericho road–Dead Sea) in two sectors:

- NZMR Brigade and the 1st Light Horse Brigade, the 1st and 2nd battalions, British West Indies Regiment and two Jewish battalions.
- 2nd Light Horse Brigade and the 20th Indian Infantry Brigade from the Dead Sea to the Auja bridgehead, including the Ghoraniye bridge.
- Additional bridgeheads at Henu and Makhadet Hajla were held by Indian infantry detachments. The 86th Heavy Brigade RGA (60-pounders) was just north of the Jericho road.

Chapter 26

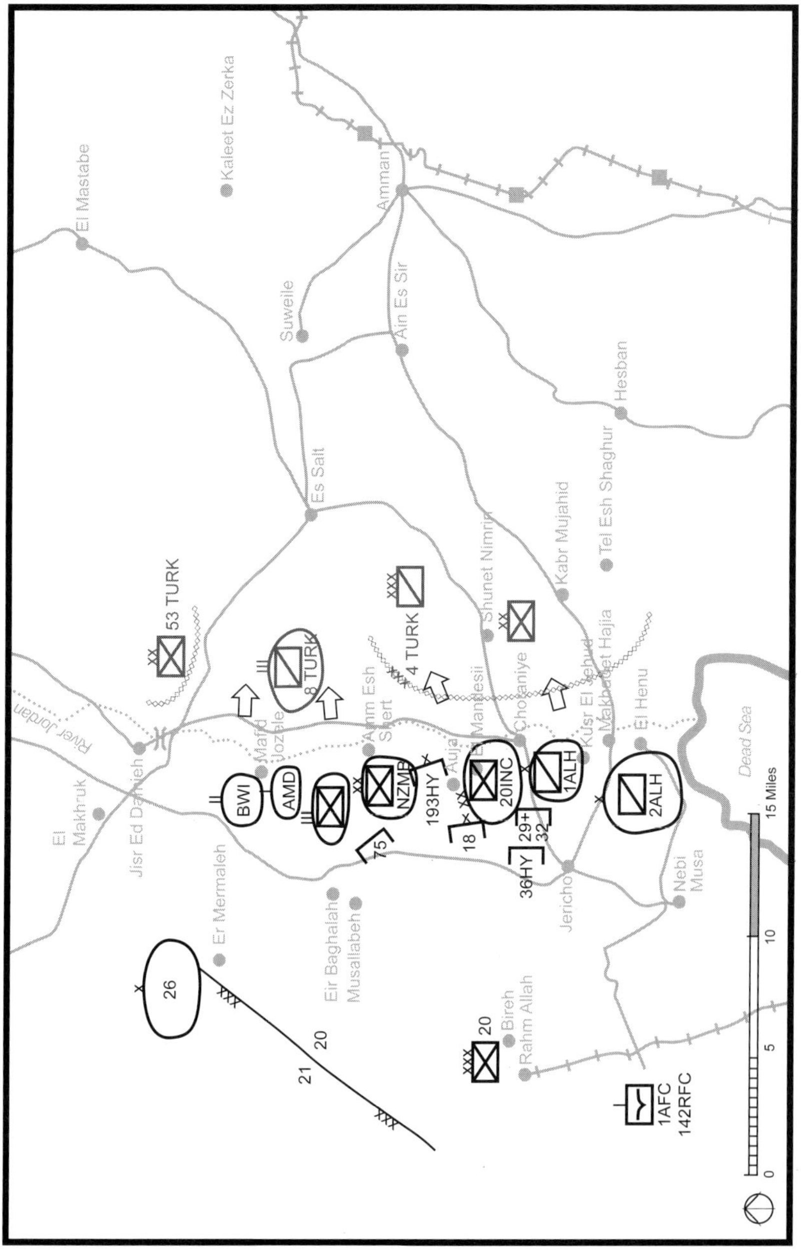

Map 21. Major General Chaytor's cavalry and infantry assault across the Jordan River prior to the force's advance north to eventually join Chauvel's cavalry.

Chaytor was also the beneficiary of the brilliance of Colonel Lawrence east of the river. As Gullett recorded, 'a substantial force of Arabs, supported by British armoured cars and a French mountain battery gathered at Kasr el Azrak, 50 miles east of Amman, as a preliminary to a series of raids on the Deraa railway.' Agents buying horse feed hinted that it was required for Allenby's cavalry when it advanced.[1]

Chaytor's force also had to protect and conform to the right flank of XXI Corps. On 19 September he ordered Brigadier Meldrum's New Zealanders and his British West Indies infantry to move north to Bakr ridge and Baghalat. His whole command was vitally interested in how the West Indies troops would perform. They need not have worried, for they earned the respect of the Anzacs with their zeal.[2] Chaytor ordered that Disr ed Dameir be taken, and the Auckland Regiment advanced up the northern Roman road, reaching its objective by 3.30 am on 22 September. With the Wellington Regiment, the Aucklanders advanced 15 miles before being stopped by resolute Turks holding the Damieh bridge. Here the Ayrshire Battery shot effectively at the defenders and the New Zealanders took the bridge undamaged. At the same time the Jewish battalions had advanced to Umm esh Shert. At this point the Turks heard that the Hejaz railway line at Deraa had been taken by Lawrence's Arabs, thus blocking one escape route. All along the front, as Chaytor's troopers moved to capture Es Salt, there were few resolute actions, yielding many prisoners. There was little work for the RHA Brigade and mountain gunners except to follow the troopers and hope for some action.[3]

Following the fall of Es Salt, Chaytor pushed along the high ground leading to Amman, familiar territory to many of the men with long memories of the debacle in May. The mountain batteries were better able to keep pace with the advance, and Chaytor ordered his regimental commanders to envelop Amman from the west and north-east. Already the enterprising Kiwis had blown up a section of rail track north of the town. He disposed his other troops to force the retreating Turks to take a much longer route and to deny them water. He ordered his less mobile troops to prepare defences at Shunet Nimrin, Es Salt and Suweile. His advance continued and his forces captured men and materiel in large quantities. The final drama of this phase of the campaign occurred at Ziza when Brigadier Ryrie resolved the high farce of 5000 Turkish troops bivouacking overnight with the light horsemen to save the Turks from the ghastly depredations of the marauding Arabs (the same Beni Sakr tribe which had 'disappeared' in May) bent on plunder and murder.

In this nine-day operation Chaytor's force captured 10,300 prisoners, 57 guns, 132 machine-guns, substantial amounts of rolling stock and much materiel. His casualties were three officers and 24 other ranks killed, and 10 officers and 95 other ranks wounded, with seven missing. This was surely the most economical military operation for its size ever conducted. For the gunners and the infantry divisions that remained in the theatre, many had fired their last shots of the war.[4]

Chapter 27
The pursuit to Damascus

And now the matchless deed achieved, determined, dared and done.
Christopher Smart, 1722–1771

The cavalry pursuit of the broken *Seventh, Eighth* and *Fourth armies* virtually sidelined the field, siege and heavy artilleries and, to a lesser extent, the engineers. The mounted troops were maintained with the sole task of remaining mobile. To this end all transport, including water carts, was left in parks. Guns, ammunition wagons and ambulance vehicles were all that accompanied the columns and the animals carried two days' rations and forage. Orders directed the cavalry to 'live off the country' until such time as the logistic tail caught up with the advance. Beirut, Tripoli and Damascus were the focus of administrative support.

So complete was the destruction of the Turkish line and communications that it further reduced the morale of the retreating soldiers, already hostage to poor provisioning and lack of water. Their animals' condition was deplorable and they suffered badly from neglect and the shortage of rations. As they retreated north there were relatively few spirited rearguard actions to delay Allenby's rampant cavalry. His intelligence staff estimated that some 45,000 enemy soldiers were withdrawing to Damascus or had already arrived, seeking desperately to flee further north. Of this number, it was believed that there were 17,000 effectives with a strength of 4000 rifles. It was invariably a rearguard comprising a battalion (around 400 men) of Turks and Germans with machine-guns, the latter accounting for around 10% of the effectives. In many minor actions they gave a good account of themselves before being overcome by the cavalry's outflanking tactics on narrow fronts, with and without artillery support. Occasionally, these tactical situations were resolved in the cavalry's favour without the horse gunners influencing the outcome. Given the opportunity, they assisted in achieving a decisive result. Aircraft, which had already contributed significantly to Allenby's successful enterprise, continued in the same role.[1]

The ascendancy gained by the 5th Air Wing RFC was most pronounced over the front, generally west from the Jordan. The German airmen had been driven from the skies over Bulfin and Chetwode's corps fronts by higher performance aircraft (particularly the Bristol Fighter) and more skilful and resolute pilots. Further east the German aviators and staff had detected the adverse effects of their bombing of the Arab levies, noting that they were easily panicked. While Salmond's force had clearly neutralised these closer to the coast, the German airmen were terrorising the Arabs to such an extent that Colonel Lawrence asked Allenby to send aircraft to shoot them down. After a short delay three Bristol Fighters from No. 1 Squadron AFC were sent and, in short order, destroyed the enemy force. This prompted more Arabs to join the winning side, a pleasing consequence of the application of psychological warfare. The Australian airmen were also instrumental in causing numerous casualties among the retreating Turkish columns. A large column of 300 horse transports and guns, 600 camels and 3000 infantry and cavalry was discovered at Marfak en route from Amman at the time the Australians attacked. The column was routed, but some of those on foot made good their escape. After 23 September no enemy aircraft appeared over the Allied armies.[2]

Allenby advanced over 400 miles from the start line on 19 September until 1 October when hostilities ceased, crossing unforgiving country that severely tested men and their horses, camels and mules. The progress of his four forces from 24 September is summarised in Table 13 below:

TABLE 13: ALLENBY'S PROGRESS 25 SEPTEMBER–11 OCTOBER 1918

	Formation			
Date	**AMD**	**A&NZ MD**	**4 CAV DIV**	**5 CAV DIV**
September				
25-9	Semakh Tiberias	Amman		
26-9		Wadi Hammam		
28-9	Jisr Benat Yakub	Iziza	Deraa	Kuneitra
			Kaubak	
30-9	Sasa Barada Gorge Damascus	Damascus		Damascus
October				
2-10		Chauvel's victory parade in Damascus		
3-10		7th Infantry Division marches to Haifa and Beirut		
15-10		Homs		
26-10				Alexandretta Road
31-10		ARMISTICE CONCLUDED		
1-11	Homs			Aleppo

The affiliated RHA batteries 'jangled along' with their regiments of light horse, mounted rifles and yeomanry. The last eight artillery and significant actions of the war are described in the remainder of this chapter, followed by a summary of this fine example of manoeuvre warfare over 400 miles. The first action was that involving the 5th Cavalry Division at Haifa.

Haifa: 22–23 September

The main Turkish escape routes and the bulk of their remaining forces were positioned inland from the coast, although Haifa itself was garrisoned. Chauvel had appreciated the logistic benefit of occupying its port and, with two Turkish armies retreating inland, he risked little, expecting a show of force from that quarter. Aerial reconnaissance reported that the town had been evacuated. Accordingly, he cobbled together a small force — a detachment of armoured cars and the 7th Light Car Patrol — command of which he entrusted to his GOCRA, Brigadier A.d'A. King. King's orders instructed him to assume the role of Military Governor and to select an Australian as his Town-Major.

Haifa is approached via the Esdraelon Plain, the town itself dominated by Mount Carmel, some four miles away. Here a Turkish rearguard was positioned, and its spirited defence from a redoubt halted King's small force. The airmen had been wrong in their assessment that the town had been evacuated, but King decided to press on despite the approaching darkness. Closer to the town a light battery opened up on the convoy from 1000 yards, destroying King's car and puncturing the armoured car tyres with accurate shellfire. A firefight developed causing casualties to both sides. King decided to call off the action, and Chauvel then ordered a more substantial effort from Macandrew's 5th Cavalry Division the next day.

He entrusted this assault to the 15th Brigade (Brigadier Harbord) which was then at Afule. B Battery HAC joined the cavalry on its march to Haifa. The Mysore Lancers in the vanguard reached Belled el Sheikh at 11.00 am and came under heavy fire, much of it from the guns on Mount Carmel. Tactically, the approach to the town was difficult, with little cover on the open plain and swampy ground around the Kishon brook, ending in a defiladed approach to the built-up area. Harbord sent the lancers to tackle the guns via the seashore, followed by the Sherwood Rangers Yeomanry of the 14th Brigade as reinforcements. The brigadier's plan called for a direct assault supported by artillery. B Battery came into action beside the road, the cavalry and machine-gunners targeting a well-concealed enemy with searching fire. The gunners found observation difficult. The naval guns on Mount Carmel maintained a steady fire and determined the brigadier's next course of action, which was to assault them with the Jodhpur Lancers. In an exciting several minutes this regiment crashed through the machine-gunners and cleared the route into town. The enemy's artillery fire became ragged as a result of accurate counter-bombardment fire and machine-gunnery. Enemy guns undetected at Karmelheim north of the town were charged and captured by the Mysore Lancers, coinciding with the Jodhpurs' attack over the swamp and plain. While delayed by shellfire and casualties, the cavalry ultimately took the town, taking 1850 prisoners and two 6-inch naval guns from the top of Mount Carmel.

The 13th Brigade was detached from the main force, pushed north and captured Acre without a shot, taking 150 prisoners and two guns. Following the battle B Battery HAC limbered up and bivouacked by the sea, the gunners unaware that they had fired their last shots of the war. The lancers had accomplished a satisfying victory, one of the few occasions when artillery support was combined successfully with the charge. While the previous day must have been a disappointing tactical outcome for King, he had been heavily involved in all the DMC's battles and artillery arrangements for 18 months and, as Military Governor, he now assumed new responsibilities. His artillery war concluded on 19 September.[3]

Semakh: 23 September

Semakh represented an action that could have been executed with fewer casualties had the artillery commander's advice been proffered and accepted. Semakh lies at the southern end of Lake Tiberias. The Haifa–Damascus railway line passes through the village from the south-east and turns south to Haifa. The River Jordan flows south from Semakh, some 1000 yards to its west. The terrain of approach is flat ground devoid of cover. The 11th and 12th Light Horse regiments advanced astride the railway until fired on at 4000 yards.

Brigadier Grant's 4th Light Horse Brigade was ordered to take Semakh as an airman's report indicated that the village was being evacuated via the lake. Three squadrons of the 11th Light Horse Regiment and two squadrons of the 12th moved forward for a right flank attack while the machine-gunners, covered by a troop, advanced parallel to the railway. Night was falling but the moon had risen and the cavalry drew swords and charged, only to be met by very effective machine-gun fire that brought down many horses and men. The defenders, mostly German, were ensconced in railway buildings and carriages with a handy supply of grenades. Repositioning machine-guns during the night brought some relief for the attackers and, when dawn broke, the enemy was overcome in close-quarter fighting, using both swords and revolvers. Survivors of the garrison then attempted to escape in a motor boat which was sunk by machine-gun fire, with one survivor. The Australians captured 23 officers and 341 other ranks but lost 43 men killed and 61 horses while 27 men were wounded. The enemy's losses were estimated at 98 killed and 364 taken prisoner, with all those killed German. Had the light horse commanders waited until daylight and used the firepower — direct or indirect — of their horse gunners, a more satisfactory outcome in terms of casualties would have resulted, and subsequent butchery avoided.[4]

Jisr Benat Yakob: 28 September

The AMD and 5th Cavalry units regrouped following the affair at Semakh, their orders to advance up the River Jordan and the western side of Lake Huleh and push on to Kuneitra and Damascus. The division moved up and Headquarters AMD was established to the west of the river alongside the headquarters of both the 4th and 5th Light Horse brigades where the panoramic view allowed the commanders to gain an appreciation of enemy strength on the eastern hills some 1500 yards from Jordan at Jisr Benat Yakob. Here enemy forces comprised two batteries and five machine-gun nests. The stone bridge had been destroyed but the troopers fashioned a ford and the crossing proceeded. The brigades had A Battery HAC and the Notts Battery in support, the latter from the northern flank, A Battery from the southern. Observers from the batteries had some difficulty pinpointing the enemy guns. A New Zealand machine-gun squadron and a French squadron were also in support. The 5th Light Horse Brigade was to envelop the ridge from both sides. The steep approach to the enemy position was crested first, but then opened up to good fields of fire for the enemy. Coming into action at 4.00 pm, the gunners demolished some machine-gun posts with 'admirable shooting', but progress was slow.

Further north, the 5th Light Horse Brigade's regiments had crossed the Jordan aiming for Deir es Saras and it was here that they halted for a brief but intense firefight. The enemy — German machine-gunners and Turkish infantry — mounted stiff resistance but were eventually overcome, with some 40 captured along with a field gun and other weapons. With their line of withdrawal now threatened, the remaining enemy troops withdrew in lorries hoping to delay the cavalry and to ensure the *Fourth Army*'s escape to Damascus.[5]

Marhardet Abu Naji: 24 September

On 24 September General Chauvel ordered Barrow's 4th Cavalry Division to block the escape route of the withdrawing Turkish *Fourth Army*, which was attempting to reach Beisan before it could be intercepted by Allenby's cavalry. Beisan had fallen on 22 September, and some remnants, including artillery, were heading north on either bank of the Jordan. Barrow ordered Brigadier C.L. Gregory's 11th Brigade to block them and the brigade moved south at 6.00 am. His Jacob's Horse and 29th Lancers and A Squadron, Middlesex Yeomanry, were sited on the eastern bank, the 21st Machine Gun Squadron and the other squadrons of the Middlesex on the western side. Gregory, who had been seconded to the Australian Military Forces five years earlier, anticipated that artillery support might be required given the strength of his force and the substantial numbers of Turks opposing him. Accordingly he ordered the Hants Battery RHA to move up from Beisan. The BC, obviously a man of considerable experience, had anticipated the order and his battery was hooked in and ready to move. It covered the six miles from Beisan to the brigade's headquarters at Ain el Beida at the trot, and arrived with 'men and horses alike covered with dust and sweat'. He positioned his battery close to brigade headquarters.

The Middlesex squadrons probing forward were soon across the Wadi esh Sherar. This wadi was overlooked by a number of hillocks ridging to the south, three of which were occupied by infantry. Gregory ordered the Turkish position to be enveloped from both flanks. The lancers and Jacob's Horse on the eastern bank were held by strong fire but the western approach by the Middlesexers brought complete success. The gunners had been engaging opportunity targets when the Turkish battery of four '5.9s' replied in kind with some accurate shooting. Guns and Hampshire gunners took shell splinters — every gun was hit but there were no casualties — and they duly limbered up and advanced across the Wadi esh Sherar to keep pace with the troopers. The cavalry and gunners continued to exert pressure and gradually pushed the Turks to the heights three miles south of the wadi. Two Turkish guns and their protection were run down with sword and lance and their guns destroyed. Upwards of 3000 prisoners were taken, all members of the *Seventh Army*. No more than a few stragglers escaped imprisonment. The *Seventh Army* had ceased to exist.[6]

Sasa: 29 September

Major General Hodgson concentrated his division at El Kuneitra for the thrust to Damascus. The 5th Cavalry was sited a few miles to the south-west and Barrow, pursuing the enemy towards Damascus, sought Chauvel's help to send a force north-east to cut their withdrawal route, but he was unable to assist. The fights at the bridge and Deir es Saras had imposed delays on his advance. A reconnaissance by armoured cars towards a ridge dominating the road to

Damascus revealed that it was occupied by 1200 Turks and 300 Germans, well protected by numerous machine-guns. Brigadier Wilson dismissed a night attack due to inadequate reconnaissance and, under pressure from Hodgson, agreed to the brigade mounting a three-point attack the following morning. By 2.00 am the attackers had dislodged the resistance, which fell back to a prepared position, only to succumb to the 10th Light Horse Regiment which took two guns, much equipment and many prisoners.[7]

Kaukab: 30 September

A similar tactical position on the Damascus road presented the next obstacle to the advance. The enemy position was occupied by infantry and cavalry approximately 2500 strong, but with no artillery. A number of machine-guns had been sited to act as a proxy for this deployment. High ridges oriented north-west 2300 yards apart separated the two forces. A Battery HAC and the Notts Battery, now attached to Brigadier Bourchier's force, managed to move their guns to the ridge top and engage the enemy over open sights at 2400 yards. Two light horse regiments and the Frenchmen were to attack both frontally and with a right hook, while another was to outflank on the west and move behind the defence. H Hour was set for 11.00 am. Both batteries had registered targets and the advance — a mounted rush — was preceded by a bombardment over the cavalry's heads until the very last minute, reminding some experienced battery hands of manoeuvres practised on field days. The divisional report noted that 'The guns gave splendid support … It was a dashing performance on the part of both artillery and cavalry against a strong dominating position.'[8] The outcome was entirely unexpected. The Germans fled without firing a shot, while 22 prisoners and 12 machine-guns were captured by the Australians without loss. The French outflanking force reached the head of Barada gorge and shot down the leading files heading for Beirut. At the same time a small force of troopers occupied a stone house close to the head of the gorge and opened fire on the ragged columns. The enemy, some 4000 in all, were confused and destitute, and quickly surrendered. This was only the first phase of a Turkish tragedy, as Chauvel planned to seize the route to Homs out of Damascus by cutting the road north of the city. The cavalry was to exploit west of the city. This proved impossible due to the terrain — the gorge was deep and only 100 yards wide — and presented a strong defensive position, so the brigade commanders headed for Dumar, five miles west on the gorge road and railway. The Australians, armed with Vickers, Hotchkiss and rifles, treated the enemy to plunging fire to try to induce them to return to Damascus. Soon the whole gorge was packed with horse and wagons, motor cars, carts and *ahmets* on foot broken in mind and body, the most horrific shambles of the campaign. The only opposition came from the German machine-gunners on top of lorries and trains who would not surrender. The following day an airman's report of a Turkish column heading for Damascus via Kiswe brought Macandrew's cavalry into the battle, his 14th Brigade rounding up 1000 prisoners. By 30 September Allenby had Damascus.[9]

Goold-Walker writes that the booty amassed by the AMD amounted to:

30,746 prisoners

74 guns

26 aircraft

340 machine-guns

38 boxes and sacks of money[10]

The campaign casualty cost is illustrated in Table 14 below:

TABLE 14: CAMPAIGN CASUALTY COUNT

AMD casualties 19 September to 2 October	KIA	WIA
3rd Light Horse Brigade	3	28
4th Light Horse Brigade	3	6
Bourchier's force	1	8
11th Light Horse Regt (Semakh)	14	29
	21	**71**

Four Australian Light Horse formations (11th Regiment, 3rd and 5th brigades and Bouchier's force) captured 31,335 Turks and Germans.[11]

Chapter 28
Damascus to Aleppo

There must be a beginning to any great matter, but the continuing on to the end until it be thoroughly finished yields true glory.

Sir Francis Drake, Letter to Queen Elizabeth I

To reach Aleppo following its spectacular advance, Allenby's force had to gird its loins for the 230-mile journey via the Rayak road. Chauvel selected the 4th and 5th cavalry divisions as his means of completing a campaign that would bring an armistice. B Battery HAC was again brigaded with the 5th Division for the trek. By this time the scourge of Spanish influenza and the ever-present malaria had begun to decimate units, leaving the 5th Division at around 30% of its strength, the 4th hit the hardest. The 5th Division was to make for Homs which could be supported logistically by a good road from the small port of Tripoli, to which a brigade from the 7th Indian Division had been sent to assist with arrangements. A railway south from Aleppo was still capable of reinforcing the Turkish front. General Macandrew organised his much-reduced division into two columns, A Column leading with command elements, the 15th Brigade, and motorised machine-guns/light car patrol. This force would be sufficiently strong to hold a reinforcing group until B Column arrived. B comprised the remainder of the division, with B Battery HAC joining it at Baalbek on 11 October. The divisional column reached Homs on 16 October, A Column having arrived two days earlier. Delays due to the repair of the blown bridge at El Rastan on the Orontes River saw B Battery HAC arrive at Hama on 23 October. On 26 October news arrived that General Macandrew had reached Aleppo with the assistance of the Arab forces. After a brief skirmish between the 15th Brigade and a Turkish rearguard, the Turkish Army melted north and, on 31 October, Turkey capitulated. The weather turned cold and the troops were able to live in sheltered accommodation, while more was 'requisitioned' for the teams. B Battery's horses were thin, having marched 567 miles in 38 days. Rest days had been few and fodder quality problematic. Attention to horse welfare had always been a high priority for successive and successful BCs, and Major Elliott and his officers and other ranks worked hard. DMC casualties were 16 officers and 109 other ranks killed, 48 officers and 317 other ranks wounded and 33 missing, a total of 523.[1]

Chapter 28

General Allenby made his official entry into Aleppo on 11 December preceded by British, Australian and New Zealand mounted detachments, including an RHA battery from each division. All formed part of his parade. Cavalry regiments lined the streets. Colonel Preston, an original BC, visited the batteries as CRA 5th Division. The 5th's artillery had been under his command for the entire duration of the war, apart from a period of some five months. He was anxious to have both HAC batteries together, and organised for this reunion when A Battery arrived in Aleppo. Together they garrisoned the city. On 9 December 1919, the battery cadres marched back into their London barracks, some five years and four months after they had first departed.[2]

The exultation felt by the troops at the magnificence of Allenby's victory was itself significant, soon to be replicated by their fellow soldiers in Europe. Much has been written of his achievement, but rather less on the efficiency and sheer fighting spirit of his cavalry and infantry, gunners, engineers and signallers and still less on the competence of his supply organisation. The military dictum of 'No A, No Q, No OPS' was emphatically confirmed by this campaign. Gullett put this into context when he wrote,

> No army was in better trim for battle, nor was a force more completely under the influence of its commander. And perhaps not since the campaigns of Napoleon had such a great decisive operation owed so much to the strategy of its leaders. But the achievement must always be regarded as a staff victory. The dazzling ride of the cavalry was dependent on the grand dash of the infantry to release the cavalry in the first place … followed by the maintenance of supplies.[3]

Chapter 29
The artillery campaign: a recapitulation

It was no coincidence that the Royal Artillery, bound as it was by its vows to its gun carriages and breech blocks, was to remain into the twentieth century the most professional Corps of the British armed forces.

J. Morris[1]

1. Heavy, siege and counter-battery artillery

The appalling conditions (climate excepted) under which the heavy and siege gunners operated were not much different to those of France, the main difference the topography and its surface composition. Sand, scrub, poorly developed tracks on pasture and mountain and bare features rising from wadis and dusty valleys restricted mobility. In two battles (Amman and the defence of Jerusalem) the terrain could be compared to muddy Flanders. The Jordan Valley was a hell-hole in its own league. The gunners' animals were the unsung heroes of the campaign, enduring privation and thirst for many hours, yet persevering until they reached their destination.

The hesitant initial approach to counter-bombardment operations in mobile warfare was to resurface in 20 years in the same theatre. The results achieved in Palestine were not characterised by the technical background and excellence of those of Lawrence Bragg and his survey and observation company colleagues on the Western Front. The Balloon Company and locating assets were latecomers to the campaign, but clearly gave Allenby an edge in the counter-bombardment war when they were protected by the RFC. It was not until Allenby's arrival and 'new broom' that artillery efficiencies took on a more significant role in the use of heavy weapons, applying the latest doctrine and its ensuing refinements as supervised by his MGRA. When used properly, the gunners were, as Farndale notes, 'magnificent. Sweat and toil to get the lumbering guns over roadless mountains. Yet they did it. Their impact was always dramatic … and its movement owed much to the Sappers and the RFC.' The record also suggests that the infantry of Palestine were made from the same mould as their brethren in France, with the notable exception of the 52nd (Lowland) Division. As the historian E.G. Keogh notes, 'This fine formation put up something of a record for hard marching, hard fighting. Every time it got near enough it promptly seized the initiative.'[2]

2. A gunnery perspective

It is instructive to analyse the effect of Turkish artillery (and its machine-gunners) on casualty lists of the eight infantry divisions in the theatre. Table 15 below provides an analysis of five battles for which figures are available, albeit from different sources:

TABLE 15: COMPARISON OF GUNS AND CASUALTIES

Turkish Guns and British Guns and Casualties

Battle	Turkish Guns	British Guns Heavy	British Guns Other	Casualties	Per Turkish Gun
First Gaza	100	6	106	4213	42[3]
Second Gaza	100	44	160	6000	60[4]
Third Gaza	320	94	226	1750	5.5[5]
Beersheba	28	85	220	1348	48[6]
Jaffa	60	88	180		3[7]
Megiddo	370	109	443	5666	16[8]

Second and Third Gaza were set-piece infantry battles in which cavalry was deployed in subordinate roles to outflank Turkish positions, to block withdrawal routes and divert enemy resources. Nonetheless, the difference between the two was statistically significant. While there were many variables involved in both battles, doubling the number of heavy/siege guns per se was a positive counter-battery investment. The 'trend line' for the other battles listed confirms this. The ratio at Beersheba suggests that, for all the élan shown by the light horse regiments in galloping Turkish trenches, it was a comparatively expensive operation in terms of battle casualties. Clearly in an event of this kind, control of the progress of the attacking horsemen and artillery fire for their protection would have been close to impossible given the methods of communication of the day, even compared to France where by this time far more sophisticated communications were employed. Subsequent operations at Jaffa and Megiddo were against an enfeebled Turkish infantry supported by resourceful gunners, whose diminishing number accompanied the surrendering infantry into captivity. Underlying these factors was a realisation that neutralisation was the key purpose of field, mountain and horse artillery fire. It was not the same as bombardments which were designed to achieve death and destruction.

The gunners also used barrages in set-piece attacks to assist the infantry onto its objective. *Field Service Regulations 1914*, the bible for every gunner, makes no mention of the barrage, failing to describe the types in use or offer any analysis of the advantages or disadvantages of creeping, block or rolling barrages. Most appear to have been a variation on what was known as the 'creeping' barrage.

In the 1918 campaigns the RFA brigades used the up-rated 18-pounder. While this weapon was still capable of firing 20 rounds per minute with a good detachment, the Mark IV, with its longer range of 9300 yards, gave the infantry more hope of continuing support during the advance. By a quirk of fate this advantage was barely needed at Megiddo. Historian John Terraine asserts that, on the Western Front, the Mark IV's capability gave it the status of 'battle winner'.

3. Horse artillery matters

Colonel Preston saw the Palestine battles both as a BC and a brigade commander. His comments on the tactical employment of horse artillery with cavalry formations differ in some respects to the conventional military wisdom of control and command. He contended that a BC attached to a brigade had 'more fun of the fair' and less drudgery than when the battery was acting as a divisional unit. However, the hard facts of the campaign revealed that greater assistance was forthcoming when batteries were under divisional orders. In most engagements a cavalry brigade needed all the available artillery and not just the attached battery — a circumstance that often occurred when a battery was in reserve and could not help in a timely manner. During the cavalry advances the view that all the horse gunners should accompany the advance guard brigade gained ground. There were objections that it made the advance column unduly long and, as Preston observed, 'at some risk of leaving the main body short of artillery'. Massed artillery fire could achieve a more decisive result than a battery, and thereby save time and casualties. There was also a belief that the divisional CRA should accompany the vanguard commander as 'vigorous artillery fire delivered after first contact on the enemy rearguard exercised a powerful effect on his morale.' This was also confirmed in a critique written once hostilities ceased by a US Army observer (Captain Stibert) who stated that 'the outstanding general conclusion that can be deduced from reading of these campaigns is the success of the bold use of [horse] artillery.'[9]

Preston noted that gunners acting in the role of escorts to a formation should also be tasked with obtaining information concerning the enemy's strength by scouting and giving early warning of an enemy approach. In this regard the cavalry performed well, Preston singling out the Australian Light Horse for praise in this role. The artillery staff also noted the requirement for a suitable howitzer, such as the 3.7-inch weapon, in a cavalry division order of battle organised as a battery of four 13-pounders and two howitzers, or a separate battery of four howitzers per division. Preston favoured the latter. In terms of ammunition, BCs preferred HE on rocky ground and shrapnel in open country. The Turks dreaded HE if they were attacking but shrapnel inflicted more casualties. Preston noted that Allied infantry and the German soldiers expressed similar opinions on this subject, and that a proportion of between 50% and 75% HE to shrapnel was preferred.

If the horse gunners had a criticism of their cavalry brethren, it was their assumption that the guns could keep pace with the troopers, which clearly they could not for obvious reasons, including the speed over the ground of a draught horse versus a charger.[10]

4. Heavy and siege artillery matters

In May 1918, with the onset of the summer heat, operations on both sides took a different course with Allenby's emphasis on the Jordan Valley as part of his 'grand design'. However, the front line remained, extending as far as the Mediterranean west of Jerusalem. The month of August receives scant treatment in the official accounts of the closing stages of the Palestine campaign. It was, in fact, a busy one for the gunners, primarily those from the 96th HAG, RGA. Commanded by Lieutenant Colonel A.H. Moberly, DSO, RGA, its organic four and two attached (for tactical purposes) siege and heavy batteries based near Et Tireh made their presence felt again after their travails as described in previous chapters. His establishment comprised the 304th, 314th and 394th Siege and 181st Heavy batteries. His attached consisted of the 189th Heavy and 43rd Siege batteries, enabling some rotation of batteries between the 95th and the other RGA group (96th) over the coming six weeks. When the gunners were told that they were moving to the coast from their inland positions there was 'great relief'. The 'pause' in operations gave the artillery staff the opportunity to mix and match ordnance after calibration shoots to ensure greater accuracy and so assist the observers in adjusting fall of shot.

In this context, the gunners regarded this period as 'business as usual'. The war diary of the 95th HAG reveals a steady but low-key period of engagement of targets. While there was little support provided to the infantries of the 60th and 10th divisions in the line, it was a fruitful time for all ranks of gunners to reach peak form for what was to become the Battle of Megiddo. It was also important for the infantry to know that these assets were at their beck and call, particularly in utilising aerial observation. Early in August 1918 their targets comprised enemy working parties and transport and a 2:1 mixture of HE and shrapnel gave good results from the expenditure of 100 rounds. Fleeting targets, which were not part of the 'bread and butter' heavy artillery regimes of the Western Front, were daily events here. On several occasions single guns were used in a 'sniping' role. In actions at the Tabsor trench lines in August 1918, some 74 rounds were fired to support a 21st Infantry Brigade enterprise. For this engagement the batteries completed a night move as, on the previous day, the enemy had engaged the firing batteries but caused no casualties. Destruction shoots also figured prominently in diary entries. The 202nd Heavy Battery joined the group, coming under command for another successful infantry 'initiative' by the 102nd Brigade.[11]

5. Technical gunnery matters[12]

In analysing the effectiveness of the larger ordnance, it is instructive to examine a bracket of ranges from the ballistic data for both the 6-inch howitzer and 60-pounder. The howitzer had a shorter maximum range of 9000 yards (the range of the 60-pounder was 12,000 yards) and its targets were usually trench lines and enemy field gun positions. The Gun Position Officer (GPO) had the choice of using five charges (1, 2, 3, 4 and Super) each of which required increasing muzzle velocities. Comparing the data for Charge 3 and Supercharge used for the majority of engagements in the 7–9000 yard range shows a much smaller length zone (and probability error) of 60 yards compared to 100 yards. The 60-pounder, with its greater range and flatter trajectory, possesses a far more extended zone at typical engagement ranges. The GPO had the 'choice' — depending on what ammunition types had been provided to him — of a full charge or a reduced charge, or two different shaped rounds. Using the full charge for a 'blunter' shell of 2 CRH (calibre radius head) at the range spread of 8000 to 10,000 yards, the length zone was 120 yards to 150 yards.[13] If, however, projectiles of 8 CRH (streamlined) were available, these lengths reduced to a more helpful 70 to 90 yards respectively. There were minor variations in the width zone (four to nine yards) at these ranges. The OPO would have to be advised what type of shell was being used.

Siege and heavy artillery positions were 3000 to 5000 yards behind the infantry forward defensive lines, their location depending on terrain and the staff's analysis of the strength and location of the enemy's guns. Where possible, alternative or roving positions were selected, surveyed, occupied or their camouflage improved. Descriptions of 'artillery duels' are rare in the diaries consulted. On the divisional fronts, the artilleries were frequently engaged in what were referred to as 'hates'. Some of the gun movements were carefully orchestrated to mislead the Turks. The OPO had to make the best of the location from his orders, irrespective of terrain. On the plains the OPO was often far more exposed, a risk that diminished in the Judean Hills.

One advantage of this situation was that the distance from the OP to the target (usually counter bombardment) dropped from 5000 yards to 3000 yards or less. It was a feature of the desert terrain that establishing a 'bracket' of around 100 yards using either HE or shrapnel required long periods before the order came to 'fire for effect'. As enemy guns were usually sited on reverse slopes, observation then passed to the RFC/AFC pilots or predicted fire for counter-battery shoots. In RA practice there was a 'rule of thumb' that applied to the length zone which was doubled if there was a danger to friendly troops. If a section or battery had been calibrated, this zone length could be reduced. Experienced airmen adept at observation work were quicker and more accurate. However, the airmen still had to contend with the length zone. They used a clock face dial of distance in yards from the target centre and a bearing from due north to indicate fall of shot, for example:

OK (or X), Y, Z, A and B, where OK/X was a round that fell within 10 yards of the target centre, Y was 25 yards, Z 50 yards, A 100 yards and B 200 yards.

What was typical of group operations in the month prior to Megiddo was the meticulous recording of ammunition expenditure and its accuracy on area/trench/earthworks and gun positions (4.5-inch, 75mm and '5.9s'). With both aerial and ground OP observers the record of the fall of shot was:

Number of shoots recorded: 17

Number of rounds fired: 2065

X/OK accuracy: 92 or 4.4%

Y accuracy: 239 or 11.5%

Z accuracy: 338 or 16.4%

A accuracy: (3 shoots only) 235 or 17.4%

B accuracy: none recorded

An analysis of the record reveals that, on three occasions in 17 shoots when aerial observation was recorded, better results were obtained. Ground observation was more difficult than aerial in judging the fall of shot relative to the target at longer ranges. The table also raises interesting gunnery questions given that siege batteries in theatre outnumbered heavy batteries 3:1, except when either genre was attached to a brigade for 'tactical' reasons. Given that a total of 24 factors (including a variety of errors) could affect the mean point of impact of a group of rounds, the fact that one round in three fell or burst close enough to the enemy section or battery to cause its neutralisation or destruction is significant. No gunner wanted his rounds to fall in the same spot. Shrapnel gave what the infantry called a wider 'beaten zone' and was preferred, notwithstanding the variability of height of burst. While further examination of the later data may reveal surprises, suffice to say the 95th HAG shot well. There appear to be no references describing the influence of meteorological data on accuracy, known latterly as 'correction of the moment'. Analysis of HAG ammunition expenditure also needs to take account of the fact that the gunners were restricted in their ammunition use as part of an overall deception plan. Generally, Moberly's management of his group was not hindered by ammunition shortage, and his aggressive use of a sniping gun would have been appreciated by his command. Over the period described above, the brigade suffered five casualties. Lieutenant T.A. Walker was wounded and returned to duty, while four other ranks were wounded, two seriously and two slightly.

5. Ammunition expenditure for five battles

Earlier in this account, tabulated numbers of and ratios of guns to casualties were used to illustrate the performance or the effectiveness and/or contribution of the artillery arm. Farndale, in his abbreviated account, sometimes overstates the effectiveness of the artillery arm, one that took some time to reach proficiency. Appendix 7 provides a glimpse of the ammunition expenditure over four periods in late 1917, early 1918 and, finally, in the biggest battle of the campaign. The three encounters selected are those that involve cavalry actions in isolation or in 'partnership' with infantry brigades in which (with hindsight) inadequate artillery support was provided. The tables show the totals for the weeks examined and do not take into account rounds used in training, calibration or losses for other reasons. For the horse gunners' 13-pounder guns, the Ordnance Service had two categories of rounds, the 6 cwt and 9 cwt. What is of interest in this differentiation was that the ratio of shrapnel to HE varied considerably between the battles. The same could be said for the RGA 2.75-inch and the 3.7-inch howitzers of the Hong Kong and Singapore mountain batteries. Note that the latter fired only HE, as did the 4.5-inch and 6-inch howitzers.

6. Casualties

No specific overall figures of artillery casualties exist, as they were subsumed in the total for the RA during the war. An entry in EEF communications that a reinforcement draft of 15 officers and 132 other ranks left the UK in January 1918 provides some indication of replacements following the Jerusalem battles. The five RHA (county) batteries incurred sizeable casualties in the predominantly cavalry battles from Romani to Rafa. The Turkish artillery fire was highly effective and generally remained so over the life of the campaign. Specifically of interest are the casualties suffered by both HAC batteries. These provide a broad indication of losses for the RHA brigades as a whole following the clearing of the coastal plain. The history of the RHA brigades records a total of 26 fatalities from their Aden foray to Damascus. Of these, five were killed or died subsequently of wounds, while 21 died from other causes, mostly illness. B Battery incurred more losses than A Battery (16 to 10), and all ranks from major (Bryant) to driver are represented. Nine drivers comprise the biggest sub-group. If the other six batteries in theatre suffered similarly, a total of 400 appears a reasonable approximation.[14] No specific record for losses suffered by the 18-pounder and 4.5-inch batteries has come to light. The official historian provides overall numbers for significant events which have been included in the text. Table 16 presents an overview:

TABLE 16: SUMMARY OF TOTAL BRITISH COMMONWEALTH CASUALTIES

Egypt, Sinai and Palestine 1914-1918

	Killed	Wounded	Missing
British	14,600	29,100	3200
Australia	1370	3550	Not Known
New Zealand	540	1150	Not Known
India	3400	6300	270
Total	**19,910**	**40,100**	**c. 3560**

Gullet records the aggregate Turkish casualty count as 200,000 killed and wounded, while 45,000 prisoners were taken.[15] The Australian casualties for this campaign totalled 1282 deaths, with 574 killed in action, 288 dying of wounds and 320 dying from other causes. Combined total casualties reached approximately 5000.[16]

Chapter 30
Artillery summary and conclusions

The proof of the pudding is in the eating.

Proverb

Despite the disparity in the generic types of operations their commanders mounted, there are several parallels to be drawn between the experiences of the Allied armies on the Western Front and the Sinai/Palestine operations. As described, until July 1917 the application of appropriate scale and accuracy of fire on enemy guns and trenches was beset by the same endemic problems in both Europe and the Middle East. It was not until the long casualty lists and tactical setbacks suffered by the infantry and cavalry divisions over more than 12 months began to bite that a change in practice was initiated. The Turk's artillery was superior from First Gaza until Megiddo 18 months later. There were exceptions — Beersheba, Wadi Hesi, Sheria and Jerusalem — battles in which Allied artillery was clearly more effective.

Allenby's strategic approach turned the Palestine campaign into one of the most brilliant of the war. Embedded in this was the influence of his MGRA, Major General S.C.U. Smith, who was Mentioned in Despatches six times. In his post-war musings, he noted somewhat pointedly that his infantry peers or brigadiers did not always avail themselves of his wisdom. His major role at this time may well have been the essential business of cajoling more guns and ammunition for the theatre from the parsimonious bureaucrats of the War Office. This changed when Allenby arrived. His career background was sound, and featured a number of senior postings including command of the New South Wales Artillery Corps prior to Federation. Tall and gregarious with a broad perspective and well-honed persuasive powers, his influence was greater for his mastery of detail, while his CRAs eventually gained the confidence of their cavalry and infantry commanders. Once Allenby arrived in theatre, Smith quickly gained his confidence, which he obviously retained. He may well have been the type of staff officer preferred by Allenby — someone he could trust rather than a man of 'brilliance' whom he felt he could not. Indeed, it was

Chapter 30

not until Allenby's appointment that Smith was even consulted on matters of artillery practice. It is also instructive to note that no GOCRA or CRA of divisions and brigades of all three branches of the RA was 'replaced', except one for health reasons. However, several were promoted.

The artillery arm also benefitted from developments of all kinds on the Western Front. Recent scholarship suggests that, all too often, the gunners in Europe had to support plans that restricted the effectiveness of their weapons. This was not limited to the Western Front and First Gaza quickly comes to mind. The gunners were eager to learn and established schools to teach advances in tactics and the application of doctrine, regarding change and adaptation as 'not the responsibility of the few but the duty of many'.[1] While several conclusions can be drawn, the fact remains that, after initial reverses, primarily at the hands of the Turkish and German gunners, their collective professionalism and regimental pride won through in the end.

In terms of ammunition consumption, brigade and divisional ammunition columns commanders and staff performed heroically to keep the batteries supplied to first line holding standard. Crossing featureless desert, trekking through the Jerusalem foothills and the desolate Jordan Valley, often at night, required excellent navigation skills and staff work, not to mention vital animal husbandry practices. These men were the unsung gunner heroes of the campaign.

The excellence of the British and Australian air arm in this campaign is also worthy of mention, particularly their contribution to victory through the establishment of aerial superiority over the Germans in late 1917. The innovative use of aerial photography and its employment in artillery observation, their bombing and strafing attacks on enemy gun positions, gun teams, ammunition dumps and transport also contributed significantly to the success of operations. Over the campaign as a whole, the air contribution was probably more effective than counter-battery artillery fire in securing the final victory. This is an obvious assessment produced by any reading of the aggressive tactics of Allied airmen once their strength reached two wings. Their efforts in reconnaissance made a crucial contribution to the intelligence picture in a land that provided the Turks few places of concealment. The air contribution to communications through message dropping and wireless was also significant and proved critical to Allied success.

The Sinai and Palestine campaigns that began in 1916 generally followed the British Army pattern of taking heavy losses and setbacks for an initial period before Allied forces eventually prevailed over their enemies. The cavalry battles from Romani to Rafa which featured seasoned Australian light horsemen and

New Zealand mounted riflemen ably supported by their horse artillery gave their higher commanders victories under capable, battle-hardened regimental and battery commanders. Subsequent operations yielded victories and defeats, the turning point the appointment of General Allenby as supreme commander. A man of absolute courage, moral and physical, fine generosity of spirit and a natural gift for command, Allenby never sought popularity. He liked to 'think things through to a finish' and his few losses, notably in several of his Jordan Valley ventures and on the coast, were due to security lapses and he was quick to determine the cause and ensure that these lapses were never repeated. Allenby's creative schemes in 1917–18 designed to mislead his enemies displayed a stroke of genius. His ability to persuade the War Office to take the battle to the Turk was remarkable and significant in itself. Some historians have characterised Allenby as belonging to the 'old Imperial school' and criticised his approach as inappropriate for the Antipodean troopers who, while they did not love Allenby, certainly trusted him. The record suggests that, two security breaches aside, Chauvel and his predominantly non-regular dominion commanders never let him down. His British cavalry and yeomanry commanders eventually restored their reputation for dash. Allenby's victory at Megiddo stands as a brilliant feat of arms, remarkable also for being the most economical in manpower given its frontage, scope and composition and the fact that this was a 400-mile advance. He was assisted by an outstanding staff and excellence in his senior gunner officers in cavalry and infantry corps and divisions. Headquarters EEF was a well-oiled machine and, certainly after the arrival of Allenby, gives lie to Gullett's remark that 'you had the impression a great man was not in charge'.

To conclude, did the British Army apply any of the lessons that were dearly learned to its 'new' post-war army? There were certainly issues with the killing power of the 13 and 18-pounders and other gunnery refinements, and the management and provisioning of large numbers of men and horses. The development of the tank, tractor, lorry and armoured car was followed by the mechanisation of artillery. This is not the place to expand on the competing forces within the British Army hierarchy where progressives pitted themselves against the die-hard 'establishment', although several of the central issues are worthy of brief mention. One of the two primary debates concerned the future of the horse within cavalry circles, and saw its eventual absorption into the Royal Armoured Corps by the then Chief of the Imperial General Staff, Lieutenant General Sir Alan Brook.

Another critical (long-term) development involved the enormous improvements made to what is now termed 'logistics'. The huge army system that supplied men, guns and the wherewithal to fight the German Army in France and Flanders had to be adapted considerably, and Allenby oversaw its adaptation during the Palestine campaign. Between the wars, the General Staff modified its logistics, doubtless helped by the lessons of 1916–18 and the need to supply its 'peacekeeping' force in Palestine and later its Eighth Army in Egypt in 1940.

Yet another crucial development occurred in ordnance with the transmogrification of the 18-pounder to the 25-pounder and later the 60-pounder which devolved into the 4.5 and 5.5-inch medium guns and finally a new weapon type, the 2-pounder (and eventually the 6 and 17-pounder) anti-tank gun. The cavalry would be equipped with scout and armoured cars, tanks and armoured personnel carriers. Some troopers would become 'lorried infantry privates' in armoured formations. All these developments were followed and implemented in whole or in part by the Commonwealth armies. Perhaps the most quintessential example of bureaucratic bloody-mindedness, however, concerned the protracted tug-of-war between the RAF and the British Army over who should 'own' the Air OP Branch. Happily, the initiative and enthusiasm of Lieutenant Colonel Bazeley, RA, prevailed and gunner-to-gunner communications resulted.

The final conclusion that can be drawn from this campaign, however, is that the Royal Regiment lived up to its motto — 'Everywhere the paths of glory lead'.

Ubique Quo Fas Gloria Ducunt

Postscript

Field Marshal Viscount Allenby of Megiddo visited Australia as a guest of the Australian government in 1932. The association between the Australians and New Zealanders and their supporting RHA batteries was continued by individuals in an informal way. The New Zealanders were frequent guests of the Somerset Battery reunions, and doubtless that applied to some of the light horsemen and their RHA batteries. The light horse's post-war repute rankled with the AIF Western Front gunners, engineers and infanteers, who averred that, save for those troopers who had served at Gallipoli, they did not know what 'real soldiering' was. Certainly the absence of exposure to prolonged barrages and concentrations made an enormous difference. Less organisationally cohesive because of their rural spread over the continent, their regiments were re-established in the country, until most were removed from the order of battle in the late 1930s. Post-World War II, some similarly identified units, now mechanised, were replaced on the Citizen Military Forces order of battle. Finally, 18-pounders were used to instruct the cadets of the Royal Military College of Australia in artillery until 1939.

As an *obiter dicta* on the campaign in the Sinai and Palestine, the failure of the General Staffs of Great Britain and Australia to invest in heavy artillery cost the Second AIF dearly for 15 months from December 1940. The lessons were there, and the pleas of Lieutenant General Chauvel following World War I to the Australian government to rectify the situation went unheeded, with the result that, for 20 years, counter bombardment and its arts were subordinated to divisional artilleries instead of belonging to the more inclusive artillery corps structure. The British Army was similarly seriously negligent in using the lessons from World War I in the BEF sent to France in 1940. Lessons learned from history are readily forgotten, and these lapses in doctrinal verities were most spectacularly replicated in France and Flanders, and in the North African battles of 1941–43 until Bernard Montgomery and his Brigadier Royal Artillery, Sidney Kirkman, restored artillery to its eventual 'master of the battlefield' status in the campaigns that followed. While many lessons and their (then) novelty resulting from the tactical use of air power in Palestine in 1918 augured well for infantry-artillery-air cooperation, the RAF/RAAF army-aircraft cooperation and techniques in 1939 were inferior to those of the *Luftwaffe*. The Germans made better use of the data and it took four years from 1939 for the British to create a tactical air force as operationally competent as that in France and Palestine in 1918.

Appendices

APPENDIX 1

CHRONOLOGY

1916	18 JAN	A&NZ Army Corps (ANZAC) formed, Major General Godley, GOC AIF
		Occupy Ferry Post, Suez Canal
	10 FEB	Lieutenant General Birdwood GOC AIF
	14 FEB	Doubling AIF divisions begins
	16 MAR	Australian Mounted Division formed GOC Major General Chauvel
	21 MAR	I ANZAC Corps GOC Birdwood
		II ANZAC Corps GOC Godley
	1 JUN	GE a/c bomb Romani
	4–9 AUG	Romani, Qatya and Bir el Abd
	6 NOV	Desert Column formed (Dobell's advance troops) Abolished Aug 1917
	21 DEC	El Arish occupied
	22 DEC	Battle of Magdhaba
1917	9 JAN	Battle of Rafa
	25 MAR	First Gaza
	17–19 APR	Second Gaza
		General Dobell sacked as GOC Eastern Force
	18 JUL	General Allenby appointed
	OCT	Desert Mounted Corps formed GOC Lieutenant General Chauvel + Camel Brigade and 7th Mounted Brigade
		XX Corps GOC Chetwode
	2 NOV	Third Gaza
		XXI Corps GOC Bulfin
	30–31 OCT	Battle of Beersheba
	6 NOV	Battles of Sheria, Hareira
	9 NOV	Northern Drive begins coastal advance Qatra–El Mughar
	11 NOV	Nahr Sukureir affairs

Appendix

	12 NOV	Khuweilfe
	17 NOV–30 DEC	Capture and defence of Jerusalem
	20–22 DEC	Battles of Jaffa, Tul Karm and Junction Station
1918	19–21 FEB	Capture of Jericho, Ghoraniye
	MAR	von Kressenstein and Falkenhayn depart
	6 MAR	Ghoraniye bridgeheads
	8–12 MAR	Tel Asur attack
	21 MAR	63, 53 and 75 Yeomanry divisions to France
	21 MAR–2 APR	First trans-Jordan raid to Es Salt/Amman
	1 APR	Loss of RHA guns
	11 APR	Turkish attack on DMC Jordan bridgeheads
	30 APR–4 MAY	Second trans-Jordan attack on Amman
	20 APR	Attack on Shunet Nimrin
	29 APR	Swords used by light horse
	14 JUL	Musallabeh, Abu Tellul, Mellahah and El Hinu
	19–22 SEP	Megiddo – battles of Sharon and Nablus (destruction of *Army Group F*)
	23 SEP	Capture of Es Salt
	25 SEP	Capture of Semakh
	25–26 SEP	Capture of Amman
	28 SEP	Crossing of Jordan at Benat Yakub
	1 OCT	Capture of Damascus
	5–26 OCT	Pursuit to Aleppo
	31 OCT	Turkish Armistice
	11 NOV	German Armistice

APPENDIX 2

AUSTRALIAN MOUNTED DIVISION — SENIOR/KEY STAFF

Brigadier R.G. Howard-Vyse, CMG, DSO, Chief of Staff	RHG
Brigadier E.F. Trew, DSO, DAA & QMG	RM
Brigadier A. d'A. King, OBE, DSO, GOCRA	RA
Colonel R.M. Downes, CMG, DDM	AAMC
Lieutenant Colonel W.P. Farr, APS, AA & QMG	
Lieutenant Colonel A.A. Corder, CMG, ADOS	AOD
Lieutenant Colonel R.E.M. Russell, CRE	RE
Lieutenant Colonel L. Partridge, DSO, CMGO	Pembroke Yeomanry
Major A.J. Love, GSO2	10 ALH
Major N.N.C. Russell, DSO, GSO2	Leinster Regt
Major R.A. Allen, MC, DAAG	RFA
Major F.G. Newton, AAG	5 ALH
Major F.P. Howell-Price, DSO, DAST	AASC
Major T.E. Robins, APM	1st City of London Yeomanry
Captain A.B.C. Neale, GSO2	RFA
Reverend W. Macfarlane-Woods, Senior Chaplain	

APPENDIX 3

ORGANISATION OF NEW ZEALAND MOUNTED RIFLES BRIGADE

The brigade's fighting forces consisted of three mounted rifle regiments: Auckland, Wellington and Canterbury and attached troops who were supported organisationally within the NZEF in the Middle East.

The **Auckland Mounted Rifles** comprised the 3rd Auckland, 4th Waikato and 11th North Auckland Mounted Rifles.

The **Wellington Mounted Rifles** comprised the 2nd Queen Alexandra's, 6th Manawatu and 9th Wellington East Coast Mounted Rifles.

The **Canterbury Mounted Rifles** comprised the 1st Canterbury Yeomanry Cavalry,

8th South Canterbury and 10th Nelson Mounted Rifles.

The Somerset Battery RHA was the most commonly affiliated RHA battery supporting the NZMB on operations, 'the men becoming to consider themselves New Zealanders although recruited in the county of Somerset'.

The following table describes the composition of NZMB and attached troops of the NZEF serving in Palestine.

CASUALTIES

The total losses to the NZMR between 1914 and 1920 amounted to 1120, of whom 599 died at Gallipoli. In the period from May 1916 in the Sinai and Palestine, a total of 306 mounted riflemen were killed in action and 1162 wounded. Disease accounted for 177 and 105 were listed as missing in action in both Gallipoli and Palestine campaigns. In the Sinai and Palestine between April 1916 and December 1918, some 1416 horses became casualties. Of these, 211 died, 184 were destroyed, 383 (27%) were killed in action and 559 'evacuated to hospital with wounds, exhaustion and sickness. 79 were listed as missing.'

(Sources: http://www.nzmr.org/campaigns.htm, pp. 1–13; Kinloch, *Devils on Horses*, p. 348.)

NEW ZEALAND MOUNTED RIFLES BRIGADE	OFFRS	R&F	HORSES
HEADQUARTERS	8	43	55
3 REGTS each of (24) (499) (616)	72	1497	1848
1st MACHINE GUN SQUADRON	8	222	321
SIGNAL TROOP	1	36	36
ENGINEER FIELD TROOP	2	50	67
No2 MOBILE VET SECTION	1	29	28
MOUNTED FIELD AMBULANCE	6	133	127
AUCKLAND MTD RFLS BAND	1	36	
No 4 COMPANY ASC	5	119	156
ATTACHED PERSONNEL			
TWO CAMEL COMPANIES ea (6) and (117)	12	234	
Offr/NCO at ZEITOUN;OR Trg Depot ISMAILIA	15	59	
2nd MACHINE GUN SQUADRON	8	221	320
NZ RAROTONGAN COMPANY	6	240	
ADMIN HQ CAIRO	3	30	
Offr/NCO at ZEITOUN;OR Trg Depot ISMAILIA	19	79	
			2958 in 1918

NOTE

To keep the brigade up to strength throughout the war a total of 17,723 all ranks left New Zealand

APPENDIX 4

SIEGE BRIGADE WAR ESTABLISHMENT

Siege artillery brigade of two batteries, each of 4.6-inch howitzers

The July 1915 establishment varied slightly from its predecessor dated 4 February 1915.

A. **Horse drawn**

						Horses			
Component	**Offrs**	**SNCOs**	**Artificers**	**R&F**	**Total**	**Rid'g**	**Draft**	**Heavy**	**Total**
HQ	2	2		17	23	6	3		9
HQ Att	2		2	4	8		2		2
Two Batteries	10	18	18	314	364	34	12	160	206
Amm Col	3	5		49	58		2		2
Amm Att	2	3	12	84	101				
Total Brigade									
Incl Attached	19	28	32	468	554	42	17	160	219

Note: Included in the total R & F (rank and file) are six trumpeters and five R & F on sanitary duties.

Brigade HQ had eight R & F trained observers and telephonists, and six batmen 'trained for duties in the ranks' and two under orders of the Medical Officer (all R & F).

The Ammunition Column's artificers included fitters and turners, blacksmiths, wheelers and an electrician. Each brigade had a base detachment of two officers, four SNCOs and 123 R & F.

B. **Horse and lorry drawn**

In a mixed brigade there were 33 petrol-powered lorries and 64 heavy draught horses for the ordnance and 96 carts and wagons. The lorries were for ammunition, luggage and supplies, workshop, stores and personnel and included 25% as 'spare'.

AMMUNITION

First line ammunition was specified as 40 rpg for 120-pound shells and 50 rpg with 100-pound shells with the battery and 45 rpg of either weight with the brigade ammunition column. A general service wagon had a capacity of 25 rounds of 100-pound shells or 20 x 120-pound shells. A lorry had a capacity of 60 rounds. Reserves with Lines of Communication was 400 rpg.

(Source: War Establishments, A Siege Artillery Brigade, WO SD 2 of 4 February and 14 July 1915 for both tables.)

WAR ESTABLISHMENTS	RHA BATTERY	RHA AMN Col	RGA SIEGE BDE HQ	RGA SIEGE AMN Col	RGA SIEGE BTY	TOTAL	RGA HEAVY BATTERY	RGA HEAVY BATTERY	TOTAL
ORDNANCE	6 x 13 pr		8 X 6 in		4 x 6 in		4 x 60 pr	AMMO	
	6 - 9 cwt		HOW		HOW		GUN	COL	
Officers	7	2	29	5	4	8	5	1	6
Other Ranks	215	115	19	49	157	545	173	51	223
Attached			8	84		92	2		
TOTAL	**222**	**117**	**56**	**139**	**195**				
Riding Horses	108	25	3	2	6		28	3	31
Mules, Heavy draft							209		
Draft Horses	132	119					2 Draft		
Drivers				74 ASC			Mules		
Bicycles	24			37 spare					
Cars				2					
2 Horsed Carts	2	1							
2 Horsed Wagons		3							
4 Horsed Wagons	2	1							
6 Horsed Wagons *	12	16	64				116 Heavy		
*Camel or Mules									
Equivalents not given									
Lorries 3 or 4 ton			33						

Ref: War Est't. Siege Bde WO 2 of 4-Feb-15 & 14 July and Detail Heavy Bty WO 2 of 10-Sep-15 & Amn Col

Appendix

NOTE In addition to those personnel on the gun line, the following 'trades' were detailed in the Establishments

- Trumpeters
- Telephonists
- Fitters & Turners
- Wheelers
- Electricians
- Blacksmiths
- Storemen
- Orderlies
- Batman
- Mechanics (Diesel)
- Mechanics (motor)
- Drivers
- Army Medical Corps
- Army Service Corps

Note: During wartime minor changes were made to take account of conditions in the Middle East theatre.

Appendix 5

ROYAL HORSE ARTILLERY GUNS

	13 Pounder MkII BC	15 pr Erhardt BL QF	15 Pounder BLC (b)
Breech			Int Screw Thread
Recuperator	Hydrospring		Hydrospring
	Constant 41 in		40 inch
	1.04 m		1.02 m
Trail			BOX
Calibre - inches	3	3	3
- mm	76.2	76.2	76.2
Weight - pounds	2236	2240	3177
- Kgs	1014		1441
Elevation - degrees	- 5 to +16		-9 to +16
Traverse - degrees	4 L & R		
Muzzle Velocity - fps	1675	1675	1590
Muzzle Velocity - mps	511	511	485
Maximum Range - Yards	5390 - 5900		5750
Maximum Range - Metres	4937 - 5392		5260
Projectile Filling	HE, Amatol		HE, Shrapnel
Charge/Fuse	80 T & P		65A
	Cordite		
Crew	9		11

Appendix

ARTILLERY BRANCH	HORSE	FIELD APPENDIX	FIELD	HEAVY 6	SIEGE	TURKISH	GERMAN	ORDNANCE
Employment Role	Cavalry Support	Infantry Support	Infantry Support	Bombardment	Bombardment	Infantry Support	Bombardment	Bombardment
ORDNANCE	13 pounder Mk II	18 pounder Mk II	4.5 inch Howitzer	60 pounder BL	6 in Howitzer	7.5 cm Gun	12 cm Howitzer	15 cm
	9 cwt			Mk II				Howitzer
Caibre inches	3	3.3	4.5	5	6	3	4.72	5.9
mm	76.2	84	114	127	152	75	120	150
Weight Pounds	2,236	2,831	3,020	9,655	9,740	2,380	2,480	3,588
Kgs	1014	1,284	1,370	4,470	4,426	1,079	1,125	1,754
Shell Weight pounds	12.5	35	35	60	86 & 100	19	44	84
Kgs	5.7	15.9	15.9	27.3	39 & 45.4	8.7	20	38
Elevation Degrees	minus 5 to + 16	minus 5 to + 45	minus 5 to +45	minus 5 to +21	Zero to 45	minus 9 to +15	0 - 42	0 - 73
Traverse in Degrees	4 Left & Right	3 Left & Right	3 Left & Right	4 Left & Right	4 Left & Right	7	5	11.5
Carriage	Wheeled Pole	Wheeled Pole	Two Wheel Box	Two Wheel Box	Two Wheel Box	Two Wheel Pole	Box	Box
Charges	1	3	5	2	5			
Rate of Fire rpm	10	10	Two	Two	Two			
Recoil inches	41					Hydro Spring		
Recoil mm	1041							
Range Maximum Yards	5,900	9,515	7,000	12,300	11,600	6,600	6,300	5,140
Metres	5,400	8,700	6,400	11,250	10,610	6,000	5,800	4,700
Muzzle Velocity ft/sec	1,675	1,614	1,026	2,080	1,330	1,790	900	787
m/sec	511	492	313	634	405	540	275	240
Detachment	9	10	10	10	10	7	8	
Shell Types	HE, Shrapnel	HE, Shrapnel, Smoke, Star & Gas	HE, Smoke Star, Gas	HE, Shrapnel	HE, Shrapnel	HE, Shrapnel	HE, Shrapnel	HE, Shrapnel

APPENDIX 6

ORDERS OF BATTLE

RHA Territorial Force 1917

Battery	Initial Equipment	Brigade	Division
A Honorable Artillery Company	4 x 13 pdr	19 RHA	DMC
B Honorable Artillery Company	4 x 13 pdr	19 RHA	DMC
1/Ayrshire	4 x 15 pdr	18 RHA	ANZMD*
2/Ayrshire	4 x 15 pdr	260 RFA	
Berkshire	4 x 15 pdr	2/20 RHA	4 & 5 Cav**
Essex		263 RFA to 20 RHA	
Hampshire		20 RHA	4 & 5 Cav**
Inverness		18 RHA	ANZMD*
Leicester		20 RHA	4 & 5 Cav**
1/Nottinghamshire		19 RHA	DMC
Somerset		18 RHA	ANZMD*

* Jordan Valley affiliations.

** In October 1917 these batteries were affiliated with the Yeomanry Mounted Division, viz the 6th, 8th and 22nd mounted brigades and armed with 18-pounders. From Megiddo to Damascus they were with the 4th and 5th mounted brigades

Note: There is some confusion in the sources regarding the ordnance with which an RHA battery was equipped at various times during the war. Farndale writes (p. 79) that B Battery HAC was equipped with 15-pounders. For the Gaza battles (p. 83) all except Notts had 18-pounders. On p. 90 Ayr and Somerset have 18-pounders. On p. 95 Inverness, Ayr and Somerset have 13-pounders. The *Official History* recorded that, in 1917, 20 RHA Brigade had 18-pounders. According to Goold-Walker, the HAC batteries exchanged their 13-pounders in 1918 for 18-pounders and then gave them back. Farndale (Annex 1) writes that, by the end of the war they were all equipped with 13-pounders. This would have been an artefact of officialdom's organisational purity. That said, the smaller shell could still be lethal given suitable ground conditions, good observation and skilled forward observers.

From time to time for (sudden) tactical responses, batteries were moved around between brigades, but this seems to have been infrequent. For example, the NZMB had the Somersets who, as one historian noted, by the end of the war regarded themselves as 'New Zealanders'. Veterans of the NZMB attended post-war reunions of the Somersets. The Essex Battery as corps troops is seldom mentioned.

Royal Field Artillery[1]

Battery	Equipment	Brigade	Division
372	6 x 18 pdrs	8	3 Indian
373	6 x 18 pdrs	8	3 Indian
374	6 x 18 pdrs	53	3 Indian
389	6 x 18 pdrs	37	75 Infantry
390	6 x 18 pdrs	37	75 Infantry
391	6 x 18 pdrs	172	75 Infantry
392	6 x 18 pdrs	172	75 Infantry
405 H	4 x 4.5 in	37	75 Infantry
406 H	4 x 4.5 in	172	75 Infantry
413 H	4 x 4.5 in	302	60 Infantry
422	6 x 18 pdrs	264	7 Indian
423	6 x 18 pdrs	264	7 Indian
424	6 x 18 pdrs	263	10 Irish Infantry
428 H	4 x 4.5 in	8	3 Indian
430 H	4 x 4.5 in	53	3 Indian
438 H	4 x 4.5 in	262	7 Indian
439 H	4 x 4.5 in	267	53 Infantry
440 H	4 x 4.5 in	271	54 Infantry
A	6 x 18 pdrs	67	10 Irish
A	6 x 18 pdrs	68	10 Irish
A	6 x 18 pdrs	261	52 Infantry
A	6 x 18 pdrs	262	52 Infantry

Battery	Equipment	Brigade	Division
A	6 x 18 pdr	264	52 Infantry
A	6 x 18 pdr	265	53 Infantry
A	6 x 18 pdr	266	53 Infantry
A	6 x 18 pdr	267	54 Infantry
A	6 x 18 pdr	270	54 Infantry
A	6 x 18 pdr	271	54 Infantry
A	6 x 18 pdr	301	60 Infantry
A	6 x 18 pdr	302	60 Infantry
A	6 x 18 pdr	303	60 Infantry
B/69	4 x 4.5 in	Unbrigaded	
B	6 x 18 pdr	67	10 Irish
B	6 x 18 pdr	68	10 Irish
B	6 x 18 pdr	261	52 Infantry
B	6 x 18 pdr	262	52 Infantry
B	6 x 18 pdr	264	52 Infantry
B	6 x 18 pdr	262	52 Infantry
B	6 x 18 pdr	264	52 Infantry
B	6 x 18 pdr	265	53 Infantry
B	6 x 18 pdr	266	53 Infantry
B	6 x 18 pdr	267	53 Infantry
B	6 x 18 pdr	270	54 Infantry
B	6 x 18 pdr	271	54 Infantry
B	6 x 18 pdr	272	54 Infantry
B	6 x 18 pdr	301	60 Division
B	6 x 18 pdr	302	60 Division
B	6 x 18 pdr	303	60 Division
C (H)	4 x 4.5 in	68	10 Irish
C (H)	4 x 4.5 in	261	52 Infantry
C (H)	4 x 4.5 in	264	52 Infantry
C (H)	4 x 4.5 in	263	10 Irish
C (H)	4 x 4.5 in	265	53 Infantry
C (H)	4 x 4.5 in	264	7 Indian
C (H)	4 x 4.5 in	266	53 Infantry

Battery	Equipment	Brigade	Division
C (H)	4 x 4.5 in	270	54 Infantry
C (H)	4 x 4.5 in	272	52 Infantry
C (H)	4 x 4.5 in	301	60 Infantry
C (H)	4 x 4.5 in	302	60 Infantry
C (H)	4 x 4.5 in	303	60 Infantry

Heavy brigades and batteries[2]

Battery	Equipment	Brigade
10	4 x 60 pdr	
15	4 x 60 pdr	100
91	4 x 60 pdr	96
181	4 x 60 pdr	95
189	4 x 60 pdr	102
195	4 x 60 pdr	97

6 brigades = 24 x 60 pdrs

Siege brigades and batteries

Battery	Equipment	Brigade
43	4 x 6 in gun	-
134	4 x 6 in how	100
205	4 x 6 in how	103
209	4 x 6 in how	102
300	2 x 6 in/2 x 8 in how	100
304	4 x 6 in how	95
314	4 x 6 in how	95
378	4 x 6 in how	96
380	4 x 6 in how	102
383	4 x 6 in how	96
421	4 x 6 in how	97
440	4 x 6 in how	96

6 brigades: 44 howitzers, 4 guns

Summary:

95 Brigade: 181, 304, 314 batteries
96 Brigade: 91, 378, 383, 440 batteries
97 Brigade: 195, 421 batteries
100 Brigade: 13, 43, 134, 300 batteries
102 Brigade: 189, 209, 380 batteries
103 Brigade: 205 Battery

Appendix

CAVALRY, CORPS, DIVISIONS ORDERS of BATTLE

A&NZ Mounted Division ALH
1st Brigade: Brig Cox — 1st, 2nd, 3rd LH regts
2nd Brigade: Brig Ryrie — 5th, 6th, 7th LH regts
NZMB: Brig Meldrum — Auckland, Wellington, Canterbury MRs
Artillery: 18 RHA Brigade — Ayr, Inverness and Somerset Btys (18-pdrs)

AMD ALH
3rd ALH Brigade: Brig L. Wilson — 8th, 9th, 10th LH regts
4th ALH Brigade: Brig Grant — 4th, 11th, 12th LH regts
5th ALH Brigade: Brig Macarthur-Onslow — 14th, 15th LH regts, French Chasseurs/Spahis (FDFA)
5th Mounted Brigade: Brig Fitzgerald — 1/1st Warwick, 1/1st Gloucester, 1/1st Worcester Yeomanry
Artillery: 19 RHA Brigade, Notts, A and B batteries HAC (18-pdrs)

Australian light horse brigades (G 48, 344)
March 1916

A&NZ Mounted Division — Chauvel

1 Bde: NSW, QLD, SA & TAS	Cox and Meredith
2 Bde: NSW, QLD	Ryrie
3 Bde: VIC, SA & WA	Royston, L. Wilson
4 Bde: NSW, QLD & SA	Meredith, Grant

1917
5 Bde: all states, 14 LHR, 15 LHR + French, Macarthur-Onslow

Machine-gun squadrons
1 — NSW, QLD, SA & TAS
2 — NSW, QLD
3 — VIC, SA & WA
4 — NSW, QLD, VIC & SA
5 — NZ (Camel Bde)
NZMB — NZ MG SQN

Each brigade had a machine-gun squadron, each eight officers, 221 other ranks

Doubled machine-gun strength during campaign from three Lewis guns per squadron increased to 13 x .303 Hotchkiss

NZMB (see Appendix 3 for more detail)
The Auckland Regt — 3 Auckland Sqn; 4 Waikato Sqn; 11 North Auckland Sqn
The Wellington Regt — 2 Queen Alexandra's Mounted Rifles (Wellington East and Wellington West); 6 Manuwatu Mounted Rifles
The Canterbury Regt — 1 Canterbury Yeomanry Cavalry; 8 South Canterbury Mounted Rifles; 10 Nelson Mounted Rifles

Camel Corps Smith, VC
1 Battalion (Anzac)
2 Battalion (British)
3, 4 Battalion (Anzac)

Light armoured batteries
Nos. 1 and 2 Vickers mounted machine-guns

Cavalry forces and artillery affiliations[3]
DIVISION
A&NZ Mounted Division: Chaytor 1 LHB 2 LHB, NZMB Meldrum
AMD: Hodgson 3 LHB 4 LHB 5 MB 19 RHA Bde (A & B HAC, Notts)
Corps Reserve: 7 MB ICC Bde + HKS Mtn Bty, Essex Bty RHA
After April/May reorg to four cavalry divisions including AMD & A&NZ Mounted Division

4 Cavalry: Barrow 10 11 & 12 MBs 20 RHA Bde
5 Cavalry: Macandrew 14 13 & 14 MBs B HAC & Essex

BRIGADES
5 Fitzgerald 6 Godwin 7 Wigan/Clarke 8 Rome 10 Green
11 Gregory 12 Wigan 13 Kelly 14 Clarke 15 Harbord
22 Fryer/Fitzgerald

Infantry and cavalry divisions
Division - Arrival and Departure
10 - 9/17 at end

Appendix

52 - 4/16 4/18
53 - 4/16 at end
42 - 5/14 2/17
54 - 4/16 4/18
3 - Lahore 4/18
7 - Meerut 1/18
60 - 6/17
75 -10/17
74 (Yeo) - 1/17 5/18 (Note: 74 Div 229, 230 and 231 Bdes)

1. April 1916
    IX Corps: 42 (East Lancs); 54 (East Anglian)
    XV Corps 11; 53 (Welsh); 52 (Lowland)
2. January 1917
    42 (East Lancs) departed for France in February
    74 Yeo Div from cav as infantry
    A&NZ Mounted Division and IMD
3. March 1917[4]
    For First GazaEEF Gen Dobell,
    53 (Welsh) Div and 161 Bde of 54 Div (East Anglian)
    54 Div (-161 Bde) ; 52 Div – not engaged
    NZMB (-1 LHB) IMD (- 4 LHB) ICB
    Right Secs 10, 15 & 91 Hvy Btys (60 pdr)
    7 Lt Car Patrol, 11 & 12 LABtys
    5 Wing RFC
4. April 1917 for Second Gaza (EEF) Dobell[5]
    DMC (Chetwode) A&NZ Mounted Division & IMD
    XXI Corps 52, 53, 54, 74 (no arty – not engaged)
    Det Tank Corps, ICC, 7 Lt Car Patrol
    10, 15 and 91 Hvy Btys, 201 Sge Bty 8" & 6" Hows
    11 & 12 Lt Armd Btys; 12 Motor MG Bty
5. 27 Oct–16 Nov Beersheba[6]
    July 1917 (after Allenby)
    Beersheba
    DMC A&NZ Mounted Division + 7 MB
    XX Corps Chetwode

60 Div (London) & 74 Div

53 Div + ICB (not engaged)

96 HA Gp Berks Bty & 10 Mtn Bty

Third Gaza 28 Oct – 9 Nov

XXI Bulfin Corps 54 Div 156 Bde

100 & 102 HA Gps + 52 Div Artillery; Army Troops 7 MB

Composite Force (Imp Indian Service, 1 Bn BWIR French and Italian contingents)

Creation of Desert Mounted Corps (Chauvel, June 1917)

March to August 1918 (in Jordan Valley)[7]

60 DIV (less 181 Bde)

6 MB (2 regts), ISCC Bde (2 regts), 20 Ind Bde

AMD

A&NZ Mounted Division, 18 RHA Inverness, Ayr and Somerset Btys

HK & S Mtn Bty RGA

91 Hvy Bty

301, 302 and 303 Bdes RFA

9 Mtn Bty

Reorg for Megiddo (summer 1918)[8]

GHQ MGRA Maj Gen Smith

DMC Chauvel GOCRA (King)

A&NZ Mounted Division & AMD

Yeomanry Cav Div, 6 Mounted Bde, 8 Mounted Bde, 20 RHA Bde Berks, Hants and Leicester RHA + DAC

AMD (Chaytor) 3 & 4 LH Bdes, 5 Mtd Bde. 19RHA Bde (A & B HAC, Notts + DAC)

Corps Troops 11 and 12 Lt Armd Car Btys

Corps Reserve ICC Bde (Smith), 7 Mtd Bde , Sherwood ,South Notts, Herts and Essex RHA + BAC

Imperial Camel Corps Bde (two Aus + 1Brit Bns, HK & S Mtn Bty, RGA)

4 Cav Division (Barrow)

10, 11 and 12 Cav Bdes, 20 RHA Bde + DAC

5 Cav Division (Macandrew)

13 & 14 Cav Bdes, B HAC and Essex Bty + DAC

XX Corps (Chetwode) GOCRA Short
10 Div, 67, 68 and 263 RFA Bdes
53 Div, 265, 266 and 267 RFA Bdes
60 Div
74 Div
Corps Troops 97 RGA Bde 421 and 387 Btys, 103 Bde RGA
10 H, 205 S and 392S and 387 (-)
39 Ind Mtn Bty, HK & S Mtn
300 and 85 AA Secs
XXI Corps (Bulfin)
HQRA GOCRA Simpson-Blaikie
AMD 18 RFA Bde, 75 Bty (x 10 Div) 29 & 32 IndMtBtys,
195 H RGA + captured 4 G and 2H
3 Div, 4, 8 and 53 RFA Bdes
7 Div, 261, 262 and 264 RFA Bdes
54 Div, 270, 271 and 272 RFA Bdes
60 Div, 301, 302 and 303 RFA Bdes
75 Div, 37, 172 and 1 SA FA Bdes
Corps Troops artillery
95 RGA Bde 181H, 304, 314 and 383 S Btys + 2Hs 150
96 RGA Bde 189 H, 202 H, and 387S & 394 S
100 RGA Bde 15H, 134 S and 334S, Sec 43S, Sec 300S (ea – one sec)
102 RGA Bde, 91 H, 209S, 380S and 440S, and Sce 43S and Sec 300 S (ea – one sec)
8 Mountain Bde RGA, 11 and 13 Mtn Btys (3.7H) and 17 Mtn Bty (2.75)
9 Mountain Bde RGA 10 and 12 Mtn Btys (3.7 H) and 16 Mtn Bty (2.75)
38, 55 and 102 AA Sections

REORGANISATIONS in July 1918

Yeomanry Mtd Div – 7 Mtd Bde and ISC (Imp Service Cav)
ICC Bde – 1, 3 and 4 Bns Aus. NZ company 2nd NZ MG Sqn
(sheds camels) 5 LH Brigade - 14th and 15th LH Regts + two sqns of Spahis and two Chasseurs Afrique replaced 5 Mtd Bde in AMD

Yeomanry Mtd Div becomes 2nd Cavalry Div
1st Mtd Div becomes 4th Cav Div, mainly Indian Cavalry
Lt Gen G deS Barrow GOC

DMC - 4th Cavalry Div ex Yeomanry Div. Mtd Bde (x 6th Mtd Bde)
11th Mtd Bde (x 8th Mtd Bde) and 12th (x 22nd Mtd Bde). 20 RHA Bde

5th Cavalry Div. 13th Mtd Bde (x 5th Mth Bde), 14th Mtd Bde (x 7th Mtd Bde) and 15th Mtd Bde (x ISC Cav Bdes). Essex Bty, RHA.

A&NZ Mounted Division – AMD (all Australian) incl 5th LH Brigade, sub. for 5th Mtd Bde
NO organic RHA

CAVALRY REGIMENTS in THEATRE
Berkshire Yeomanry
Buckinghamshire Hussars
City of London 1st
County of London Yeomanry, 1st and 3rd
Dorsetshire Yeomanry
East Riding Yeomanry
Gloucestershire Yeomanry
Hertfordshire Yeomanry
Lincoln Yeomanry
Middlesex Yeomanry
Sherwood Rangers
Stafford Yeomanry
South Notts Hussars
Warwickshire Yeomanry
Westminster Dragoons
Worcester Yeomanry
6th Cavalry
9th Hodson's Horse
2nd Lancers
18th Lancers
19th Lancers
29th Lancers

38th Central India Horse
36th Jacob's Horse
Deccan Horse
Poona Horse
Johdpur, Mysore and Hyderabad Lancers

REORGANISATION OF THE FORCE[9]
Sent to France in March/April 1918

Two infantry divisions, 52 & 7 Division exchange artilleries

52 Division embarked 14 Apr for France
74 Division embarked 1 May for France

Nine Yeomanry regts

Five siege batteries

23 infantry battalions

ARRIVALS
3 Indian Div 14 Apr 1917

AIR FORCE DATA

Until Dec 1917, the air force comprised:
1 Sqn AFC
14 Sqn RFC

July 1918[10]
Palestine Brigade (with GHQ Sarona)

5th Corps Wing HQ at Ramleh
14 Sqn to XX Corps at Junction Station
113 Sqn to XXI Corps at Sarona
142 Sqn to DMC at Sarona, less one flight at Jerusalem for Chaytor
(142 to move to Jenin)

Tasks: co-op with artillery, contact patrols and tactical recce
10,000 m in advance of corps front

40th Army Wing HQ at Ramleh
1 Sqn AFC = strategic recce, bombing and photography
111 Sqn = fighter/scouts
143 Sqn = escorts and offensive patrols
144 Sqn at Junction Station – bombing ops.

21 Balloon Coy (49, 50 and 57 sections) = XXI Corps

RHA BATTERIES

Battery	Raised/Located	Affiliated
Ayrshire	Ayr	18 RHA Bde
Berkshire	Ascot	22 MB 1917, 20 RFA Bde, 6 Mtd Bde 1917
Essex	Chelmsford	263 RFA > 20 RHA Bde
	Colchester	7 Mtd Bde
	Ingatestone	
Hampshire	Southampton	263 RFA > 20 RHA Bde
Amm Col	Basingstoke	
Inverness	Inverness	18 RHA Bde
Amm Col	Nairn	
Leicester	Leicester	20 RHA Bde
Notts	Nottingham	19 RHA Bde
	Wilston	
Somerset	Taunton	Taunton
	Glastonbury	
HAC		
A Battery	London	19 RHA Bde
B Battery	London	19 RHA Bde

Hong Kong & Singapore Battery 6 x 9-pounder
Personnel - 240 Sikhs and Moslems

ARTILLERY DETAILS
10 Hvy Bty Capt Clarkson
Strength: officers and other ranks 980, horses 894 and mules 172
60 pdr team 14 horses (put 13 rds within a circle at Beit Abu Taha)

May 1917 CRA Marquis of Exeter
SC Capt H. McCall-Pollock

A Battery HAC OC Maj O.D. Eugster
B Battery HAC OC Maj The Hon R.P. Preston
Berks Battery OC Capt H.V. Landenberg (actg)
Notts Battery OC Maj J.S. Lambert
Inverness OC Maj Fraser (KIA), Major Rushbrook 1918

Average battery strength:
8 officers, 228 other ranks, 220 horses and 60 mules

YEOMANRY MOUNTED DIVISION
6th Mtd Bde: Brig C.A.C. Goodwin 1/1st Bucks Yeo, 1/1st Berks Yeo, 1/1st Dorset Yeomanry

8th Mtd Bde: Brig C.S. Rome, 1/1st County of London Yeo, 1/1st Midsx Yeo, 1/3rd County of London Yeomanry

22nd Mtd Bde: Brig F.A.B. Fryer, 1/1st Lincoln Yeo, 1/1st Staffs. Yeo, 1/1st East Riding Yeo

Artillery: 20 RHA Brigade - Berks, Hants and Leicester Batteries (18-pdrs)[11]

ORBAT OCTOBER 1917 (after Allenby)
As above, except that 20 RHA Brigade only had 18-pdrs.[12]

Appendix 7

	GAS	AT		GAZA
Date	**Guns**	**Shells**	**Type**	**Main Targets**
30-31 Oct	Heavy	1,709	VN+PS	Xroads North & East of
				Gaza; two btys North of Gaza
5-Oct	Field	2,310	CBR	Labyrinth, El Arish, Bivouacs
				West of Gaza
31-Oct	Heavy	899	VN+PS	Same Xroads, 3 btys in Gaza
				and Kh. Sihan
1-Nov	Field	1,200	CBR	Labyrinth, El Arish
1-2 Nov	Heavy	2,245	VN+PS	Same Xroads, 10 btys in Gaza
				and West of Kh. Sihan
				Trenches & installations
	Field	600	CBR+SK	Roman Hill -trench Left of
				Labyrinth
2-3 Nov	Field	600	SK	Labyrinth
3-4 Nov	Field	600	SK	Labyrinth
	Total:	Heavy	4,853	
		Field	5,310	

(Source: Sheffey, p. 831)

Appendix

BATTLE	DATES FROM - TO	TOTAL ROUNDS	RATIO SHRAPNEL: HE	MAX DATE W/E	MIN DATE W/E
TABLE 1					
ADVANCE TO,	3 DEC 17 to				
CAPTURE & DEFENCE	3-Jan-18				
OF JERUSALEM	13 pr 6 cwt	13838	3 to 1	9-Dec	21-Dec
	13 prt 9 cwt	3144	1 to 3	9-Dec	28-Dec
	18 pr	74654	4 to 1	21-Dec	13-Dec
	4.5 in How	30995	NA	3-Jan	21-Dec
	60 pr	5270	1 to 1	28-Dec	21-Dec
	6 in How	5004	NA	28-Dec	9-Dec
TABLE 2					
AMMAN & ES SALT	20 Mar 18 to				
	5-Apr-18				
	13 pr 6 cwt	38		27-Mar	5-Apr
	13 pr 9 cwt	1403	1 to 3	20-Mar	5-Apr
	18 pr	45495	2 to 1	20-Mar	5-Apr
	4.5 in How	13867	NA	20-Mar	5-Apr
	60 pr	6302	1 to 5	20-Mar	5-Apr
	6 in How	4698	NA	20-Mar	5-Apr
TABLE 3					
BERUKIN &	10 APR to				
SHUNET NIMRIN	18-Apr-18				
	13 pr 6 cwt	3159	6 to 1	18-Apr	NA
	13 pr 9 cwt	3082	1 to 1	10-Apr	
	18 pr	38247	2 to1	18-Apr	
	4.5 in How	11777	NA	18-Apr	
	60 pr	4006	NA	18-Apr	
	6 in How	4653	NA	18-Apr	

BATTLE	DATES FROM - TO	TOTAL ROUNDS	RATIO SHRAPNEL: HE	MAX DATE W/E	MIN DATE W/E
TABLE 4					
ES SALT					
W/E 2 MAY to	13 pr 6 cwt	3043	only shrapnel	all	calibres
8 MAY !8	13 pr 9 cwt	4829	1 to 2		
	18 pr	35397	2 to 1		
	4.5 in How	12485	NA	firing	steadily
	60 pr	4428	1 to 5		
	6 in How	5972	NA		
TABLE 5					
MEGIDDO					
A.W/E 4 SEP 18		Registering targets,	calibration,		
B.W/E 11 SEP 18		and 'schemes'			
C.W/E 18 SEP 18		Etc.			
W/E 27 SEP					
	13 pr 6 cwt	409	2 to 3		
	13 pr 9 cwt	258	1 to 4		
	18 pr	37857	2 to 1		
	4.5 in How	14952	NA		
	60 pr	2317	1 to 1		
	6 inHow	10031	NA		

Ammunition expenditure

Table 1

The Capture of Jerusalem and its Defence: 3 December 1917 to 3 January 1918

The terrain of the Judean Hills over which the attacking forces crossed on their way to assault Jerusalem was the most formidable in Palestine. It required cavalry flank protection and infantry assaults lasting around a week. The busiest week ended on 9 December 1917. During the assault, the horse artillery gunners used three times more 6 cwt shrapnel rounds than HE. Their use of 9 cwt rounds saw the ratio reversed. This begs the question of whether the OPOs or BCs decided on the mix, since their engagements were not coordinated at brigade headquarters. War diaries do not provide an answer. The cavalry actions primarily relate to the attack phase, a period in which the gunners fired a total of 16,982 rounds in five weeks. During the defence phase the RFA and RGA 'heavies' came to the forefront. The critical dates for this phase are the last two weeks in December/January. The busiest week was that ending 21 January in which the infantry's supports fired 24,106 of the 105,649 rounds, half of which was shrapnel (4:1 for the 18-pounders) in a mix of friendly attacks and Turk counter-attacks. As noted in the narrative, the heavy and siege batteries were busy in the defence of the city, with 10,274 rounds fired, the 60-pounder round type mix being even.

Table 2

Amman and Es Salt: 20 March to 5 April 1918

With one exception, Allenby's spring offensives involving the 60th Division and the DMC provided a different perspective to expenditure for which the terrain and climatic conditions provide explanations. Shea's artillery (RFA) and the big guns (RGA) despatched 78,246 and 16,357 rounds respectively. In this instance the ratio of shrapnel to HE was 2:1 for the 18-pounders and, for the heavies, 1:4 during the week ending 20 March. For the week ending 5 April 1918 as noted in an earlier chapter, the RHA and Indian gunners' consumption was severely affected by supply problems, terrain and weather, the enemy's offensive spirit and good gunnery. At the end of the first week of April, as Shea's force was recrossing the Ghoraniye, the Indian gunners fired mostly shrapnel (7:1) and the RHA batteries fired a mere 9109 rounds, predominantly HE (5:1).

Table 3

Berukin and Shunet Nimrin: 9–10 April and 11–18 April

The 75th Division's bold attempt to capture the vital ground at Berukin ultimately failed. Ammunition expenditure for this two-day foray, including the opening bombardment, was estimated at 15,000 of the 65,000 rounds for the fortnight's operations. Based on previous records, most of this usage was by the 18-pounders. For the Jordan Valley salient, the spotlight was on Major General Shea's 60th Division and included the RHA's loss of nine guns. The ratios of shrapnel to HE are quite high for the 6 cwt gun, but over both types it was about even as would be expected in a defensive battle. It was significant that the infantry's howitzers, siege and heavy guns relied on HE to help Shea's Londoners.

Table 4

Es Salt: 2–8 May 1918

This engagement did not go well for the Eastern Egyptian Force of infantry and cavalry and this second battle for the Jordan Valley followed a similar pattern to the first. While weather conditions were not a factor, the terrain and enemy responses were familiar to the combatants: advance to contact, encounter battle, withdrawal in the face of superior forces. What is noteworthy is that, during the last week (8 May), expenditure by all types of ordnance except the 60-pounder, was at its highest weekly total of rounds fired to that point in time. One outcome was that the Turks believed that Allenby would try again — which he did in the decisive battle of the campaign — and later deployed their artillery accordingly.

Table 5

Megiddo: 4–19 and 27 September 1918

This climactic battle is fascinating in the way the staff misled the Turks over the number of guns facing them on the coastal sector. As described in the narrative, the overall Berukin plan became a template for a significantly expanded version on 18/19 September. The major differences lay in the fact that the cavalry role was pre-eminent, its task to debouch across the Esdraelon Plain and cut off the Turks' right wing and escape routes north. Accordingly, RHA consumption was generally limited to thickening the opening bombardment and later to expenditure associated with the numerous cavalry skirmishes. Following the relatively quieter summer months, Allenby retained the initiative with aggressive forays, 'schemes' to confirm Turkish gun dispositions. Other initiatives had limited objectives, their principal purpose to convince the Turk that Allenby's next big thrust would be eastwards. As described, this led enemy intelligence to place its opposing force on the coastal sector deploying 70 guns, with 300 others facing east. In sum, these forays always had an objective and the records show that ammunition expenditure was considerable over a two and three-week period, as illustrated in the table below:

Appendix

Weekly and Daily

Ammunition Expenditure	4 – 18 SEP 1918		27 SEP 1918	
Branch	Total Expended	Average per day*	Total Expended	Average per day*
Cavalry's Batteries:	7842	341	6059	1200
Field Artillery Batteries:	28,657	1250	52,709	10,500
Heavy and Siege Batteries:	8407	364	12,348	2470
	44,906		**71,116**	

*Over five days, with the peak consumption in the first two days: 2400, 21,000 and 5000.

The Turkish staff appears to have deduced that the consumption of approximately 2000 rounds a week equated to 70 guns of mixed ordnance. The most unusual statistic is that of the latter category of ordnance, and the 6-inch howitzer's contribution to the opening barrage. It was 10,031 rounds. The 18-pounders laid down smoke from 1108 shells.[1]

ORDNANCE in the THEATRE @ 18 MAY 1918

	Ref: WO 33/946		
13-pounder	40	3-inch Stokes mortars	138
2.75-inch gun	14	6-inch Newton mortar	12
13-pounder AA	12		
13-pounder 9 cwt	22		
18-pounder	216		
4.5-inch howitzer	68		
3.7-inch howitzer	16		
60-pounder	28		
6-inch gun	2		
6-inch howitzer	2		

1 WO 33/935 and 33/936, EEF Weekly Ammunition Returns, dated entries, August 1918.

MEGIDDO AMMUNITION EXPENDITURE

W/E	2.75"	3.7" How	13pr	13pr	18pr	4.5" How	60pr	6" How
4 September 1918								
Shrapnel	956		432	179	7190	15	1376	
HE	392	1404	321	335	420	4031	494	2700
	1348	**404**	**753**	**514**	**7610**	**4046**	**1870**	**2700**
11 September 1918								
Shrapnel	426		196		2698	20	686	
HE	124	1132		88	2799	1892	352	1132
	550	**1132**	**196**	**88**	**5497**	**1912**	**1038**	**1132**
TOTAL(1)	**1898**	**2536**	**949**	**602**	**13107**	**5958**	**2908**	**3832**
18 September 1918								
Shrapnel	895		7	19	3174		557	
HE	301	438	35	62	3326	3192	473	803
	1196	**438**	**42**	**81**	**6500**	**3192**	**1030**	**803**
27 September								
Shrapnel	1040		164	62	24402		1096	
HE	1230	3122	245	196	13455	14952	1221	10031
	2270	**3122**	**409**	**258**	**37857**	**14952**	**2317**	**10031**
TOTAL(2)+	**3466**	**3560**	**451**	**339**	**51312**	**14952**	**3347**	**10031**
4 October 1918								
Shrapnel	56		601		2329	576		
HE	1464		423		405	158 (8in How)		
TOTAL(3)	**1520**		**1024**		**2734**	**734**		
GRAND TOTAL (4)								
4 Sep to 4 Oct								
Shrapnel	3373		1400	260	39793	576	3943	
HE	3511	6096	1024	112	20000	24102	2946	14666
TOTAL	**6884**	**6096**	**2424**	**372**	**59793**	**24678**	**6889**	**14666**

Appendix

For the three weeks prior to the commencement of the battle on the evening of 19 September the periodic differences were:

Week ending 4 September: 20245 rounds, 2900 rounds per day
" " 11 September: 11670 rounds, 1670 " " "
" " 18 September: 13300 rounds, 1900 " " " .

The staff assumption was that this volume of fire would represent approximately 70 artillery pieces. This led to the Turkish/German intelligence deducing that Allenby's thrust would be to his east, and not the coastal/north-eastern sectors.

For the latter two periods of 18 and 27 September, 87,458 rounds were expended on all fronts. For the week ending 4 October, the total was 6012.
For the remainder of the campaign to Aleppo it was very much less.

APPENDIX 8

RFA battery – stores list and camel loads

The logistical tail of an RFA battery was considerable and, for camel loading, a matter of trial and error. Battery necessities would require a 1-ton capacity wagon and eight camel loads, as follows:

	Items	Weight in pounds
A	In a locker: lamps, handcuffs, reins and shoeing tools	35
B	Body of wagon: mobilisation boxes for saddlers, fitters and forge tools, stationery and 56 fathoms of cordage (3/4 inch, tarred)	275
	veterinary chest, horse shoes, Dubbin and lubricating oils	88
	field forge, tools and anvil, 20 sets horseshoes	530
	signal pannier and saddler's kit	228
	mobile sanitary equipment	150
	buffer oil, picketing and rope gear	220
	wireless apparatus and spares	684
	Total:	**2240**
C	Five baggage camels carrying: 3 camels: men's bivouac sheets and forage 1 camel: officers' kit and bivouacs 1 camel: two miles of cable and sanitary equipment	
D	Three baggage camels for HQ DAC, carrying: 1 camel: office materials 1 camel: Q stores and stationery 1 camel: officers' kits	

(Source: 54th Division Operation Instruction, 13 September 1918, Appendix A)

Endnotes

Chapter 1

1 J.B.A. Bailey, *Field Artillery and Firepower,* US Naval Institute Press, 2004, p. 116.

2 The reputation of the Turkish infantry was 'sky high' after their success at Gallipoli, one source claiming that they were better fighters than those of any other nation. See C.E.W. Bean, *Official History of Australia in the War of 1914–1918*, Vol. III, *The AIF in France*, pp. 959–65.

3 See Appendix 1 for a chronology of the campaign.

4 T. Kinloch, *Devils on Horses: Anzacs in the Middle East 1916-1919*, Exisle, Auckland, 2007.

5 H.S. Gullett, *Official History of Australia in the War of 1914–1918*, Vol. VII, *Sinai and Palestine*, Angus & Robertson, Sydney, 1941, p. 42. Lieutenant General Sir Archibald Murray had to make the point to the War Office that he could not defend the delta without Australian and New Zealand troops given the low value he placed on the fighting qualities of the New Army divisions he had been sent.

6 Ibid., p. 52; J. Grenfell, 'Lieutenant General Sir John Maxwell', *Oxford Dictionary of National Biography*, Vol. XXXVIII, Oxford University Press, UK. Maxwell retired in 1922 and died at Newlands, Cape Province, on 21 February 1929. He was a strongly built man, a heavy smoker, and had a prominent nose that earned him the sobriquet 'Conky'. He was regarded as 'a limited, self important and lazy man' whose career plateaued when he was sent to Ireland to make sense of 'The Troubles' in 1916–19, which he did not manage sufficiently well to satisfy his political masters.

7 Gullett, *Official History*, Vol. VII, *Sinai and Palestine*, p. 48.

8 Both Maxwell and Murray were critical of the worth of some Yeomanry regiments, more so after the debacle at Oghratina on 24 April, when three and a half squadrons of cavalry lost 24 officers, 252 other ranks and 425 horses. See Marquess of Anglesea, *A History of British Cavalry*, Vol. 5, *1816 –1919*, Les Cooper, London, 1994, pp. 21–24.

9 Gullett, *Official History*, Vol. VII, *Sinai and Palestine*, Chapter II, describes Maxwell's and later Murray's problems raising the forces and standing firm against the War Office's strictures.

10 P. Chasseaud, *Artillery's Astrologers*, Maps Press, Lewes, 2002, pp. 6, 12.

11 M. Farndale, *The Forgotten Fronts and the Home Base, 1914-1918*, Royal Artillery Institution, London, 1998, pp. 69–70.

12 F.M Cutlack, *Official History of Australia in the War of 1914–1918*, Vol. VIII, *The Australian Flying Corps*, Angus & Robertson, Sydney, 1941, p. 68. There were two squadrons, No. 1 AFC (Australian Flying Corps) and No. 14 RFC, each of 24 machines.

Chapter 2

1 S. Badsey, 'The Boer War (1899-1902) and British Cavalry Doctrine: A Re-Evaluation', *Journal of Military History*, Vol. 71, No. 1, pp. 81, 85; J. Bou, 'Firepower, and Swords: The Australian Light Horse and the Tactical Lessons of Cavalry Operations in Palestine, 1916-1918', *Journal of Military History*, Vol. 71, No. 1., pp. 101–03.

2 Badsey, ibid., p. 77.

3 Bou, 'Firepower, and Swords', p.110.

4 Gullett, *Official History*, Vol. VII, *Sinai and Palestine*, p. 403.

5 Bou, 'Firepower, and Swords', p. 115; Anglesea, *A History of British Cavalry*, Vol. 5, p. 116.

6 War Office, *Field Service Regulations 1914*, Part 10, Operations.

7 Gullett, *Official History*, Vol. VII, *Sinai and Palestine*, p. 393.

8 AWM 25 327/5/1, Establishment of a Light Horse Regiment, 1917. British 1914–18 Cavalry Regiment.

9 I. Jones, *The Australian Light Horse*, Time-Life Australia Books, Sydney, 1987, pp. 94–95. A loaded trooper had two belt pouches of .303 rounds, rifle and bayonet, special military saddle, leather horseshoe and nail case, grain bag (7 pounds/3.6 kilograms), canvas water bucket, grooming gear, picket line and stake. Personal items included a billy, mug, plate, spoon and mess tin, blanket, greatcoat wrapped in a groundsheet, water bottle and canvas haversack. A spare bandoleer was draped over the saddle, and a leather muzzle to prevent the horse eating sand. Long sticks ('bivvy poles') were used for shelter. The British cavalry regiment, when mounted for operations, adopted its own selection of useful equipment (not restricted to government issue).

10 Gullett, *Official History*, Vol. VII, *Sinai and Palestine*, pp. 30, 69, 110. The Vickers gun was water cooled and mechanically operated (450–600 rpm) with an effective range of 800 yards. Its maximum range was 4400 yards firing on 'fixed lines'. The Hotchkiss was air cooled, gas operated and fired 500–600 rpm from strips of 24 rounds, with a similar effective range.

11 Ibid., pp. 59–61.

12 Ibid., pp. 34–36.

13 See Appendix 3 for details of the NZMR Brigade.

14 Bou, *Light Horse: A History of Australia's Mounted Arm*, Cambridge University Press, Melbourne, 2010, Chapter 8.

Chapter 3

1 RHA brigade establishments varied if the brigade was part of a cavalry division rather than operating as a cavalry brigade. See Appendix 4 for the Establishment Tables of British and other artillery units. See Appendix 6 for RHA orders of battle.

2 B. Gudmundsson, *On Artillery*, Praeger Publishers, Westport, US, 1993, pp. 17, 31, 34.

3 Appendix 5 provides a description of the guns and their vital statistics.

4 Source: War Office *Field Service Manual QF 18-pounder 1914*.

5 Source: Siege and Heavy Brigades Establishments, p. 106. See Appendix 4 for additional detail.

6 Gullett, *Official History*, Vol. VII, *Sinai and Palestine*, p. 169.

7 *Handbook of Artillery Instruments*, 1914, HMSO, London, Chapter VI, Telemeters; Chapter VII, One Man Range Finders.

8 *Field Service Regulations*, Chapter 7, pp. 236–40.

9 The other RHA brigades also arrived in the delta at this time.

10 G. Goold-Walker, *The Honourable Artillery Company in the Great War, 1914-1919*, Seely, Service & Co., London, 1930, chapters I and II, pp. 108–54, passim.

11 Ibid., p. 125. The battery's veterinary officer, an elderly Scot, oversaw a 'procession of a sorry collection of equine wrecks' with a melancholy expression and a fixed idea that 'side bones, spasms and broken wind were indispensable qualities of an artillery draught horse.'

12 Ibid., A Battery, chapters I and II, pp. 155 –02, passim.

13 Ibid., p. 170. However the battery's good fortune was confined to the battlefield. Only five men from B Battery escaped illness and/or hospital treatment at or after Aden with several men dying from malaria and similar infections. The battery was 'struck off strength' from Headquarters EEF for a month to recuperate.

14 Ibid., pp. 124–25. The brigade commander was Meredith, who was described as 'a splendid type of man, who appeared to combine all the best attributes of a British General Officer with Colonial geniality and practical sympathy.'

15 Ibid., pp. 180–82.

16 R.M.P. Preston, *The Desert Mounted Corps*, Houghton Mifflin, London, 1921, p. 325. Camel trains were not used by cavalry formations. Camels were usually formed into trains and worked along a 'route' of supply dumps. See Appendix 8 for a description of the loads carried by camels.

Chapter 4

1 See Appendix 6 for a comprehensive outline of the various orders of battle for the Sinai and Palestine campaign.

2 H.G. MacMunn and Cyril Falls, *Military Operations in Palestine and Egypt*, Vols. 1 and 2, HMSO, London, 1927, p. 194; AWM 13/17/5 HQRA ANZMD Intelligence Report — this was the assessment that placed Turkish strength at 30 guns. See A. Bruce, *The Last Crusade*, J. Murray, London, 2002, pp. 48, 49, 80, 85. The German presence was considerable. In addition to their *60th Battalion* heavy mountain batteries, the 'Pasha' comprised: a machine-gun battalion of five companies, five anti-aircraft groups, No. 300 Flight Detachment and aircraft, a wireless detachment, two trench mortar companies, three railway companies and two field hospitals. See Anglesea, *A History of British Cavalry*, Vol. 5, *1816 –1919*, p. 59.

3 See Appendix 6 for the RFA order of battle.

4 A.J. Hill, *Chauvel of the Light Horse*, Melbourne University Press, 1978, pp. 72–74, 80; Anglesea refers to this 'new' force under Chaytor's command as 'Section Mounted Troops'. Ibid.

5 Gullet, *Official History*, Vol. VII, *Sinai and Palestine*, p. 156.

6 E.G. Keogh, *Suez to Aleppo*, Australian Military Forces Directorate of Training, Wilke, Melbourne, 1955, pp. 44–56.

7 MacMunn and Falls, *Military Operations in Palestine and Egypt*, p.176; Keogh, *Suez to Aleppo*. The 42nd Division troops helped build the Scots' redoubts, some of which were never finished. The Scots were unable to completely wire their front due to a shortage of wire and a lack of time.

8 R.R. Thompson, *The History of the 52nd (Lowland) Division, 1916-1919*, Macleuse, Glasgow, 1923, pp. 275–76.

9 MacMunn and Falls, *Military Operations in Palestine and Egypt*, p. 194.

10 Ibid., pp. 186–89. The German gunners cut down cactus bushes to place under the gun wheels to provide better traction.

11 Gullett, *Official History*, Vol. VII, *Sinai and Palestine*, pp. 149–52; J.D. Richardson, *History of the 4th Light Horse Regiment, 1914-1919*, E.N. Birks, Sydney, 1923, pp. 29–30.

12 Thompson, *The History of the 52nd (Lowland) Division, 1916-1919*, pp. 284–85. In front of No. 1 Section, the Scots gunners counted 205 enemy dead, most killed by shrapnel. Troops from the 158th Brigade helped construct the defensive works.

13 Gullett, *Official History*, Vol. VII, *Sinai and Palestine*, pp. 153–62.

14 Ibid., p. 157; Keogh, *Suez to Aleppo*, p. 54.

15 Farndale, *The Forgotten Fronts and the Home Base, 1914-1918*, pp. 72–74.

16 Hill, *Chauvel of the Light Horse*, p. 80.

17 Keogh, *Suez to Aleppo*, p. 57.

18 MacMunn and Falls, *Military Operations in Palestine and Egypt*, p. 177; Gullett, *Official History*, Vol. VII, *Sinai and Palestine*, p. 161; A.C.N. Olden and A. McCubbin, *Westralian Cavalry in the War: The Story of the 10th Light Horse Regiment in the Great War*, self-published (McCubbin), Perth, 1923, pp. 18–20, 90.

19 Gullett, ibid., pp. 167–69; Anglesea, *A History of British Cavalry*, Vol. 5, *1816 –1919*, p. 69.

20 Gullett, ibid., p. 173.

21 Farndale, *The Forgotten Fronts and the Home Base, 1914-1918*, p. 75.

22 Gullett, *Official History*, Vol. VII, *Sinai and Palestine*, p. 179. This was noted by the 10th Light Horse Regiment.

23 Ibid., p. 183; B. Woerlee, 'Magdhaba and Kress', *Sabretache*,Vol. XLIX, No. 4, p. 11.

24 MacMunn and Falls, *Military Operations in Palestine and Egypt*, p. 377; AWM 13/17/5. The 3rd Light Horse Regiment's casualties were 14 killed, 36 wounded and 4 missing, with 95 horses killed or wounded.

25 Gullett, *Official History*, Vol. VII, *Sinai and Palestine*, p. 186.

26 Ibid., p. 192.

27 Ibid., pp. 162, 190–93; Olden and McCubbin, *Westralian Cavalry in the War*, pp. 18–20.

28 Hill, *Chauvel of the Light Horse*, p. 81; A. Murray, *Sir Archibald Murray's Despatches, June 1916 to June 1918*, Naval and Military Press, UK, 2010, p. 73.

29 Gullett, *Official History*, Vol. VII, *Sinai and Palestine*, p. 192.

30 Murray, *Despatches*, p. 75; Gullett, ibid., pp. 186, 190.

Chapter 5

1 Gullett, *Official History*, Vol. VII, *Sinai and Palestine*, pp. 215–17.

2 Woerlee, 'Magdhaba and Kress', pp. 5, 8. Von Kressenstein wrote a minute on his inspection of the defences at Magdhaba on 22 December 1916; Cutlack, *Official History*, Vol. VIII, *The Australian Flying Corps*, p. 49; R. Williams, *These Are the Facts: The Autobiography of Sir Richard Williams*, Australian War Memorial and Australian Government Publishing Service, Canberra, 1977, p. 47. At this time plate cameras were fixed to the side of the aircraft, and after each exposure (from c. 3000 feet) the pilot had to renew the plate quickly to have around a one-third overlap with the next exposure. Later model aircraft had a hand-operated camera mounted behind the pilot which used strip film. Better cameras and photographs from greater heights, vertical and oblique angles (eg. around 13,000 feet) gave more accurate maps for survey purposes.

3 Gullett, *Official History*, Vol. VII, *Sinai and Palestine*, p. 217; Hill writes that his Assistant Quartermaster General, Guy Powles, flew over the settlement in an AFC aircraft and dropped a note, 'The bastards are there alright.' This landed close to Chauvel's headquarters tent. Later, a German pilot dropped a message on Chauvel's 'doorstep', asking him to clearly identify his 'hospital'. Chauvel mused that he hoped the German could not drop his bombs with such accuracy. See Hill, *Chauvel of the Light Horse*, p. 88.

4 Farndale, *The Forgotten Fronts and the Home Base, 1914-1918*, p. 77.

5 Gullett, *Official History*, Vol. VII, *Sinai and Palestine*, pp. 219–21; Anglesea, *A History of British Cavalry*, Vol. 5, *1816 –1919*, p. 87.

6 Gullett, ibid., pp. 227.

7 Ibid., p. 46; Keogh, *Suez to Aleppo*, pp. 74–76.

8 Woerlee, 'Magdhaba and Kress', pp. 4–21.

9 Cutlack, *Official History*, Vol. VIII, *The Australian Flying Corps*, p. 46.

Chapter 6

1 Gullett, *Official History*, Vol. VII, *Sinai and Palestine*, p. 243. The 7th Light Car Patrol was a British unit commanded by a New Zealander, Lieutenant W.H.P. McKenzie. Seven Model T Ford cars each carried a Vickers machine-gun, adding to the troopers' firepower 'with sporting elan'.

2 Goold-Walker, *The History of The Honorable Artillery Company in the Great War*, p. 184. According to Farndale, B Battery, HAC, was initially equipped with 15-pounders when employed in the Western Desert, but changed to 18-pounders in 1916. Farndale, *The Forgotten Fronts and the Home Base, 1914-1918*.

3 Farndale, ibid., p. 79. One of the AFC observers was Lieutenant Ross Smith, a former 3rd Light Horse Regiment participant at Romani, and later a famed Australian aviator alongside his brother Keith.

4 Goold-Walker, *The History of The Honorable Artillery Company in the Great War*, pp. 185–87; Anglesea, *A History of British Cavalry*, Vol. 5, *1816 –1919*, p. 90. The ICC Brigade comprised four battalions of 18 companies (each with three Lewis guns), a machine-gun squadron of eight Vickers machine-guns and a mobile veterinary unit of 142 Egyptians. The ICC Brigade was the equivalent of two light horse brigades.

5 Gullet, *Official History*, Vol. VII, *Sinai and Palestine*, p. 239; Olden and McCubbin, *The Westralian Cavalry in the War*, p. 108.

6 Gullet, ibid., p. 242.

7 Goold-Walker, *The History of The Honorable Artillery Company in the Great War*, pp. 189–90; Cutlack, *Official History*, Vol. VIII, *The Australian Flying Corps*, p. 50.

8 Only the Inverness Battery's actions are recorded in Gullett's *Official History*. The others are from Farndale, *The Forgotten Fronts and the Home Base, 1914-1918*, pp. 78–80.

9 In relative terms, the differences were significant, even allowing for the 'hard ground' v 'sand' effect.

10 Farndale, *The Forgotten Fronts and the Home Base, 1914-1918*, p. 80.

11 Gullet, *Official History*, Vol. VII, *Sinai and Palestine*, p. 242; N.C. Smith, *The Third Light Horse Regiment, 1914-18*, Mostly Unsung Military History Publications. Victoria, 1993, p. 59. The 3rd Light Horse Regiment lost 10 killed and 49 wounded in this encounter.

12 Olden and McCubbin, *The Westralian Cavalry in the War*, p. 108.

13 Sources: Gullett, *Official History*, Vol. VII, *Sinai and Palestine*; Woerlee, 'Magdhaba and Kress'.

14 See Appendix 7 for details of ammunition expenditure.

15 A. Wavell, *Allenby in Egypt*, Harrop, London, 1944.

Chapter 7

1 Gullett, *Official History*, Vol. VII, *Sinai and Palestine*, pp. 259–60.

2 Farndale, *The Forgotten Fronts and the Home Base, 1914-1918*, p. 81; Williams, *These Are the Facts*, pp. 64, 71. General Murray came to the front by train with a three-aircraft escort. Williams incorrectly names the '8 inch howitzers' — they were 60-pounders.

3 Y. Sheffy, 'Chemical Warfare and the Palestine Campaign 1916-1918', *Journal of Military History*, Vol. 73, No. 3, pp. 803–44.

4 19th RHA Brigade War Diary, WO 95/4544.

5 Goold-Walker, *The History of The Honorable Artillery Company in the Great War*, p. 129.

6 Ibid., p. 130; Farndale, *The Forgotten Fronts and the Home Base, 1914-1918*, p. 84.

7 Gullett, *Official History*, Vol. VII, *Sinai and Palestine*, pp. 273–77, 280–81; Goold-Walker, ibid., p. 197; I. Jones, *A Thousand Miles of Battles: The Saga of the Australian Light Horse in WWI*, Anzac Day Commemoration Committee of Queensland, 2007, pp. 61–62. Light Horse machine-gun squadrons had been issued with the strip-fed (24 rounds) Hotchkiss gun.

8 Farndale, *The Forgotten Fronts and the Home Base, 1914-1918*, p. 81;Keogh, *Suez to Aleppo*, p. 88.

9 Gullett, *Official History*, Vol. VII, *Sinai and Palestine*, p. 258–59; Jones, *A Thousand Miles of Battles*, p. 63.

10 Farndale, *The Forgotten Fronts and the Home Base, 1914-1918*, p. 84; MacMunn and Falls, *Military Operations in Palestine and Egypt*, pp. 296–97; Keogh, *Suez to Aleppo*, p. 90. The 53rd Division's attack was supported by just twenty-four 18-pounders, twelve 4.5-inch howitzers and six 60-pounders.

11 MacMunn and Falls, ibid., p. 271.

12 Farndale, *The Forgotten Fronts and the Home Base, 1914-1918*, p. 82; Keogh, *Suez to Aleppo*, p. 93.

13 Gullett, *Official History*, Vol. VII, *Sinai and Palestine*, pp. 273–75.

14 Farndale, *The Forgotten Fronts and the Home Base, 1914-1918*, p. 83.

15 Ibid.

16 AWM Item 13/17/15, 26 March 1917. The ammunition expended was:

Battery	Shrapnel	HE
Ayrshire	52	8
Leicester	18	1
Somerset	75	48
Inverness	112	0
	257	57

17 Farndale, *The Forgotten Fronts and the Home Base, 1914-1918*, p. 83; MacMunn and Falls, *Military Operations in Palestine and Egypt*, p. 299; Bruce, *The Last Crusade*, pp. 96–97.

18 Gullett, *Official History*, Vol. VII, *Sinai and Palestine*, pp. 273–75.

19 Jones, *A Thousand Miles of Battles*, p. 66; MacMunn and Falls, *Military Operations in Palestine and Egypt*, p. 300.

20 Gullett, *Official History*, Vol. VII, *Sinai and Palestine*, p. 287; Jones, ibid., p. 65. The 10th Light Horse lost 22 men.

21 Goold-Walker, *The History of The Honorable Artillery Company in the Great War*, pp. 195–202.

22 Gullett, *Official History*, Vol. VII, *Sinai and Palestine*, p. 289; Farndale, *The Forgotten Fronts and the Home Base, 1914-1918*, pp. 82–83.

23 MacMunn and Falls, *Military Operations in Palestine and Egypt*, p. 316; Gullett, ibid., pp. 274, 288, 292; Farndale, ibid., p. 84.

24 MacMunn and Falls, ibid., p. 314; Gullett, ibid., p. 291.

25 Gullett, ibid., p. 288; MacMunn and Falls, ibid., pp. 318–19.

26 WO CAB 45/80; notes made by MGRA S.C.U. Smith for the official historian in November 1925; MacMunn and Falls, ibid., pp. 318–19. Biographical details of Major General Sydenham Campbell Urquhart Smith are taken from 'Historical Record of the NSW Regiment of Royal Australian Artillery', *RA Journal*.

27 British casualties as cited in Murray's *Despatches*, p. 153; Jones gives British casualties as 6444, of which the Desert Column incurred 1166. He cites fewer Turkish casualties (2013) than the *Official History*.

Chapter 8

1 Lloyd George quoted by J.J. Norwich, *The Middle Sea*, Random House, London, 2010, p. 591.

2 Bruce, *The Last Crusade*, pp. 80–81; Farndale, *The Forgotten Fronts and the Home Base, 1914-1918*, p. 87; H. StG. Saunders, *The History of the Royal Air Force, 1914-1939*, Oxford University Press, 1939, p. 182. Observers were aboard the vessels *City of Oxford*, *Raven II* and *Empress*.

3 Gullett, *Official History*, Vol. VII, *Sinai and Palestine*, p. 297.

4 MacMunn and Falls, *Military Operations in Palestine and Egypt*, pp. 425–26.

5 Ibid., p. 375.

6 Ibid., pp.334–37. Eastern Force Order No. 41, 16 April 1917.

7 Sheffy, 'Chemical Warfare and the Palestine Campaign', pp. 818–19; WO 95/4617, 53rd Division, CRA War Diary. Artillery Order No. 11 of 18 April. See Appendix 7 for details on the use of gas at Gaza.

8 MacMunn and Falls, *Military Operations in Palestine and Egypt*; Appendix 2, Eastern Force Order No. 41; Farndale, *The Forgotten Fronts and the Home Base, 1914-1918*, p. 125.

9 Sheffy, 'Chemical Warfare and the Palestine Campaign', pp. 818–19. Murray recorded '3,000 rounds, 52nd Division 2,000 rds and 53rd Artillery fired' from '0557 to 0645'.

10 MacMunn and Falls, *Military Operations in Palestine and Egypt*, p. 337.

11 Farndale, *The Forgotten Fronts and the Home Base, 1914-1918*, pp. 88–89; Gullett, *Official History*, Vol. VII, *Sinai and Palestine*, p. 302; Thompson, *The History of 52nd (Lowland) Division in World War 1*, p. 317.

12 Gullett, ibid., p. 307.

13 Farndale, *The Forgotten Fronts and the Home Base, 1914-1918*, p. 87. This attack was supported by tanks. The 91st Heavy Battery fired 281 rounds.

14 WO 95/4617, War Diary, CRA 53rd Division log; Thompson, *The History of 52nd (Lowland) Division in World War 1*, p. 328.

15 WO 95/4617, War Diary, CRA 53rd Division log, 19 April entry.

16 MacMunn and Falls, *Military Operations in Palestine and Egypt*, p. 337.

17 Goold-Walker, *The History of The Honorable Artillery Company in the Great War*, pp. 132–33.

18 Gullett, *Official History*, Vol. VII, *Sinai and Palestine*, pp. 319–21; Farndale, *The Forgotten Fronts and the Home Base, 1914-1918*, p. 89.

19 Goold-Walker, *The History of The Honorable Artillery Company in the Great War*, pp. 204–07.

20 Gullett, *Official History*, Vol. VII, *Sinai and Palestine*, pp. 323–24.

21 Goold-Walker, *The History of The Honorable Artillery Company in the Great War*, p. 206. The OP officer, Lieutenant Phillips, was awarded the Military Cross.

22 Kinloch, *Devils on Horses*, p. 171.

23 Goold-Walker, *The History of The Honorable Artillery Company in the Great War*, p. 208.

24 MacMunn and Falls, *Military Operations in Palestine and Egypt*, p. 329; Williams, *These Are the Facts*, p. 64. The cost was one aircraft and one pilot.

25 Gullett, *Official History*, Vol. VII, *Sinai and Palestine*, p. 333.

26 Ibid., pp. 331, 334.

27 Ibid., p. 304. The German air arm inflicted many casualties. The 2nd Light Horse Regiment lost six killed, 12 wounded and 30 horses before the battle started.

28 Farndale, *The Forgotten Fronts and the Home Base, 1914-1918*, p. 89.

29 Smith, CAB 45/80.

30 Thompson, *The History of 52nd (Lowland) Division in World War 1*, pp. 332–33; the 52nd Division infantry suffered 1914 casualties, 1026 in the 155th Brigade alone.

31 Sheffy, 'Chemical Warfare and the Palestine Campaign', pp. 809–19.

32 Ibid., pp. 821–23.The infantry and gunners were easier to convince through realistic training than the cavalry, one trooper going so far as to ask 'whether death was preferable by suffocation in the masks or by gas out of them'.

33 WO 95/4599, CRA 52nd Division War Diary, entries for 0530-0700; WO 95/4634, 54th Division Artillery Order No. 5, 16 April 1917, and WO 95/4617, 53rd Division, CRA Artillery Order No. 11, 18 April 1917. This is based on a comparison between data on the actual allocation of shells to the firing units and pre and post-engagement ammunition levels.

34 Sheffy, 'Chemical Warfare and the Palestine Campaign', pp. 821, 832–33.

35 CAB 45/80, S.C.U. Smith Report, paras 5, 6, 7.

Chapter 9

1 Gullett, *Official History*, Vol. VII, *Sinai and Palestine*, pp. 24–25, 357; Cutlack, *Official History*, Vol. VIII, *The Australian Flying Corps*, p. 52.

2 See Appendix 2 for a list of senior/key staff of the AMD.

3 Farndale, *The Forgotten Fronts and the Home Base, 1914-1918*, p. 93.

4 Ibid., pp. 94–95. The Essex Battery RHA was assigned to the 7th Mounted Division. See comparison with 13 and 15-pounders.

5 Ibid., p. 98. Allenby's artillery now comprised: 40 x 13-pounders and 18 x 2.75-inch howitzers in RHA brigades and RGA mountain batteries; 288 x 18-pounders and 52 x 4.5-inch howitzers in infantry divisions; 28 x 60-pounders in heavy batteries; 46 x 6-inch howitzers, 10 x 8-inch howitzers, and 2 x 6-inch Mk VII guns. See Appendix 4 for heavy and siege batteries/brigades establishments.

6 Gullett, *Official History*, Vol. VII, *Sinai and Palestine*, p. 356.

7 Figures for both tables taken from WO SD2 of 4 February and 14 July 1915. See Appendix 4 for details of the establishment of a heavy artillery battery.

8 B. Gardner, *Allenby*, Cassell, London, 1965; Bruce, *The Last Crusade*, pp. 126–27; Gullett, *Official History*, Vol. VII, *Sinai and Palestine*, p. 369; M. Hughes, 'Viscount Allenby', *Oxford Dictionary of National Biography*, Vol. I, Oxford University Press, p. 837. Allenby's son was a subaltern with the Royal Field Artillery and was killed in action by a piece of German 5.9-inch HE shrapnel that pierced his steel helmet and entered his forehead.

9 Jones, *A Thousand Miles of Battles*, p. 90; Gullett, ibid., p. 357. British Army Headquarters staff officers lived at Shepheard's Hotel and their offices were in the Savoy Hotel. Many had wives and families 'on active service' with them. Wavell, Allenby's biographer, merely noted that the staff lacked ability (too junior and too inexperienced) to adequately fulfill their responsibilities. More detailed 'glimpses' of Allenby's personal traits that fitted him for high command are provided in the final chapter. See Wavell, *Allenby in Egypt*.

10 Allenby was not mentioned by Murray in his *Despatches*. Chetwode's famous 'Notes' were drafted by Colonel Dawnay, his chief of staff, using the allusion of 'Nelson's General' — The Duke of Wellington's campaigns in the Iberian Peninsular Wars of the 1790s to 1804 as 'Nelson's general'; i.e., to sustain the army by a secure sea route from the UK and France and to the Middle East.

11 Gullett, *Official History*, Vol. VII, *Sinai and Palestine*, p. 366.

Chapter 10

1 Farndale, *The Forgotten Fronts and the Home Base, 1914-1918*, Annex 8, p. 412.

Chapter 11

1 Goold-Walker, *The History of The Honorable Artillery Company in the Great War*, Chapter V, pp. 210–15, passim.

2 WO 95/4504, 19th RHA Brigade War Diary, dated entries.

Chapter 12

1 Gullett, *Official History*, Vol. VII, *Sinai and Palestine*, p. 374; Saunders, *The History of the Royal Air Force, 1914-1939*, p. 182.

2 Jones, *The Australian Light Horse*, p. 92.

3 Gullett, *Official History*, Vol. VII, *Sinai and Palestine*, pp. 375–76; AWM 40/58 'Notes'; Richardson, *History of the 4th Light Horse Regiment, 1914-1919*, p. 55. The 7th Light Horse Regiment assisted in this 'rescue'.

4 M. Hughes, *Allenby and British Strategy in the Middle East, 1917-1919*, F. Cass, London, 1999, pp. 46–47. Turkish strength of three corps, *III*, *XX* and *XXII* was given as 23,000

with divisional strengths at approx. 1500 rifles, with a sick rate of 25%. Another Turkish figure gives average divisional strength at 3000 or 21,000 along the whole front.

5 Jones, *The Australian Light Horse*, p. 93; Gullett, *Official History*, Vol. VII, *Sinai and Palestine*, p. 377.

6 Farndale, *The Forgotten Fronts and the Home Base, 1914-1918*, pp. 98–99. The 53rd Division (XX Corps) fielded the 265th, 266th and 267th RFA brigades, the latter's C Battery replaced by the 439th Battery. The 60th Division provided the 301st, 302nd and 303rd RFA brigades and the 74th Division the 44th and 117th RFA brigades. The division deployed X and Y medium trench mortar batteries.

7 Bruce, *The Last Crusade*, pp. 126–27.

8 Farndale, *The Forgotten Fronts and the Home Base, 1914-1918*, p. 96. The batteries fired: 6-inch howitzers [96th HAG (1)], 60-pounders [Yeomanry (1) and 60th Division (1), 96th HAG (1)], 4.5-inch howitzers [96th HAG (1)], 3.7-inch howitzers [74th Division (1)] and 18-pounders [53rd and 74th divisions (10)].

9 Gullett, *Official History*, Vol. VII, *Sinai and Palestine*, p. 389; Smith, *The Third Light Horse Regiment, 1914-18*, p. 62: 'Our artillery did excellent work dislodging machine guns.' Richardson, *History of the 4th Light Horse Regiment, 1914-1919*, pp. 56–57, 'The Ayrshire Battery shot without success and the enemy 77's put a hole in their limber.'; Preston, *The Desert Mounted Corps*, p. 25.

10 Jones, *The Australian Light Horse*, p. 97; E.L. Sibert, 'Campaign Summary and Notes on Horse Artillery in Sinai and Palestine', *RA Journal*, Vol. LV, No. 4, p. 536.

11 18th RHA Brigade War Diary, WO95/4504; Gullett, *Official History*, Vol. VII, *Sinai and Palestine*, pp. 393–99. Water was Chauvel's overriding consideration. His troops were taking casualties from accurate German bombing even when dispersed. The 3rd Light Horse Regiment lost one officer and 10 troopers killed and 18 wounded (p. 405), the 9th Light Horse Regiment lost three officers wounded, while 13 troopers were killed and 13 wounded, with 32 horses killed and 26 wounded. Preston, in his *The Desert Mounted Corps*, p. 29, noted that, had demolition charges that had been placed in the railway station been detonated, they would have inflicted very high casualties on the mounted riflemen.

12 Gullett, ibid., pp. 399–402; Goold-Walker, *The History of The Honorable Artillery Company in the Great War*, pp. 135–36, p.218; Jones, *The Australian Light Horse*, pp. 96–104. The Notts Battery was now commanded by Major Price-Harrison. Captain A. Smith, Ayrshire Battery, was promoted to OC BAC and Captain N.M. Elliott, Hants Battery, to BC B Battery, HAC.

13 Goold-Walker, ibid., pp. 217–18.

14 Gullett, *Official History*, Vol. VII, *Sinai and Palestine*, pp. 405–07. The 8th Light Horse Regiment, which lost five killed, 18 wounded and 27 horses, had its revenge the next day when a trooper shot down a German machine with rifle fire.

15 Ibid., p. 403.

16 The term '*arme blanche*' — literally 'white arm' — referred to skill with bladed weapons, the sword or lance. See Bou, *Light Horse: A History of Australia's Mounted Arm*, p. 6.

17 Ibid., pp. 113–15; Badsey, 'The Boer War (1899-1902) and British Cavalry Doctrine: A Re-evaluation', p. 96.

18 J. Coates, *An Atlas of Australian Wars*, Oxford University Press, Melbourne, 2006, p. 103. Mention was also made of the need for heavier guns.

19 Hughes, *Allenby and British Strategy in the Middle East, 1917-1919*, pp. 47–49. The Turks could do little to offset the superior artillery of the EEF. Allenby, the War Office and Cabinet also made mistakes in three key areas: overestimation of Turkish strength, misreading of Turkish tactics and intentions, and an unsuitable plan for Beersheba.

20 Bruce, *The Last Crusade*, p. 133.

Chapter 13

1 MacMunn and Falls, *Military Operations in Palestine and Egypt*, Appendix 1, p. 651.

2 WO 33/935, GHQ Ammunition Returns, No. 8472 for 28 October 1917 and No. 8511 for 29 October–4 November 1917. See Appendix 7 for details of ammunition expenditure.

3 Hughes, *Allenby and British Strategy in the Middle East, 1917-1919*, p. 46; Saunders, *The History of the Royal Air Force, 1914-1939*, pp. 181, 184; Williams, *These Are the Facts*, pp. 73–74. No. 1 Squadron (RE8c 'Harry Tates' machines) in 40th Army Wing was joined by No. 111 Squadron, RFC (Bristol fighters). They were then joined by No. 113 Squadron, RFC, at Shellal airfield the following month. At this time Brigadier Geoff Salmond was replaced by Brigadier Sefton Brancker for four months, Salmond returning to command in January 1918.

4 J.M. Bourne, 'Lieutenant General S.M. Bulfin', *Oxford Dictionary of National Biography*, Vol. VIII, Oxford University Press, UK, pp. 571–73. Bourne mistakenly identifies 'Chetwode's rapier' as a cavalry formation — it was an infantry corps with an attached brigade of cavalry. Chauvel's command was 'all rapier' (author's metaphor).

5 Gullett, *Official History*, Vol. VII, *Sinai and Palestine*, pp. 408–09. Allenby's plan was impractical because of water constraints. This later resulted in unseemly, chaotic scenes at water points where men and beasts literally fought each other for water, often with dire medical consequences.

6 Ibid., p. 410. Soft sand on the western side of the front 'made a cushion for British shells, and only occasional hits gave concern to the defenders.' It also neutralised wire-cutting fuses (No. 106) so that many more rounds were needed to cut a useful gap, given the 'beaten zone' of the shell at a given range and 'angle of arrival'. This would suggest that a large number of HE rounds Fuse 106 were used. The preponderance of shrapnel (> 3:1) is evident in the table at endnote 16.

7 WO 95/4635, 54th Division Artillery Narrative, Section A.

8 Ibid., paras 4 to 8. Materials required were 200,000 sandbags, 2000 filaries (reels of barbed wire) and 2000 sheets of corrugated iron.

9 Ibid., Sections B and C — Preliminary Bombardment and Attack, passim; MacMunn and Falls, *Military Operations in Palestine and Egypt*, Vol. 2, p. 651.

10 WO 95/4490, BGGS Heavy Artillery Group, XXI Corps, Order No. 11, 24 Oct 1917; Hughes, *Allenby and British Strategy in the Middle East, 1917-1919*, p. 170 gives the EEF a total of 462 guns — full divisional complements plus 90 heavy guns. The latter figure includes 4.5-inch howitzers, not all of which were employed in the battle. If only Bulfin's 54th Division and 156th Brigade affiliated artilleries are counted, they add up to 68 pieces plus 72 from the 97th HAG, 140 in all. MacMunn and Falls' total of 148 comprises 62 heavy plus the 52nd and 54th divisions' artilleries. See MacMunn and Falls, ibid., Appendix 1, p. 651.

11 MacMunn and Falls, ibid., Appendix 7 - 3, p. 677; Farndale, *The Forgotten Fronts and the Home Base, 1914-1918*, p. 100. HMS *Raglan* had 14-inch guns and M15 had 9.2-inch guns. The other calibres (French) ran from 150 to 210mm or equivalent.

12 Thompson, *Fifty Second (Lowland) Division, 1914-1918,* p. 360.

13 MacMunn and Falls, *Military Operations in Palestine and Egypt*, Vol. 2, p. 651. This was the same quantity of artillery as that expended on the first day of the Battle of the Somme.

14 WO 95/4683 75th Division, Ammunition Expenditure, 2 pp.; MacMunn and Falls, ibid., Vol. 1, pp. 45, 65; Thompson, *Fifty Second (Lowland) Division, 1914-1918,* p. 360; Farndale, *The Forgotten Fronts and the Home Base, 1914-1918*, p. 100. Two 6-inch guns were also ordered to attack the Turkish railhead at Beit Hanum using balloon observation.

15 WO 95/4490, BGGS Heavy Artillery Group, XXI Corps, Order No. 11, dates noted.

16 WO 33/935, Ammunition Returns Nos. 8472 and 8511 respectively:

Week to 28 October

Ordnance	Shrapnel	HE	Total	Ratio
Light (a)	551	167	718	3.3:1
Field (b)	5645	3813	9558	1.5:1
Heavy (c)	207	2011	2218	0.1:1
Total	6403	5991	12394	1:1

Week 29 October to 4 November

Ordnance	Shrapnel	HE	Total	Ratio
Light (a)	5010	2164	7174	2.3:1
Field (b)	73306	23694	97000	3:1
Heavy (c)	3248	27207	30445	1:9
Total	81564	53065	134629	1.5:1

(a) 2.75-inch, 6 and 13-pounder (6 and 9 cwts)

(b) 18-pounder, 3.7 and 4.5-inch howitzers

(c) 60-pounder, 6-inch and 8-inch howitzers

4.5-inch fired 4746 rounds of chemical shell and 60-pounders 3991 rounds during the week. Six 6-pounder guns were lost.

17 Farndale, *The Forgotten Fronts and the Home Base, 1914-1918*, pp. 101–02. The attacks by the 163rd Brigade were less successful and here the tanks proved their worth.

18 Bruce, *The Last Crusade*, pp. 134–35; WO 95/4368 for infantry cooperation.

19 The 53rd and 54th Kite Balloon sections provided balloon observation from their base at Kantara.

20 WO 95/4490.

21 Gullett, *Official History*, Vol. VII, *Sinai and Palestine*, p. 412. At this time Chetwode's force was eight miles north of Beersheba.

22 WO 95/4638 Section B, paras 3–12, Tables.

23 Hughes, *Allenby and British Strategy in the Middle East, 1917-1919*, p. 49.

24 Farndale, *The Forgotten Fronts and the Home Base, 1914-1918*, p. 102.

25 Sheffy, 'Chemical Warfare in the Palestine Campaign', p. 827. Only 24 of 29 Turkish regiments in the line had adequate protection, whereas all British soldiers did.

26 Ibid., pp. 830–32.

27 Source: Sheffy, 'Chemical Warfare in the Palestine Campaign', p. 831. See Appendix 7.

28 WO95/4684. CRA 75th Division War Diary 30–31 October, 3–7 November 1917; WO 95/4484 WD 10th Heavy Battery 30 Oct–1 Nov 1917;WO 95/4635 CRA 54th Division, Artillery Narrative 15 November 1917;WO 142/120 EEF Chemical Advisor, Report on Gas Training. According to EEF ammunition returns the gunners fired 9410 chemical shells (4650x60-pounders and 5350x4.5-inch howitzer). This compares with the Chemical Advisor's figures of 4760 and 5300 respectively.

29 Sheffy, 'Chemical Warfare in the Palestine Campaign', pp. 835–36.

30 AWM 40/58, Gullett Papers, p. 9, item 12; MacMunn and Falls, *Military Operations in Palestine and Egypt*, Vol. 2, p. 651; Sheffy, ibid., p. 835.

31 Sheffy, ibid., p. 839.

32 This group includes Turkish official historian Husnu Emir, Lieutenant Colonel Archibald Wavell, Generals Murray, Bulfin and historian MacMunn.

33 Farndale, *The Forgotten Fronts and the Home Base, 1914-1918*, p. 102; Thompson, *Fifty Second (Lowland) Division, 1914-1918*, pp. 370–71.

Chapter 14

1 WO 95/4504 War Diary, 20th RHA Brigade.

2 MacMunn and Falls, *Military Operations in Palestine and Egypt*, Vol. 2, p. 651; Goold-Walker, *The History of The Honorable Artillery Company in the Great War*, p. 221.

3 WO 95/4505, passim, 3–7 November.

4 Gullett, *Official History*, Vol. VII, *Sinai and Palestine*, pp. 421, 444, 462-89; Preston, *The Desert Mounted Corps*, pp. 39–40.

5 WO 95/4617 War Diary XX Corps, 53rd Division CRA; Gullett, ibid., p. 418; Jones, *The Australian Light Horse*, Chapter 2, passim; Keogh, *Suez to Aleppo*, p.163; Preston, ibid., p. 45 noted that at Hureira German artillery destroyed a convoy of ambulance camels.

6 Farndale, *The Forgotten Fronts and the Home Base, 1914-1918*, p. 104.

7 WO95/4617; Gullett, *Official History*, Vol. VII, *Sinai and Palestine*, p. 423; Farndale, ibid., p. 105.

8 Farndale, ibid., p. 104; WO 95/4617, 11 November 1917.

9 Gullett, *Official History*, Vol. VII, *Sinai and Palestine*, p. 437.

10 MacMunn and Falls, *Military Operations in Palestine and Egypt*, Vol. 2, p. 651; Saunders, *The History of the Royal Air Force, 1914-1939*, p. 184.

11 MacMunn and Falls, ibid., p. 97; Farndale, *The Forgotten Fronts and the Home Base, 1914-1918*, p. 105.

12 Gullett, *Official History*, Vol. VII, *Sinai and Palestine*, p. 428.

13 Ibid.

14 MacMunn and Falls, *Military Operations in Palestine and Egypt*, Vol. 1, p. 108, Vol. 2, p. 651.

15 Farndale, *The Forgotten Fronts and the Home Base, 1914-1918*, p. 106; MacMunn and Falls, ibid., Vol. 1, p. 109.

16 Farndale, ibid., pp. 105–06.

Chapter 15

1 WO95/4504 WD of 20 RHA Brigade, 1–30 November 1917. Disruptions to logistic support came in many forms at this time, including an Orderly Officer losing his way with orders. Goold-Walker, *The History of The Honorable Artillery Company in the Great War*, pp. 136–37, 229.

2 Preston, *The Desert Mounted Corps*, p. 52.

3 Gullett, *Official History*, Vol. VII, *Sinai and Palestine*, pp. 442–43; MacMunn and Falls, *Military Operations in Palestine and Egypt*, Vol. 2, p. 651. Major General Shea, a Newfoundlander, was serving with the Indian Army. He used Chauvel's Rolls Royce tourer to complete his own reconnaissance and decided to test the Yeomanry cavalry.

4 Gullett, ibid., p. 452.

5 WO 95/4454 WD 20 RHA Brigade, 7 to 20 November 1917; Gullett, ibid., pp. 447–48, 453, 457; L.C. Wilson, *Narrative of Operations of the Third Light Horse Brigade (1917-1919)*, Naval & Military Press-Imperial War Museum, 2010, p. 12.

6 Goold-Walker, *The History of The Honorable Artillery Company in the Great War*, p. 137; Wilson, ibid., p. 15. Lieutenant Thompson's troop shot more than 60 horses.

7 WO 95/4454 WD 20 RHA Bde, 7 to 20 November 1917; Gullett, *Official History*, Vol. VII, *Sinai and Palestine*, pp. 447–48, 453, 457; Wilson, ibid., p. 12.

8 Wilson, ibid., p. 138. Wilson's regiments had not bathed since 28 October. WO 95/4454, Notts Battery War Diary 12–13 November.

9 Farndale, *The Forgotten Fronts and the Home Base, 1914-1918*, p. 107.

10 Ibid., p. 108.

11 WO 95/4505, 19 Bde RHA. The Berks Battery required 1000 rounds to replenish its stock. Farndale, ibid., p. 109.

12 Goold-Walker, *The History of The Honorable Artillery Company in the Great War*, p. 230.

13 Farndale, *The Forgotten Fronts and the Home Base, 1914-1918*, pp. 108–09.

14 Gullett, *Official History*, Vol. VII, *Sinai and Palestine*, pp. 471–72.

15 Farndale, *The Forgotten Fronts and the Home Base, 1914-1918*, p. 109.

16 Goold-Walker, *The History of The Honorable Artillery Company in the Great War*, p. 231.

17 Gullett, *Official History*, Vol. VII, *Sinai and Palestine*, p. 475.

18 Ibid., p. 473.

19 Ibid., p.480. Here there was water, food and grain for the occupying batteries and cavalry, an excellent way (for some) to end a campaign.

20 Ibid.; MacMunn and Falls, *Military Operations in Palestine and Egypt*, Vol. 2, pp. 652–53,

Chapter 16

1 Gullett, *Official History*, Vol. VII, *Sinai and Palestine*, p. 487.

2 Ibid., p. 488.

3 Ibid., p. 489.

4 Preston, *The Desert Mounted Corps*, p. 90.

5 WO 95/4504, 20th RHA Brigade War Diary.

6 Preston, *The Desert Mounted Corps*, p. 90.

7 20th RHA Brigade War Diary; Thompson, *The History of the 52nd (Lowland) Division, 1916-1919*, p. 412.

8 Gullett, *Official History*, Vol. VII, *Sinai and Palestine*, pp. 489–90; Wilson, *Narrative of Operations of the Third Light Horse Brigade (1917-1919)*, p. 17.

9 Gullett, ibid., pp. 486–89; 499–500.

10 Ibid., pp. 492–95.

11 Thompson, *The History of the 52nd (Lowland) Division, 1916-1919*, pp. 405–06.

12 Ibid., pp. 438–39.

13 Farndale, *The Forgotten Fronts and the Home Base, 1914-1918*, pp. 112–13, Map 35; Thompson, ibid., p. 446.

14 20th RHA Brigade War Diary.

15 Ibid. The balloon was one of the three balloon sections in theatre. This one was shot down not long after it had been hoisted at Sakia.

16 Farndale, *The Forgotten Fronts and the Home Base, 1914-1918*, p. 112; Gullett, *Official History*, Vol. VII, *Sinai and Palestine*, p. 494.

17 Farndale, ibid., p. 112. This artillery comprised one section from each of five batteries, under command of the 264th RFA Brigade.

18 Thompson, *The History of the 52nd (Lowland) Division, 1916-1919*, pp. 446–47; Farndale, ibid.

19 Thompson, ibid., p. 455.

20 Farndale, *The Forgotten Fronts and the Home Base, 1914-1918*, Map 35 and p. 113; Thompson, ibid., p. 447.

21 Thompson, ibid., pp. 472–75; Wilson, *Narrative of Operations of the Third Light Horse Brigade (1917-1919)*, pp. 21, 472. On 1 December, when the 3rd Light Horse Brigade was in the El Burj area with the 52nd Division, Wilson submitted to the brigade commander that Second Lieutenant J.H. Boughay, 5th Royal Scots Fusiliers, be recommended for the award of the Victoria Cross. Gullett, *Official History*, Vol. VII, *Sinai and Palestine*, pp. 498–504.

22 Gullett, ibid., p. 467; Farndale, *The Forgotten Fronts and the Home Base, 1914-1918*, p. 112.

23 Gullett, ibid., p. 508. In describing this incident he refers to the presence of German 'storm troops', some of whom were embedded in Turkish formations. See also Wilson, *Narrative of Operations of the Third Light Horse Brigade (1917-1919)*, pp. 21–22. They were Galician Turks, wearing German-style helmets who, according to Brigadier Wilson, were 'the best we had ever seen among Turkish prisoners'.

24 Gullett, ibid., p. 503.

25 Farndale, *The Forgotten Fronts and the Home Base, 1914-1918*, order of battle XX Corps, pp. 96–97.

26 Ibid., p. 113 mentions casualties to 15 officers and men in the 301st RFA Brigade.

27 Gullett, *Official History*, Vol. VII, *Sinai and Palestine*, p. 515.

28 Ibid., pp. 516–19. Gullett also provides a graphic account of the first four days of occupation and the events that ensued.

29 Williams, *These Are the Facts*, p. 77. The Air Brigade now comprised 5th (Corps) Wing: Nos. 14, 113 and 142 squadrons RFC; 40th (Army) Wing: Nos. 111, 144 and 145 squadrons RFC and No. 1 Squadron, AFC; No. 21 Balloon Company (49, 50 and 57 sections). Cutlack, *Official History*, Vol. VIII, *The Australian Flying Corps*, p. 68.

30 Gullett, p. 489.

Chapter 17

1 Farndale, *The Forgotten Fronts and the Home Base, 1914-1918*, pp. 116–17.

2 F.P. Hutchinson, 'The Work of the Heavy Artillery of XXI Corps in Palestine', *Journal of the Royal Artillery*, Vol. XLVI, No. 6; MacMunn and Falls, *Military Operations in Palestine and Egypt*, pp. 283–85. The 74th Division artillery sub-units were commanded by Lieutenant Colonel W. Kinnear, RA. MacMunn and Falls mention 'supply difficulties' in siege battery ammunition.

3 Farndale, *The Forgotten Fronts and the Home Base, 1914-1918*, p. 116; WO 33/960 EEF Ammunition Return, Week Ending 5 January 1918. See Appendix 7.

4 Cutlack, *Official History*, Vol. VIII, *The Australian Flying Corps*, p. 68.

5 MacMunn and Falls, *Military Operations in Palestine and Egypt*, p. 291.

6 Farndale, *The Forgotten Fronts and the Home Base, 1914-1918*, p. 109.

Chapter 18

1 Gullett, *Official History*, Vol. VII, *Sinai and Palestine*, pp. 535–36.

2 MacMunn and Falls, *Military Operations in Palestine and Egypt*, pp. 303–05.

3 Farndale, *The Forgotten Fronts and the Home Base, 1914-1918*, p. 117; Preston, *The Desert Mounted Corps*, pp. 127–29. The track zigzags to the valley floor 3000 feet below, one section a cliff 1000 feet high. Gullett, *Official History*, Vol. VII, *Sinai and Palestine*, p. 537.

4 Gullett, ibid., pp. 536–40; MacMunn and Falls, *Military Operations in Palestine and Egypt*, pp. 303–05.

5 MacMunn and Falls, ibid., pp. 307, 655. XXI Corps casualties were:

Casualties	KIA	WIA	MIA
Officers	5	22	-
Other ranks	75	404	4
Total	80	426	4

Turkish prisoners of war numbered 144.

Chapter 19

1 Gullett, *Official History*, Vol. VII, *Sinai and Palestine*, p. 547; Hughes, *Allenby and British Strategy in the Middle East, 1917-1919*, pp. 78–87.

2 MacMunn and Falls, *Military Operations in Palestine and Egypt*, p. 655, Appendix 16. The 1st Light Horse Brigade was located 18 miles south-east of Amman and 18 miles south-east of Ghoraniye.

3 Gullett, *Official History*, Vol. VII, *Sinai and Palestine*, pp. 546–47; MacMunn and Falls, ibid., pp. 331–47.

4 Gullett, ibid., p. 552.

5 Ibid., p. 554; Farndale, *The Forgotten Fronts and the Home Base, 1914-1918*, pp. 119–20.

6 Hughes, *Allenby and British Strategy in the Middle East, 1917-1919*, p. 79.

7 Gullett, *Official History*, Vol. VII, *Sinai and Palestine*, p. 561. The troopers resorted to chopping down shrubs with their bayonets to make a fire.

8 Ibid., pp. 566–84 passim; MacMunn and Falls, *Military Operations in Palestine and Egypt*, pp. 347–77.

Endnotes

Chapter 20 Part 1

1 Gullett, *Official History*, Vol. VII, *Sinai and Palestine*, pp. 589–90.

2 MacMunn and Falls, *Military Operations in Palestine and Egypt*, p. 355.

3 Gullett, *Official History*, Vol. VII, *Sinai and Palestine*, pp. 586–93.

4 Ibid., p. 596; MacMunn and Falls, *Military Operations in Palestine and Egypt*, p. 362. The ammunition expenditure for these two battles and contemporary actions was prodigious and is provided in Table 4, Appendix 7.

Chapter 20 Part 2

1 MacMunn and Falls, *Military Operations in Palestine and Egypt*, p. 352. The *Pasha* was less the German *703rd Battalion*.

6 Ibid., pp. 708–09, Appendix 21. Naval gunnery was controlled by HMS *Grafton*.

7 Ibid., p. 352; Farndale, *The Forgotten Fronts and the Home Base, 1914-1918*, p. 121.

8 MacMunn and Falls, *Military Operations in Palestine and Egypt*, p. 357.

9 Ibid., pp. 352–55.

10 Ammunition expenditure for the period 10–18 April is described in Appendix 7.

11 MacMunn and Falls, *Military Operations in Palestine and Egypt*, pp. 352–55.

Chapter 21

1 Goold-Walker, *The History of The Honorable Artillery Company in the Great War*, p. 141. At this point the battery was asked to nominate gun detachment commanders for officer training.

2 Gullett, *Official History*, Vol. VII, *Sinai and Palestine*, p. 599.

3 Goold-Walker, *The History of The Honorable Artillery Company in the Great War*, p. 141.

4 Gullett, *Official History*, Vol. VII, *Sinai and Palestine*, p. 604.

5 Ibid., pp. 605–06.

6 Ibid., pp. 610–11; Goold-Walker, *The History of The Honorable Artillery Company in the Great War*, p. 142.

7 Goold-Walker, ibid., pp. 143–44.

8 Ibid., p. 245.

9 Ibid., p. 245; Farndale, *The Forgotten Fronts and the Home Base, 1914-1918*, p. 435.

10 Goold-Walker, ibid., p. 246; Farndale, ibid., p. 436.

11 Goold-Walker, ibid., p. 247; Gullett, *Official History*, Vol. VII, *Sinai and Palestine*, pp. 620–34; MacMunn and Falls, *Military Operations in Palestine and Egypt*, p. 388.

12 Goold-Walker, ibid., pp. 243–44. Another wagon overturned during the afternoon and could not be retrieved.

13 Ibid., p. 251.

14 MacMunn and Falls, *Military Operations in Palestine and Egypt*, p. 389.

15 Gullett, *Official History*, Vol. VII, *Sinai and Palestine*, p. 635; Hughes, *Allenby and British Strategy in the Middle East, 1917-1919*, pp. 92–93.

16 Goold-Walker, *The History of The Honorable Artillery Company in the Great War*, p. 251. Ammunition expenditure for the period 10 April to 8 May 1918 is provided in Appendix 7, Table 3.

Chapter 22

1 MacMunn and Falls, *Military Operations in Palestine and Egypt*, p. 312.

2 Ibid., p. 313.

3 Farndale, *The Forgotten Fronts and the Home Base, 1914-1918*, p. 118.

4 Ibid., p. 119.

5 Gullett, *Official History*, Vol. VII, *Sinai and Palestine*, p. 657.

6 Ibid.

Chapter 23

1 Gullett, *Official History*, Vol. VII, *Sinai and Palestine*, p. 638.

2 Ibid., p. 641.

3 Goold-Walker, *The History of The Honorable Artillery Company in the Great War*, p. 254.

4 Ibid., pp. 255–57. The temperature in the Headquarters RA tent ranged from 132^0 to 140^0 Fahrenheit.

5 Ibid.

6 Ibid., pp. 145–47.

7 Ibid., p. 259.

8 Ibid., p. 258. Sergeant Davis was awarded the MM.

9 MacMunn and Falls, *Military Operations in Palestine and Egypt*, p. 429.

10 Ibid., p. 431.

11 Gullett, *Official History*, Vol. VII, *Sinai and Palestine*, p. 663; MacMunn and Falls, ibid., p. 657.

12 Gullett, ibid., p. 671. One of the attackers was carrying an explosive charge which was ignited by small arms fire and the victim became a 'beacon', providing light for the defenders.

13 Ibid., p. 673.

14 Ibid., pp. 673, 667 n.; MacMunn and Falls, *Military Operations in Palestine and Egypt*, p. 437.

15 Gullett, ibid., pp. 669–70.

16 Goold-Walker, *The History of The Honorable Artillery Company in the Great War*, p. 264.

Chapter 24

1 Bou, 'Firepower, and Swords: The Australian Light Horse and the Tactical Lessons of Cavalry Operations in Palestine, 1916-1918'; Bou, *Light Horse: A History of Australia's Mounted Arm*, pp. 153–99.

2 Bou, *Light Horse: A History of Australia's Mounted Arm*, Chapter 6, passim.

3 History of the 4th Light Horse Brigade, AWM 445/67, RS 25.

4 Bou, *Light Horse: A History of Australia's Mounted Arm*, p. 114.

5 Ibid., p. 118; Notes on enemy attack on DMC, 14 June 1918, AWM 941/1, RS 25.

6 Bou, ibid., p. 122; Anglesey, *History of British Cavalry*, Chapter 5.

7 Bou, ibid., p. 122; AMD Tactical Narrative, 2 October 1918, AWM 455/7, RS 25.

8 Sarona was the most suitable town for the siting of Allenby's large headquarters.

9 MacMunn and Falls, *Military Operations in Palestine and Egypt*, pp. 453–55; Preston, *The Desert Mounted Corps*, p. 197.

10 Gullett, *Official History*, Vol. VII, *Sinai and Palestine*, p. 680.

11 Preston, *The Desert Mounted Corps*, p. 198; Anglesea, *A History of British Cavalry*, pp. 237–57 passim.

12 Saunders, *The History of the Royal Air Force, 1914-1939*, pp. 241–43: Williams, *These Are the Facts*, p. 89; Preston, ibid., p. 193; Gullett, *Official History*, Vol. VII, *Sinai and Palestine*, p. 716.

13 WO95/4599, 4639, 4661 and 4683 divisional CRA's papers, dated entries.

14 Bridging trains were provided by the Royal Canadian Engineers.

15 MacMunn and Falls, *Military Operations in Palestine and Egypt*, pp. 459–510.

16 Ibid., Appendix 26, para 7(c).

17 Gullett, *Official History*, Vol. VII, *Sinai and Palestine*, p. 772; MacMunn and Falls, ibid., pp. 335, 431, 459.

Chapter 25

1 Bruce, *The Last Crusade*, p. 215, notes that Allenby had 35,000 infantry, 9000 cavalry and 383 guns. The enemy had 10,000 infantry, some 1000 cavalry and 130 guns. Most RFA brigades had A and B batteries of 18-pounders and C batteries of 4.5-inch howitzers; MacMunn and Falls, *Military Operations in Palestine and Egypt*, p. 722, para 3(iv); WO 95/4511 20th RHA Brigade, dated entry; Farndale, *The Forgotten Fronts and the Home Base, 1914-1918*, pp. 124–27. Farndale's calculations suggest 552 guns of all types.

2 Preston, *The Desert Mounted Corps*, p. 194; Gullett, *Official History*, Vol. VII, *Sinai and Palestine*, pp. 686–87.

3 Farndale, *The Forgotten Fronts and the Home Base, 1914-1918*, p. 131; WO 95/4511 20 Bde RHA War Diary, dated entry. They collected mules and remounts from Ludd. See Gullett, ibid., pp. 694–97.

4 MacMunn and Falls, *Military Operations in Palestine and Egypt*, pp. 453–57; Bruce, *The Last Crusade*, pp. 221–37 passim; Cutlack, *Official History*, Vol. VIII, *The Australian Flying Corps*, pp. 155–58; Saunders, *The History of the Royal Air Force, 1914-1939*, p. 24; Williams, *These Are the Facts*, p. 89.

5 WO95/4639 CRA 54th Division, dated entries; MacMunn and Falls, ibid., pp. 476–79; WO95/4511, 20 RHA Bde, dated entry; Goold-Walker, *The History of The Honorable Artillery Company in the Great War*, p. 149.

6 MacMunn and Falls, ibid., pp. 453–57; Goold-Walker, ibid., p. 149; WO95/4661, 60th Division, dated entries.

7 Farndale, *The Forgotten Fronts and the Home Base, 1914-1918*, p. 132; MacMunn and Falls, ibid., pp. 476–79; Hutchinson, 'The Battle in Palestine (Commencing 19 August 1918)', pp. 370–74.

8 WO95/4683, 75th Division CRA, dated entries; WO95/4498, 95th RGA Brigade, hostile battery data.

9 Farndale, *The Forgotten Fronts and the Home Base, 1914-1918*, p. 132. The Royal Canadian Engineers Sound Ranging and Flash Spotting Section locations had been within an average accuracy of 30 yards. It also reflected excellent calibration technique.

10 MacMunn and Falls, *Military Operations in Palestine and Egypt*, pp. 476–79, 501–02; WO95/4639, 54th Division CRA. Gullett, *Official History*, Vol. VII, *Sinai and Palestine*, p. 701. Total (division) ammunition expenditure (rounds) for the barrage was:

18-pdr shrapnel: 802
18-pdr HE: 2065
18-pdr smoke: 1015
4.5-in howitzer HE: 3775
3.7-in howitzer HE: 2019
4.2-in Hun bty: 700 (captured ammunition). See Appendix 7.

11 MacMunn and Falls, ibid., pp. 496–501.

12 Gullett, *Official History*, Vol. VII, *Sinai and Palestine*, pp. 690–92; MacMunn and Falls, ibid., p. 502.

13 MacMunn and Falls, ibid., pp. 496–501; Farndale, *The Forgotten Fronts and the Home Base, 1914-1918*, p. 132; The 53rd (East Anglian) Division was the only division comprised entirely of British troops. All the others were one-third British and two-thirds Indian.

14 MacMunn and Falls, ibid., p. 502; Gullett, *Official History*, Vol. VII, *Sinai and Palestine*, p. 701; Farndale, ibid., p. 132.

15 See Appendix 7 for full details and analysis.

16 Gullett, *Official History*, Vol. VII, *Sinai and Palestine*, p. 698.

17 MacMunn and Falls, *Military Operations in Palestine and Egypt*, pp. 496–97.

18 Goold-Walker, *The History of The Honorable Artillery Company in the Great War*, pp. 148–50. By 11.00 am on 20 September, A Battery, HAC, had advanced 40 miles.

19 Gullett, *Official History*, Vol. VII, *Sinai and Palestine*, pp. 695–99; Cutlack, *Official History*, Vol. VIII, *The Australian Flying Corps*, pp. 155–59.

20 Gullet, ibid., p. 708.

21 Ibid., p. 711.

Chapter 26

1 Gullett, *Official History*, Vol. VII, *Sinai and Palestine*, p. 686.

2 Ibid., p. 714. Gullett noted that the British West Indies troops did very well in action; the same could not be said for the Jewish battalions, which showed 'no military promise'.

3 Ibid., p. 716.

Chapter 27

1 Gullett, *Official History*, Vol. VII, *Sinai and Palestine*, p. 767.

2 Ibid., p. 739; Cutlack, *Official History*, Vol. VIII, *The Australian Flying Corps*, pp. 166–67.

3 Gullet, ibid., pp. 711–12; Goold-Walker, *The History of The Honorable Artillery Company in the Great War*, pp. 267–69.

4 Gullet, ibid., pp. 730–33; Preston, *The Desert Mounted Corps*, pp. 248–251. This action at Semakh was noted for the retribution exacted by the Australians because of the treachery of the German defenders who had pretended to surrender and subsequently continued to fight.

5 Gullet, ibid., pp. 771–73. For further details of cavalry actions on the advance to Damascus, see Preston, *The Desert Mounted Corps*, Chapter XIX.

6 MacMunn and Falls, *Military Operations in Palestine and Egypt*, p. 539. This force was commanded by German Colonel Oppen, who had escaped encirclement at Nablus.

7 Gullett, *Official History*, Vol. VII, *Sinai and Palestine*, pp. 746–47.

8 Goold-Walker, *The History of The Honorable Artillery Company in the Great War*, p. 151. This was A Battery's last action of the war.

9 Gullett, *Official History*, Vol. VII, *Sinai and Palestine*, pp. 749–55; Goold-Walker, ibid., pp. 275–76.

10 Goold-Walker, ibid., p. 152.

11 Gullett, *Official History*, Vol. VII, *Sinai and Palestine*, p. 772. The 3rd Light Horse Brigade captured 11,025, the 5th captured 7523, Bourchier's force 12,423 and the 11th Light Horse Regiment at Semakh captured 364, a total of 31,335.

4 Ibid., pp. 725–27.

Chapter 28

1 Anglesea, *A History of British Cavalry*, p. 317.

2 Goold-Walker, *The History of The Honorable Artillery Company in the Great War*, pp. 282–83; Gullett, *Official History*, Vol. VII, *Sinai and Palestine*, p. 776; MacMunn and Falls, *Military Operations in Palestine and Egypt*, pp. 570–72.

3 Gullett, ibid., p. 782.

Chapter 29

1 J. Morris, *Heaven's Command: An Imperial Progress*, Faber & Faber, London, 1973, p. 333.

2 Keogh, *Suez to Aleppo*, p. 187.

3 Farndale, *The Forgotten Fronts and the Home Base, 1914-1918*, p. 89.

4 Ibid., p. 93.

5 MacMunn and Falls, *Military Operations in Palestine and Egypt*, Appendix 1, p. 651.

6 Ibid., p. 650. The 91st Heavy Battery was the only sub-unit to assist in this battle.

7 Ibid., p. 452.

8 Ibid., p. 657; Farndale, *The Forgotten Fronts and the Home Base, 1914-1918*, p. 129.

9 Keogh, *Suez to Aleppo*, p. 188.

10 Preston, *The Desert Mounted Corps*, pp. 303–09.

11 WO 95/4484 and 4498, war diaries of the 95th and 96th brigades, RGA.

12 See also Appendix 7, Ammunition statistics.

13 For a 2 CRH 6-inch shell the radius of the nose was 12 inches. An 8 CRH radius was 48 inches and was streamlined.

14 Goold-Walker, *The History of The Honorable Artillery Company in the Great War*, Appendix A, pp. 482–528.

15 J. Ellis and M. Cox, *The World War I Data Book*, Aurum Press, UK, 1993, pp. 270–71, Table 6.2, Aggregate Casualties by Nationality on the Various Fronts.

16 Bou, *Light Horse: A History of Australia's Mounted Arm*, p. 222.

Chapter 30

1 A. Palazzo, Review of 'British Artillery in the First World War – The Infantry cannot do with a gun less' by Sanders Marble, *US Journal of Military History*, Vol. 77, No. 4, pp. 1505–07.

Appendix 6

1 Source: Farndale, *The Forgotten Fronts and the Home Base, 1914-1918*, pp. 380-84.

2 Ibid., p. 387.

3 Source: Preston, *The Desert Mounted Corps*, Appendix 1, pp. 331–35.

4 Source: Gullet, *Official History*, Vol. VII, *Sinai and Palestine*, Appendix 1, p. 379.

5 Ibid., Appendix 1, p. 379.

6 Ibid., Appendix 1, p. 655.

7 Ibid.

8 Source: Preston, *The Desert Mounted Corps*, pp. 331–35.

9 Source: Gullet, *Official History*, Vol. VII, *Sinai and Palestine*, pp. 413–16.

10 Source: Cutlack, *Official History*, Vol. VIII, *The Australian Flying Corps*, p. 68.

11 Ibid., p. 661.

12 Ibid., Appendix 2, pp. 660–61.

BIBLIOGRAPHY

Documents

British Army

1914-1922 WO 95 Palestine Campaigns

RA WO 95/5494 Divisions and Corps

1527 18 Brigade RHA Jul 17 to Dec 1918
4555 19 Brigade RHA Jul 17 to Mar 1919
4504 20 Brigade RHA Jul 17 to Aug 1919
4450 BGGS EEF to 52nd, 53rd and 54th Divisions Oct-Nov 1917
4368 52 Division CRA War Diary Nov 17
4450 BGGS to GOCs 52,53,54 & 74 Divisions ES 129 Apr 17
4479 GS XX Corps Instructions
4490 BGGS XXI Corps Heavy Artillery Part IV – Nov 1917
4491 GS XXI Corps, Part IV Nov-Dec 1917-18
4484 96 HAG -10 Heavy Battery Mar-May-Jul 1918
4494 CRA XXI Corps Part IV; Oct -Nov 1917, Apr and Sep 1918
4498 95 HAG Apr Sep 1918 Mar-May-Jul 1918
4504 20 RHA Brigade War Diary Nov 17, Apr-Nov 1918
4505 20 RHA Bde Oct 1917
4511 20 RHA Bde Sep 1918
4544 19 RHA Brigade War Diary – A & B Bty HAC, Apr, Oct –Dec 1917
4555 19 RHA Bde Apr – Nov 1917
4571 10 Div CRA Sep 1917 ; Jun - Sep 1918
4614 53 Div CRA Nov 1917
4617 HQ 53 Division, Artillery Order No.3 1-12 Nov 1917
4634 53 Div CRA, Narrative
4635 54 Division Ops Order No.11, Heavy Artillery Oct 1917; Artillery Appreciation –Narrative - 27 Oct to 7 Nov 1917
4636 54 Division Artillery – Warning Order No.3 Nov 1917
4639 54 Div CRA , Sep 1918
4661 60 Division CRA, Sep - Nov 1917
4674 74 Div CRA Dec 1917 - Apr 1918

4683 75 Division CRA , Oct-Nov 1917, Apr 1918, Sep 1918
4707 7 Indian Div CRA May – Jul 1918
4728 4.7 inch Gun Battery RGA

WO 319 Palestine Administration
WO 33/935 GHQ Weekly Ammunition Returns
WO 33/946 GHQ Weekly Ammunition Returns

AIR 1/2336/2/35 – Operations of 5th Wing, RFC, April 1917
WO 33/960 and WO 33/946 Weekly Ammunition Expenditure
WO 319 - PALESTINE

AWM and National Archives Canberra

AWM 40/58 Gullett Papers, AWM 40/58 (p. 9 Gas at Gaza) and
AWM 45/12/7 Eastern Egyptian Force Special Instructions, Artillery 9 APR 1917
13/16 HQ IMD
13/17 ANZACMD
13/19 HQ 5 RFA Bde
13/ 20 HQ 11 RFA Bde
13/21 HQ 18 RFA Bde
13/23 HQ 18 Bde RHA, ANZMD
13/24 HQ 19 Bde RHA
13/25 HQ 36 HAG
1/56 GS IMP MTD DIV 2-6/17
4/1/6 GS GHQ EEF
4/1/62 GS HQ DMC
4/1/64 GS HQ Desert Mtd Column
13/16/4 HQ IMD 4-16 to 6-17
45/7/21 Gas at Gaza
AWM 40/58 Gullett's Campaign Notes

Microfilm Reel No:
855 AWM 1/56 GS IMD 2-6/17
749 754 GS GHQ EEF 4/1/6
863 AWM 4/1/62 GS HQ DMC
864 AWM 4/1/64 GS HQ Desert Mounted Column
212 AWM 13/16/4 HQ IMD Artillery Details

Bibliography

The Regimental Journal of the 1st Light Horse Regiment.

Other AWM war diaries

13/16 HQ IMD
13/17 ANZACMD
13/19 HQ, 5, 11, 18, Bdes RFA
20
21
13/23 HQ 18 Bde RHA, ANZMD
13/24 HQ 19 Bde RHA
13/25 HQ 36 HAG
REEL NO:
AWM 1/56 GS IMP MTD DIV 2-6/17
855 AWM 4/1/6 GS GHQ EEF 749-754
4/1/62 GS HQ DMC 863
4/1/64 GS HQ Desert Mtd Column 864

AWM 13/16/4 HQ IMD 4-16 to 6-17

National Archives Kew (UK)

Cabinet Papers:
CAB 45/80 – Maj. Gen. S. C. U. Smith, MGRA to Historical Branch, 27 NOV 1925, First and Second Gaza Battles

Official manuals

Field Artillery Training 1914, General Staff, WO 2016.
Field Service Regulations, 1914.
Range Table BL 6 inch 21 cwt HOWITZER, MARK I.
Range Table 60 PR, GUNS, ALL MARKS.

Notes on Probability Errors in Ballistics, Table 1, 'Errors which affect the range tothe MPI in predicted fire'; Table 2, 'Errors which affect accuracy in line'; Table 3, 'Wear, EFC and MV' and Table 4, 'Errors which affect the dispersion in predicted and observed fire', 10 pp.

Books

Anglesea, Marquess of, *A History of British Cavalry,* Vol. 5, *1816 –1919,* Les Cooper, London, 1994.

Bailey, J.B.A., *Field Artillery and Firepower*, Naval Institute Press, US, 2004.

Bean, C.E.W., *Official History of Australia in the War of 1914–1918*, Vol. III, *The AIF in France 1916*, Angus & Robertson, Sydney, 1939.

Bou, J., *Light Horse: A History of Australia's Mounted Arm*, Cambridge University Press, Melbourne, 2010.

Bourne, G.H., *The History of the Second Light Horse Regiment*, John Burridge Military Antiques, Swanbourne, Western Australia, 1994.

Bourne, J.M., 'Lieutenant General S.M. Bulfin', *Oxford Dictionary of National Biography*, Vol. VIII, Oxford University Press, UK.

Bruce, A., *The Last Crusade*, J. Murray, London, 2002.

Chasseaud, P., *Artillery's Astrologers*, Maps Press, Lewes, 2002.

Coates J., *An Atlas of Australian Wars*, Oxford University Press, Melbourne, 2006.

Cutlack, F.M., *Official History of Australia in the War of 1914–1918*, Vol. VIII, *The Australian Flying Corps*, Angus & Robertson, Sydney, 1939.

Edmonds, J.E., 'General Sir A.J. Murray', *Oxford Dictionary of National Biography* (revised J.M. Bunton), Vol. XXXIX, Oxford University Press, UK.

Ellis, J. and Cox, M., *The World War I Data Book*, Aurum Press, UK, 1993.

Farndale, M., *The Forgotten Fronts and the Home Base, 1914-1918*, Royal Artillery Institution, London, 1998.

Gardner, B., *Allenby*, Cassell, London, 1965.

Goold-Walker, G., *The History of The Honorable Artillery Company in the Great War, 1914-1919*, Seely, Service & Co., London, 1930.

Grenfell, J., 'Lieutenant General Sir John Maxwell', *Oxford Dictionary of National Biography*, Vol. XXXVIII, Oxford University Press, UK.

Gudmundsson, B., *On Artillery*, Praeger Publishers, Westport, US, 1993.

Gullett, H.S., *Official History of Australia in the War of 1914–1918*, Vol. VII, *Sinai and Palestine*, Angus & Robertson, Sydney, 1941.

Hammond, E.W., *History of the 11th Light Horse Regiment, 4th Light Horse Brigade*, W. Brooks, Brisbane, 1942.

Hill, A.J., *Chauvel of the Light Horse*, Melbourne University Press, 1978.

Hogg, I.V., *Illustrated History of Artillery*, Quarto, London, 1987.

Hughes, M., *Allenby and British Strategy in the Middle East, 1917-1919*, F. Cass, London, 1999.

——, 'Viscount Allenby', *Oxford Dictionary of National Biography*, Vol. I, Oxford University Press, UK.

Bibliography

Hunter, D.J., *My Corps Cavalry: A History of the 13th Light Horse Regiment*, Slouch Hat Publications, McCrae, Victoria, 1999.

Jones, I., *The Light Horse*, Hodder & Stoughton, London, 1985.

——, *The Australian Light Horse*, Time-Life Books, Sydney, 1987.

——, *A Thousand Miles of Battles: The Saga of the Australian Light Horse in WWI*, Anzac Day Commemoration Committee of Queensland, Brisbane, 2007.

Keogh, E.G., *Suez to Aleppo*, Australian Military Forces Directorate of Training, Wilke, Melbourne, 1955.

Kinloch, T., *Devils on Horses: Anzacs in the Middle East 1916-1919*, Exisle, Auckland, 2007.

Liddell Hart, B.H., 'Field Marshal Sir Philip Chetwode (Bt)', *Oxford Dictionary of National Biography*, Vol. XI, Oxford University Press, UK.

MacMunn, H.G. and Falls, C., *Military Operations in Palestine and Egypt*, Vols. 1 and 2, HMSO, London, 1927.

Matthews, M.C.G. and Harrison, B., 'Allenby', *Oxford Dictionary of National Biography*, Vol. II, Oxford University Press, UK.

Morris, J., *Heaven's Command: An Imperial Progress*, Faber & Faber, London, 1973.

Murray, A., *Sir Archibald Murray's Despatches, June 1916 to June 1918*, Naval and Military Press, UK, 2010.

Norwich, J.J., *The Middle Sea*, Random House, London, 2010.

Olden A.C.N. and McCubbin, A., *The Westralian Cavalry in the War: The Story of the 10th Light Horse Regiment in the Great War*, self-published (McCubbin), Perth, 1923.

Powles, C.G. and Wilkie, A., *Official History New Zealand's Effort in the Great War*, Vol. III, *The New Zealanders in Sinai and Palestine*, Whitcombe & Tombs Ltd., Auckland, 1922.

Preston, R.M.P., *The Desert Mounted Corps*, Houghton Mifflin, London, 1921.

Richardson, J.D., *History of the 4th Light Horse Regiment, 1914-1919*, E.N. Birks, Sydney, 1923.

Saunders, H. StG., *The History of the Royal Air Force, 1914-1939*, Oxford University Press, 1939.

Savage, R., *Allenby of Armageddon*, Bobbs-Merrill, USA, 1926.

Simpson, C.V., *Maygar's Boys: A Brief History of the 8th Light Horse Regiment, 1914-1919*, Just Soldiers Military Research and Publications, Victoria, 1998.

Smith, N.C., *Men of Beersheba: A History of the 4th Light Horse Regiment, 1914-1919*, Mostly Unsung Military History Publications, Victoria, 1993.

——, *The Third Light Horse Regiment, 1914-18*, Mostly Unsung Military

History Publications, Victoria, 1993.

Thompson, R.R., *The History of the 52nd (Lowland) Division, 1914-1918,* Macleuse, Glasgow, 1923.

Wavell, A., *Allenby in Egypt*, Harrap, London,1944.

Williams, R., *These Are the Facts: The Autobiography of Sir Richard Williams*, Australian War Memorial and Australian Government Publishing Service, Canberra, 1977.

Wilson, L.C., *Narrative of Operations of the Third Light Horse Brigade (1917-1919)*, Naval & Military Press-Imperial War Museum, 2010.

Wilson, L.C. and Wetherell, H., *History of the 5th Light Horse Regiment*, Motor Press, 1926.

Journal articles

Anon (A Battery commander), 'The Taking of Jerusalem', *Journal of the Royal Artillery*, Vol. XLV, No. 3.

Badsey, S. ,'The Boer War (1899-1902) and British Cavalry Doctrine: A Re-evaluation', *Journal of Military History*, Vol. 71, No. 1.

Bou, J., 'Firepower, and Swords: The Australian Light Horse and the Tactical Lessons of Cavalry Operations in Palestine, 1916-1918', *Journal of Military History*, Vol. 71, No. 1.

Hall, B.N., 'Technological Adaptation in a Global Conflict: The British Army and Communications Beyond the Western Front, 1914-1918', *Journal of Military History*, Vol. 78, No. 1.

Hutchinson, F.P., 'The Work of the Heavy Artillery XXI Corps in Palestine, February to September 1918', *Journal of the Royal Artillery*, Vol. XLVI, No. 6.

——, 'The Battle in Palestine (Commencing 19 August 1918)', *Journal of the Royal Artillery*, Vol. XLV, Nos. 11 & 12.

Palazzo, A., Review of *British Artillery in the First World War – The Infantry cannot do with a gun less* by Sanders Marble, *US Journal of Military History*, Vol. 77, No. 4, pp. 1505–06.

Sheffy, Y., 'Chemical Warfare in the Palestine Campaign', *US Journal of Military History*, Vol. 73, No. 3.

Sibert, E.L., 'Campaign Summary and Notes on Horse Artillery in Sinai and Palestine', *RA Journal*, Vol. LV, No. 4.

Woerlee, B., 'Magdhaba and Kress', *Sabretache*, journal of the Military History Society of Australia, Vol. XLIX, No. 4.

Electronic media

Cavalry Regiment Organisation, New Zealand Mounted Rifles website at: http://www.nzmr.org/campaigns.4/26/2010.3pp

Terraine, J., 'Indirect Fire as a Battle Winner/Loser', Artillery in the First World War, Tactical Doctrine Retrieval Centre Disc 07250, Ref. p. 3. The same disc has similar comment from Shelford Bidwell.

Index

1st Light Horse Brigade 75, 79, 111, 131, 169, 171, 173, 174, 250, 311
  Amman and Es Salt 201
  Beersheba 132, 134
  Gaza 103
  Great Northern Drive 160
  Jordan Valley 231, 234, 268
  Katia 55, 56
  Magdhaba 63
  Romani 46, 47, 48, 51
2nd Light Horse Brigade 68, 75, 111, 170, 175, 194, 197, 214, 250, 311
  Amman and Es Salt 200, 201
  Beersheba 130
  Bir el Abd 56
  Gaza 83, 92, 100, 103
  Great Northern Drive 158, 159, 160
  Jordan Valley 231, 234–5, 268
  Katia 55
  Magdhaba 63
  Romani 46, 47, 48, 50, 51
3rd Indian Division 249, 250, 253, 254, 256, 261, 307, 313
3rd Light Horse Brigade 75, 111, 126, 165, 167, 170, 175, 265, 279, 311
  Amman and Es Salt 200
  Beersheba 131, 134
  Bir el Abd 57, 59
  Es Salt (second raid) 212, 213
  Gaza 80–1, 87, 89, 102
  Jerusalem, capture of 178, 179, 180, 185
  Katia 54–6
  Magdhaba 63
  Romani 47, 48, 50, 52
4th Cavalry Division 248, 250, 280
  Damascus, advance to 273, 276
4th Light Horse Brigade 28, 44, 75, 111, 124, 165, 169, 170, 175, 211, 231, 243, 276, 311
  Beersheba 131, 132, 240, 241
  Es Salt (second raid) 211, 212, 213, 214, *216*, 220
  Gaza 79, 100, 101, 102
  Jerusalem, capture of 179, 183, 185
  Megiddo 263, 265
  Semakh 275
5th Cavalry Division 248, 250, 280, 281
  Damascus, advance to 273, 274, 276, 277
5th Light Horse Brigade 23, 101, 200, 227, 235, 276, 279, 311
  Megiddo 249, 250, 253, 263, 265
5th Mountain Brigade 175, 177
5th Mounted (Yeomanry) Brigade 44, 111, 124, 165, 168, 170–1, 173, 311
  Beersheba 131, 132
  Es Salt (second raid) 214
  Gaza 80, 83, 87, 100–2
  Katia 55, 56
  Rafa 68, 69, 75
  Romani 46, 52
6th Mountain Brigade 179, 218
6th Mounted (Yeomanry) Brigade 75, 80, 100, 102, 111, 182
7th Division 184, 208, 247, 248, 249, 250, 263
7th Indian Division 207, 209, 250, 253, 254, 258, 261, 280, 307, 308, 313
7th Mountain Brigade 175
7th Mounted (Yeomanry) Brigade 112, 115, 131, 139, 158, 170–1, 183, 231
8th Mountain Brigade 209, 251
8th Mounted (Yeomanry) Brigade 111, 157, 178–9, 182
9th Mountain Brigade 141, 171, 180, 181, 191, 197, 251
10th Division 113, 128, 137, 157, 160, 161, 162, 183, 186, 188, 191, 209, 210, 224, 285, 307, 308, 312
  Megiddo 250, 251, 252, 260, 262
  road building 194
10th Mountain Brigade 191, 247
11th Cavalry Brigade 267, 277
13th Cavalry Brigade 263, 265, 275
14th Cavalry Brigade 263, 274, 279
15th Cavalry Brigade 263, 274, 280
18th Brigade RHA 113, 131, 197, 204, 250, 251, 306, 311
19th Brigade RHA 79, 111, 113, 124, 130, 131, 155, 165, 206, 211–12, 218, 228, 306, 311
  Megiddo 250, 251, 258
20th Brigade RHA 44, 79, 113, 131, 155, 250, 251, 306
21st Brigade 44, 258
22nd Mounted (Yeomanry) Brigade 75, 84, 103,

Index

111, 178, 182, 226
29th Brigade 191, 261
30th Brigade 191, 261
31st Brigade 160, 162, 191
37th Brigade RFA 181, 250, 251, 307
42nd Division 45, 48, 53, 57, 59, 61, 75, 149, 313
44th Brigade 112, 120, 161
52nd Division 112, 114, 168, 170, 173, 282, 308, 309, 313
Bir el Abd 57, 61
Gaza 79, 84, 94, 96–9, 105, 106, 120, 137, 140, 141, 145, 151, 158
Jerusalem, capture of 177, 179, 182, 183, 184, 185
Romani 45, 48, 50, 52–4, 61
Wadi Auja 223
53rd Division 51, 112, 113, 118, 119, 194, 222, 307, 308, 313
Beersheba 126, 129, 161
Berukin 209
Gaza 79, 84, 85, 90, 92, 94, 96, 97, 99, 106, 137
Great Northern Drive 157, 159
Jericho 195
Jerusalem 175, 177, 185, 186, 188, 191
Megiddo 250, 252, 260–2
Wadi Auja 224, 225
54th Division 51, 112, 114, 117, 171, 308, 309, 313
Berukin 207, 208, 209
Gaza 79, 84, 86, 90, 94, 96–7, 99, 124, 137, 140–2, 145, 147, 152, 158
Jerusalem, capture of 177, 183, 184
Megiddo 250, 252, 253, 260, 261
Wadi Auja 223
60th Division 112, 113, 128–9, 130, 137, 192, 242, 248, 285, 307, 308, 309
Amman and Es Salt 197, 199
Berukin 207
Es Salt (second raid) 212, 217, 220
Great Northern Drive 155, 157, 159, 160, 162
Huj 167
Jericho 194, 195, 196
Jerusalem, capture of 177, 180, 183, 184, 185, 186, 188
Jordan Valley 204, 206, 227, 232
Megiddo 249, 250, 251, 253, 254, 256, 263
Wadi Auja 224, 225
61st Brigade 144
67th Brigade RFA 191, 224, 250, 261, 307, 308
68th Brigade RFA 162, 191, 224, 250, 261, 307, 308
74th Division 75, 112, 113, 313
Beersheba 128–9
Gaza 84, 94, 96, 97, 99, 100, 102, 112, 113, 120, 137
Great Northern Drive 157, 159, 160, 161
Jericho 195
Jerusalem 177, 183, 184, 185, 186, 188, 191
Wadi Auja 224
75th Division 112, 114, 120, 137, 144–5, 158, 168, 170, 171, 307, 313
Berukin 207, 208, 209, 210
Jerusalem, capture of 177, 178–83
Megiddo 249, 250, 253, 254, 256, 260
Wadi Auja 223–4
91st Brigade 253
95th Brigade 114, 223, 251, 254, 256, 285, 288, 309, 310
96th Brigade 114, 129, 186, 191, 251, 254, 285, 309, 310
97th Brigade 114, 143, 152, 309, 310
100th Brigade 114, 143, 152, 223, 251, 254, 309, 310
102nd Brigade 114, 143, 152, 223, 250, 251, 253, 254, 256, 286, 310
103rd Brigade 250, 262, 310
117th Brigade 161
155th Brigade 50, 51, 52, 98, 148, 170, 173, 183, 184
156th Brigade 51, 52, 140, 141, 142, 152, 171, 182, 184
157th Brigade 170, 181, 183, 184, 185
158th Brigade 85, 128, 159, 191, 224, 262
159th Brigade 85, 128, 262
160th Brigade 84, 85, 99, 128
161st Brigade 85, 86, 91, 100, 121, 141, 147, 183
162nd Brigade 141, 147, 225, 261
163rd Brigade 141, 145, 147, 261
164th Brigade 261
169th Brigade 191
172nd Brigade RFA 224, 250, 307
179th Brigade 129, 182, 199, 200, 253, 258
180th Brigade 162, 182, 195, 201, 207, 253
181st Brigade 129, 130, 162, 192, 200, 224, 227, 253
212th Brigade 55
224th Brigade 171
229th Brigade 75, 161–2, 191, 192
230th Brigade 75, 129, 161, 186, 224
231st Brigade 75, 129, 186
232nd Brigade 171, 209, 260

233rd Brigade 171, 209, 260
234th Brigade 145, 182, 209, 224, 260
239th Brigade 84
260th Brigade RFA 47, 306
261st Brigade RFA 84, 141, 173, 307, 308
262nd Brigade RFA 47, 50, 57, 84, 141, 170, 181, 307, 308
263rd Brigade RFA 47, 50, 52, 84, 97, 102, 186, 224, 250, 262, 306, 307
264th Brigade RFA 118, 141, 170, 171, 173, 180, 181, 258, 307, 308
265th Brigade RFA 84, 85, 99, 158, 250, 308
266th Brigade RFA 84, 85, 99, 147, 158, 250, 261, 308
267th Brigade RFA 96, 99, 158, 250, 307, 308
268th Brigade 161, 162, 163, 185
270th Brigade RFA 84, 117, 119, 141, 148, 225, 236, 250, 308, 309
271st Brigade RFA 84, 86, 117, 118, 141, 142, 148, 183, 250, 307, 308
272nd Brigade RFA 97, 141, 183, 250, 308, 309
273rd Brigade 96, 181
301st Brigade RFA 185, 188, 197, 206, 232, 250, 253, 308, 309
302nd Brigade RFA 129, 185, 188, 197, 224, 228, 250, 253, 307, 308, 309
303rd Brigade RFA 118, 129, 162, 185, 195, 232, 250, 253, 308, 309
310th Brigade 129
372nd Brigade 250
373rd Brigade 250
374th Brigade 250
422nd Brigade 250
423rd Brigade 250
XX Corps 84, 113, 117, 164, 195, 207, 222, 224, 226, 243
  Beersheba 125–6, 128–9, 131, 149–50
  Great Northern Drive 155, 157, 160, 162
  Jerusalem, capture of 179, 183, 186, 188
  Megiddo 250, 251, 254, 260
  Third Battle of Gaza 137, 144, 152
XXI Corps 76, 113, 117, 119, 135, 139, 164, 195, 196, 243, 244, 248
  Berukin 207–10
  Great Northern Drive 155, 157, 162
  Jerusalem, capture of 177, 178, 183, 185
  Megiddo 249–63, 265, 270
  Third Battle of Gaza 125, 128, 137, 138, 143–4, 150, 152, 155
  Wadi Auja 223

A
Abasan el Kebir 123
Abbalete 143
abbreviations 12–13
Abu Aweigila 67
Abu Hamra 53, 54
Abu Hureira 77
Abu Shukheidin 194
Abu Shushe 173, 179, 263, 265
Abu Tellul 206, 222, *223*, 226, 229–32, 268
  defences 230–2, *233*
Acre 275
Aden 16, 41, 42, 43
Afule 244
ahmets 30–1, 147, 149, 151, 162, 185, 197, 206, 279
Ain el Beida 277
Ain es Sir 200
Ain Kolah 158
air support 41, 94, 105, 294
  AFC *see* Australian Flying Corps (AFC)
  reconnaissance 39, 46, 62–3, 67, 78, 99, 103, 120, 125, 138, 246, 260, 267, 274, 291
  RFC *see* Royal Flying Corps (RFC)
Aleppo 19, 28, 115, 264, 280–1
Alexandria 42
Ali el Muntar 77, 79, 84, 85, 86, 90, 96–7, 147, 149
Allen, Major R.A. 213, 214, 215, 218, 298
Allenby, General Edmund 9, 23, 24, 25, 76, 118, 121, 122, 126, 135, 136, 150, 154, 170, 226
  Aleppo 281
  appointment and arrival 106, 112–13, 117
  Australia, visit to 294
  background 115–16
  command style 116, 290, 292
  Damascus, advance to 272–9
  Jerusalem, capture of 175–90, *176*, *187*, *189*
  Megiddo 249–50
  strategy 155, 157, 164–5, 170–1, 174, 175, 177, 183, 185, 192, 194, 197–8, 203, 206, 207, 211, 236, 242, 243–8, 268, 285, 290, 292
Ameidat 160
Amman 9, 18, 19, 154, 194, 196, 207, 211, 217, 220, 221, 226, 244, 249, 267, 270, 273, 282
  raid 197–203, *202*, 228, 236, 321, 323
ammunition 102, 106
  captured 59, 66, 234, 251, 260, 263, *266*, 267, 270–1

Index

expended 66, 71, 74, 105, 108, 142–5, 188, 192, 209, 215, 260, 263, 267, 287, 288, 291, 320–7
shortage 23, 84, 85, 105, 128, 158, 179, 180, 209, 220, 229, 288
siege brigades 302–3
supply 34, 35–6, 38, 42, 44, 74–5, 106, 120, 124, 126, 130, 140, 141, 144, 147, 155, 160–1, 178, 181–2, 192, 195, 208, 210, 213–14, 215, 228, 230, 246, 251, 253–4, 257–8, 263, 272, 291
types 34, 285, 286
Amwas 178, 180
Anatolia 16
Anebta 253, 258
Antill, Brigadier J.M. 48, 52, 53, 54–5
Anzac Mounted Division *see* Australian and New Zealand (A&NZ) Mounted Division
Arab uprisings 16, 18
Arak el Menshiye 167, 190
armoured cars 22, 68, 104, 160, 174, 175, 197, 201, 206–7, 214–15, 270, 274, 277, 292, 293
Light Armoured Motor Battery 79, 160, 180, 197, 239, 240
Arsuf 191
Ashkelon 170
Asluj 128
Asyferieh 100
Ataweina 163
Auckland Mounted Rifles 38, 102, 132, 173–4, 183, 199, 224, 270, 299, 311
Australia Hill 77, 97
Australian Flying Corps (AFC) 9, 45, 69, 138, 245–6, 287, 291, 317–18
No. 1 Squadron 39, 63, 78, 102, 103, *139*, 192, 245–6, 251, 267, 273
Australian Imperial Force (AIF) 33, 294
I Australia Corps 25
II ANZAC Corps 25
1st Division 22, 25, 31
2nd Division 22, 25
3rd Division 22
4th Division 22, 25, 33
5th Division 22, 25, 33
reorganisation 8, 18
Australian Light Horse 8, 11, 22, *30*, 33, 205–6, 229, 232, 285, 291 *see also by brigade number*
composition of regiments 29–31
Australian Mounted Division (AMD) 111, 128, 137, 157, 162, 164, 167, 170, *198*, 206, 208, 209, 214, 226, 236, 243, 312 *see also* Imperial Mounted Division (IMD)
booty 279
brigades *see by brigade number*
Damascus, advance to 273, 276
Jerusalem, capture of 175, 178, 179, 183
Megiddo 250
senior/key staff 298
Australian and New Zealand (A&NZ) Mounted Division 44, 60, 62, 68, 113, 157, 164, 167, 170, 311, 312
Amman and Es Salt 197
Beersheba 128
brigades *see by brigade number*
Damascus, advance to 273
Gaza 79, 83, 92, 100, 103, 106, 137
Jericho 194–5, 196
Jerusalem, capture of 177
Jordan Valley 206–7, 227
Megiddo 250
Romani 45, 46, 47, 50
swords, use of 241, 243
Avara 209
Ayrshire Battery 8, 41, 111, 113, 171, 183, 211, 250, 270, 306, 311, 318
Amman and Es Salt 197
Beersheba 134
Bir el Abd 56, 57
Gaza 79, 86, 101, 102
Great Northern Drive 155, 158
Jordan Valley 204
Katia 55
Magdhaba 62
Romani 46, 47, 48, 52
Azmut 261

B

Baalbek 280
Bada 56
Badich 56
Baghalat 270
Baghdad 115
Baiket el Sana 104
Baissan 222
Bakr ridge 270
Balata 261, 267
Bald Hill 183, 184
Balin 169
Balkan Wars 19, 37
Ballah 43

ballistic data 286–8
Bamford Smith, Major 211
barbed wire 27, 148
Barney, Lieutenant 168, 171
Barrow, General G.deS. 111, 173, 248, 263, 265, 267, 276–7
battery guns
  2-pounder 293
  2.75-inch howitzers 114, 251, 288
  3-pounder 67
  3.7-inch howitzers 79, 129, 285, 288
  3.75-inch howitzers 114
  4.5-inch howitzers 36, 47, 84, 96, 107, 112, 113, 117, 129, 140, 142, 143, 150, 181, 182, 186, 192, 204, 232, 288, 289, 293
  5.5-inch howitzers 38, 293
  5.9-inch (German/Turkish) howitzers 38, 51, 53, 55–7, 73, 81, 103, 120–1, 141, 165, 168, 170
  6-inch howitzers 37, 38, 96, 113, 114, 118, 119, 129, 140, 144, 246, 253, 254, 258, 286, 288
  6-inch Mark VII guns 144, 246, 251
  6-pounder 293
  8-inch howitzers 96, 113, 114, 118, 140, 144, 247
  11.5-pounder 200
  13-pounder 34, 41, 47, 68, 73, 74, 79, 104, 106, 111, 112, 132, 155, 165, 178, 181, 228, 229, 232, 285, 292
  17-pounder 293
  18-pounder 34, 36, *37*, 42, 47, 52, 61, 68, 73, 79, 84, 96, 98, 111, 112, 113, 117, 129, 140–3, 155, 165, 181, 182, 185–6, 188, 192, 195, 206, 225, 245, 247, 252, 261, 284, 289, 292, 293, 294
  25-pounder 293
  60-pounder 25, 37, 38, *39*, 47, 78, 113, 114, 129, 144, 150, 161, 180, 195, 204, 206, 228, 230, 245, 246, 247, 251, 252, 253, 254, 257, 258, 263, 268, 286, 293
  Krupp 75mm 229
  'three-group' configuration 140–1
  Turk 7.7cm 229
bayonet charges 73–4, 162, 240–2
Bazeley, Lieutenant Colonel 293
Beersheba 1, 19, 22, 28, 67, 77, 123, 139, 157, 161, 164, 165
  Battle of 8, 113, 114, 115, 116, 122, 125–36, *133*, 154, 240, 241, 283, 290
Beirut 272, 278
Beisan 244, 250, 262, 263, 265, 267, 277
Beit Anan 181
Beit Duras 168
Beit Durdis 80, 87, 88
Beit el Tatha 183
Beit Hanum 144
Beit Iksa 186, 191
Beit Izza 181, 183, 192
Beit Jibrin 170, 177
Beit Lid 258
Beit Likia 184
Beit Naqquba 181
Beit Nuba 185
Beit Sira 194
Beit Surik 186
Beit ur el Foka 186
Beit Ur el Tahta 179, 184, 185, 191
Beituniye 182, 192
Belah 148
Belled el Sheikh 274
Benet-Mercie machine guns 30
Beni Sakr horsemen 198, 203, 221, 270
Berfilya 185
Berkshire (Berks) Battery 41, 42–3, 44, 111, 113, 171, 173, 218, 306, 318
  Beersheba 129, 131
  Gaza 79, 80–1, 87
  Great Northern Drive 155, 157
  Jerusalem, capture of 179
  Megiddo 250, 251
Berkshire Yeomanry 173
Berukin 19, 207–10, 243, 261, 321, 323
Berukin ridge 262
Beshshit 173
Bethlehem 191, 198
Biddu 180, 181, 183, 186, 191
Bidya 208, 249, 261
Bir el Abd 38, 54, 56–60, *58*, 67, 73, 241
Bir el Lafan 63
Bir el Mazar 60
Bir el Nuss 54
Bir es Sqati 157
Bir ez Zeit 194
Bir Nagid 55
Bir Sale-Abu Igreig 131
Birdwood, Lieutenant General 25, 31, 59
Bireh 175, 177, 178, 182, 191, 192
Birein 177
Blazed Hill 118, 120
Boer Wars 26–7, 40, 115, 138
Bolton, Trooper 134

Index

Borbridge, Lieutenant 168
Bourchier, Brigadier 278, 279
Boyce, Brigadier H.A. 145
Bragg, Lawrence 282
Bridges, Major General 31
Bristol Fighter 116, 138, *139*, 192, 272, 273
British Army 16 *see also by brigade and division number*
cavalry 22, 26–33, 45
class distinctions 33
Egypt, in 18–19
Honourable Artillery Company *see* Honourable Artillery Company (HAC)
numbers 31
Royal Field Artillery *see* Royal Field Artillery (RFA)
Royal Garrison Artillery *see* Royal Garrison Artillery (RGA)
Royal Horse Artillery *see* Royal Horse Artillery (RHA)
Territorial artillery units 8, 41–2
Brook, Lieutenant General Sir Alan 292
Brown, Lieutenant Colonel J.G. 31
Brown Hill 180, 256
Bryant, Major 183, 289
Budrus 188
Bulfin, Lieutenant General Edward S. 113, 119, 128, 157, 169, 170, 196, 222, 244, 247, 248, 272
Berukin 207–10
Jerusalem, capture of 178, 180, 182, 183, 185
Megiddo 252, 260
Third Battle of Gaza 138 9, 140, 142, 143, 150, 151, 152
Wadi Auja 223
Bunker Hill 77
Burbera 170
Bureir 167
Burej 168
Burg Bardawil 224
Burj el Beiyara 160
Burka 170, 180
Burkusie 169
Burney, Brigadier P.deS. 224
Burqa 171, 173
Byar Adas 208
Byng, Major General Julian 21

C

Cain, Captain J.R. 159
Cairn Hill 200
Cairo 22, 93, 107, 116, 126, 138
camouflage 246
Campbell, Major 184
Canadian Army 9, 25, 247, 260
Canterbury Hill 48
Canterbury Mounted Rifles 38, 65, 131, 183, 299, 311
cartography 40
casualties 27, 28, 31, 34, 61, 118, 271, 280, 283–4, 288–9
Abu Tellul 235
Amman and Es Salt 201, 203
Beersheba 130, 135, 136, 283
Berukin 210
cavalry charges 241, 242
comparison with guns 283–4
Damascus, advance towards 279
El Mughar 171, 173
Es Salt (second raid) 218, 220
Gaza 92, 101, 105, 106, 151, 152, 283
Great Northern Drive 162, 163
illness 120
Jaffa 174, 283
Jericho 196
Jerusalem 179, 181–2, 183, 184, 185, 192–3
Jordan Valley 205, 206, 235
Magdhaba 66, 67, 74
Megiddo 260, 261, 262, 265, 283
NZMR 299–300
Rafa 73, 74
Romani 51, 53, 54, 57, 59, 61, 74
Semakh 276
Wadi Auja 225
cavalry 281
British 26–33
charges 28, 132, 134, 135, 149, *166*, 167, 240–2
communications 40–1
doctrine 26–8
horse artillery 240–3, 284–5, 292
regiments 316–17
tactics 239, 240–3
Central Powers 16, 154, 238
Chauvel, Lieutenant General Sir Harry 8, 9, 11, 29, 31–3, *32*, 38, 73, 75, 111, 115, 122, 139, 164, 169, 170, 174, 175, 207, 242, 244, 247–8, 276, 277, 280, 292, 311
Beersheba 125, 126, 128–30
Bir el Abd 56–60
command style 31–2, 264–5

Es Salt (second raid) 211, 213, 217–18, 220
Gaza 79, 80–4, 90, 100, 103, 104, 106
Great Northern Drive 155, 157, 160, 162
Haifa 274
Jerusalem, capture of 178, 188
Jordan Valley 206–7, 226, 227, 229–31, 234
Katia 54–6
Magdhaba 62–3, 66–7
Megiddo 263–7
Rafa 68, 71
Romani 46, 47–8, 50, 52, 53
Chaytor, Major General E.W.C. 46, 47, 52, 54, 63, 65, *65*, 90, 111, 170, 173, 200, 217, 243, 244, 248–50, 263, 267, 312
Beersheba 128, 132
Jericho 195, 196
Jordan Valley 204, 227, 268–71
Chetwood, Major General Sir Philip 73, 75, 76, 111, 113, 116, 139, 222, 224, 252, 260, 262, 272
Beersheba 128, 130
Gaza 79, 80, 83, 85–6, 90–1, 100, 103, 144, 152
Great Northern Drive 155, 158, 160–1
Jerusalem 185, 188, 191–2
Magdhaba 62, 66, 67
Rafa 68, 69, 71, 72
Chipp Hill 224
Chirmside Battery 8
chronology 296–7
Clarke, Sergeant A.J. 218
Clay Hill 86
Clowes, Major 132
Cockburn, Captain W. 25
communications 40–1, 67, 96, 119, *198*, 243, 244, 291
mistakes 86, 91
signals network 247
Corder, Lieutenant Colonel A.A. 298
counter-battery artillery 9, 38, 84, 99, 105, 113, 230, 234, 252, 282–3, 291
counter bombardment 29, 152, 210, 247, 282–3
Coutlas 143
Cox, Brigadier Charles 32, 160, 195, 205, 234, 311
Amman and Es Salt 201, 217
Gaza 104
Magdhaba 63, 65–6, *65*
Cyprus 125

D
Dallas, Major General G. 79, 83–6, 90, 91, 106
Damascus 19, 45, 240, 242, 243, 244, 262, 268, 280, 289
advance towards 272–9
Damieh 201, 212, 217
Daniel, Major 102
Dardanelles 18
Dead Sea 194, 195, 196, 227, 230, 268
Deir Belah 22, 80, 81, 89, 90, 112, 119
Deir es Saras 276, 277
Deir Ibizia Ridge 192
Deir Saide 158
Deir Sineid 80, 125, 143, 158, 164, 168
Denbigh, Lord 42
Deraa 19, 242, 244, 249, 268, 270
Desert Mounted Column (DMC) 8, 9, 11, 25, 29, 62, 111, 113, 155, 170, 243, 246, 248, 275, 280, 314–15
Amman and Es Salt 197, 199
Beersheba 130–1
cavalry charges 242
Gaza 79, 85, 92, 94, 100, 137, 139
Jerusalem, capture of 177
Jordan Valley 204, 206, 226, 227, 236
Megiddo 249, 253, 262, 263–7, *264*, *266*
Dhaheriye 139, 175
Dhareriyeh 159
Disr ed Dameir 270
divisional ammunition column (DAC) 35, 36
Dobell, Lieutenant General Sir Charles 61, 107–9, 110
First Battle of Gaza 78–9, 83, 84, 86, 90, 92
Second Battle of Gaza 93, 94, 96, 100, 101, 104, 106, 122, 135
Dorset Yeomanry 173, 218
Dotham Plains 249
Downes, Colonel R.M. 298
Dueidar 46
Dukka 181
Dumar 278
Dunbar, Lieutenant Colonel 141
Dunckley, Major 188

E
Eastern Frontier Force (EFF) 61
Ebdis 168
Egypt 16
British Army in 18–19
first operations 41

Index

Egyptian Expeditionary Force (EEF) 16, 18, 46, 76, 92, 106, 107, 112, 115, 116, 143, 150–1, 292
El Afule (Affule) 19, 246, 250, 265
El Arish 19, 22, 57, 62, 66, 71, 75, 76, 93, 96, 99, 120, 141, 145, 152
El Auja 22, 62, 67
El Buggar 130
El Burj 185, 186
El Butani el Charibye 171
El Faluje 157
El Ferdan 122
El Haud 212
El Hinu 231, 232, 235
El Huwej 200
El Jabry 158
El Jib 181, 182, 186
El Kossaima 22
El Kubeibe 170
El Kubri 43
El Kuneitra 277
El Kustine 171
El Lubban 263
El Madhbeh 231, 232
El Maghruntein 68
El Mejdel 170
El Mughar 164, 170–3, *172*
El Muntar 182
El Rabah 53, 55
El Rafa 62
El Rastan 280
El Ruag 56
El Shellal 123
El Sheluf ridge 85
Elliott, Major M.N. 124, 155, 215, 218, 280
Elwis, Captain 104
Es Salt 19, 197, 201, 207, 270, 321, 323
  second raid 211–21, *219*, 322, 324
Es Sawiye 263
Es Shire ridge 84, 85, 96, 97, 98, 99
Esani 124, 130
Esdraelon Plain 185, 242, 244, 264, 274
Esdud 169, 171, 180
Essex Battery 41, 131, 168, 171, 250, 306, 318
Et Taiyibe 258
Et Tine 173
Et Tireh 186, 208, 209, 210, 249, 252, 256, 257, 258, 260, 285
Etmaler 47, 48, 51
Eugster, Lieutenant Colonel Oliver J. 42, 113, 124, 155
Exeter, Marquis of 44, 80

F

Falkenhayn, General 115
Faluje 169
Fane, Major General Sir V.B. 253
Farndale, Sir Martin 8, 11
Farquhar, Lieutenant Colonel 141
Farr, Lieutenant Colonel W.P. 298
Ferrikhiye 247
Ferry Post 25, 44
Ferweh 267
field artillery brigades 35–7
Field Service Regulations 28, 40, 284
Fig Grove 121
FitzGerald, Brigadier 69, 103, 132, 311
Flanders 21, 38
Foka 191
France 16, 21–2, 23, 38
Franco-Prussian War (1870–71) 37
Fraser, Major 55
Frauconnau 143
French, Colonel Sir John 26, 110
French Army 115, 278
  Megiddo 249, 253, 260
Fryer's Hill 77, 96, 140
Furqa ridge 261, 262

G

Galilee 264
Gallipoli 8, 16, 18, 21, 22, 23, 25, 31, 33, 46, 106, 294
Gamli 123
gas warfare 79, 96, 106–9, 143, 150–2, 320
Gaza 20, 22, 76, 77, *78*, 116, 120, 125, 159, 236, 243, 320
  First Battle 75, 77–92, *82*, 98, 283, 290, 291
  gas, use of 106–9, 320
  Second Battle 93–109, *95*, 111, 112, 117, 283
  Third Battle 113, 114, 115, 117, 125, 137–52, *146*, 155, 164, 283
German airforce 67, 190, 246, 266, 272–3
Germany Army 16, 19, 197, 203
  Abu Tellul attack 234–5, 236
  artillery 38–9
  spring offensive 154
Ghoraniye crossing 196, 198–201, *199*, 204, 206–7, 211, 212, 214, 218, 222, 227, 231, 236, 249, 268
Gilead 242

Girdwood, Major General 161
Girheir 165
Gloucester Yeomanry 168, 185, 311
Godley, Lieutenant General 25
Godwin, Brigadier 179, 218
Goold-Walker, Major G. 11, 122, 221, 229, 266, 279
Goz El Bazar 124
Grant, Brigadier William 28, 32, 132, 134, 135, 165, 211–13, 215, 217, 220, 241, 275, 311
Granville, Lieutenant Colonel 212, 234
Great Northern Drive 155–63, *156*, 243
Green Hill 77, 96, 149
Gregory, Brigadier C.L. 277
Gulf of Aqaba 19
Gullett, H.G. 11
Gun Hill 145

H

Hache 143
Haifa 274–5
Haig, Douglas 26, 238
Hama 280
Hamame 168
Hamilton, Captain Ian 26
Hamisah 54, 55
Hampshire Battery 111, 113, 250, 306, 318
Hamshaw-Thomas, Lieutenant 138
Handley-Page bomber 246, 251
Hants Battery 41, 131, 277
  Great Northern Drive 155, 157
  Jerusalem, capture of 179
  Megiddo 251
Happy Valley 119
Harbord, Brigadier 274
Hare, Major General S.W. 140, 147, 148, 252
Hareira 81, 83, 87, 103, 157, 158, 161, 162, 163, 168
Hargraves, Lieutenant L.M.S. 168
Harris, Captain C.L. 214
Hatrick, Lieutenant 132
Heart Hill 118
heavy artillery 37–9, 84, 282–3, 285–6, 309
Heavy Artillery Group (HAG) 143, 186, 208
  61st Brigade 144
  95th Brigade 114, 223, 251, 254, 256, 285, 288, 309, 310
  96th Brigade 114, 129, 186, 191, 251, 254, 285, 309, 310
  97th Brigade 114, 143, 152, 309, 310
  100th Brigade 114, 143, 152, 223, 251, 254, 309, 310
  102nd Brigade 114, 143, 152, 223, 250, 251, 253, 254, 256, 286, 310
Hebron 19, 139, 157, 175
Hejaz railway 154, 194, 221, 226, 270
Hejaz tribes 16
Henu 268
Herbie 170
Hereford Ridge 119
Hext, Brigadier General L.J. 161
Hill 70 48
Hill 265 174
Hill 405 80, 87
Hill 1070 129, 130
Hill 3039 200
HM *Aphis* 143
HM *Comet* 143
HM *Druid* 247
HM *Forester* 247
HM *Ladybird* 143
HM *Staunch* 143
HMS *Aphis* 42
HMS *Grafton* 143
HMS *Raglan* 125, 143
Hod el Aras 48
Hod el Enna 48, 50, 52, 53, 54
Hod Um Ugba 46
Hodgson, Major General H.W. 75, 79–81, 83, 100, 101, 103, 106, 111, 169, 170, 175, 226, 242
  Beersheba 128, 130
  Berukin 208, 209
  Es Salt (second raid) 211, 218
  Great Northern Drive 155, 162
  Jerusalem 180, 191
  Sasa 277–8
Hog's Back 192
Homs 278, 280
Hong Kong and Singapore Mountain Battery 34, *35*, 60, 261
  Es Salt (second raid) 213
  Gaza 79, 81
  Jerusalem, capture of 179, 182, 185, 186
  Jordan Valley 232, 235
  Magdhaba 63
  Rafa 69, 71, 72
Honourable Artillery Company (HAC) 41–4, 111, 113, 155, 165, 167, 168, 169, 171, 173, 265, 280, 289, 318
  Beersheba 131, 132, 134

Index

Damascus, advance to 274, 276, 278
Es Salt (second raid) 211, 213–15, 217, 218
Gaza 79, 80, 81, 83, 87–8, 101–3, 111, 113
Jerusalem, capture of 180
Jordan Valley 227, 228, 229–30, 232, 234, 235, 236
life of a gunner 122–4
Megiddo 250, 251, 252
Rafa 68–9, 73, 75
horses *30*, 241 *see also* cavalry
care of 19, 42, 123, 169, 173, 227, 280
Waler *see* Walers
Hoskins, Major General 253
Hotchkiss machine guns 30, 205, 213, 278
Howard-Vyse, Brigadier R.G. 247, 298
Howell-Price, Major F.P. 298
Howes, Major C.G. 141–2
Hudson, Trooper 134
Huj 28, 77, 80, 83, 87, 135, 160, 162, 164–7, *166*, 242
Hutchinson, Colonel 257, 260
Hutton, Major General Sir Edward 26, 29, 59
Huwara 261

I

Ijseir 171
Imperial Camel Corps (ICC) 60, 62, 63, 66, 68, 113, 164, 312
Amman and Es Salt 200
Gaza 79, 80, 89, 100, 106, 128, 137, 139
Great Northern Drive 155, 158, 159
Jordan Valley 206
Imperial Mounted Division (IMD) 25, 79, 97, 100, 111, 231 *see also* Australian Mounted Division (AMD)
brigades *see by brigade number*
Imperial Service Cavalry 158
Indian Army 8, 21, 154, 213, 226, 227, 231, 238, 249, 268
Berukin 207–8, 209
cavalry 33
Imperial Indian Service Troops 115, 206, 235, 250
intelligence, field 126, 229–31, 246, 260
leaks 198, 203, 209, 243
misleading 244–5, 250, 252, 267
Inverness Battery 41, 113, 169, 174, 306, 311, 318
Amman and Es Salt 197
Beersheba 131, 132
Bir el Abd 56
Gaza 79, 102
Jordan Valley 204
Katia 54, 55
Magdhaba 66
Megiddo 250
Rafa 68–9, 71
Romani 47
Irgeig 165
Ismailia 21, 22, 46, 53, 61, 67, 93, 110
Ismet Bey 126, 128, 136
Italian Army 15

J

Jaffa 19, 164, 173–4, 175, 177, 185, 194, 196, 244, 283
horse race 245
Jaljulye 209
Jebel Ekteif 195
Jebel el Kahmum 195
Jebel Kuruntul 195
Jemah 167, 168
Jemmameh 160, 164, 167
Jenin 243, 245, 251, 263, 265, 266–7
Jericho 194–6, 198, 207, 211
Jerusalem 19, 22, 116, 125, 139, 152, 154, 164, 165, 173–4, 194–5, 227, 231, 244, 245, 285
capture of 175–90, *176*, *187*, *189*, 243, 290, 291, 321, 322–3
defence of 191–3, 195, 282, 321, 322–3
Jiljulieh 244, 247, 261
Jisr Benat Yakob 276
Jisr el Damieh 211, 214, 222, 263, 267
Jones, Lieutenant 168
Jordan Valley 9, 194, 197, 203, *205*, 236, 245, 282, 285, 291, 292
April 1918 204–7
May–July 1918 226–36
September 1918 268–71, *269*
Jozele 201
Judean Hills 19, 128, 155, 157, 159–60, 164, 177, 178, 194, 221, 226, 241
Julis 192
Junction Station 154, 164–5, 168, 170, 173–4, 177, 178

K

Kabr Mujahid 212
Kantara 42, 46, 47, 48, 53, 59, 93
Karm Ibn Musleh 71
Kashim Zanna 130

Kasr el Azrak 270
Katia 22, 23, 38, 46, 47, 54–6, 60, 236
Katib Ganiel 48
Katib Gannit 48, 53, 54
Kaukab 278–9
Kelab 116
Kemal, Mustapha 115
Khan Younis (Yunis) 71, 80, 90
Khasala 128, 130
Khasif 124, 128
Kheir Jibert 262
Kheir Kakun 195
Khirbet Buteihah 165
Khirbet er Reseim 80
Khurbet Erk 100, 104
Khurbet Um Adrah 104
Khuweilfe 139, 149, 157, 158–60, 161, 163 *see also* Tel el Khuweilfe
King, Brigadier d'Arcy 113, 155, 274, 297
Kirkman, Brigadier Sidney 294
Kiswe 279
Kolonieh 227
Kubeibeh 181
Kufra Qasim 208, 261
Kuneitra 276
Kurd Hill 99, 118
Kuryet el Enab 177, 181, 182
Kustine 167, 169
Kut 16, 60

L

Labyrinth 77, 85, 86, 96–7, 147, 149, 151, 147, 149
Lambert, Major 100
Latron 168, 175, 178, 179–80, 186, 198
Laurie, Lieutenant Colonel R.M. 117, 141, 142
Lawrence, Lieutenant T.E. (Lawrence of Arabia) 23, 154, 221, 249, 268, 270, 273
Lawrence, Major General the Hon. H.A. 46, 47, 48, 50, 51, 54, 59, 79
Laycock, Colonel Sir Joseph 68, 84, 91, 94, 113
Le Mottee, Brigadier R.E.A. 85, 91, 94, 119, 120
Lee Enfield .303 rifle 27, 31
Lees Hill 118, 120
Leggett, Brigadier A.H. 52
Leicester Battery 41, 113, 165, 218, 306, 318
  Beersheba 131
  Bir el Abd 56
  Gaza 79, 86, 104
  Great Northern Drive 155, 157
  Katia 55
  Megiddo 250, 251
  Rafa 68, 69
  Romani 47, 48, 51
Lewis machine guns 29, 30, 162
Libya 19
Lifta 188
Light Armoured Motor Battery 79, 160, 180, 197, 239, 240
Lilley, Lieutenant W.H. 168
logistics 18, 22–3, 36, 41, 47, 62, 72, 75, 76, 93, 110–11, 116, 129, 160, 173, 177–8, 185, 186, 197, 203, 209, 236, 243, 246, 265, 272, 274, 280, 292–3
  camel loads 328
  stores list 328
  supply chain 16, 41, 62, 68, 76, 160, 181, *228*, 272
Londoners 129, 162, 168, 188, 196, 197, 199, 204, 211, 213, 217, 224
Longley, Major General 252, 261
Lorry-equipped Siege (Power) Brigade 114
Love, Major A.J. 298
Ludd 174, 177
Lydda 244

M

Maan 207
Macandrew, General 248, 263, 265, 274, 279, 280
Macarthur-Onslow, Brigadier 32, 311
Macfarlane-Woods, Reverend W. 298
McGregor, Lieutenant F.J. 168
Mafid Jozele 212
Magdhaba 19, 61, 62–7, *64*, 72, 74, 96, 241
Mageibra 54
Mahmudiyah 48
Majdal Yaba 225
Makhadet 199
Makhadet Abu Naj 267
Makhadet Hajla 268
malaria 227, 230–1, 280
Mansura ridge 77, 85, 97, 120
Marfak 273
Marhardet Abu Naji 276–7
Marne 116
Massy, Brigadier E.C. 44, 180
Maud, General 16
Mayall, Major 81
Maygar, Lieutenant Colonel 134

Index

Maxim machine guns 27, 29
Maxwell, General Sir John 21, 22, 23, 25, 38, 41, 110
Mazar 96
measurements 11
Mediterranean Expeditionary Force (MEF) 26
Megiddo 9, 11, 19, 152, 207, 210, 220, 221, 239, 242, 244
  Battle of 249–67, *255*, *259*, 283, 286, 290, 292, 322, 324, 327–8
  DMC at 249, 253, 262, 263–7, *264*, *266*
  XXI Corps operations 249–63
Meinertzhagen, Major 126
Mejdel 192
Meldrum, Brigadier 195, 270, 311
Mena Camp 43
Mendur 87, 102, 103
Mersa Matruh 42
Meshrefe-Aseiferiyeh-Hill 310 103
Mesopotamia 16
Middlesex Hill 77, 97
Middlesex Yeomanry 126, 277
Midie 188
Miskeh 257, 260
Moab Heights 242
Moberly, Lieutenant Colonel A.H. 285
Mogg Hill 207
Mogg Ridge 209
Money, Colonel 84
Monitor M15 143
Monitor M21 125
Mons 31
Montgomery, Bernard 294
Mott, Major General 175, 177, 188, 224
Mount Carmel 244, 274–5
Mount Meredith 48, 52
Mount Royston 48, 51, 53
Mudros 107
Mueller, Lieutenant G.L.H. 168
Mughar 28
Mulebbis 208, 251
Munkeilleh 101
Murray, General Sir Archibald 16, 21, 22, 24, 38, 59–60, 62, 67, 112, 154
  commander, as 110–11, 116
  Gaza 76, 78, 79, 83, 92, 93, 106, 107–9
  Romani 46, 48, 50, 51, 53
Musallabeh *205*, 206, 222, 226, 231, 232
Musmus Pass 244, 265
Mutton, Captain 144
Muweileh 158
Muzeir'a ridge 225

N
Nabala 251
Nabi Belan 261
Nabi Musa 195
Nabi Tari 225
Nablus 175, 177, 192, 207, 222, 243, 244, 246, 249, 253, 261–2, 265
Nahr Auja 175, 177, 183–4, 239, 240, 245, 247
Nahr el Faliq 208, 209, 249, 253, 256
Nahr Iskanderuneh 265
Nahr Rubin 170, 173
Nahr Sukherier 170
Nalia 170
Nalin 183
Naur 200
Nazareth 19, 263, 265
Neale, Captain A.B.C. 298
Nebi Samwil 175, 177, 180, 181, 182, 183, 184, 185, 186
New Zealand Army 25
New Zealand Expeditionary Force (NZEF) 16
New Zealand Mounted Rifles (NZMR) 8, 11, 32, 33, 38, 75, 111, 155, 173, 231
  Amman and Es Salt 200
  Beersheba 131, 132
  Bir el Abd 56
  casualties 299–300
  Gaza 83, 100
  Jericho 195
  Jordan Valley 268
  Katia 54, 55, 56
  Megiddo 250
  organisation of brigade 299
  Rafa 68
  Romani 46, 47, 52
Newton, Major F.G. 298
Nichol, Brigadier W.D. 25, 113
Niven, Lieutenant Colonel 96
Nott, Major General 99
Nottingham (Notts) Battery 41, 44, 111, 113, 165, 167, 169, 173, 266, 306, 311, 318
  Beersheba 131, 132, 134
  Damascus, advance to 276, 278
  Es Salt (second raid) 213, 214, 215, 218
  Gaza 79, 80, 87, 100
  Jerusalem, capture of 180

Jordan Valley 228, 232, 234
Megiddo 250, 251

O

Oghratina 22, 28, 46, 50, 56, 57
Onslow, Lieutenant Colonel George 212, 227
Orontes River 280
Outpost Hill, 96, 98, 118, 120, 145, 149

P

Palestine 8, 9, 16, 19, 115, 116
chronology 296–7
climate 22, 227
logistics infrastructure 22
map *127*
terrain 19, 21, 28, 159–60, 178, 194, 211–12, 226, 227–8, *228*, 241, 244, 261, 282
Palin, Major General 253
Parker, Brigadier 50
Partridge, Lieutenant Colonel L. 298
Pasha, Ali Faud 161
Pasha, General Refet 138, 152, 170, 207
Paterson, Major Andrew 'Banjo' 116
pedrails 44, 265
Pelusium 47, 52
The Pimple 204–5
Pollok-M'Call, Brigadier 52
Port Said 52
Port Suez 22
Prescott, Colonel 232, 234
Preston, Colonel R.M.P. 11, 42, 124, 131, 227–8, 281, 284–5
Preston, Major 103
Price-Harrison, Major 134
prisoners 167, 168, 196, 235, 243, 249, 260, 262, 265, 266–7, 270, 275, 277, 279

Q

Qaliye 208
Qalonye 186
Qalqile 207
Qatra 170, 173
Qatya 54, 55, 56, 73, 241
Qawuqa 159
Qubeibe 191
Queen's Hill 120
Qule 225
Qusra (Quza) 261

R

Rafa 18, 62, 96, 116, 145
Battle of 68–72, *70*, 73, 75, 86, 289, 291
Rafat 209, 252, 253
railways 22–3, 111, 154, 164, 174, 175, 194, 221, 245
Ramallah 182, 186, 195
Ramleh 164, 173–4, 175, 181, 244, 251
range, calculating 40
Ras el Ain 253
Ras el Nagb 158, 159
Ras et Tawil 262
Rawlinson, Colonel Henry 27
Red Hill 212–13, 214, 230
Requin 93, 96, 105, 125, 143
rifles 30–1, 240–3
types *see by name*
River Jordan 194, 195, 196, 198–201, *199*, 211–12, 213, 218, 220, 222, 226–7, 229–30, 238, 240, 244, 245, 248, 265, 268, 272, 276, 277
Roberts, General Lord 27
Robins, Major T.E. 298
Romani 19, 22, 43, 44, 56, 96
Battle of 9, 45–54, *49*, 57, 59, 60–1, 62, 72, 79, 93, 289, 291
Rosenthal, Colonel Charles *20*
Royal Field Artillery (RFA) 74, 85, 97, 101, 144, 162, 168, 191, 200, 224, 232, 254, 261 *see also by brigade number*
order of battle (1917) 307–9
Royal Flying Corps (RFC) 9, 23, 25, 45, 46, 57, 62, 65, 84, 91, 93, 99, 105, 120, 138, 190, 201, 245–6, 267, 272–3, 282, 287, 291, 317–18
No. 14 Squadron 39
No. 111 Squadron 192, 245
No. 113 Squadron 246
No. 114 Squadron 138
No. 144 Squadron 245
No. 145 Squadron 245
Royal Garrison Artillery (RGA) 21, 34, 45, 47, 141, 268 *see also by name of battery*
Megiddo 250, 253–4, 261
Royal Horse Artillery (RHA) 8, 11, 21, 18, 28, 34, 45, 54, 80, 104, 130, 131, 168, 178, 179, 206, 220, 227, 250, 252, 270, 274, 281, 289 *see also by name of battery or brigade number*
critique 72–5
guns 304–5
order of battle (1917) 306–7
Royal Inniskilling Fusiliers 192
Royal Naval Air Service 41
Royal Navy (RN) 43, 208, 238, 247, 252

Royal Scots Fusiliers 52, 180, 185
Royal Welsh Fusiliers 224
Royston, Brigadier 51, 56–7, 65
Rupertswood battery 8
Rushbrooke, Captain 69, 227
Russell, Lieutenant Colonel R.E.M. 298
Russell, Major N.N.C. 298
Russian Army 16, 154, 238
Russo-Japanese War (1904–05) 37
Ryrie, Brigadier 32, 80, 81, 90, 130, 139, 174, 184, 200, 270, 311

S
sabres 31, 168
Salmana 57
Salmond, Brigadier 138, 167, 190, 230, 245, 263, 273
Salonika 16, 21, 60, 110, 112, 238
Samaria 263
Samson's Ridge 121, 148
Sandilands, Brigadier H.G. 118
Saris 180, 182
Sarona 244, 252, 264
Sasa 277–8
Sausage ridge 100–1, 103, 169
Scott, Lieutenant Colonel 81
Seaforth Hill 253
Sebustiye 249
Selmeh 211, 236
Semakh 243, 275–6
Senussi tribes 16, 18, 34, 41, 42
Serapeum 25
Sharon Plain 206, 249, 264, 265
Sharta 97, 101
Shea, Major General 162, 167, 188, 197–8, 200, 203, 204, 206, 211, 213, 242, 253
Sheikh Abbas 91, 97, 118
Sheikh Aljin 94, 120, 121, 148
Sheikh Hasam 141, 142
Sheikh Othman 42
Sheikh Redwan 149
Sheikh Subi 209
Sheikh Zowaiid 62, 68, 71, 72, 76, 96
Sheria 83, 128, 149, 155, 157, 160–3, 164, 290
see also Tel esh Sheria
Sherwood Rangers Yeomanry 274
Shibleh 267
Shilta 179
Short, Brigadier A.H. 78, 79, 113, 161
Shunet Nimrin 200, 205, 206–7, 211, 212, 217–18, 220, 235, 270, 321, 323
siege artillery 37–9, 282–3, 285–6
siege brigades 93, 96, 158, 159, 161, 164, 171, 195, 204, 206, 209, 222–4, 226, 250, 251, 260, 261, 263, 285, 287, 309
  ammunition 302–3
  order of march 256–8
  war establishment 301
Simpson, Lieutenant Colonel G.S. 50
Simpson-Baikie, Brigadier H.A.D. 113, 143, 147, 148, 207, 251
Sinai 8, 9, 16, 19, 265
  area of operations (map) *17*
  chronology 296–7
  climate 22
  Honourable Artillery Company (HAC) 43–4
  logistics infrastructure 22
  terrain 19, 21, 28, 241, 244
Smith, Brigadier 47, 184, 206, 227
Smith, Captain A. 155
Smith, Lieutenant Ross 78
Smith, Major A 211
Smith, Major General Sydenham Campbell Urquhart 24, *24*, 25, 79, 91–2, 94, 105, 108, 113, 290–1
Smith, Major General W.E.B. 47–8, 50, 53, 63
Smith, Second Lieutenant P.D. 218
Somerset Battery 41, 111, 113, 174, 294, 306, 311, 318
  Amman and Es Salt 197, 200
  Beersheba 131, 132, 134
  Bir el Abd 56, 57
  Gaza 79, 86, 101
  Jordan Valley 204
  Katia 55
  Magdhaba 66
  Megiddo 250
  Rafa 68, 69
  Romani 47, 52
Somme 27
sources 11
South African Field Artillery Brigades 145, 171, 209, 224, 250, 260
Spanish influenza 280
SS *Japanese Prince* 42
SS *Karoa* 42
SS *Minnesota* 42
Sudan 16, 110
Suez Canal 16, 18, 19, 21, 45, 47, 60, 164
Sukereir 194

Summeil 169, 174
supply chain 16, 41, 62, 68, 76, 160, 181, *228*, 272
  camel loads 328
  stores list 328
Suweile 270
swords, use of 27, 28, 135, 168, 240–3, 266, 275–6, 277

T
Tabsor 208, 209, 253, 260, 286
tactics 238, 239
  cavalry 239, 240–3
Taibiye 222
Tala Bey 86
Talat ed Dumm 195, 226
tanks 107, 135–6, 293
  Mark I 98
  Mark V 97
  Mark VI 97
Tel Abu Dilkah 165
Tel Abu Zeitun 183
Tel Afule 251, 263, 265
Tel Asur 224
Tel el Fara 94, 100
Tel el Jemmi 100
Tel el Khuweilfe 139, 157, 158 *see also* Khuweilfe
Tel el Marakeb 122
Tel el Nejile 83
Tel el Saba 130, 131, 134, 135
Tel el Sakati 130, 131, 139, 159
Tel el Turmus 173
Tel el Ujul 84
Tel esh Sheria 77, 81, 139, 158, 161, 162 *see also* Sheria
Tel Jezar 179
Three Bushes Hill 209
Tin Hat Hill 210
Tooth, Lieutenant Owen 167
Towaiil el Emir 71
Towal el Jekwal 158
Townshend, General 16
transport 22–3 *30*
trenches 19, 43, 57, 60, 69, 73–5, 84, 91, 96–106, 108, 120, 128, 134–5, 139–40, 148–9, 158, 230, 249, 253
Trew, Brigadier E.F. 298
Tripoli 272
Tubl el Keuneitrah 195
Tul Karm 251, 253
Tul Keram 222, 244, 246, 249, 253, 256, 257, 258, 265
Turkish Army 16, 22, 115, 238
  III Corps 128, 137, 186, 223
  XX Corps 137, 161, 170, 223
  XXII Corps 137, 170, 207–8, 260
  1st Division 223
  3rd Division 47, 77, 94, 139, 145, 147, 177, 223
  7th Division 137, 139, 170, 177, 223
  16th Division 94, 128, 137, 161, 209
  19th Division 207
  20th Division 207
  24th Division 128, 137, 186, 223, 236
  26th Division 137, 161, 186, 223
  27th Division 63, 128, 137, 161
  48th Division 212
  53rd Division 77, 94, 137, 139, 147, 186, 196, 223, 236
  54th Division 137
  artillery *72*
  Asia Corps 207
  Central Army 222
  Eighth Army 137, 155, 170, 177, 178, 183–4, 222, 223, 251, 272
  Fourth Army 197, 198, 221, 272, 276
  Gallipoli, lessons from 18–19
  morale 249
  numbers 30–1, 47, 87, 113, 128, 137, 152, 193, 198, 207–8, 223
  Seventh Army 175, 177, 193, 222, 223, 251, 267, 272, 277
Turner, Lieutenant 81
Turtle Hill 148

U
Um el Kelab 177
Umbrella Hill 118, 119, 140, 141, 142, 145
Umm esh Shert 212, 217, 218, 235, 270
United States of America 154, 238

V
Vickers machine guns 30, 68, 240, 278
visual signalling 27–8
Voltigeux 143
von Falkenburg, Colonel 207
von Kressenstein, Major General Friedrich Frieherr Kress 47, 62, 67, 77, 86, 94, 108, 115, 126, 128, 135, 136, 139, 157, 170
von Sanders, Liman 244

Index

W
Wadi Arah 265
Wadi Auja 174, 175, 183, 222, 226
Wadi Deir Ballut 224, 225
Wadi el Arish 63
Wadi el Fara 103, 260, 267
Wadi el Khubb 171
Wadi el Kuffrein 200
Wadi el Saba 128, 135
Wadi es Sabe 128
Wadi esh Sherar 277
Wadi Faliq 253
Wadi Ghuzze 76, 77, 80, 83, 84, 87, 89, 90, 93, 94, 100
Wadi Hesi 125, 162, 169, 290
Wadi Ihan 100
Wadi Khalil 131
Wadi Imleih 104
Wadi London 128
Wadi Mellahah 231, 232, 235
Wadi Mirtaba 128
Wadi Nimrin 204, 211, 268
Wadi Nueiame 231
Wadi Nukhabir 97
Wadi Retem 215
Wadi Saba 131, 134
Wadi Saleh 167
Wadi Sheria 103, 128, 161, 165
Wadi Sihan 100
Wadi Sukereir 171, 173
Wadi Surar 170
Wadi Uxbridge 162
Walers 19, 22, 200
Warwickshire Yeomanry 57, 88, 167, 311
water 19, 21, 47, 51, 63, 68, 76, 111, 126, 155, 158, 165, 168, 169, 171, 174, 205, 230, 234, 247, 272
Watson's Force 250, 260, 262
Wellington Mounted Rifles 65, 103, 231, 234, 270, 299, 311
Wellington ridge 48–53
West Indies troops 115, 245, 250, 268, 270
Western Desert 16, 18, 19, 41, 110
Western Front 22, 107, 110, 154, 238
  comparisons with 149, 152, 203, 236, 244, 282, 284, 286, 290, 291
Western Frontier Force 18
Wiggin, Brigadier 46, 83, 87–8
Wilhemnia 174, 183, 184
Williams, Major R. 63, 102
Williamson-Oswald, Brigadier O.C. 144, 223
Wilson, Brigadier Leslie 167, 212–13, 217, 266–7, 278, 311
Worcestershire Yeomanry 167, 262, 311
Worthington, Lieutenant 182

Y
Yalo 180
Yeomanry and Mounted Rifle Training Manual 27
Younis 148

Z
Zerqiye 208
Ziza 270
Zuheillah Wadi 167